The Friday Project
An imprint of HarperCollins*Publishers*
77–85 Fulham Palace Road
Hammersmith
London W6 8JB

www.thefridayproject.co.uk
www.harpercollins.co.uk

This edition published by The Friday Project 2011

1

Part 1 first published as *Blood, Sweat and Tea* by The Friday Project in 2006

Part 2 first published as *More Blood, More Sweat and Another Cup of Tea* by
The Friday Project in 2009

A catalogue record for this book is available from the British Library

978-0-00-741981-4

Printed and bound in Great Britain by Clays Ltd, St Ives plc

MIX
Paper from
responsible sources
FSC® C007454

FSC is a non-profit international organisation established to promote the responsible
management of the world's forests. Products carrying the FSC label are independently
certified to assure consumers that they come from forests that are managed to meet the
social, economic and ecological needs of present and future generations. Find out more
about HarperCollins and the environment at
www.harpercollins.co.uk/green

This book is dedicated to my mum and my brother, who have tolerated me with astonishing patience and love for almost forty years. It is also dedicated to all my work colleagues in the London Ambulance Service who do their best for the people who call them under some very difficult situations.

Finally to anyone and everyone who works for any of the emergency services – those people who bring calm to chaos, peace to despair and aid to the injured and frightened while working under incredible pressure and yet who rarely get the thanks that they deserve.

'Tom Reynolds' was the pen name for Brian Kellett, an EMT for the London Ambulance Service. Once upon a time he wrote a blog about his work which mostly involved speeding around the streets of East London while dealing with the sort of people who call ambulances.

This book is based on his blog 'Random Acts of Reality' and is the collection of his two previous books *Blood, Sweat and Tea*, and the imaginatively titled *More Blood, More Sweat and Another Cup of Tea*.

These books have now been made into what he hopes will be a hit TV show for Channel 4 that will make him a lot of money so he can retire to a sunny island and never have to think about (or smell) pustulating sores ever again.

Until then he still finds himself working in healthcare in East London.

SIRENS

Tom Reynolds

There are a number of terms found in this book that may be unfamiliar; for the assistance of the non-medical reader there is a short glossary at the back.

In the interests of confidentiality patients have been made anonymous and identifying characteristics may have been altered or removed.

Read more at http://randomreality.blogware.com

🚐 Prologue: Too Young

Yesterday started well, we had the only new 'yellow' vehicle on the complex, and it really is an improvement on the old motors. But then we got a job that should have been routine, but unfortunately was not.

We were given a '34-year-old male, seizure' at a nearby football pitch in the middle of a park. Also leaving from our station was the FRU (a fast car designed to get to a scene before the ambulance). As we had a new motor, we were able to keep up with the FRU.

Arriving at the top of the street, we were met and directed by some of the patient's football team-mates. Unfortunately, the patient was 200 yards into the park, and there was no way we were going to get the ambulance onto the field – the council had built a little moat around the park to stop joyriders tearing up the grass in their stolen cars.

The FRU paramedic had reached the patient first and I ran across the field to get to the patient as the paramedic looked worried, and this isn't someone who normally worries.

As I reached the patient, carrying the scoop which we would use to move him, the paramedic asked me if I thought the patient was breathing.

The patient was Nigerian, and it is not racist to say that sometimes detecting signs of life on a black person is harder than if the patient is Caucasian. White people tend to look dead; black people often just look unconscious. Also, a windy playing field at dusk is not the ideal circumstance to assess a patient.

'He's not breathing,' I told the paramedic, just as my crewmate reached us. 'Shit' replied the paramedic, 'I left the FR2* in my car'.

---

* An FR2 is a defibrillation machine, which is used to shock a heart back into a normal rhythm: in the UK emergency medical technicians (EMTs) are allowed to use this piece of equipment, and rapid defib' shocks are essential in certain forms of cardiac arrest.

I had to run 200 yards back to our ambulance to get this, now vital, piece of kit.

On my return my colleagues had started to 'bag' the patient (this means using equipment to 'breathe for' the patient and performing cardiopulmonary resuscitation, or CPR), which is the procedure to keep blood flowing around the body in the absence of a pulse. Attaching the defib pads I saw that the patient was in 'fine VF' (ventricular fibrillation) – this is a heart rhythm which means the heart is 'quivering' rather than pumping blood around the body to the brain and other vital organs. Technically, the patient is dead and without immediate treatment, they will remain dead.

We 'shocked' the patient once and his heart rhythm changed. It changed to asystole (this means that the heart is not moving at all, and it is much more difficult to restore life to the patient with this form of rhythm). We decided to 'scoop and run' to the nearest hospital. The paramedic secured the patient's airway by passing a tube down the windpipe, and we got the patient onto the scoop, all the time continuing the CPR and giving potentially lifesaving drugs. We then carried him, with the help of his team-mates, to the ambulance and rushed him to hospital.

Unfortunately, the patient never regained consciousness, and died in the resuscitation room.

Thirty-four years old, normally fit and healthy – and he drops dead on a football pitch. Despite our best efforts there was nothing more we could have done for him; the treatment went according to plan and the resuscitation attempt went smoothly. This was a 'proper' job, but one job we would have happily done without.

PART I

🚑 Why Won't They Let Me Do This?

Here is a moan about something that I am not allowed to do. I'm not allowed to run people over in my job. I could really clear the streets of a lot of stupid people if I was able to do that.

Picture the scene: there I am, driving through the streets of London in a big white van, with blue flashing lights, loud sirens running and the word Ambulance written in rather large letters. As a pedestrian, what would you do? Would you think 'Hmm, being run over by that would really hurt, I think I'll wait the 12 nanoseconds that it takes him to drive past before I cross the road'. Or would you, as most of the people in my area apparently do, think 'Hmm, an ambulance on his way to an important job, I bet I can run across the road in front of him before he can hit me'.

During the last job, three people tried to dive under my ambulance. If I was allowed (by government grant or some such) to keep driving and splat them across my windscreen, that would mean three less idiots being allowed to breed tonight.

Oh well, I might get lucky later tonight.

☕ Dear Mr Alcoholic

… Can all alcoholics please just get drunk in their houses and fall asleep there? Why do you insist that you drink your Tennent's Super in a public place where some do-gooder will think you are ill and call for an ambulance?

… Can you also have a bath once in a while? I know it's nice to roll around in the road while drunk, but it would be nice if you were at least a bit clean to start with.

… Would you mind awfully not swearing at me, taking a swing at me or

3

exposing yourself to me? I have quite enough abuse from the non-drunks out there ... Still at least your fists are easy to dodge, and if I stop holding you up, you fall over.

... If you have a medical condition, please don't use it as an excuse to get taken into hospital. If you tell me 'I'm drunk and need to sleep it off', I have less work to do than if you tell me that you have 'Chest pain, Angina, Cancer and Difficulty in Breathing'. The more tests I have to do the longer it will be before you get to hospital, and the more I have to come into physical contact with you. If you are just drunk, then I can just be a taxi.

... When you have been sick, at some point in the next week or so could you please change your clothing? Give them to someone who hasn't knackered their brain on booze to wash. Dry vomit on the clothing, while advertising your love for beer, doesn't endear you to me thankyouverymuch.

... Please keep your weight down either through diet or through terminal liver failure. I'm the poor bastard that has to lug the dead weight of your unconscious body into the ambulance.

... You don't have to tell me 'I'm an alcoholic', and sound so proud about it. I *do* have a nose, and can smell for myself.

... Finally, although Tennent's Super Strong lager, White Lightning, and for the rare rich alcoholic Stella Artois are perfectly acceptable drinks, could you please come up with something less damaging? I think lighter fuel is better for you and contains fewer chemicals.

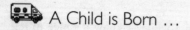 A Child is Born ...

The story of the first baby I delivered — I can still remember it now. I can also remember my feeling of relief when it all went smoothly. Yet still managed to turn it into a rant about midwifery.

Just in from my late-shift and feeling more upbeat than normal. Tonight I delivered my first baby … and yet I can still turn this happy event into a rant.

Picture the scene: you are a midwife (this means you have a chip on your shoulder the size of the African debt), and a lady comes in to your maternity department in the second stage of labour. Do you …

(a) Say hello, take a room and we'll have that baby out as soon as we can,

or …

(b) Tell them to go home and come back when the pain gets worse.

Guess which answer results in your baby being delivered by an ambulance bloke who has 1 day's training in maternity (and who, to be honest, slept through most of it)?

Then when I take mother and baby into the same maternity department are you …

(a) Vaguely apologetic, or …

(b) Snotty towards the ambulance crew who did your work for you?

Can you guess that tonight I got (b) for both questions?

Otherwise it was a nice simple delivery, with dad shooting pictures on his mobile phone sending them to all and sundry while his wife was lying, bloodstained and naked on a leather sofa. Blood went all over that sofa, which come summer will start to smell just a little rank. Blood also went all over me (note to self – must remember to pack Wellington boots next time) and my acting skills ('Don't worry mum, all normal, I've done hundreds of deliveries') were tested to the limit.

… and I didn't have to pick up any alcoholics.

Why Would People Even Think It?

I have sometimes been astounded by the bloodymindedness of people, and sometimes by their stupidity. Now I am astonished at their petty nastiness.

I'm driving my 'big-white-van-with-blue-flashing-lights-and-a-siren' to a 1-year-old child with difficulty in breathing. While passing a group of youths on the pavement, one of them thinks that it would be a good idea to throw his bottle of coke at the ambulance, thus spraying my screen, obscuring my vision and nearly causing me to swerve into oncoming traffic.

All I can say is that it is lucky for them that I was going to a call, because if I hadn't I'd have shoved my boot up their arse.

Where in the tiny recesses of their minds does it seem like a good idea to throw something at an ambulance running on lights and sirens?

All I hope is that one day they need me – something likely, given the amount of people like that who get stabbed in my neck of the woods – and I'm just that little too slow to save their worthless skins.

Payment Point

I get called to a lot of RTAs (that is, for the uninformed, 'Road Traffic Accident'). I'd say that 90% of these are diagnosed as 'whiplash' (which is a muscular sprain of the neck – this is a minor injury that is treated with painkillers); I'd suggest that over half of these are an attempt to gain insurance money. In the ambulance trade we call this the 'Payment Point', referring to the point in the neck that is painful, and pays out the money.

Tonight I saw the most blatant attempt to get money from an 'accident'.

I was called to a flyover where two cars had been in a near collision, yes, a near collision. There was no damage to either vehicle, neither were there any skidmarks on the road. The 'patient' was the passenger of the car, and complained of pain on the right side of his neck. He was desperate to go to hospital, for what reason I did not know, as there was obviously no injury.

This was made even more evident when he forgot what side of his neck the pain was on. When I called him on this he pretended not to know what I was talking about.

Even the police were not above making fun of this idiot.

It probably didn't help that he was 10 years younger than me and cruising around in a red sports car.

Of course RTA is now RTC (Road Traffic Collision), because if it's an 'accident' then the police can't prosecute anyone.

☕ Single

Although I do love my job dearly, there are a number of disadvantages. At the moment I am a 'relief' worker, which means although I have a main station, I can be sent anywhere in London to cover absences and holidays in the 'Core' staff. I also don't have a regular crewmate ... I am essentially the whore of the London Ambulance Service.

So, at the moment I am sitting on my backside at my main station with no-one to work with, watching daytime TV.

Bored, Bored, Bored, Bored ...

Of course, at some point in the next 12 hours I could be rushing off anywhere in London. Being on strange stations is actually quite good fun, as you get to meet new people and, let's face it, in this job moving around London just means 'same shit, different scenery'.

... But at the moment I'm bored ...

Daytime TV, the ambulance relief's worst enemy. Thankfully I'm no longer a relief – I'm 'Core' staff now, which means I have a regular partner and I work mainly out of one station.

Some People Just Can't Wait

So, there I am in my ambulance helping a bloke who was actually quite ill, when all of a sudden the back doors fly open and some idiot decides to start berating me because I'm blocking the road. Needless to say I am not pleased at this, not only because it is embarrassing for the patient, but also because of the sheer bloody cheek of this person. When I tell her (very politely mind you) to bugger off, she replies with the old favourite 'I'm a taxpayer and I pay your wages'. At this I remind her that my patient, my crewmate and I also pay taxes. At this she is a bit nonplussed, yet still she continues to moan that there is no need for me to block the road.

In any event, I did need to block the road, I don't do it on purpose, but it is more important to get to the patient quickly.

This woman's moaning then gets other drivers upset and they start honking their horns, and the only way I get rid of the woman who was in such a hurry was to pull the door shut after me and tell her to imagine her relative in the ambulance ...

I didn't hurry treating the patient either.

The same thing has happened on more than one occasion. Now I simply ask the complainer that if it was them rolling around in agony, would they like to have to wait while I find a better place to park?

Maybe it's Because I'm a Londoner

Research carried out by the London Ambulance Service for our 'No Send' policy has shown that 59% of Londoners think that they will get seen quicker in A&E (Accident and Emergency department) if they arrive in an ambulance.

This ... Is ... Not ... True ...

In fact, if you come to A&E after calling an ambulance for something minor, the nursing staff will be more inclined to send you out to the waiting room and forget about you.

I was an A&E nurse for a long time – just trust me on this ...

Also, Londoners call for three times the number of ambulances for 'flu than in any other English city. Half the time the patient has got a cold and not 'flu at all, and just needs to work it out of their system. Even if they did have 'flu, there is little the hospital could do for them anyway.

Coupled with high population densities, lack of staff and vehicles, speed-bumps everywhere and heavy traffic, is it any wonder we are having trouble hitting the 8-minute deadline we have to make 75% of calls in?

Nice New Motors

The London Ambulance Service is giving us poor ambulance staff shiny new ambos to drive … well, puke yellow rather than shiny … but they *are* new. These are Mercedes Sprinters outfitted in 'EURO RAL 1016 Yellow' which is apparently the most striking colour available and is used throughout the European Union. They have lots of nice new bits for us to play with. Most importantly, they have a tail lift so now we don't need to break our backs lifting some 20-stone lump into the back of the motor (20 stone is 127 kilograms for those using 'new money').

I was asked by a friend what I thought of them, and having just finished my 'Familiarisation Course' (4 hours of playing with the new toy) I must say I do like it. Not only is the engine more responsive when moving off, but the brakes also work that bit better than our old LDVs (Leyland Daf vans) and the interior is much more professional looking.

The only real problem I foresee is that the tail lift needs around 4 yards to unload the trolley and around London this means that we will have to park in the middle of the road, blocking off other traffic. So, if you do see one of us blocking your way, please realise that there is no way we can park the things and be sure of being able to load a patient on board as well.

These things also cost £105 000 each and if we get the slightest scratch on them they have to be taken off the road and repaired (unlike the ones we have at the moment where they are beaten up until they stop working). Since our insurance has a £5 000 excess it'll mean a lot more money going to vehicle maintenance.

Should be fun, but I can't see management ever letting me drive one … I estimate if I can squeeze through gaps by driving until I hear the crunch …

While I thought that parking to allow the tail lifts space would be a big problem, our biggest problem would turn out to be the regular breaking down of the lifts.

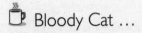 My (So-Called) Exciting Life

I had my hair cut today, which has become a weighty decision in my mind. It goes something like this …

(a) Do I get a crop or not? If I get a crop I'll look like I've just been released from a concentration camp; if I don't then I'll look like a paedophile.
(b) Will my mum like it? If not then I'll have to put up with 3 weeks' worth of moaning about how terrible I look.
(c) Will this cut enhance my ability to attract members of the opposite sex? To be honest, no haircut has ever done this but I live in hope.
(d) If I go to my local hairdressers will I get the trainee … and if I do will it be possible to get a refund?

Anyway, I went in and got a 'short-back-and-sides' and rather unfortunately I'm deaf as a post when I'm not wearing my glasses (for those who have 20/20 vision, you don't wear your glasses when getting a haircut). So when the whole place erupted in fits of laughter I didn't know if it was because of a rapidly growing bald-spot.

(*Still while I can't see it, it doesn't exist.*)

The best I can say is that I'm not having to brush my hair out of my eyes with a pair of gloves covered in someone else's vomit.

Which is nice …

Bloody Cat …

I'm sitting here single on station (you need two people to man an ambulance, and if you haven't got anyone to work with you are 'single' and therefore unable to work. However, you need to stay on station in case they find someone else in London who is single. In that case you find yourself trekking across London to work in a place you've only seen on telly). I'm hungry and bored, partly because it's night-time, and partly because there is no-one else on station.

However I have a plan …

To counter the boredom I have a DVD I can watch on the station's new DVD player (bought out of staff funds, so no we haven't been defrauding the NHS). The hunger problem will soon be solved by the microwave curry I have sitting in my car.

Let us now introduce a new member into the cast: when I said I was alone that was a bit of a lie, there is the station cat. Well at least I think it's a cat as it is so threadbare it could be anything. This cat is so stupid it lies in front of your ambulance just when you need it the most, and refuses to move until you physically have to ~~kick~~ lift it gently out of the way. However, it is intelligent enough to realise that when someone is using the microwave there will be an opportunity to beg for food 5 minutes later (13 minutes if the food is frozen).

I nearly fell over the damn thing stepping away from the microwave, only to spend the next 10 minutes discussing with a mouth full of chicken korma why it wouldn't like to jump up on my lap and make off with my dinner. It went a little something like this …

Miaow.
'No you can't have any.'
Miaow.
'You wouldn't like it.'
Miaow.
'Go eat your own dinner.'
Miaow.
Gets up, plate in hand, to check that the cat does indeed have food/water/ toy mouse.
Miaow.
'Will you bugger off!'
Miaow.

At this point I put the plate (still with some of my food on it) on the floor, which the mangy beast sniffs and turns his nose up at. Said 'cat' then goes and hides under a table.

Horrible bloody creature.

It's now dead; there is only one person on station who misses the bloody thing.

Why This Is a Good Job

My crewmate and I went to a man having a fit on Christmas day; he was a security guard and built like a brick out-house. This fit wasn't your 'normal' epileptic fit, but instead the man was punchy and aggressive. To say it was a struggle to get him on the back of the ambulance is to say that Paris Hilton may have appeared in an Internet video download. Cutting a long story short, the patient is diabetic and his blood sugar has dropped to a dangerously low level. Luckily, we carry an injection to reverse this, and after wrestling with him in order to give him this drug he made a full recovery before we even reached the hospital. This is a nice job because we actually helped someone rather than just drove them to hospital.

Other benefits of the job include (but are not limited to …)

Working outside in the fresh air. I don't know how office workers put up with air conditioning.

For much of the time you are your own boss – do not underestimate this.

Driving on the wrong side of the road with blue lights and sirens going; it's not about the speed it's about the *power*.

Being able to poke around people's houses and feel superior even though you haven't done the washing up in your own house for 2 days.

No matter how annoying the patient is, knowing that within 20 minutes it'll be the hospital's problem.

Meeting lots of lovely nurses, and knowing that I get paid more than them.

On the rare occasion, being able to help people who are scared or in pain.

Every time I have a bad day, or feel fed up at work I think back to this list and soon start to feel better — although I no longer get paid more than the nurses I meet.

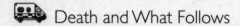 Death and What Follows

There are some people, who despite being lovely people, you dread working with; one such person is Nobby (not his real name). He is what is known in the trade as a 'trauma magnet'. He's one of those people who will get the cardiac arrests, car crashes, shootings and stabbings; by contrast I am a 'shit magnet', meaning I only seem to pick up people who don't need an ambulance. Other than having to do some real work for a change I really enjoy working with him.

I was working with him a little time ago and we got called to a suspended (basically this is someone whose heart isn't beating and they have stopped breathing). It's one of those jobs that require us to work hard trying to save the punter's life. We got to the address and found relatives performing CPR on their granny. You might have seen it on TV as a 'Cardiac Arrest'.

(Let me correct a few ideas you might have about resuscitation. First, it rarely works; 'Casualty' and 'ER' have led people to believe that you often save people: I can count on the fingers of one hand the number of people who have survived an arrest and most of them arrested while I was watching them in hospital. Second, it isn't pretty: when someone arrests there is often vomit, faeces, urine and blood covering them and the area around them. Finally, people never suspend where you can reach them:

if there is an awkward hole, or they can find some way to collapse under a wardrobe they will do so.)

This poor woman was covered in body fluids and was properly dead; there was no way we were going to save her. One of our protocols says that we can recognise someone as beyond hope and not even commence a resuscitation attempt. Unfortunately, we couldn't do it this time as the relatives had been doing CPR (which is the right thing to do) and so we had to make an attempt.

Nobby and I got to work and tried to resuscitate the patient for 30 minutes. Our protocol goes on to say that if we are unsuccessful after attempting a resuscitation for 'a specified time' we can end it and recognise death, which is what we did.

However, during our resuscitation attempt it seemed that the entire extended family had arrived and there were well over 20 people in this little terraced house with much wailing and gnashing of teeth. It's always hard to tell someone that their mother has died, but it has to be done, and if you can manage it well you can answer some of their questions and hopefully provide some healing for them.

The GP (general practitioner) was informed, as were the police (a formality in sudden deaths). The family had called a priest and he was there before the police arrived, while the GP was going to 'phone the family'; what he expected to be able to do over the phone puzzled me.

We tidied up and went onto another job.

Two weeks later, Nobby was called to a chest pain. He turns up and finds himself in the middle of a wake, surrounded by 20 familiar-looking people.

Can you guess who the wake was for? Its a funny old world …

I worked with Nobby again for the first time in 2 years. He still remembered the job, and what happened after it. I told Nobby that he'd be included in this book but he wasn't happy with his pseudonym and told me that he would prefer to be referred to as 'George Clooney'. I refused.

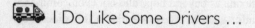

I Do Like Some Drivers ...

Although I often moan about the idiocy of other people's driving when faced with a big white van with blue flashing lights on top, I am sometimes pleasantly surprised at the lengths some people will go to in order to get out of the way. For example, yesterday we had people nearly grounding their cars on roundabouts and roadside verges, squeezing into parking spots I wouldn't be able to fit a Mini Cooper in and swearing at other drivers who wouldn't move out of the way. I've had workmen stand in the middle of the road and stop traffic, lollipop ladies fence off crossings with their 'lollipops', and van drivers who I have clipped while squeezing past them wave me on and tell me, 'don't worry about a little damage'.

Yesterday we had all the above on one call (except hitting a van driver), it was like the Red Sea parting before us. It was a beautiful thing to behold; it left us in awe and wonder.

Shame we were going to 2-year-old with a cough.

This is a rare occurrence.

The Dangers of Prostitution

Occasionally you get a job that makes you laugh, normally because the person you are picking up is an idiot. We got called to a chip shop in one of the main roads in Newham – unfortunately there are about 20 chip shops on this road, but we managed to narrow it down by looking for the shiny white police car parked outside. The call had been given as an 'assault' which can mean anything from a slap on the face to a fatal stabbing.

In this instance it was a young lad, the spitting image of 'Ali G', who was complaining that he had been hit on the nose; needless to say there wasn't a mark on him, and it turned out that he had been hit by his girlfriend. The police wanted to take statements, but he wasn't interested and when I tried to assess him he told me that the ambulance wasn't needed as 'I'm St Johns innit, and a security guard'. This fella couldn't scare a toddler, so I suspected he was telling a little bit of a lie. As he wasn't hurt and 'refused aid' my crewmate and I retreated to a safe distance to do our paperwork …

In the course of the night we found ourselves at the local hospital (dropping off yet another ill person) when who should walk in with another crew from my station, but our earlier 'Ali G' lookalike. I asked him why he decided to call an ambulance when he'd already sent us packing and it turned out that another woman had hit him … the prostitute he'd hired after his girlfriend had slapped him. Turns out she had hit him and then robbed him of his jewellery. He couldn't have put up much of a fight because he only had one scratch on him.

It's pillocks like these we have to put up with … and call 'sir' …

However, it is also jobs like this that we can use to have a good laugh with our workmates. So people like him do serve some purpose.

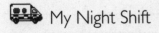 My Night Shift

Much fun and games last night, working in the Poplar/Bow area. Not only did some German bloke graffiti on the back of one of the ambulances, but he also called the crew from a payphone and ran off, repeating it twice.

There are a *lot* of strange people out there …

MacMedic (an American ambulance blog) gave a rundown of what his shifts are like, so I thought I'd do the same, in honour of our brothers in foreign climes.

All these people called an ambulance last night by dialling '999'.

(a) Fractured wrist – young lad at the Boat Show.
(b) An alcoholic 'frequent flyer' who has just been released from prison … We thought we'd got rid of him for good.
(c) A 15-year-old with a runny nose.
(d) Very minor RTA.
(e) Domestic Assault, with no actual injury, but police already on scene.
(f) 'Facial Injury' which turned out to mean 'Some bloke kicked my door.'
(g) Assault with a cut hand – actually a decent injury with tendon involvement (which means surgery and physiotherapy).
(h) Varicose Vein that had burst – plenty of blood everywhere.
(i) A 29-year-old with chest pain, hyperventilating, with very upset relatives.
(j) A suicidal overdose in a house filled with young men with short hair and tight T-shirts (ifyouknowwhatImean).
(k) RTA with a traffic light pole coming off the worse in a two-car collision.
(l) An 8-month pregnant female who had fallen earlier that day.
and …
(m) A fitting 9-year-old; only one parent spoke English, and they decided to stay at home and send the father who *doesn't* speak English with us, because 'The hospital has interpreters …'

Now, out of these thirteen jobs, only five actually went to hospital …

This counts as a 'good shift', reasonably interesting jobs, and no-one tried to hit me.

I Hate Psychiatric 'Services'

Sorry folks, bit of a rant here ... but I last slept 22 hours ago ...

We got a call to a patient who was 'Depressed – not moving': normally with this type of call it's some teenager having a strop, but this time it was a little different. Basically, the patient, who suffers from depression, was discharged from the local psychiatric unit 3 weeks ago and recently had her dose of antidepressants reduced. Yesterday, she was crying all night, and tonight she was just sitting staring into space, refusing to make eye contact and not talking at all.

One of the things that we as an ambulance crew cannot do is physically remove someone to hospital if they don't want to go – that would be kidnapping and is frowned upon by the law. This young girl was not going anywhere despite my best attempts to persuade her – she just wasn't communicating.

The solution would be simple: call the Community Psychiatric Nursing (CPN) team to come and assess her and, if needed, arrange her compulsory removal to the psychiatric unit (called a 'Section' under the Mental Health Act). The problem? It was 10 p.m. ...

First off I phoned the psychiatric unit that she had received treatment under. After talking to two idiots who had trouble understanding plain English, I finally managed to get the number of the CPN team. Now, the London Ambulance Service (LAS) is quite smart: when we want to arrange an outside agency we go through our Control because all the telephone conversations are recorded ... so if someone says they are going to attend they damn well better. I got onto Control, passed the details to them and waited for them to get back to us.

I'd just like to say that in all my years of medical experience I have never had a simple referral to a psychiatric service: they always seem to try shirking any form of work by 'forgetting' you or by being just plain obstructive. Maybe I'm just unlucky and get the idiots every time.

Needless to say we waited … and waited … and waited … from 22:20 until 23:00 we waited; then at 23:02 Control got back to us. Apparently the CPN team all goes home at 23:00 and hadn't answered the phone until 23:00 on the dot. So they refused to visit the patient. The moral so far is if you are going to have a psychiatric breakdown in Newham don't do it after 22:00.

So we switched to plan 'B', which is to arrange the out-of-hours social worker to come and visit, as they double as Psychiatric Liaison. Again we went through Control and waited … and waited … and waited … Finally we heard back that the social worker would ring the family and would like to talk to me. (Outside agencies try this trick, as they know the patient's phone isn't being recorded, and so can say whatever they want, with any disagreement being my word against theirs.) The social worker explained that she was very busy and so would prefer not to come to see the patient and have I tried the out-of-hours GP?

Back to Control I went and got them to try and contact the out-of-hours GP (a GP, for those not in the UK, is the patient's family doctor). Can you guess what we then did? We waited … and waited … and waited … Finally, Control got back to us and informed us that the out-of-hours GP hadn't arrived for work yet and that when they did, they would have to see two other patients first.

All through this time the family of the patient were very understanding and were happy when I explained that the GP would call at some point in the night. All I could do was advise them to remove anything that the patient could use to hurt herself, and keep an eye on her, calling us back if they felt the need.

Total amount of time an ambulance was tied up trying to get outside agencies to DO THEIR DAMN JOB – 2 hours and 19 minutes … and not the world's most satisfactory outcome.

As I mentioned to our Control, sometimes you feel very lonely out there on the mean streets of Newham.

It is still the case that as soon as the sun goes down, various community services disappear and people in trouble need to rely on the ambulance service and the A&E department, even if it isn't the best place for them.

 ## Sticky Feet

There is something deeply disturbing about walking on a sticky carpet – especially when the flat is in a complete mess and the punter has called an ambulance 4 times in the last 2 days for a pain in the chest that has lasted 2 *years*. I'd like the jury to note that the pain hasn't changed in any way, it's not worse, or moved around the body, he has no other symptoms. But the patient just seems to like calling ambulances. I wanted to wipe my feet on the way out of the flat.

It also doesn't help when the patient smells so bad that I want to leap out the side window. We didn't have any air freshener (and apparently, neither does the hospital).

When we got to the hospital the triage nurse took one look at the patient, muttered 'Not him again' and sent him out to the waiting room. I suspect that it may just be a ploy to use biological warfare to empty the waiting room.

I still keep getting called back to him for the exact same 'problem'.

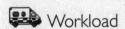 ## Workload

Once again I know a lot of visitors here are from America, so I'm going to explain how the LAS works on a day-to-day basis. This will either be very boring or immensely interesting – your choice.

Ambulances run out of dedicated stations, we don't share stations with the Fire Service. In fact, some years ago, when it was suggested the idea was shot down as we would be disturbing the firecrews' sleep throughout the night. Each station has its own call-sign 'K1', 'J2', 'G4' for example, then each ambo has a suffix that is attached to this, so one ambulance running out of station J2 would be called J201, while another would be J207.

The stations are spaced approximately 5–6 miles apart, and you mainly service the area surrounding the station; however, with interhospital transfers and other irregularities you can quite easily find yourself across the other side of London.

It's an old joke that when asking if we need to travel so far the dispatcher will ask us if it still says *London* on the side of the ambulance.

There is a main station, and two or three 'satellite' stations; the main station will normally have between three and six ambulances running from it, while the smaller stations have between one and four. There is less cover at night, and you can easily find yourself being the only ambulance running from a given station.

Across London we deal with more than 3 500 calls per day, and with a fleet of 400 ambulances of which perhaps only three-quarters are manned, we seldom get a rest. Where I work we average 1 job an hour, and are supposed to transport every one of those patients to hospital.

The longest shift we officially do is 12 hours, in which we can expect 10–13 jobs, which doesn't sound like a lot but is enough to keep us busy … We spend 97% of our time away from station (compared with 3% for the fire service).

However, it *is* a fun job.

☕ Night Shifts

There has been a discussion over on another medical blog's forums over which shift we prefer to work. Like many of the others I have a preference for working through the night. The reasons for this are many but include:

(1) I'm single, I can lie in bed as long as I want. And breakfast is dinner … and kebabs are lunch … and an icecream is supper.

(2) You get empty streets, and so can drive like someone out of 'The Fast and the Furious'.

(3) You also get the strange jobs: 'sex-toy accidents', criminal behaviour, stabbings …

(4) It feels as if you 'own' the world: there is no-one else around, and anyone you do meet is normally shocked to be awake at night.

(5) You get to work a lot of jobs with the police, who are generally excellent people to work with.

(6) I get to sleep through early morning television – I'm sorry but I can't see the attraction of 'Trisha' or 'This Morning'.

(7) I don't have to go into a school, and be surrounded by 400 screaming children just because a kid has sprained their ankle.

(8) There is less management around – actually there is no management around (always a good thing); I like to avoid management as much as I can: I worked this job for 6 months before they remembered my name.

(9) On a cold winter morning, I'm going home to my warm comfortable bed, while everyone else is trudging to work.

I still like nights, which makes me a rarity in the LAS. Most of my most interesting jobs occur at night.

Busy, Busy, Busy

No sooner do I post why I like night shifts than I get two 'proper' emergency calls, one after another. The first was a 76-year-old Male 'Suspended'. Unfortunately, despite our best efforts there was little hope for him, and he died later in hospital without his heart ever restarting. His wife of 50 or more years was disbelieving of the whole situation, and I was too busy doing CPR to be able to comfort her much. It is one of the few things that I miss about nursing – sometimes you want to spend time with a relative. If you can't do anything for the patient, the relatives then become your concern. For the first time in 50 years she was going to sleep alone and the nurse who would be looking after her is not someone that I would call the most sympathetic person in the world. I spent a little longer at hospital talking to the wife. The only consolation that I could give her was something that I've practised many times over the years – that her husband never suffered, and that he wouldn't have felt anything that we did.

The next job was a man who, after drinking too much, fell over in the street. He had a greatly altered level of consciousness, possibly due to the alcohol but also possibly due to the large head injury which was leaking a frankly excessive amount of blood over the tarmac.

He could have been worse – he was lying in the middle of the road and could have easily been run over. It is important in such a job that you should 'collar and board' them. This is a way of immobilising someone in order to prevent any damage to the spinal cord. Unfortunately the patient was quite combative and so the only safe way to secure his head was for me to hold it during the transport – all the time blood was leaking through the dressing we had put on him, all over us, the trolley bed and the floor of the ambulance. Some managed to flick up onto my crewmate's face, which is something you don't really want happening to you.

I've just come back from the hospital (after dropping off yet another assault) and our patient is doing fine – seems that his altered consciousness was indeed as a result of the alcohol. He still isn't sober enough to have a meaningful conversation, but he is looking a lot better than when we picked him up.

I still like wrestling with drunks, and writing about blood being flicked up into your face set the stage for a future set of posts.

New Uniforms (But Still Green)

The LAS has got some new uniforms. These include 'combat trousers' and a fleece, which is nice seeing as it can get a bit nippy around here. The only problem is that we use 'Alexandra', who doesn't have the best reputation, for our uniforms. We'll forget that they can't measure you up correctly – I am not a 38-inch waist no matter how many kebabs I eat. Instead, let us consider that the buttons on their shirts tend to fall off at the worst possible moment. Having a button drop in a dead man's mouth when you are trying to resuscitate him is not something that inspires confidence in the relatives watching. I was supposed to have eight shirts; two of them have been cannibalised, so that I have six shirts with the right number of buttons.

The new uniform actually seems quite nice. We have a little NHS logo in case the big motor with 'Ambulance' written on the side is not enough of a clue to our identity, and the shirts have a mesh in the armpits so we can let our sweat out. The combat trousers have 'Permagard' (their spelling, not mine) which is designed to kill bacteria, which is nice considering the state of some of the houses we visit. The high-visibility jackets are … well … visible and we now have a green 'beanie hat' (I think it's green so that people won't wear them anywhere except at work).

There is a rumour that we will be getting new boots soon … 'Magnums'. We are a bit like the army in that we buy our own boots because the ones supplied are a bit shoddy.

Anyway the uniform 'goes live' on the 12th but those who have uniform that actually fits have been wearing them early. The bosses are moaning a bit but haven't actually told anyone off about it.

I now have five shirts with the right number of buttons. People are still buying their own boots.

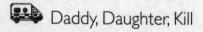 Daddy, Daughter, Kill

Picked up an assault yesterday. While sitting in the back of the ambulance he told his 2-year-old daughter that 'daddy is gonna fucking kill the people who did this to me', then complained when the nurse at the hospital told him to moderate his language.

I love this job.

We then went to someone who started hitting his own nose in order to prove that it had been bleeding earlier, and then went to a woman who had a bleeding varicose vein that had stopped bleeding, but wanted to pick at it to prove that it had been bleeding.

Then we went to a 14-year-old girl who was 'fitting' but when we got there was confused and combative – she was a diabetic so we checked her blood sugar, which was low. Being confused is one of the symptoms of a low blood sugar and we normally give them an injection that brings them out of it. We gave the injection and waited for it to work and receive the grateful thanks of the parents.

But it didn't work.

We checked the blood sugar again, and it had come back up to normal levels, yet the condition of the girl was unchanged.

So we (rather quickly) took her into hospital – we haven't been back there yet to find out what had caused her confusion. Was it drugs, alcohol, psychiatric problems, CVA (cerebrovascular accident) or even just a bad nightmare? Once we get back to the hospital which we took her to we will no doubt be able to find out. She didn't have a high temperature, didn't have any medical history besides the diabetes, her pupils were normal and responsive; all observations were normal.

We spend a lot of time dealing with things that are simple to cope with. You can fix them almost by rote thinking, but every so often you get a job that throws you off balance. Normally you 'wake up' and deal with it by going back to basics, but other jobs just completely confuse you, and this was one of those jobs.

This post got me a large number of people coming to my site looking for the search term 'Daddy fucking daughter'. Sometimes the Internet is a scary place. It turned out that the girl had been drinking vodka, and that this was the reason behind her confused and combative state.

ORCON!

ORCON – the biggest problem with the ambulance service, and the biggest cause of staff/management friction. Every so often I will revisit this topic, as it's of such importance.

I'm single at work at the moment (which means I don't have anyone to work with – so am sitting on station twiddling my thumbs), so I thought I'd tell you all about the great God ORCON and how he rules the life of every EMT/paramedic in England.

This is really boring, so I'll not be hurt if you don't bother reading any further.

The government likes to give everything targets, from school grades, the waiting time for breast cancer referrals to the number of trains on time.

The ambulance service has only one main target to reach, that of ORCON. ORCON was started in 1974 and governs how fast we are expected to respond to 'Cat A' calls. ('Cat A' calls are our high-priority calls, although because of the way calls are assessed, they are rarely seriously ill patients).

Essentially, for every 'Cat A' call in London we have to be there within 8 minutes.

Simple really.

It doesn't matter what actually happens to the patient, just so long as we get there within 8 minutes. For example, if we get to someone who has been dead for 2 days within 8 minutes, that counts as a *Success*. If we get to a heart attack in 9 minutes, provide life-saving treatment and ensure that their quality of life is a good as possible it counts as a *Failure*.

For those who don't live in London, let's just say that traffic is often heavy, and there are speed-bumps and tiny side-roads. We have more than 300 languages spoken in London, which may delay getting the location we are needed at. We are hideously overused and understaffed, we face delays at hospital owing to overcrowding and delays on-scene because of the ignorant people we have to attend to.

None of this matters – all that matters is the 8-minute deadline. If we make 75% of all calls in 8 minutes we get more money from the government, which means more staff, vehicles that work etc. … If we don't make 75% then we don't get any more money and we continue to struggle. This year it looks like we are going to make it, but only just.

There isn't any reason behind 8 minutes being the time we need to get to people: brain death occurs after 4 minutes or so; trauma, while needing to be treated as quickly as possible, has the 'Golden Hour'. The current rumour is that it is how long MPs have to vote when the Division Bell rings in parliament – who knows? No-one I have spoken to has any decent answers.

Well, that should be the last of my posts on the boring 'day to day' running of the London Ambulance Service.

You may all rejoice now.

🚐 Oh ... Bollocks ...

Rather obviously this topic dominated my weblog for some time – I'm including only some of it here, because I'm sure that you didn't want to pay good money to read about me being horribly ill. I haven't edited this post for this book – it's much how it originally appeared on my website. I started writing it less than 2 hours after I was exposed.

There is a fear that every health-care worker has. Tonight that fear jumped up and slapped me in the face.

Second job of the shift, we were called to '50-year-old male – collapsed in street'. Normally this is someone who is drunk, but we rushed to the scene anyway, just in case it isn't (we rush to *everything* – it's the only way to be sure you are not caught out). We reach the scene and see the male laying on the floor talking gibberish. He is bleeding from a cut on his face and possibly from his jaw. Bystanders tell us that he 'just dropped'. He then starts to vomit, and because it's dark we get him on our trolley and into the back of the ambulance.

Our basic assessment finds that he has no muscular tone on his right side, although all his observations are within normal limits. Deciding against hanging around we start transport to hospital. Halfway to hospital he starts to vomit and cough – part of this vomitus/blood flies unerringly across the width of the ambulance ...

... right into my open mouth.

Pretty disgusting, but what can you do? The patient then starts to come around, now able to move all limbs and to talk. This is good, it means I'm able to get some history from him. So I get his name, date of birth, address. Then I ask this 50-year-old if he is normally fit and well.

'No', he says, 'I have AIDS (acquired immune-deficiency syndrome)'.

Bollocks.

I've never had anything from a patient in my mouth before (apart from the odd chocolate when I was a nurse), so of course the first time is with an HIV (human immunodeficiency virus)-positive patient.

My crewmate looks in the rear view mirror, and that look passes between us. Ambulance people will know what I mean – it's the 'Oh shit' look that you give/get when something goes horribly wrong.

We get to the hospital and the patient is looking a lot better, fully orientated, full strength and starting to feel the pain from a probably busted jaw. So I get to hand over to the nurse, which turned into a bit of a comedy moment …

Me: 'Patient witnessed collapse, had right-sided hemiparesis, now resolved. Previous history includes AIDS'.
Handover Nurse: 'Fine'
Charge Nurse: 'You can't say that'
Me: 'Pardon?'
Charge Nurse: 'You can't say AIDS – people will be prejudiced against him'
Me: 'Well they shouldn't be, and this is medical stuff. It's a syndrome like any other'
Charge Nurse: 'You have to call it something else'
Me: 'I don't really care for political correctness, besides I'm a patient as well – I swallowed some of his blood'
Charge Nurse: 'Oh, well … lets get you sorted out then'

I then went through the rigmarole of having blood taken, then I asked to be put on PEP, which the charge nurse agreed I should be put on. PEP is 'Post Exposure Prophylaxis' – basically a cocktail of antiretroviral drugs that, taken over a 4-week period, will hopefully reduce any live virus to non-infective amounts. Common side-effects include nausea, vomiting, headache, diarrhoea, cough, abdominal pain/cramps, muscle pain, tiredness, flu-like symptoms, difficulty in sleeping, rash and (*I love this one*) flatulence.

Other more uncommon side-effects are … pancreatitis, anaemia, neutropenia, peripheral neuropathy, and other 'metabolic effects'.

I'm in for a barrel of laughs for these next 4 weeks …

The charge nurse looked really sympathetic when he offered me stuff to look after the side-effects – he used to work in an HIV clinic so I guess he knows better than me what I'm in for …

Then we talked about rates of infection, which is why I'm feeling kinda relaxed here. HIV is a tough virus to catch (compared with hepatitis, which is the one that worries me). If I were to stab myself with a needle after drawing HIV-positive blood I would have a 0.004% chance of catching the virus. Swallowing a bit of blood/vomitus is less risky than that, especially as I have no mouth/stomach ulcers. With the PEP my chances of 'seroconverting' are as close to zero as you can get. I knew all this before I set foot in the hospital, which probably explained why I wasn't a quivering wreck.

So far 'only' two medical workers have seroconverted after needle-stick injuries. I greatly doubt that I'll be the third.

So 'The Plan' is that I go to see Occupational Health on Monday, and they will advise me on what happens next. I've been told already that I'll have to avoid sexual contact for the next 3 months (not a hardship – I've managed 'no sexual contact' for 2 years before now) and that I'll probably need to take 4 weeks off work due to me feeling too ill from the side-effects of the antiretrovirals.

We'll see about that … I don't 'do' ill.

Anyway, if I do need to take time off it'll give me a chance to read some books I've got sitting on my shelf – and complete 'Zelda – Windwaker'.

Gotta go now, I feel flatulent already …

I never got around to completing 'Zelda'.

'Donor' Takes on New Meaning

I got a lot of support over the previous post, and to be honest I would have been a lot less calm if I didn't have my blog where I could offload some of my worries.

First, thanks to everyone who has contacted me over my 'exposure', I appreciate it all, even if I haven't personally replied to you (you'll find out why I might not have answered you a bit later in this post …).

I went to Occupational Health on Monday, basically to let them know about my exposure, and that I was on PEP. The LAS showed how nice they are by lending me a spare ambulance to drive to my appointment – GPS navigation comes in handy when you don't know where you are going.

Occupational Health is south of the river at King's College Hospital, which is a bit of a trek. 'Occy Health' took baseline blood samples, so they would know if there was any effect on my liver/kidneys/white cell count, and filled in a couple of forms about my exposure. Then they told me that they would get in contact with the 'donor' to see what his virus load and hepatitis status was.

Until now I always thought of 'donor' as a 'nice' word – heart donors and the like – I never really thought it would happen to include this circumstance.

During the consultation they told me that I'd need blood tests every fortnight for the next month and a half, and that my first HIV/hepatitis status check would be in 3 months, with an additional one in 6 months. Should they both be negative then I would be in the clear.

They also told me of the side-effects of the antiretrovirals that I am taking, and seemed surprised that all I was experiencing was similar to a mild hangover.

That was yesterday – today was spent vomiting/sleeping to avoid nausea/ and experiencing the joys of explosive diarrhoea.

My station officer called up and asked me how I was. When I told him, he basically told me to take it easy and go back to work when I felt better.

However, there was some good news when the Occupational Health nurse contacted me, and told me that the donor's viral load was low, that there were no resistances to the PEP drugs I'm taking and that in 2002 he was free of hepatitis. That has eased my mind somewhat.

Some people have commented that I'm taking it rather well. There are a number of reasons for this, not least that the chances of me becoming HIV-positive are less than 1 in 5 000. The other thing is that I can't do anything now to change those odds, apart from continue to take the PEP.

The other side-effect of the meds I'm taking are that I'm having a certain 'vagueness': my mind isn't operating on all four cylinders, so if this seems disjointed, I've got an excuse …

Even today I'm not sure that the PEP drugs didn't permanently 'disjoint my mind'.

☕ Pavlov's Dog

Well, the PEP is still going down, unfortunately I've developed a Pavlovian response to the hours of 8 o'clock. Every 12 hours I need to take the pills – I start to get nauseous just thinking about it, the familiar copper taste hits my mouth and I just want to lie down.

I also seem to have lost any control over my circadian rhythms, I'm sleeping for 14–16 hours straight and I'm drowsy for the rest – doesn't matter whether it is day or night.

At the moment the rather wonderful 'Scissor Sisters' album is chilling me out nicely, particularly 'Return to Oz' (which has a bit that puts me in mind of The Kinks' 'Lola').

I am, however, losing the motivation for cooking food, not least because of the large amount of washing up accruing in my sink. It makes me feel like a student again.

Also, my PC is screaming out for a complete overhaul – I just can't be bothered.

Mothering Sunday

Well, Saturday was the last day I worked but Greenfairy (another blogger) mentioned something that I wanted to write about – but forgot, for some bizarre reason …

The first call of Saturday was to a '?Suspended'.*

So we hack along the road, knowing full well that because it is the first job of the day the patient is definitely going to be dead.

We arrive at the house and the FRU is there before us – I grab my kit and bound up the stairs past the daughter who called us and into the bedroom. Where a very dead lady was lying on the bed while the Rapid Responder was completing his paperwork.

One look is all you need to tell if someone has been dead for some time – and this lady had that look. It turned out that the daughter last saw her mother alive an hour ago, but that she was feeling a little unwell and took to bed. The daughter had checked on her half an hour later and found her not breathing. She then waited 20 minutes to call us as she was in such a 'tizzy'. A quick look told us that even if we had been there when it had happened it was unlikely we could do much: various clues led us to think that a stomach ulcer had ruptured and she had bled out into her stomach.

---

* '?Suspended' means 'Query Suspended' which means that the patient might be suspended (a.k.a 'dead') – we don't know, they might just be asleep, or drunk, or have a high temperature or a cut finger, but the person calling us is a twit.

All around the house were flowers and cards – the next day being Mothering Sunday.

No sooner than we had informed the daughter that her mother had died than the doorbell went and my crewmate went down to see who it was. It was only a bleedin' flower delivery man, delivering flowers to the (now) dearly departed. My crewmate told the delivery guy that now, perhaps, wasn't the best time to bring flowers but took them in anyway, hiding them in the kitchen.

Perfect!

Then we had to wait an hour for the police to turn up, which is normal procedure for any death in the home and is nothing to worry about. I then helped the police turn her body (to look for anything strange) and put my hand in a puddle of urine[*] – something that wouldn't bother me, IF I was wearing any gloves.

Oh well.

The Other Guy

I'm feeling a little better, the side-effects of the PEP seem to have subsided somewhat, although the flatulence is reaching epic proportions, which, coupled with the diarrhoea, makes every bowel motion an adventure

I have my second date with Occupational Health on Friday, for a blood test to make sure that the PEP isn't battering my liver/kidneys/pancreas and that my white cell count hasn't lowered. Work have said they'll do everything they can to supply a vehicle to get me down to south-east London.

---

[*] There are two things that I can't smell – alcohol on someone's breath and urine that isn't infected with bacteria.

I've been thinking a bit about the 'donor'; I wonder how he feels – he's lying in bed after having a rather frightening collapse in the street, with a broken jaw and the reason for the collapse unknown. Then a couple of days later the medical team ask him to consent to some more blood tests because he may have infected the EMT who helped him out.

If it were me I'd be absolutely mortified.

When I talk to Occupational Health I'll ask them if they can get a message back to him, letting him know that I'm fine and that I don't blame him for anything. I know his name and address, but I don't think it'd be right to turn up on his doorstep to talk to him.

I hope *he* is alright and that the collapse was something simple – I suspect a 'TIA' (transient ischaemic attack), which can be a precursor to a stroke, but with the right medications hopefully the threat of that can be controlled.

I never got to see him again, so he never found out the results of my blood tests. I kind of hope that he gets to read this, so he knows that I'm fine.

Twelve Hours to Go

In 12 hours I will have stopped PEP. Those seven pills are the last ones that I am going to take.

I am extremely happy about this.

It has been a month since my stomach didn't feel as if I were waiting to vomit, a month since my thought processes have seemed even remotely like mine. A month since I last worked – good grief, am I bored! A month of wondering if my life is about to change for the worst. A month of my mates looking sideways at me when I had to take the pills in front of them (but still friends enough to laugh and joke with me about it). A month of having to get out of bed to eat breakfast, because the pills need food in my stomach. A month without shaving (why bother, I'm not allowed to have sex!). A month of feeling just the tiniest bit isolated. A month of people who I have never met, from places around the globe I have never seen, wishing me well. A month of always feeling grateful to those people, for this is the kindness of strangers – in itself a random act of reality.

All over now.

In two months I get to go for my HIV test, which should be fun and giggles.

But for now – I'm happy.

I really think that if it wasn't for my blogging and the support of my friends around the globe I'd have gone mad from boredom. My next book should be Blogging as a Mental Health Exercise.

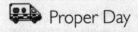 Proper Day

My first 'proper' day back at work, working with my new crewmate on a proper ambulance.

The first job was a 66-year-old male who had been fixing tiles on his shed roof and had fallen off the ladder, probably around 10 feet. He was shut behind his front door and all I could hear through his letterbox was 'I've broken my leg'.

The police are much better than me at getting into locked premises (the last time I tried I fell on my arse in front of a crowd of 20 people) so we waited for them to arrive and use their specialised equipment (screwdriver/size 12 boot) to force open the door.

Gaining access to our customer it was pretty obvious that he had fractured his femur (thighbone) as it had a new bendy section just above the knee. The pulse was good in his foot and he didn't complain of pain anywhere else in his body. This brave man had crawled, with this fracture, from his garden through his kitchen to the living room where he kept his phone. All throughout our treatment he didn't complain once. We splinted his leg and 'collared and boarded' him from the house (a fall of 10 feet can easily break your neck, and the pain from his leg could easily distract him from a neck injury). We could have set traction on his leg, but we were only 5 minutes from the hospital; so we 'blued' him into Newham General Hospital, where he was 'attacked' by the local trauma team.

The next job we got was a dinner lady at a local primary school who had dropped a knife on her foot. There was a tiny cut to the foot, and after cleaning, dressing and checking her tetanus status we left her at work. What depressed us was that there were no scraps of food left we could have.

Driving back from the last job we saw four workmen chasing another man who ducked into the local mosque. We ignored this until we got a call to the area the men had run from – apparently a man had been assaulted with a 'Car-lock'. HEMS (our emergency helicopter service) had been activated and were going to make their way to the scene. When we did a quick U-turn and rolled up to the scene it soon became obvious that HEMS was not needed so we cancelled them. The man had been clamping an illegally parked car when the owner and his wife returned. The car owner then pulled a large aerosol can from his boot and hit our patient around the back of the neck, causing a short period of unconsciousness. His wife had also put up a fight, but the owner of the car had run (into the aforementioned mosque) leaving his wife behind. (What a gent!) At one point we thought it was going to turn into a riot as 30 youths from the mosque were adamant that the four workmen doing the chasing weren't going to set foot in the mosque.

Again, we had to collar and board him, and lift him onto our stretcher, which wasn't much fun as the man weighed at least 20 stone. Subsequent treatment at hospital showed no serious injuries.

Final job (after having to get our nice, new, shiny ambulance fixed – a problem with the side-door) was a 60-year-old female collapsed at a bus station with slurred speech and 'not drunk'. Remember that, 'not drunk', it's important.

What could it be? Could it be a stroke? Could it be hypoglycaemia? Could it be cardiac related? So we turned up to find 'Mary' having fallen over, smelling strongly of alcohol and with a 5/6ths empty bottle of whisky in her purse. (*My crewmate had to tell me about the smell of alcohol, as I've mentioned before, I'm pretty much unable to smell it myself.*)

'Not drunk' – why did the callmaker say that? It's bloody obvious she was pissed as a fart. I'd guess it was the bus station staff who wanted her gone and were afraid we wouldn't turn up if we knew she was drunk. Still, it was an easy last job of the shift, even if she did keep grabbing at my balls and kissing my (thankfully) gloved hand.

This counts as a good day.

Now I'm off for some endorphin-releasing Bailey's ice-cream.

Can you tell I was deliriously happy to be back at work?

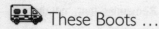 These Boots ...

These Boots ...

Have walked along train tracks

Have been washed in the blood of murder victims

Have kicked in doors to get to unconscious women

Have stepped in more urine, in more tower blocks, than I'd care to think about

Have kept my feet warm and comfortable on long nights

Have been allowed into a mosque

Have climbed fences to reach dead bodies

Have run across football fields to try to save a life, and failed

Have been spat on, vomited on and shat on

Have stood in 'remains'

Have tried to find purchase while walking backward down narrow stairs

Have defended me from drunks and druggies

Have been run over by a 22-stone trolley

Have been stared at by a daughter when I was telling her her mother had died

For Pixeldiva who denies she has a shoe fetish.

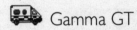 # Gamma GT

I went to Occupational Health today – it seems that the last time they checked my blood (because of being on PEP) my liver enzymes were a bit elevated. Most significantly my gamma-GT (gamma-glutamyl transpeptidase) was at 164 (it should be between 0 and 55). PEP is well known as having effects on the liver, so this isn't completely unexpected.

More blood was taken today to check that the enzymes have returned to normal. The nurse was very concerned that I was alright in having my blood drawn, and that I wouldn't faint. She was asking me this while I'm sitting opposite her in full uniform …

The nurse was also a bit surprised that I'd had aural hallucinations and looked at me as if she thought I was turning schizophrenic – I assured her that the 'voices' were now leaving me alone and that it wasn't a problem. She'd never heard of this symptom before, so at least I entertained someone today.

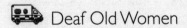 # Deaf Old Women

Nobby is working tonight from our main station. He is always a good laugh and always seems to have a joke whenever he works. Tonight I met him outside the hospital and he told me about a deaf old woman he had just brought in.

It was raining as he started to wheel her out her house so he made the comment 'It's raining, you picked a fine time to be ill'.

'Eh?' was the reply.

'The rain … it mucks up my hair'.

'Eh?'

'MY HAIR!'

With this she took a long hard look at Nobby's very short, and very receding hair and asked him, 'Is it because of cancer?'

It is now 3 a.m. and already every other patient we have picked up has been drinking – from the 38-year-old male having a panic attack, who didn't want to talk to us, to the 50-year-old female who slipped on some steps coming out from the pub and cut her head. This has so far ended with our last call being one of our smelly 'frequent flyers', who thankfully decided not to hang around and wait for us to turn up.

Then there was the police car that managed to accidentally force another car into someone's garden – one of those jobs where every passing car slows down to stare. Thankfully, there were no injuries, apart from the house-owner's disturbed sleep. (At least I assume it was the owner – he was dressed in no shoes and a dressing gown.)

With a bit of luck people are now wrapped up nice and snug in bed – away from the rain – and the only calls we will get will be the 5 a.m. 'I'm in labour' call that will result in a baby around 11 a.m. (long after I'm in bed).

Hand Over Mouth

No sooner do I hope for a quiet hour or two than the activation phone goes; it's sending us 200 yards up the road to a 'Collapsed Male'. We are met by two police officers who tell us that the patient was walking along the street, saw the policemen and then collapsed.

We get to the patient and my crewmate can't smell any alcohol on him, but he is coughing and spluttering like an Oscar winner. He complains of a headache, coughing, leg pain, back pain and an inability to walk.

Other than that he is refusing to talk to us. Examination is normal and the patient is obviously play-acting.

He then does one of the things that I really hate (given the prevalence of tuberculosis in Newham); he coughs all over us and the vehicle *without putting his hand over his mouth*. Then he starts to spit on the floor of the ambulance, again something I take a dim view of – but I'm driving so I leave it to my crewmate to sort out.

Forty seconds later and we pull up outside the hospital, and our patient decides to roll around the floor. By now our patience is wearing thin, so we haul him up and throw him in a wheelchair.

In the hospital he refuses to speak to the nurses, says he cannot stand and doesn't acknowledge any requests. We leave him there and within 30 seconds are back on station.

While at the hospital I indulged in a little bit of teaching. The nurse who was assessing our patient was trying to check his pupil response (by shining a light in each eye and making sure that it reacts to light) but the eyes don't appear to be reacting. I then suggest turning off the ceiling light that the patient is lying on his back staring at.

I still have patients who insist on coughing without putting their hand over their mouth. I've given up asking them to stop – instead I just give them oxygen, via a nice tightly fitting oxygen mask. I got a lot of people coming to this post searching for 'Hand over mouth'. I swear I don't know why.

Essential, Not Emergency

One of the bizarre things about the Ambulance Service is that, in the eyes of the government, we are an 'essential' service but not an 'emergency' service. We are 'essential' because the emergency services (Police, Fire Brigade and Coastguard) are run by the Home Office but Ambulance

Services across the country are run by NHS Trusts, and as such do not have access to the same resources as the true 'emergency' services. The distinction is often slight, but can sometimes have quite important considerations for our safety.

Last night was a case in point. We were called to a patient with abdominal pain; however, further information was given that the patient could be violent. There was something in this information that triggered my 'danger-sense', so I was happy to wait for police assistance to arrive before approaching the house.

Four police officers turned up – normally only two are sent to assist us – and they told us that their computer system, and their personal experience with the householder, showed him as a nasty piece of work. We followed the police to the patient and they told him that they were going to search him, and that they wanted to put him in handcuffs first. The patient had obviously been involved with the police before, as once he was handcuffed they checked to see if he had any *new* warrants out for his arrest …

Searching him they found a large stick, and a rather worrying-looking (5-inch) knife on his person.

All through this the 'lady' of the house was shouting abuse, mainly at the patient, but occasionally at the police officers present. One quick examination showed nothing life-threatening, so we offered a trip to hospital, which the patient accepted. However, as we left the house the woman shouted a few final obscenities at the patient and he then told us he couldn't be bothered to go to hospital and stalked off into the night. (*This was not a problem for either my crewmate or myself.*)

Police computers had information that he was dangerous (a number of rather vicious assaults) but our computers are not allowed to have such data. A police dispatcher has told us that they have all sorts of information on addresses, from animal liberation protesters to Members of Parliament. Again, our computers don't have any information of that sort unless we enter it manually *after* an ambulance crew has been threatened assaulted.

Needless to say, one such report has been sent to central office.

I later found out that the patient was addicted to crack cocaine – which explains a lot.

Return of Pavlov's EMT

Last night we picked up an alcoholic who is HIV positive. I (still) have no real fear of HIV patients, even when they are bleeding a bit and this patient was not (although they had wet themselves). The only problem is that I seem to have turned into one of Pavlov's dogs. When we found out the patient was HIV positive my stomach churned as if I were back on the PEP. It was really rather strange because it wasn't fear (I'll only have that when I'm due for my HIV test) but instead something more ... biological.

The son of the patient was extremely embarrassed at the antics of his parent, and my crewmate spent some time making sure that he was alright.

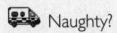 Naughty?

Is it naughty to take someone to hospital, who doesn't really need to go, just in order to get a fry-up breakfast there?

It's a lot simpler to take everyone to hospital whether they need it or not. It means that I have to do less paperwork, the patient feels validated and it means that if I'm missing something nasty (which is likely to happen at 6 a.m.) then the hospital has a chance to catch it.

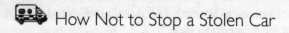 Too Darn Busy

I am extremely busy at the moment; I'm often posting from my PDA (Personal Digital Assistant) and mobile phone. I should be catching up with stuff on Friday (including answering all those comments people have left).

Got some blood results (post PEP stuff), seems my white cell count is still going down. I think they have a life-span of 120 days, so it might get lower before it gets better. Still, it gives me an excuse to see the rather pretty occupational health nurse.

Today we did the usual of little old ladies who feel unwell calling their GP and the GP calling us to take them to hospital because they are too busy to drag their arses out of their office to visit sick people. On the radio it seems that lots of people are dropping dead – the weather is quite a bit warmer (24°C) so the old are placed under a bit more physiological stress.

I have a 101 things to do, and no time to do it – simple stuff like paying bills can be incredibly hard when you are single and a shift worker.

And I think I'm moaning too much …

I'm off to bed now. Goodnight all.

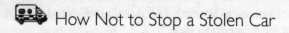 How Not to Stop a Stolen Car

So damn tired …

I'm currently at that point where I wonder whether I am hungry enough to cook dinner before I go to sleep. Which biological urge will win out?

Today, our Control wanted us to go to an emergency call when we were the other side of the Thames – I rather politely asked them if we were the nearest motor as we weren't actually a boat, the reply was, 'Yes, do you have your water wings?' So we ended up going a couple of miles out of our way to cross the river.

The call was a faint, probably from the heat that is roasting London at the moment – at least the women are wearing revealing clothes, which makes our job of cruising through the streets a bit more enjoyable.

Picked up two psychiatric drug-using patients in a row who were drunk and lying in the road perhaps 500 yards away from each other. Some children were poking one with a stick …

Then there was the 51-year-old 4-foot-4 Asian grandmother who, upon seeing her husband's car being stolen, jumped on the back and hung onto the rear windscreen wiper. She was flung off and, thankfully, not seriously hurt – mainly bruising and gravel rash. Unfortunately, the car that was stolen also contained her house keys and bank books. The A&E was so busy they had to put her out in the waiting room – something that annoyed me no end, especially as the nurse that put her out there had annoyed me earlier in the day by suggesting that I didn't know what the symptoms of bulimia were.

Now to eat/sleep … then lather/rinse/repeat tomorrow.

☕ Sunday

Sunday alone in my flat, no work, no stress, some decent stuff on telly = Good.

No chocolate in the fridge, uniform to be ironed, work tomorrow = Bad.

Phone call from Occupational Health telling me my blood values are back to normal = Excellent (only HIV/hep test to go now).

Eight … Nine Down

Our complex is EIGHT ambulances short today, so it comes as no surprise that we are running around like the proverbial blue-arsed fly. Control keeps broadcasting jobs for which they have no ambulances, this means that a lot of crews are more unhappy than usual, as Control hassles us about 'greening up' quicker. It doesn't bother me, if I'm busy doing jobs it makes the shift go quicker.

As I'm typing this an ambulance has had a blow-out on the fast lane of the A102 – a very busy road. The crew are alright, but it means we are now nine ambulances down for the next 2 hours at least.

The jobs I've been doing are the usual Monday morning sort of stuff: 97-year-old women having heart attacks, 10-year-old boys with cut heads (a rather impressive 3-inch cut, mind you) and 88-year-old men from nursing homes who have 'high blood pressure' (they invariably have a better blood pressure than I do).

Now some silly sod has stabbed himself in the stomach with a pair of scissors.

Health Copyright

I've been on a 'Guidelines' course. Essentially, this is a course that tells us that we are already doing the right thing; it also introduces us to a book with our new treatment guidelines. It takes 2 days and tomorrow will include learning about child abuse (do we have to bring our own child?). So far the course has been a trainer telling us that this course changes nothing, and we are to continue doing what we are doing at the moment. At least the days are short, 8 a.m. until 2 p.m. At the start of every Powerpoint presentation is the same definition of 'Clinical Governance'.

We had to write our own scenarios then swapped them around to other groups (this is a really easy teaching technique, since you don't have to plan anything). There was also a chat about how our complaints to compliments ratio is about 50/50, and that most of the complaints are because of 'staff attitude'. So far I have had no complaints, and no compliments – I'm a strong believer of flying under the radar.

However there is a problem – the Guidelines book we should be getting is version 3.0, but the book we are actually getting is version 2.2.

The reason for this?

Copyright!

It seems that the LAS wants to change a few bits to make it more relevant to London. But because the organisation that wrote it maintains the copyright it can't be changed for us. Lawrence Lessig's *Free Culture* states that you get value added when others can build on your work. This is a perfect example of this principle.

So, the people of London are not getting the best clinical care because of copyright.

Clinical Governance is about getting the best care to the public, so it's a bit of a mixed message.

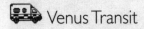 Venus Transit

There is a Transit of Venus today – all these special astronomical phenomena remind me of the eclipse we had in the summer of 1999 …

(Cue wobbly flashback video effects)

I was working in A&E at the time of the eclipse and thought that there would be no way I'd get to see it. Like all A&E departments this place had no windows and could be perhaps best described as a bunker. Today, however, the department was empty for the first time in living memory. Normally by that time of the day we would be packed full, but today ... not a soul. One person had been in earlier with a painful foot, but there wasn't the normal 'trolleys in the corridor' effect that was normal for that time of day.

We learned that day that CT (computed tomography) films make excellent sunglasses.

So, the whole department stood outside on the grass staring at the sun slowly disappearing – very spooky, and one of the few strong memories I have from that long ago. I suspect that many of the wards were empty as well: there was a procession of people wearing dressing gowns and holding tight to their drip stands wandering around the hospital grounds.

As soon as the eclipse finished we immediately had two cardiac arrests brought in by ambulance, it was as if they had waited until after the eclipse before deciding to keel over dead ...

Life also tends to be a bit quiet around FA cup finals, royal marriages and important soap storylines.

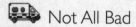 Not All Bad

I often carry a camera around with me. I was talking to some kids recently – they were happy little buggers, enjoying the sunshine on a lazy Sunday.

It's not all bad this job.

This picture still makes me smile.

🚐 Wedding Saga + Pub Fight

Some calls are a pain in the arse, not because anyone is particularly ill, but instead because you can see complaints coming in, and there being a high possibility of losing your job.

Tonight was a case in point. We got called to a wedding reception where the bride had collapsed; a quick history revealed MS (multiple sclerosis), and that it was likely that this was the cause of the collapse. Unfortunately, the patient and the patient's new husband were adamant that she wasn't going to go to hospital, particularly the hospital that was nearest. Things were not helped because they had called an ambulance for an aunt who had collapsed, but had cancelled it before it had arrived because it was 'taking too long'.

While we were getting a history from the patient, the new husband was generally acting like an arse: he was questioning everything that we did, interfering with our talking to the patient and generally getting in the way. We managed to get rid of him for a short period and the rest of the family came over to us and apologised for his behaviour.

Luckily, the patient's hotel was next door to the hospital so, after 45 minutes of persuasion, I managed to get the patient to agree for us to take her towards the hotel, and if she felt better then we could, in good conscience, leave her there. En route I called up on the radio, and arranged for the Duty Officer to meet us at the hotel. He did and the responsibility of leaving her without treatment now fell on his shoulders (thus, saving our jobs should anything go horribly wrong).

I know MS is a horrible disease. I know it isn't fair that it would strike on your wedding day, and I can understand why you might not want to go to hospital ... but if you can't move half of your body, then please understand why the ambulance people might be a bit unhappy to leave you lying in the middle of the street.

It then all kicked off in the Hackney/Homerton area. There was a big fight in a pub, with everything in it being smashed – multiple casualties with various head and facial injuries from flying bottles and broken glass. We were first on scene, and I needed to call up to let Control know that at least another 3 ambulances were needed. At least it gave me a chance to practise my '5-second triage' skills. None of the drunks there were particularly aggressive, but there was a ton of police there pulling me from one casualty to another around the pub, and even 300 yards up the street. This was just a taste of what was to come as another pub was attacked and it basically overloaded our resources. It got so busy that our Duty Officer was transporting severe asthmatic attacks in his car (and he doesn't carry much more than a defibrillator and oxygen) and Control was holding 35 calls across the area. That is, 35 calls at 3 o'clock in the morning. That'll teach me to wonder if it will be busy in a previous post.

Tomorrow England play their first 'Euro 2004' match – Alcohol + Patriotism + Recent History (we are playing the French) + Me Working = Recipe for Disaster

Watch this space …

I never got a complaint from that job, although for some time I was holding my breath about it.

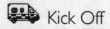 Kick Off

Well it looks like I was right, the nice weather with people in the pubs from an early hour, coupled with England losing 2–1 in the football, has led to what can, in best tabloid fashion, be described as 'an orgy of violence'.

It started out with a couple of 'glassings', which we have been getting over our vehicle computer screens as 'stabbing to the head' for some reason.

A couple more assaults, including one who was set upon by a number of drunks who were intent on stealing his car. Luckily he was not too badly injured – more shook up. Other crews were 'blueing' in a number of assaults, including at least one stab victim.

The police were running from call to call, and once more there are not enough ambulances to deal with the large number of calls we have been receiving. Our Duty Officer has been telling crews that we should be wearing our stab-vests constantly – but he isn't the one who has to lug a 20-stone unconscious patient down 4 flights of stairs in this heat …

Good job I'm not searching for a quiet life.

I am, however, off to bed now.

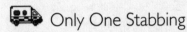 ## Only One Stabbing

For the first night in ages it has been reasonably quiet on the streets of East London – only one stabbing and that was to the patient's arse …

However, while adults are no doubt nursing hangovers the children are out causing mischief. The first two calls we got yesterday were to kids (8 and 10 years old) who had been hit by cars. The first was a 'classic': child running out towards an ice-cream van. He was alright apart from a broken right ankle. No sooner than he was safely ensconced in hospital than we find ourselves dealing with a child who has run out in front of a car (in the absence of an ice-cream van) and has broken his *left* ankle.

Tie in a hyperventilating adult, a 14-year-old with hay-fever and a drunken Colles' fracture and you have a pretty good night.

We had one serious job, someone who had a CVA (a CVA is a 'stroke') on a train. The CVA wasn't so much the problem as the extrication of the patient, who couldn't move, and yet was combative with his unaffected side. To start off, the space between the seats on the train was not large enough to allow our carry-chair to pass. The man was large and heavy so we basically had to manhandle him (in a very undignified manner) through some connecting doors and out onto the platform. The train station has a big flight of stairs towards street-level and only one lift, and the lift was not on the platform we were on. It would have been unsafe to carry this man up the stairs because of his weight and combativeness. In a rare spark of genius I realised that if we waited for a district line train we could carry him through the train onto the other platform. We 'blued' him into hospital as his pulse-rate was 40 (should be 60–100).

When I went to see the patient later in hospital he had started to regain his speech and wasn't confused. He was about to go for a CT scan so, with a bit of luck, he might make a good recovery …

This is just another part of the job that I like – that sometimes I have to out-think problems. I can't see me doing this in an office job.

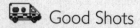 Good Shots

There is something that I've learned over many years of health-care work. When you are lifting little old ladies with senile dementia, they will sometimes grab you by the testicles.

And squeeze …

This hurts.

I swear, the greater the degree of dementia, the greater the accuracy and the stronger the grip.

And for the love of all that is holy …

Don't drop them.

That hurts even more …

Ethnic Dress

When I went to the Clap Clinic for my HIV test, I was referred to a 'Health Adviser', which is a new name for Counsellor. I am, as regular readers may appreciate, a fairly simple, pragmatic person: within hours of my HIV exposure I was aware of transmission rates, odds of infection and the rates of death caused by electrocution (1 in 5 000) and shooting in America (1 in 2 500). So, to be honest, counselling was the last thing I needed.

I did a counselling course when I was a nurse, and it did nothing to disabuse me of the notion that all counsellors are hippies who consider themselves 'worthy'.

She asked me a load of questions about how I would cope if I were to be found HIV positive (answer: get over it), and cautioned me not to tell anyone I was testing, unless I was happy for them to know the result (answer: the whole world could know – if they read this site). There was some other stuff that is just too dull for words, and definitely too dull to read.

The thing that amused me the most, however, was not that the 'Advice Room' had the only comfy chairs in the place but that the counsellor was wearing a sari (the Indian dress). In and of itself not unusual, except that the woman wearing it was 'whiter' than me.

I'm well used to 'white' women wearing various Muslim dresses – it's a religion after all – but as far as I'm aware a sari is a cultural thing. I'm guessing that in her 'equal-opportunities, worthy, multicultural' world that she is proving how non-racist she is. This is handy because to be honest out of the 20 or more people at the clinic I was in a race/culture minority of one. Not a problem, I know Newham well … it's very diverse, but I wonder if Asian people would be impressed or nonplussed by her wearing a traditional Indian dress?

Maybe I should start wearing nothing but a Papuan penis sheath?

The HIV test result should be received by the 28th …

I've tried as hard as possible to make this sound as non-racist as possible – at no point have I meant to cause offence. I hate no 'race' more than another – I hate them *all*.

'I hate them all' – a philosophy to live by.

Small Victories

Our second call of the day was to an address where the elderly woman who lived there was believed deceased – the neighbours had called the police, and the police had called us. What this often turns into is us struggling to gain entry to the house, normally resulting in an injury to me, only to find someone who has been dead for some time.

We rolled up to the house and met with the neighbours who led us around to the back garden where, peering through the rear window, we could see the old woman sitting in her chair looking pale, still … and very dead.

Simultaneously, my crewmate and I jumped back in shock as we saw her take a breath!

She was breathing about six times a minute, and surely didn't have much longer left to live – I rushed around the front and kicked in the front door (in one hit – something I've never managed before) and we got her out to the ambulance in double-time. We quickly decided that it would be wrong to 'stay and play', instead opting to ventilate her via 'Ambubag' and to monitor her cardiac rhythm and her pulse (which was strong and regular).

The hospital had a team standing by, as we had notified them of the patient on leaving the scene. The transport time to hospital was about 2 minutes, and on arrival the A&E team leaped into action, intubating and ventilating her, gaining venous access and running the various blood tests. Family members were contacted and plans for her treatment were drawn up. At no time did I feel that this 88-year-old woman was receiving anything other than the best treatment possible.

We cleaned the ambulance and restocked before going onto our next job; each time we returned to the hospital we popped our head into the Resus' room to check how she was doing; there were plans to CT scan her head and to move her to ITU (intensive treatment unit). The family arrived and after some discussion it was decided that the best care for her was going to be palliative (that is to make her comfortable, but not to do any invasive procedures and to allow her to die). This was, I feel, the right course of action – the lack of oxygen would make any survival short and probably result in serious brain damage.

It has been a very long time since I've felt a great deal of sympathy towards someone, but this was one patient that I did actually care about, and not just because I'm soft on 'little old ladies'. She had little chance of recovery, but we hoped for it anyway. She fought for her life, and had probably been doing that for the whole of the night. Because of our actions, and the actions of the hospital team, she wasn't going to die alone, and she wasn't going to die without her family saying a final goodbye to her.

It's a small victory, but sometimes those are the only ones you get.

Right to 'Load and Go'?

Yesterday we got a call to a 27-year-old male, diabetic having a fit. It was only 4–5 miles away, but travelling through Newham on a Saturday afternoon is always slow business – this was compounded by one of the roads which we use as a shortcut being closed for resurfacing. It took us 14 minutes to travel those 4 miles. Then it was up 5 flights of stairs into a flat where the first thing we could hear was hysterical sobbing. As I've mentioned before it's one of those sounds you know means trouble.

Squeezing past a large bed we entered the bedroom to find a First Responder 'bagging' the young man, who was lying motionless on the floor. Sitting on the bed wailing, was a young woman who we discovered later to be his fiancée. The patient was connected to one of our cardiac monitors and it was showing sinus rhythm. Kneeling on the floor I did a quick pulse check – beat, beat, beat … then nothing, no pulse for 10 seconds. During the pulse check I was getting a history. Apparently the patient was an insulin-dependent diabetic, who had possibly been neglecting to take his insulin injections. He had become more agitated during the morning until he collapsed and started fitting after having an argument with his fiancée.

With a monitor showing an apparent sinus rhythm the patient was in 'pulseless electrical activity' – we can't 'shock' this rhythm so I started CPR. From out of his mouth flew some bloody saliva, straight towards my face, luckily impacting on my forehead rather than ending up being swallowed (I don't want to make *that* a habit).

One round of CPR (3 minutes later) and we got a pulse – the patient started 'cramping up', all his muscles had gone into spasm. A very quick blood sugar measurement reading showed 'HI' (a reading of over 32.0 mmols of sugar – the normal is 4–7 mmols). Immediately I started thinking of DKA (diabetic ketoacidosis) – a condition that occurs when blood sugar goes too high – a life-threatening condition that could explain his cardiac arrest. There was little that we could do on-scene as he needed immediate medical treatment beyond what we could provide.

With a 'Load and Go' order my crewmate set up the chair and the three of us dead-lifted him over the bed that was blocking the door and into the chair – I felt the familiar trickle of urine down my leg and looking at the patient he seemed to lose all colour. Another pulse check followed – his heart had stopped again.

I had to make a decision then: would we start CPR again only for him to continue this cycle of pulse/arrest, or do we make a run for the ambulance – all the time starving his brain of oxygenated blood – so that we could get him into hospital to correct the cause of his arrest?

I decided that we should 'run for it': if we got a pulse back it would be a purely temporary measure until his high blood sugar could be corrected. It was a very difficult removal – my back was spasming as we carried him down the 5 narrow, dark, winding flights of stairs and ran him across the 100 yards of pavement to our ambulance. Throwing him and his fiancée in the back of the ambulance we started the long run back to the nearest hospital. For 10 minutes I did CPR in the back of the ambulance while my crewmate tried his best to get through the exceptionally busy traffic – stopping and starting, swerving across the road, over pavements; he drove to the limit.

Throughout transport the only rhythm we had was 'asystole', which is when the heart isn't beating at all. With our First Responder 'bagging' him and myself doing CPR we were doing all we could to support his life. During the transport the fiancée told us that he had had a previous arrest when he had stopped taking his insulin, but that he had, obviously, recovered.

Rolling up to the hospital we were met by the 'Arrest Team' – senior doctors from across the hospital. They descended on the patient, trying to get IV access, a secure airway and running diagnostic checks. It seemed, however, that the team leader didn't want to listen to our handover. I was later told that he was concerned about getting the audit times right. The first thing he said was 'the patient is biting on the airway' suggesting that the patient wasn't actually in cardiac arrest – because he hadn't listened to my handover he didn't know about the cramping episode earlier. The hospital staff did their own 'pulse check' and were confused about feeling a pulse (in a stressful situation doctors often feel their own pulse rather than the patient's). It was only after some time that I could actually give the team leader a complete handover that he paid attention to.

The team worked on him for over an hour. His blood tests showed that his potassium was a sky-high 7.5; this was probably the main cause of his arrest. It transpired that the patient had renal failure and the high potassium and high blood sugar probably meant that the normal biochemical reactions in the body were being interfered with, leading to his fitting and cardiac arrest.

One hour later the patient was declared dead.

His fiancée was distraught; the patient's parents had to travel 170 miles to the hospital and so it was necessary to tell them what had happened over the telephone – I can only imagine the drive down to London. The fiancée was convincing herself that it was her fault, that it was the argument that killed him, or that she should have recognised his symptoms of a high blood sugar before they became fatal. Both I and the nursing staff tried to console her, to tell her that it wasn't her fault – but would the parents blame her?

I was thinking, would he have survived if we had remained on scene longer? Was making a run for it the right decision, given that I knew we had to carry him down the stairs? Would he now be alive if he had lived in a house rather than a flat? Did he die because he was an 'angry young diabetic' who didn't want to comply with this treatment? He did have a history of taking an insulin overdose 2 weeks before.

It was a bad job, travel time was longer than it should have been, the flat was awkward to reach, it was difficult to remove the patient and the return journey to hospital was too long. It could have gone so much better. Although the patient might still have died it would have made us feel better. The job has left my crewmate and me a little depressed. Two deaths in as many days, one a 'victory', the other a real loss. I have today off so I'm going to relax and prepare for the joys of a night shift tomorrow.

One question for my medical readers: in the same situation would you 'Stay and Play', or would you 'Load and Go'?

I got a couple of replies to the question above when I originally posted it online. The best was a mnemonic that I have taken to heart: L.A.T.E.R (Load And Treat En-Route). I don't want to fool around on scene with a sick person who needs to be in hospital.

🚐 The Climax Draws Near ...

I'm feeling a bit fragile at the moment – these nights are really taking it out of me for some reason. I think the main thing that is getting me down is that I should be getting my HIV test result on Friday; as predicted, I haven't been worrying for the past 3 months (is it really that long ago?) but with the result due, it is sitting at the back of my mind nagging away. I'm confident that I'll test negative – even so I have the framework for two blog posts, one Negative, and one Positive.

Either way, I think I'll be having a drink or two after I get the result.

At the moment there is some confusion about how I actually get the result. The receptionist at the clinic didn't know if their telephone text messaging trial was still being used – I suspect that on Friday I'll hang around the ambulance station after the end of my last night shift and then walk down to the clinic and get them to give me the result at 9 o'clock. It would be cruel to make me wait until after the weekend ...

... So it'll probably happen, or they will have lost the sample or something similarly evil ...

Tonight, the only job to really stick in my mind was a 'purple plus' (someone who has died and is beyond our help because of the amount of time they have been dead). It was an 85-year-old female who died, leaving behind her husband of nearly 70 years holding her hand. A very sad job, he was putting on a brave face, but I think later today it'll sink in. Hopefully, his son will be with him when it does.

So, dear readers, the next update to this blog (unless my leg drops off) will be after I get my HIV result; I'm not in a frame of mind to write anything legible at the moment (as I'm sure you have noticed). Hopefully, my next post will be Friday, but I'm a strong believer in the inherent evil of the Universe ... so I'll talk to you on Monday.

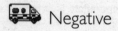 Negative

Yep, the *title* says it all: the HIV test is negative, the syphilis test is negative and hepatitis tests are negative.

Needless to say I am so far beyond 'relieved' as to be numb with it all.

I spent the last 20 hours awake, first at work, then in the 'Clap Clinic' waiting room; I now think I deserve a deep relaxed sleep.

Goodnight, I'll write more when I wake up …

Posted at 11:13 a.m. local time.

 Fallout

Well … I've had some sleep so I can now post in a slightly more focused fashion.

First off, thanks again to everyone who has shown support, either through the comments box, or via personal emails – it's all gratefully received. It looks like I'm going to have to find something else to die from now.

Tomorrow my brother and I shall be going for a nice relaxing drink, the first proper pub visit in over 3 months – there may well be a hangover involved.

I only had to wait 45 minutes at the 'Clap Clinic' for the test result – pretty hard to stay awake, but I think the emotional numbness that comes with exhaustion only helped me deal with the wait. The 'consultation' was over in less than 15 seconds: led into a room, asked to sit down and then told by a shaved-head counsellor that everything was fine. I didn't have a massive flood of emotion (possibly owing to the aforementioned exhaustion), but afterwards I sat on a stone outside the hospital, rang my mum and brother, text messaged my old crewmate and breathed a sigh of relief. (Old crewmate told me that I had to go and repopulate Newham – something I don't think I'll be doing quite yet ...)

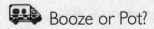 Booze or Pot?

I didn't sleep well last night – I think a total of an hour and a half – so if I'm a bit incoherent I'd like to register that as excuse number one. No real reason for the lack of sleep, it's a disadvantage of rotating shifts that every so often your body clock just throws up its hands in despair and goes to sulk behind the sofa, leaving you suffering insomnia and/or intense fatigue.

Last night was actually quite pleasant. The first job of the shift (at around 4 p.m.) was given as an 80-year-old male collapsed in the street. Making our way there we were beaten by not only the police and fast response car, but also by a Duty Officer who had taken an interest in the job. It turned out to be a drunken Russian, actually in his early fifties, who had decided to lie down and sleep it off in an alley. I suspect he was very surprised when he woke up to find himself surrounded by three police officers and four ambulance bods of various ranks. He was a pleasant enough fellow, who didn't speak a word of English, so to be on the safe side we loaded him onto the ambulance and took him to sunny Newham hospital. When we got there (and remember that this is around 5 p.m.) the crew before us, and the crew who followed us, both had people who were worse for wear for drink. Luckily for both our patient and the hospital a Russian nurse was working, so he could translate that the patient had indeed just drunk too much and would very much like to be left alone so he could go home. I'm always impressed by people who can speak another language, two people talking what sounds like utter gibberish, yet making complete sense to each other never fails to entertain.

When taking this gentleman to hospital I drove past six known drunks in the space of one street. Alcohol and alcoholism is a big blight on our society. On some shifts the only jobs we have are those influenced in some way by alcohol. Most assaults can be attributed to alcohol, frequent callers (sometimes 6 times in one day) are very often alcoholic, and the amount of 'collapse ?cause' jobs that turn out to be drunks is frankly astounding.

My personal view (and not the view of the LAS by any means) would be to prohibit alcohol, but legalise cannabis. Not only would it cut our workload by, at my estimate, 60–70%, but I've never had anyone high on cannabis try to hit me. Cannabis users are very rarely violent, tend to be generally easier to handle and seldom get loud and annoying. It's true that there are long-term health consequences, and that heavy 'stoners' can waste their life away, but the same holds true of alcohol and alcoholics.

On the rare occasions that I get called to someone on cannabis, it's normally because it is their first time and they feel 'dizzy'. Often a pat on the head, and an explanation that this is what is *supposed* to happen is enough to calm them down, and they will rarely require a trip to hospital. Because the intoxicant effects are fairly self limiting, people tend not to overdose on cannabis, unlike alcohol (which is why you find drunk people collapsed in the street).

There is one problem with the use of cannabis – I'm never sure what to call it in order to sound 'hip to the kids', the slang just befuddles me. Is it 'green', 'pot', 'hash', 'reefer' or 'draw'? At least alcohol is just 'booze'.

And now the government has made it even easier to get hold of alcohol with extended 'open hours'. Oh well …

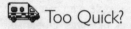 Too Quick?

(What I'm going to post about might come across as being heartless, or myself being lazy – I don't think I'm either of them, but if you disagree with this post, as always, feel free to visit the blog and leave a comment.)

Tonight we got called to a residential home for an 87-year-old female with 'difficulty in breathing'; once again it was way out of our area of coverage, but we made good time to get there. I've been to this home before, and it is one of the better ones I've visited; the residents are always clean, and appear well looked after. The care staff know their 'charges', and are always friendly, helpful and courteous towards ambulance crews.

I knew there was something wrong from the face of the member of staff who met us. She had a look of total concern, and I don't like to see that look on someone's face – it never bodes well. We went through the clean corridors and busy lounge of the home into one of the residents' rooms. There were three nurses there, one of whom was crying (something I don't think I've ever seen before); lying in the bed was a little old lady who was extremely close to death. Her pulse was weak, and thready, something I could have guessed by the patient's colour. I very quickly told the staff that, yes, she was extremely ill and that she would have to go to hospital unless she had a 'Do Not Resuscitate' order. The staff said that it would be best to take her to hospital. We scooped her up, and her heart and breathing stopped in the lift to the ground floor.

I don't believe in a 'slow blue' (where CPR is performed by 'going through the motions' knowing that the patient will not survive and that the CPR is for the benefit of the relatives), so I started active, aggressive treatment while my crewmate drove us the 5 minutes to hospital. The patient remained in asystole (no heart activity at all) and on reaching hospital the doctors there declared her dead.

I may have previously mentioned the study that showed that 'out of 185 patients presenting with out of hospital asystole arrests, none survived to be discharged'. Both my crewmate and myself – and the hospital staff – knew that this patient had no chance of survival and that the reason we started CPR was because of our policy to commence resuscitation except in certain tightly defined circumstances.

If we had got there a minute later, the patient would already have died – in her bed surrounded by people that cared for her (although not her family) as opposed to being hoisted out onto a chair and then suffering the indignities of CPR in the back of an ambulance. While trying to resuscitate her during the transit to hospital I found myself looking into her dead blue eyes, apologising to her and hoping that she couldn't feel anything that I was doing to her.

I don't know if it is because I've had one and a half hours' sleep in the past 38, but it made me feel bad to put her through the indignity of pointless CPR. I know the policies are there to protect us (and members of the public), but sometimes I wish we could use some discretion.

Now I'll see if I can get some sleep.

I can still remember her sparkling blue eyes looking up at me.

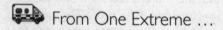 From One Extreme …

So, two nights ago I was dealing with death, people collapsing on the DLR (Docklands Light Railway), young men vomiting blood and looking like death warmed up, and women having miscarriages. Basically everyone I attended to on Wednesday night needed an ambulance.

Last night we had …

One patient with indigestion (for 2 years – FRU on scene when we got there as it was given as a 'chest pain').
One 'gone before arrival' (a drunk who phoned 999 complaining of a broken arm, but had wandered off before we got there).
One overdose 'acting violent', who also had gone before we turned up (driven to hospital by her brother).
One 'facial injury' (a woman slapped by her husband: no injury and she didn't want to go to hospital – her husband was taken away by the police).
One patient with ascites and chronic alcoholism, who was referred to hospital by the GP (could have travelled in her husband's car).

One call to a police station for an accused who had swallowed some drugs – he denied everything and the police doctor cleared his health.
And one patient with an arthritic knee …

The patient with an arthritic knee was a 70-year-old male who had called out his GP. Said GP had then diagnosed arthritis and decided that the patient needed hospital treatment. We got the call, and had to go out of the area we are supposed to be covering to pick the patient up. The booked hospital was even further out of our area – so much so it was in another sector.

When we got there the patient's son was present and as we loaded his father into the ambulance we were told that 'I'll follow up in the car'.

The look of sheer despair my crewmate gave me had me in fits of laughter; thankfully, I was outside the ambulance so neither the patient, nor his son, who had gone to get the car, could see me.

There was no reason why the patient couldn't have been driven by his son, yet here we were, out of area, going even further out for someone who didn't need an ambulance.

Still, after the past few days it was nice to have a shift where no-one was actually 'ill', and so we could spend the shift in a fairly relaxed state.

We often get patients in this sort of situation. I've given up worrying about it, even if it does mean that an ambulance is tied up doing non-essential work. I just wonder how many people have died because of a delay getting an ambulance because we are forced to do these types of jobs.

🚐 Driving for the LAS (For Dummies)
Part I (Assessment)

When you apply for a job as ambulance personnel for the LAS, one of the things that they look for is that you are a competent driver. Therefore, as part of the interview process they throw you into the most run-down, barely working 14-seater lump of crap they can find, and tell you to drive around Earls Court. For those not from London, Earls Court is a congested area with fairly small streets, constant roadworks and the sort of people who think it is amusing to leap out in front of scared-looking interviewees on their driving assessment.

Before you see a vehicle you are given a piece of paper that tells you what the assessor is looking for, the crossing over of hands when steering is a big no-no, as is over-confidence (along with under-confidence), speeding, going too slow, incorrect use of gears, incorrect use of signalling and a myriad of other things you haven't worried about since you passed your driving test as a teenager.

When I first went for my driving assessment I noticed the 'over-confidence' bit, so I thought I'd be sure not to come across as too aggressive a driver. I was a model gentleman, I let people out of side turnings, allowed pedestrians to cross in front of me and didn't hassle people who were driving too slow: I failed my assessment for being 'under-confident'. 'Come back in 3 months' I was told.

Three months later and I was determined not to make the same mistake (an additional 3 months stuck in A&E nursing will make you ever so slightly determined). So, I got into the worst piece of crap in the fleet, and off we went. Leaving the yard I hit a kerb and about 200 yards down the road I did the same thing. 'Turn around and go back' I was told; I slunk back to the yard and vowed to do better in another 3 months.

Three months later, and I thought 'Sod it! I'm going to drive how I normally drive'. So I crossed my hands turning the wheel, sped up to stop signals, refused to let anyone out of a side road and drove as if I were driving my 1.0-litre Ford Fiesta.

I passed. Needless to say I was more than happy, and fairly skipped out of the yard that morning.

Of course this double failure didn't help my confidence when it came to the driving part of my training course.

All I can say is that I haven't run over any pedestrians, although I have reversed into some stationary objects.

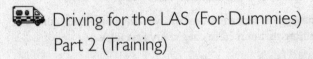 Driving for the LAS (For Dummies)
Part 2 (Training)

When you train to be an ambulance technician, you have to do 2 weeks of 'driving instruction' where you are split into groups of four, get given a 17-seater van that has been hired for you and you learn how to drive your ambulance using this equipment.

Perhaps the most important differences between an ambulance and the 17-seaters that we are given are that ambulances are automatic, while the 17-seaters are manual (I believe the American term is 'stick'), and that 17-seaters just don't 'feel' like an ambulance.

The training course consists of 2 days of fun, and the rest is chasing each other around the countryside at high speed.

The two days of fun include driving around a racing track, spinning around a skid-pan and swerving around traffic cones at high speed – both forward and in reverse.

Then, for the next 2 weeks, you learn some theory in the classroom, such as the 'limit point' and the forces that act on a vehicle (and why sometimes speeding up when you are losing control is a good thing). The rest of the time is spent driving at high speed around the countryside, making sure that you have the correct gear, speed and suchlike for high-speed cornering.

There are a few things that make this training course less than effective: the first is that as the *London* Ambulance Service, it is extremely rare that you find yourself driving in the countryside, it is also rare that you drive at any speed above 40 m.p.h. and, as mentioned earlier, ambulances are automatic vehicles and as such don't have gears.

I drove an actual, real ambulance a grand total of once during training. I sat in the driver's seat, pointed to the lever in the middle of the floor and said, 'what's that, and where is the clutch pedal?'

Luckily for me learning to drive an automatic was pretty easy.

At no point during the driving course did we drive on 'blue lights and sirens' – something that may have caused my first RTA.

(Insert wobbly flashback special effect here ...)

The first day out on the road out of training school went well. I was attending (A&E nurse for some years) and my crewmate was driving (his previous job? 'Man and Van' – driving a removal van around London doing odd jobs). So the driving went well, as did the attending (dealing with sick people). The next day our roles were swapped, I warned our supervisor that I'd never really driven an ambulance before, but he said that we'd be fine if we worked like yesterday.

So, on my first emergency job, blue lights went on, sirens went on and people started moving out the way – it was then that I realised that you can't fit a 7-foot-2-wide ambulance through a gap made by two cars which is only 6 feet and 6 inches wide. This was the first time (and hopefully the only time) I've been sworn at by a boss, although to be fair, the only time I think I've deserved it. I learned how to fill in accident forms that day ... and how to judge distances a bit better. (An ambulance is wider, longer and taller than a 1.0-litre Ford Fiesta.)

Soon my training came to an end and I was thrown into the world of emergency driving in Newham ...

(End wobbly flashback sequence, cue end title 'To Be Continued …')

The boss who swore at me was right though. Even now I think that this is why I like the ambulance service over nursing. With nursing the boss would call you into the office to discuss your 'problem', and how I might 'reflect on what happened'. So for me, being sworn at was a breath of fresh air.

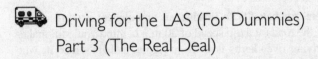

Driving for the LAS (For Dummies) Part 3 (The Real Deal)

After the assessment, the training and the first time racing around the streets of London being sworn at, you finally end up on your own, in a new part of town where you are expected to get to emergency calls in 8 minutes.

I got posted to Newham, which is a 10-minute drive from where I live; unfortunately, I'd never driven there and my navigation was awful. When I told my new workmates where I lived they thought, 'Good someone who knows the area' (and just after that they probably thought, 'If he lives *there* I wonder if he'll steal my car?'). This was before the days of satellite tracking where you just have to follow the dulcet tones of the computer (sometimes in Danish if some bright spark has reprogrammed the computer); in those days you had a mapbook and were expected to get on with it.

Gradually, you get to know the streets, where the regulars live, the pubs that are 'trouble' and where the 6-feet-6-inch width restrictions are. You then have to counter every threat the 'natives' throw at you.

For example, I might be driving a big white (or bright yellow) van, covered with flashing lights and 'ambulance' written on the side, occasionally – if I feel like pushing out the boat – I'll even have the sirens going. You might expect people to get out of the way; instead, pedestrians will be drawn to run out in front of you, like particularly dim-witted moths to a flame. People in cars will suddenly develop selective blindness, and idiots with Drum 'n 'Bass pounding out from stereos worth more than their car will argue that I should make way for them.

Drivers will pull out from side streets in front of you, and as for the bizarre ideas some people have as to the best way to clear a path for us (jump on the brakes, swerve in front of us, sit there and panic), well, it's a good job we often don't have far to travel.

However, there are benefits to driving an ambulance: driving on the wrong side of the road (at a top speed of 20 m.p.h. mind you) still makes me happy, driving over kerbs is often a giggle, and let's face it, who wouldn't like to treat red lights as a 'Give Way'?

Despite popular belief, we don't actually go that fast – we can't, we never know when some young mother is going to push her baby buggy out in front of us. At best I think we have a maximum speed of 40 m.p.h., not only for our safety and the safety of other people, but purely because the worn-out ambulances that we drive have an acceleration that would embarrass a milk float, and a top speed of … oh … about 42 m.p.h.

I once got on a motorway and 'opened her up', we got up to 70 m.p.h. (downhill naturally) before the front of the ambulance started lifting up and the steering became a trifle 'unresponsive'. Luckily I managed to stop screaming in sheer terror for long enough to regain control.

Most of our accidents (as a firm) come from reversing, I've – cough – occasionally reversed into pillars and lampposts; one person I worked with managed to reverse into a low-flying balcony. I have on at least two occasions got stuck in a width restriction (I swear, one day I'll get our 7-foot-2 ambulance through a 6-foot-6 restriction – I just need to get up to a decent speed before tackling it). Thankfully, our ambulances are so old and battered that small amounts of damage just add to the character of the vehicle.

Of course all that has changed with the new yellow Mercedes Sprinters.

Or at least it would if they haven't all started getting faults around the 5 000 mile mark. Our station had three of the new ambulances, now we have none. They are all either being patched up, or shipped back to Germany to have major repairs done. Current reports are that the fibreglass back is splitting from the metal chassis – possibly because of the number of speed-bumps we have to contend with.

Speed-bumps – a good idea in theory, but in practice they slow us down by a hell of a lot, wreck the ambulances, and in 5 years' time I intend to go on permanent sick leave because my kidneys have been shaken out through my mouth. My plan to get local councillors thinking a little more sensibly about speed-bumps would be to strap them down on a spinal board and drive them through the streets – I think they would be begging for mercy after 5 minutes.

Parking is a nightmare in Newham as well. We often have a line of traffic parked on either side of the road, making side streets effectively single track routes. When we get a call for a 'chest pain' (you know, the sort of thing that could be a heart attack), then we have no choice but to park in the middle of the road, blocking any other traffic. At no point do we engage in the 'how much traffic can I stop' game. We don't like confrontation at all, we like a nice quiet life, so we are not trying to wind people up on purpose.

Unfortunately some people don't see it like that and will sit there honking their horn at us to get a hurry on. To be fair, I tend to spend a maximum of 10 minutes on scene, and if you honk your horn at me, I'll then change my working speed to 'go slow' (assuming that this won't affect the patient's condition).

I think it's incredibly rude to think that your journey is more important than that of an emergency ambulance.

Don't you?

I'm off to work now to drive around those selfsame streets … wish me luck, and if you see me in your rear view mirror, please get out of the way by pulling over and stopping on the left of the road.

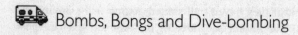 Bombs, Bongs and Dive-bombing

Some unusual jobs today, the first call was to a concrete company (which will remain nameless – no doubt they have better lawyers than I). We were told to meet with the Police and Fire Service at an RVP (meeting point). It turns out that some animal liberation types have taken offence to this company (rumour being they are supplying concrete to a new animal testing laboratory) and have sent some deactivated incendiary devices to various branches in order to scare them. Today, in three of the offices across London, some 'suspicious packages' had turned up and we were being sent to cover the defusing of one of these devices. Two ambulances, one Duty Officer, three fire engines and countless police were there, standing around the now evacuated offices.

Our Duty Officer started allocating 'Major Incident' roles to everyone. I don't think he was best pleased when I asked him why, when major incidents are designed to deal with multiple casualties, we needed to play that game when the only person in any danger in the now deserted office was the bomb disposal officer.

He sent me to arrange the parking of the emergency vehicles. We were soon stood down, however, when it was discovered that the 'device' was actually a packet of envelopes.

The next call was to two brothers who had fought over possession of a bong, with one brother trying to sell it to a third brother. Both we and the police were sent; when we got there both brothers had calmed down and there were no serious injuries. One policeman was confused about what a bong was used for, until I explained that it was 'drug paraphernalia'. One of the brothers told the policeman that he was selling it because he didn't use it – he much preferred smoking his cannabis in a spliff.

Luckily for him the policeman ignored this massive blunder (and me collapsing in tears of laughter at this idiot essentially confessing his drug habits).

Our next interesting job was to a man in Docklands who had a head injury caused by trying to avoid an attacking seagull. It turns out that there is a seagull living there who likes to dive-bomb people passing by. This man had ducked the avian attack, then tripped and fell flat on his face, knocking himself out. He had only minor facial injuries, but the loss of consciousness will mean a short stay in hospital being watched. My old crewmate suggested that he sell his story to the newspapers.

The rest of our jobs were rather boring after this early excitement.

Shouldn't You Be Dead?

One of the things that will constantly amaze me is that some people will drop dead at the drop of a hat (so to speak), while others will survive injuries that would kill us mere mortals.

Today was a case in point: we got called to a 39-year-old female who'd been hit on the head by a brick that had fallen *seven* floors. We turned up at the location fully expecting to see someone with less of their brains inside their head than would be considered healthy. Instead, the woman was sitting in a chair (having had a C-spine collar applied) with her head supported by a BASICS doctor (a doctor who volunteers to respond to calls in the community).

This woman, who should have been dead, had a 1-inch cut on the top of her head.

… And that was it.

The brick had hit her on the head, then had hit the floor with such force that it had shattered. Yet, here she was with no injury other than complaining of the cut being painful. There was no loss of consciousness, but we treated her as if she had a neck injury, purely because of the 'mechanism

75

of injury'. It's been a while since I've had to do a 'standing take-down' (where you get a standing patient onto a spinal board by placing it against their back and laying it flat with them on it) but it all went smoothly, the doctor travelled with us and was a pleasure to work with.

Although she was 39 the woman actually looked like she was in her early twenties – perhaps she has some witchy super powers? Either way she was discharged later in the day.

She was exceptionally lucky – if you can call getting beaned by a brick 'lucky'.

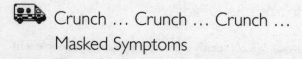 Crunch ... Crunch ... Crunch ...
Masked Symptoms

I discovered yet another reason to avoid alcohol, namely that it can mask the symptoms of otherwise obvious illnesses and injuries.

We got called to a 60-year-old man who had fallen in the street: as it was 2 a.m. we could guess that alcohol was involved. When we arrived on scene the patient was standing against a wall very much the worse for drink. Admitting he was an alcoholic he told us that he had tripped over and now his right leg hurt. While he was standing there I gave him a quick examination, he had no bony tenderness and was able to bear his weight on his leg. He could feel his toes wriggling in his shoe and there was no obvious deformity to the leg. We helped him walk the few steps to the ambulance, but he was unable to manage the stairs at the back of the ambulance so we put him in our carry-chair and lifted him into the ambulance. Further examination showed little else of note; his pulse was a tad on the high side but otherwise his blood pressure and other observations were well within normal limits.

We transported him to hospital, where the nurse gave him a quick examination, essentially repeating the examination I'd given him in the field, and she sent him out to the waiting room.

When we returned to the hospital a little later we were told that he had a fractured neck of femur – essentially he'd broken his hip.

He was so drunk that he felt little pain, and for various reasons none of the normal signs of a broken hip were present. Luckily, I'd documented that I'd examined for the possibility of this type of fracture and found negative signs all the way along, so should he complain (which I doubt he would do) both I and the admitting nurse would be covered.

So … don't drink, or you may find yourself walking around on a broken leg.

Now I'm off to sleep. Two very long night shifts and I'm ready to collapse.

It's one of the main differences between A&E nursing and ambulance work – in an A&E department you have good lights, can undress the patient and can put them on an examination table. In ambulance work you can find yourself down dark, unlit streets, in the rain and with the patient lodged under a car. I did feel a little bad about this patient, mind you …

An Excellent Bad Day

Have you noticed how much I talk about being tired or needing sleep? The benefits of shift work …

First off, I'm bloody knackered, frazzled, chin-strapped, and generally tired. If I ramble just poke me in the ribs with a stick.

Today was both bloody awful and rather good fun, which despite sounding like the ramblings of a madman is a perfectly sane way to describe today, although I'll be glad for it to be over.

The day started badly: I woke 3 minutes before my alarm was due to go off so I turned it off and woke for the second time 10 minutes before my shift was about to begin. I didn't get much sleep last night so I suspect my body overruled my brain to give me an extra 50 minutes of sleep.

Luckily, when I wake up with an adrenaline jolt like that I can get washed, dressed and speed through the streets of Newham like an Olympic sprinter on methamphetamine.

Turning up at the station I found out that my regular crewmate was ill, and instead a 'Team Leader' was being sent to work with me. Team Leaders are on the lowest rung of management: they are the people who are supposed to keep the troops in trim, and so spend considerable time moaning about the speed at which we get to jobs, and the poor quality of our paperwork. I'm of the belief that if management don't know about me, I can't get in any trouble, so working with a new Team Leader was something I was less than happy with.

I had barely gotten to say hello to 'Team Leader' than we got our first call of the day, a 'Suspended' (cardiac arrest) a couple of miles from station. Manoeuvring a big yellow taxi through rush-hour traffic is no fun at the best of times, but as I was driving I gave it my best shot – we got to the scene shortly after our First Responder who was already bagging and giving CPR to an obese woman in her eighties. As we were in one of the new yellow ambulances I lowered the tail lift, got the trolley out and nearly ruptured myself lifting the patient onto the trolley bed. Rolling her out to the street, we got her on the tail lift and raising it, rolled her into the back of the ambulance. All that was left was for me to raise the tail lift the rest of the way and rush to hospital.

You may notice that I spent some time discussing the tail lift; this is because as I went to lift it, the hydraulics failed and it was stuck, sticking 7 feet out from the rear of the ambulance at a height of about 4 feet from the floor.

I gave it a kick, a shake and then resigned myself to manually lifting the bloody thing up, all while the crying relatives were watching me pumping the manual handle like an idiot. Finally, it was raised to the closed position, so I made my way rapidly to hospital while 'Team Leader' and 'First Responder' worked on the patient in the back. I'll not mention the road closure that forced me to make a painfully wide detour, but otherwise we reached the hospital with some speed where the woman was, unsurprisingly, declared deceased.

After a quick tidy-up of the back of the ambulance (which after a cardiac arrest always looks like a bomb site) we got a job to an 'unwell child'. The 15-month-old child was indeed unwell, although not life-threateningly so. The assessment was made harder by the mother having very poor English and the child having 'Development Delay', which encompasses a multitude of syndromes and genetic/biological causes.

The next job was a transfer from the local maternity department to a maternity department in another county. This is a hospital that I had no idea how to get to (the details of why there was a need for transport are too boring to go into; also, I think I might say something about the mother I'd regret in the morning). I set our travel computer to give me directions to the hospital and we set off. The journey was supposed to be 9.8 miles, but after following the computer's directions to the letter we had travelled *37 miles* along rather crowded motorways.

We had taken 30 minutes longer than we had planned. It's the last time I trust that bloody machine. 'Team Leader' was not happy about the computer but we laughed it off.

The next job was a simple maternity which we drove into the London Hospital. This was fine until I managed to drive into another ambulance when trying to leave the hospital. No damage to my ambulance, and minor damage to the other, but as my first accident in over 18 months, it was obvious that it would happen when 'Team Leader' was sitting next to me …

Returning to fill in the accident paperwork, Control asked us to attend to another call – this time it was an obese unconscious 70-year-old female. She was extremely heavy and, because of her 'floppiness', was a complete dead weight. Once more I nearly killed myself lifting her. All her body functions and observations were normal so it was a complete mystery why she was unconscious, although I could confirm that she had been incontinent of urine …

… after I put my arm in it.

All these problems throughout the day meant that we worked harder than we needed to – and yet, throughout the day we had a great time as we laughed and joked between patients and vowed never to work together again. I said that I'd take sick leave, saying I was 'stressed' and 'Team Leader' said she would make sure I got sent to the other side of London before she worked with me again.

And so, at the end of the shift we parted, laughing at the thought that it was possible we could be repeating the experience tomorrow.

I'm looking forward to that possibility.

'Team Leader' is still on our complex and is still a good laugh. Thankfully, I haven't had to work with her again.

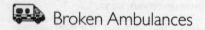 Broken Ambulances

One of the main problems with the LAS at the moment is the lack of vehicles. In the past this has come to mean that there are not enough staff to man the vehicles that we have, or fill the rota to maintain safe cover over our area. Lately, however, we haven't had the vehicles physically present. At the moment, I am typing this from work and looking out the window at the fitters whose job it is to maintain the fleet in our area of London. There are 13 ambulances waiting to be fixed. There are 3 crews sitting on station unable to take any calls because their vehicles have broken down.

Someone has just visited us in the staff car (a nice little Corsa) and, on attempting to leave, its clutch has broken.

Today I took an ambulance from West Ham over to Poplar to replace a vehicle whose steering had broken. Two management brought over a spare vehicle from Newham for me to work on – a vehicle that had just had a broken rear suspension fixed.

Let me tell you, riding on an ambulance with no suspension is an 'interesting' experience – you get thrown around and the cupboards fly open spraying bandages and other, less soft, equipment around the cabin.

This 'fixed' ambulance lasted three jobs before the suspension died again and I was bouncing around the cabin. It also stalled if you closed the choke.

So now I'm sitting on station twiddling my thumbs, unable to continue my daily grind of ~~saving lives~~ picking up drunks.

The fleet is just falling to bits, the new Mercedes have faults developing around the 5 000 miles mark and the tail lifts are extremely temperamental (like my experience yesterday – they fail at the worst possible moment). The LAS needs a cash injection so that it can have a fleet of basic, but reliable ambulances, fully equipped and fully manned.

Things haven't changed much since I wrote this, although with a few extra vehicles the turnaround for crews without a vehicle is a bit better.

An Apology to A&E Departments

I would suggest that a lot of the people who read this are doctors and nurses of one persuasion or another. I also guess that many of these readers have some experience of A&E departments.

So, as an EMT I wish to apologise.

I'm sorry that throughout the shift I will continue to bring fresh meat to the grinder, that is, I will be forced to transport patients from 'outside' into your department, where they will need to be looked after and assessed by your own good selves.

I'm sorry that I have to sometimes bring their relatives who will harass you about waiting times, the pain their relative is in and about why you are drinking that cup of coffee while their dearly beloved is 'at death's door'. I'm also sorry that sometimes I couldn't bring the only relative who can translate the patient's moaning and groaning into English, thus making assessment a thousand times easier.

I'm sorry for the dross that I bring to you: the cut fingers, the bellyaches and the spotty backs. I'm sorry that the primary health-care workers (the GPs) are often so useless as to be a liability. I'm sorry that you have to cope with the fallout that occurs because there are so few good GPs and you have to become the first point of call for coughs, colds and diarrhoea

I'm sorry that the schools don't teach basic health and first aid to their students, preferring to waste time on the history of glaciers or the solving of quadratic equations. This means that the population wouldn't know the difference between a minor cut and an arterial spurt if it jumped up and hit them over the head with a hammer, neither do they know which of these two injuries warrants a trip to the local Emergency Department.

I'm sorry that our communities where our Elders teach our Youngsters and the Youngsters listen no longer exist, resulting an influx of first-time mothers who think that when a baby vomits it is a precursor of death.

I'm sorry that the protocols and guidelines that we adhere to don't allow us to leave patients at home. In England at least, we have to transport to hospital. The government thinks that we cannot tell the difference between serious cases and the aforementioned cut finger.

I'm sorry that the police cannot look after drunks on a Friday night; they worry that they will choke to death in the cells, and so we get called. We have nowhere else to take them to but your department. Sorry.

I'm sorry that I bring in those serious cases 5 minutes before your shift finishes. If it's any consolation it's probably 5 minutes to the end of our shift that people decide to have their heart attacks, their amputations and their dissecting aortic aneurysms. Like you, this means we get off late as well.

I'm sorry, but it's not my fault.

I wrote this in part because we do sometimes get dirty looks from A&E staff as we drag in the umpteenth drunkard of the shift. It's not my fault that the government made 999 so easy to dial.

🚑 Knee Trouble

Gillick competency is the ability of youngsters under the age of 16 to give informed consent for medical treatment. Essentially, we have to assess whether a child is competent enough to make decisions about their own body. This is, as you might guess, an ethical minefield.

Back to work with the rather enjoyable 18:00–01:00 shift, where you tend to get lots of drunks, and very few *serious* cases that require me to do some actual work.

However, you do occasionally come across a job that is tricky, not because I worry about the patient's illness, but instead for reasons that to the non-ambulance person are hard to understand.

Our first job of the day was one of those very jobs. The call we were given was 13-year-old female with a dislocated knee. Nice and easy I hear you say, but lots of minor problems can build up to make a job less than ideal.

We arrived on scene and found a patient who had a rather obvious dislocated knee – just imagine your kneecap shifted 2 inches to the left, so much so that it casts a shadow on the rest of your leg. Simple enough to deal with: if you are feeling brave you can slide it back into place yourself, or go the more recommended route which is to take the patient into hospital and let the doctors fiddle with it.

Then the problems started piling up. To start with there were no adults present, just another (unrelated) teenager; neither the patient nor this other teenager were what you would exactly call brain surgeons. We are not supposed to deal with children without an adult present, but what else can you do in those circumstances? The father had been called, but he was travelling from another hospital where he had been undergoing outpatient treatment. So we had to decide whether it was 'safe' for us to take the patient to hospital – we use 'Gillick competency', but it's always a bit of a gamble on our part.

The patient had fallen from her bunkbed so her friends (who had run off) had lifted her *back* onto the top bunk. She was screaming in pain (which is fair enough I suppose), and wouldn't let us near her. This little problem was solved by giving her a lot of Entonox (known to some people as 'laughing gas'). After enough of this stuff she started laughing and we essentially 'grabbed' her off the bed.

Then she refused to sit in the carry-chair, but because we were upstairs she needed to go in it. After a *lot* of persuasion, and a lot of her screaming very close to our ears, we managed to get her to sit down; this had the rather excellent side-effect of popping the kneecap back in place.

This would normally mean that the amount of pain goes down by a lot, but this girl had a touch of 'hospital phobia' so she continued screaming. While screaming she was also arguing with the teenager who was with her, telling him that he needed to come to hospital with her but he was refusing because 'How am I gonna get back home?' I must admit I really wanted to tell him to walk it, because the hospital was only about 1 000 yards away. Despite her pleading with him, he wasn't for budging. He set his Burberry baseball cap square on his head and refused. I don't think she is going to be too happy at him next time she sees him.

Once that argument had run its course (and my crewmate and I managed to stop laughing), we had to get the patient downstairs – this was made more difficult by a sideboard that was in the upper hallway by the stairs. To counter this problem, we had to lift her completely over the banister. Luckily she was a lightweight, and my crewmate and I are – *cough* – both strapping, good-looking men.

We saw her later in hospital, having a plaster cast put on her leg, so that the kneecap wouldn't slip out of place. She was much happier and surrounded by her parents. She even managed to give us a smile, which, in the end, made the job worthwhile.

So, this is what we occasionally have to deal with, not so much the life-threatening stuff, but more the silly little things that can make an 'easy' job much trickier.

Drunk and Disorderly

We got called to a pub (which is always promising), to a 24-year-old female who was having 'difficulty breathing'. When we turned up at the pub, we were met by a man who, after letting us know he was a 'first aider', told us that she was fitting and that she had stopped breathing, but that mouth to mouth resuscitation had 'brought her back'.

Entering the pub we found the woman thrashing around on the floor. She wasn't having a fit, it was more like a temper tantrum. Throwing himself on top of her was her husband, who was reluctant to let us approach her. People in the pub told us that they had both been drinking heavily.

We near enough had to force the man off of his wife just so we could examine her properly, and it soon became apparent that she was just very, very drunk. Out of the corner of my eye I saw sudden movement and ducked quickly as the husband threw his wife's shoe at a man standing behind me. We decided that loading her onto the ambulance would be the best thing to do. The husband demanded to be let in, but we told him that we needed room to properly examine his wife. He banged on our windows twice, but then left, apparently running up the road – possibly as a result of him throwing a pint glass at another of the pub's customers. (This was very unwise of him, because half of Newham police force were 200 yards up the road dealing with an armed incident.)

By this time a second crew had turned up, as someone had called 999 and told our Control that the woman had stopped breathing. We stood them down, although, on reflection, they could have been of help keeping the woman on the trolley because she was still throwing herself around, refusing to lie still, and generally making life difficult. We managed to get a blood sugar, pulse and blood pressure (all of which were normal) but she refused to stay on the trolley and wouldn't sit on a chair – so we let her lie on the floor.

At times like these, I think I'd give my eye-teeth to be able to put people like her in a 4-point restraint, but it's something we are not allowed do.

Later, while I was driving to hospital, she made an attempt to leap out the back of the ambulance, and it was only the rugby skills of my crewmate that prevented her escaping under the wheels of a following car. The rugby tackle was all the more impressive given that my crewmate is 5-foot-nothing tall.

We finally managed to get the patient to hospital, where she threw her vomit bowl (with vomit) over the floor and tried to hit a nurse. Luckily I was standing behind her and grabbed her before she could damage any of the staff, or even a patient.

To cut a long story short, the nurses let her phone her sister to come and pick her up, and then kicked her out the department.

Two things about this job that bring a smile to my face: (1) one of her shoes is still lying in the gutter, where we picked her up from, and (2) her husband got out of prison today and, given his attitude and behaviour, he'll soon be back inside.

So, it's not just weekend nights we get the violent drunks, it's every damn night …

We are not taught how to restrain patients who might be violent but sometimes it is essential – for example, in the event of someone having a serious head injury and becoming violent. So, we have to make it up as we go along and hope that it turns out alright.

Favourite Job

The other night I had my favourite type of job, the type of job that meant I wasn't upset to be late leaving work.

People who are diabetic sometimes have very low blood sugar; this makes them confused, agitated and sleepy, and this can lead to unconsciousness and even death. Their blood sugar can become low for any number of reasons. Most often they have done more exercise than normal and not eaten enough to raise their blood sugar.

The treatment for this condition is to either give them sugar or an injection that 'frees up' some sugar that is stored in their liver.

Our patient last night normally controls her diabetes very well; so much so that her family had never seen her with a dangerously low blood sugar (the medical term for this is hypoglycaemia). They called us because she was acting confused and was unable to speak properly or stand upright. We arrived, and found out she was a diabetic; checking her blood sugar we got a reading of 1.6 mmols (the normal range for a diabetic is around 4.5–12.0 mmols) – this is very low and explained why she was losing consciousness.

The family were understandably upset, as they had never seen this before. They saw her slipping into a coma in front of our eyes, so we explained what was going on as I prepared the injection that would raise her blood sugar. I gave the injection (this injection is called glucagon) and waited for it to take effect, all the time reassuring the relatives.

Within 10 minutes she was up and talking, we then gave her some sugar jelly which raises the blood sugar some more. Soon she had made a full recovery, with her blood sugar reading 5.6 mmols. We gave her some carbohydrates (for 'slow-burn' energy) and left her in the care of her exceptionally happy family.

The reason why this is such an enjoyable type of job is that we are actually saving a life (for a change) with the treatment that we can give, and that the recovery is normally rapid, and always impressive. From unconsciousness to 100% fitness in the space of about 15 minutes really impresses onlookers … and it does our ego good to be praised every so often.

Notting Hill – *Stabby, Stabby*

Yesterday was the last day of the Notting Hill Carnival. The police are calling this year's carnival a success, with little reported crime, but I would tend to disagree: it's just that the crimes all happened to people as they travelled home.

Our second call of the night started worryingly when Control told us that a male had been stabbed in Stratford shopping centre, and that he could still hear shouting in the background of the call. The stab vest went on and we made our way down there, meeting up with a lot of police officers trying to control a rather large crowd of post-carnival spectators.

We found a 15-year-old male lying on the floor, with a policeman holding some paper tissues over an upper abdominal stab wound. There was no external bleeding, and the patient was alert, calm and talking. He also had a small wound to his right leg, which again was not bleeding significantly. I ran through a primary survey (a very quick examination of the patient to rule out anything that is going to kill him in the next 5 minutes) and then concentrated on making sure his chest and lungs were not damaged. On clearing them I turned my concentration to the belly wound.

We don't like stab wounds: they can do a lot of damage leaving only a tiny entry wound. One stab wound can easily kill you, whether it is in the leg, the arm, the chest or the belly. After my examination I decided that, although he needed exploratory surgery, he wasn't critically ill. There was a bit of 'something' poking out of the wound, I had no idea what it was (I initially thought it was part of the policeman's dressing) so I soaked one of our dressings in saline and applied it to the wound. We then got a phone call from what I took to be the HEMS road team (a doctor and paramedic) letting us know that they would be on scene in 12 minutes and that the patient should go to the Royal London Hospital. The problem with this is that the Royal London is some way further away than Newham, and that I knew that if the HEMS crew got on scene they would want to 'stay and play' securing IV (intravenous) lines, considering intubation and running a full examination on the roadside. In my opinion, having assessed the patient, his best option would be to go immediately to the nearest hospital and let the surgeons there deal with him.

So, we loaded the patient onto the ambulance and made a run to Newham hospital which took us less than 5 minutes.

The result of which was the patient got to theatre, was 'packed' as he had a lacerated liver and gall bladder and is now in ITU for recovery.

I wonder if the HEMS crew will moan. I suspect they won't because around the corner was another young lad who had been stabbed in what later turned out to be a connected series of battles between two schools. The HEMS crew played around on scene with that patient before taking him to the Royal London Hospital (who really love their trauma jobs). There were then reports throughout the night of other crews picking up more teenagers injured during the fight. The patients were spread fairly evenly between the two hospitals, so no one department became overloaded.

A couple of things struck me as amusing, the first was that when we were about to leave for hospital the patient's girlfriend and cousin were fighting amongst themselves over who loved him more and should go to hospital with him. The patient's brother was also there and was fighting with police to get to the patient. He then vanished, and my prior experience would suggest that he was planning revenge and a counterattack.

While going to hospital, the patient's girlfriend was talking about the other lad who had been stabbed (apparently his name is 'Biggy G') and how it seemed that the fight had been planned at the carnival.

As always when I got to the hospital it seemed that the doctors weren't interested in my handover ... on which I will post/moan more later.

As we were going to hospital another crew, this time in North London, were putting in a priority call to their local hospital. They had two young men (aged 19 and 20) who had been stabbed, luckily in a non-serious manner.

A night full of people getting stabbed. Just a coincidence that it is the last night of Notting Hill? The media said that the carnival passed without serious incident. Either they were not looking very closely, or they decided not to report the violence around the capital.

 ## Sad Stories That Stay With You

Some jobs will just make you sad, and it's those that you'll find yourself carrying around with you for a time. It isn't always the death and horror that affects you, and you can be surprised by the things that haunt you.

We got a call to a block of flats, it was given as a 69-year-old female who was unresponsive and who had a history of schizophrenia. Her condition could be caused by any number of things, so you carry all the equipment up the flats as you never know what you are going to encounter.

We were met by the woman's husband who led us through to the bedroom where our patient lay. She was on the bed and was not talking to anyone; with one hand she was 'fidgeting' and plucking at her clothes. This was normal for her, and could be due to the antipsychotics she uses to treat her schizophrenia. Looking at her prescription sheet we found out that she was also a diet-controlled diabetic, but her blood sugar test showed a normal amount of sugar in the blood. The patient was unable to talk, and looked very scared. Was this episode related to her schizophrenia?

Our physical exam, however, showed a complete loss of function and muscle tone down the right side of her body; this led us to think that she had had a CVA, or stroke, and that this had affected her speech and muscle function. We rapidly removed her to hospital, and, to be honest, the job itself went like clockwork.

The thing that stays with you though, is her husband telling you that they have been married for 50 years, and for the last 20 of them he has stuck by her while she was suffering first from manic depression and then schizophrenia. To have stayed by her side while she was under the shadow of these illnesses shows true love. Every so often, during the transport to hospital, her husband had to wipe a tear from his eye; he was sitting holding his wife's hand, trying to provide some comfort to her and ease the scared expression on her face.

If she survives the stroke she will probably be permanently disabled and will require quite intensive care for the rest of her life.

I think her husband will continue to stand by her.

In unrelated news ... I was so tired driving home this morning that I took the wrong turning to go home and went down the wrong street. Aren't you glad I'm looking after the health and well-being of people?

Update on Last Posting

Lots of people want to know what happened to the lady in my previous post, so tonight I spoke to the nurse who was looking after her.

The patient continued to be unable to talk, although (perhaps sadly) she could understand everything that was happening to her, and around her. She was also unable to use the entire right side of her body. It seems that the stroke was caused by an infarct (or clot) in her brain and not the more life-threatening cerebral bleed. She went to one of the better wards in the hospital after spending some time in the Resus' room, during which her husband constantly stayed by her bedside. The nurses looking after the pair of them felt a lot of sympathy towards them, and I think they all fell a little in love with the husband.

I mention that the nurses looked after the *pair* of them, because that is what good nurses do, they look after *everyone* affected by the illness.

Sometime later today or tomorrow she will have a CT scan of her brain to determine the extent of any infarct, and then she will start the long road to a hopeful recovery.

I used to work in a medical ward, and we would have a lot of stroke patients. Unfortunately, there is no magical medical treatment for a stroke once it has taken place; instead, it is a long gruelling slog through physiotherapy, speech therapy and occupational therapy. It can take months to recover some function, and many do not recover at all: they remain chair- or bed-bound and are discharged into a nursing/care home until they succumb to an infection that kills them.

Unfortunately, given the type and strength of the stroke this lady has had I would not hold much hope for a recovery. Miracles do sometimes happen, and I suspect that this entire woman's family will be praying for such a miracle.

Tricky Extraction

I think I've mentioned on more than one occasion how, when working in a hospital, the patients are often nicely 'packaged' ready for examination, this can often hide the trauma that the ambulance crew has gone through in getting the patient into hospital in such a condition.

My crewmate and I got called to a 'collapse', and we made good time getting there to be met by relatives of a 72-year-old female who had vomited altered blood (probably from a stomach ulcer) and had collapsed to the ground hyperventilating. The woman was around 20 stone in weight (280 pounds to the Americans in the audience). She was in a bungalow, so we had no stairs to get in our way, and the relatives were willing to be helpful. The patient was lying on the floor and had just finished an episode of hyperventilation (a panic attack).

Should have been a nice easy removal, even with the weight of the patient and reduced ability to walk. We had our carry-chair and after struggling a little to get the patient on it, we didn't expect any trouble.

Heh …

It turned out that the patient was an agoraphobic and hadn't left her house in 20 years …

Sweating profusely, the patient fought us the entire way out of the house; she grabbed at anything tied down, at door-frames and at the handrail she had installed in her house. Trying to get a sweaty 20-stone patient out of a house is tough enough without them fighting you the whole way.

We had explained that she needed to go to hospital, and she had logically agreed, but this didn't stop her panicking when we started to move her. When we finally managed to get her into the open air her panic rose to a dangerous level.

She was shaking, her eyes rolled back into her skull, sweat was pouring off of her and her thrashing about in the carry-chair got worse (if such a thing was possible). Both my crewmate and myself thought that she was going to have a heart attack; in fact, she had all the classic symptoms of a massive myocardial infarction (posh medical term for a heart attack). Then she started a strange screaming/moaning call that sounded completely unearthly. I could just see the next day's newspaper headline, '*Ambulance Crew Scare Patient To Death!*'

All I could think about was to try and calm her down, so I tried using some hypnosis techniques that I just happen to know, which helped a little, but by then she was in such an agitated state that horse tranquillisers probably wouldn't have affected her.

We managed to get her into the ambulance, where we shut the doors very quickly and made as smooth a transport to hospital as possible. During the transport my crewmate and the patient's family worked constantly to calm the patient down, but they were only having a fairly limited success; every so often I would hear her moan in that alien fashion and my crewmate babbling at her to calm down.

When we got to the hospital, we nearly threw her off the ambulance into the A&E department; actually, she was so slicked with sweat we could have slid her off the trolley. She calmed down a bit once she was in hospital, which only made our exhausted faces seem over-dramatic to the nursing staff.

You never know what you are going to get in this job, but nine times out of ten it isn't the illness that surprises you, but the circumstances around the job.

I can't drive past that address without thinking about the trouble we had with that call.

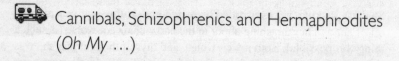 Cannibals, Schizophrenics and Hermaphrodites (*Oh My ...*)

We got called as a 'second crew' to an address. Sometimes, when a situation is beyond the capability of one crew to deal with, they will request another crew; normally this is because they have two patients, or the one patient that they have is too heavy for one crew to lift on their own.

We got the job as 'female giving apple to 7-day-old baby', which had us wondering …

As we turned up we saw the other ambulance and a police car. On entering the flat we saw two policemen standing in the corner, with a 5-foot 2-inch tall female paramedic *sitting* on a young woman (Patient Number 1); her crewmate was dealing with a male who had a nasty bite on his arm (Patient Number 2). The police were talking between themselves deciding what to do, as we got a quick briefing from the crew who was sitting on the woman.

It turned out that the woman (who had a previous mental illness episode), had given birth by Caesarean section 7 days earlier, and today had tried to feed the baby apple pie; she had then 'freaked' (note the professional medical terminology), shouting that the man wasn't her husband, and had attacked him. The ambulance crew had been called and, as they arrived, the woman had sunk her teeth into her husband's arm. The crew had fought the woman to – ahem – disengage her teeth, and this is why they were sitting on her. The police had been called, but were reluctant to do anything (I got the impression that they were a rather crap pair of coppers) and the second crew (us) had been called to deal with the husband (with new teeth-mark wound) and baby.

This woman was (brace yourself for more medical terms) 'completely bonkers', she had the rolling eyes, the delusional thoughts and the inability to communicate that separates the mildly strange from those who need immediate medication. It was actually quite sad to see this family come apart at the seams; the husband was shell-shocked, the wife was completely detached from reality and the police weren't being very helpful (which is unusual).

We got the husband and baby out of the house and into the back of our ambulance, and then returned to see the police (finally) manhandling the woman out of the house and into the back of the first ambulance. She was securely strapped down (although we don't have restraints, so she could have easily gotten free if she so desired); we had to lend the first crew a belt-strap as the one on their trolley was broken. The first crew then forewarned the hospital about what they were bringing in (violent schizophrenic female) and we all set off for the hospital.

We got there first and advised the nurse in charge that this was a 'real' warning and that security guards would be needed, along with the private 'psychiatric' room. It took her 20 minutes to arrange both, while the ambulance took less than 5 minutes to get to the hospital. So, while the secure room and security was being arranged this very disturbed woman was lying on the ambulance trolley … Not a good situation, and it made the job a lot harder than it should have been.

The husband was completely stunned; he had no idea how to look after a baby and quite simply couldn't cope. Social services were informed, and the child was admitted to the paediatric ward for a while, until the husband could be taught how to look after a baby. The woman was sent to the local psychiatric unit for assessment and treatment; hopefully, this is a temporary condition brought on by childbirth (puerperal psychosis). The husband had his wound treated, and was sent home.

Oh, and the baby is a hermaphrodite.

There are jobs that you can recount around a dinner table (or at the pub) when people ask you what your job is like. This is one of those jobs, although for some reason people seem to prefer hearing about me being injured by little old ladies.

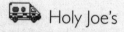 Holy Joe's

The London Ambulance Service doesn't just deal with emergency calls to people's houses, we also do hospital transfers – patients who go from hospital to hospital because the original hospital hasn't the expertise to deal with that person's medical problems. An example of this would be the transfer I recently did from Newham to the Royal London because Newham's CT scanner was broken, and the patient needed an emergency scan.

One of the regular places that we find ourselves transferring people to is St Joseph's Hospice, or as we call it Holy Joe's. Sometimes we will be picking up patients from one of the nearby hospitals, sometimes from the patient's own home. Its one of those jobs most of us don't mind doing. The patients are, by definition of needing hospice treatment, actually sick, and we are not so hard-hearted that we would begrudge an ambulance to someone who is ill. Then there is Holy Joe's itself …

Holy Joe's is a religious place, it used to be run by nuns, but now they are a bit few and far between. To be honest, I saw my first nun there yesterday, and she was picking her nose … But, you walk into the place and it just seems nice, it is clean, the staff are all friendly, the patients all seem happy and there is a really good social atmosphere there. I don't know if it is because of its ties to the religious orders (I hate all religions, but the best nursing homes always seem to have nuns running the place), but the hospice just seems to exude calm.

My crewmate and I had just transferred a terminally ill patient into Holy Joe's and were having a cup of tea in their tea bar (hot drinks are free to the LAS – another reason to love Holy Joe's). Sitting in this clean, comfortable area, we were watching the patients chat with relatives, staff and other patients, giving the place a real friendly atmosphere quite unlike anywhere in the NHS. It is very rare to see a doctor sitting down with a patient, chatting about nothing in particular and having a cup of tea with them. We both agreed that this has got to be one of the better places to see out the end of your days, and that it is a real shame that there are not more places like this.

It is a shame that in this increasingly 'technical/evidence-based/audit/professional development/governmental targets' style of health service, we seem to have forgotten that sometimes we simply, and honestly, need to care.

I went back there for the first time in 18 months. It's even better now.

I'm thinking that the NHS should poach the board of directors and point them at some of our local hospitals.

Assaulted and Happy About It

I got assaulted yesterday, which made me smile …

We got called to 'Male collapsed outside park', which immediately set my 'drunk-o-detector' bleeping. This is the sort of call that is nine times out of ten a drunk who has decided to have a sleep in a public place as opposed to going home. In a case like this we tend to wake them up, and get them to move on before another 'good Samaritan' calls us out again.

We woke him up, so he stood up and started moaning that we had woken him up. Both my crewmate and myself were actually being quite nice towards him – mainly because it was towards the end of our shift and being nasty to people takes energy that we just didn't have. Then he decided to take a swing at my crewmate, then he decided to have a swing at me … the next thing that I knew I had him in an armlock up against the side of the ambulance. My mate called on the radio for urgent police assistance, and the radio controller asked if we were both alright, to which my crewmate replied 'I'm alright, but my crewmate is restraining him'.

The police were quick to turn up, and I had just enough time to tell them that he was drunk and had taken a swing at us before he was under arrest and carted off to the local police station. It was then I realised that in the struggle I'd managed to hit myself in the chest, right where I've got a broken rib. It was a bit painful. It had already gotten a whack from a heavy trolley yesterday, so I'm wondering if it will ever manage to heal.

I can tell you what went through my mind as I was pinning him to the ambulance: the first thing was 'Oops, I hope I haven't over-reacted', the next thought (about 5 seconds later) was, 'By the time I return to station and fill in the "incident form" my shift will be over ... Result!' I'd imagined that, going by the speed that the police arrested him, they were close to the end of their shift as well.

I'm just waiting for a Team Leader to read the incident form and call me into the office to ask if I need counselling ...

A police friend of mine emailed me a couple of months later telling me that he had been in court providing evidence and the case before his was of a drunk assaulting an ambulance person. After a further description I could tell him that it was me who'd been assaulted. The drunk was found guilty, but had no penalty to pay as he was homeless. It would only have bothered me if he had actually connected with his punch.

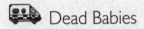 Dead Babies

One of the jobs that we find ourselves going on (perhaps once or twice a day) is that of vaginal bleeding, in a woman who is around 8 weeks pregnant. This invariably turns out to be a miscarriage. Unfortunately, it is normal for the body to 'reject' a foetus that has no chance of developing into a full-term baby. I would suppose that this stops a woman from carrying to term an infant that would not survive outside the womb.

While dealing with such patients (some of whom have been trying to get pregnant for some time), I always try to be sympathetic, and explain that what is happening is not anyone's 'fault', and that it is a normal happening.

Because of the number of people we have with this problem, and the rate at which hospitals deal with them (when working in A&E we would have about 12–18 cases of this *every day*), we have all become a little blasé about it. We feel some sympathy, but deep down in our hearts, we know that there is nothing we can do, and that it is a good thing that this is happening now, rather than in 6 months' time. Nonetheless, we are worn down by the sheer numbers, and at the end of the day, perhaps we stop caring that these women are losing babies.

I have no intention of getting into the whole abortion argument, I've seen them done, don't like them and would rather have the whole thing stay out of my world view.

I first thought that it was just me, and that as a male I was not best placed to pass comment. However, after having a chat with some female colleagues, it seems that they feel the same way I do, that it is natural, and that it is not worth worrying about. But it worries me a little that I seem to have come to care so little for the dead babies.

GCS 3/15 Outside the Door

There were two interesting jobs today, I'll tell you about one now and let you wait until tomorrow for the other one.

We got called to the very common 'Male Drunk – Police on scene'. I'll not moan about how often we get called to this type of job, you've heard it all before …

We arrived on scene and were met by a policeman who first apologised before leading us to a man who was approximately 30 years old. The man was obviously drunk, and my crewmate told me that he smelt heavily of alcohol; along his arms were the scars of a 'cutter' – something else we are seeing more and more of these days. The policeman told us that the patient was refusing to give his name or medical details, only that he was called 'John'.

We approached 'John' and he agreed to come to hospital with us. I got him into the back of the ambulance and he refused to let me touch him, so I couldn't do my usual battery of tests. In fact, he didn't want to talk to me at all, and sat in the back of the ambulance not talking; at one point he threatened to leave the ambulance but I managed to persuade him otherwise. (Don't ask me why, I normally let drunks go as soon as they say they don't want to go to hospital.)

All went as normal until we rounded the corner to the hospital, where he got off of the chair and laid on the trolley-bed. One hundred yards later and we pulled up to the hospital and I told him to get up, then I told him louder, then I did a sternal rub to wake him up – and there was no response! I then slipped an oropharyngeal airway into his mouth, this would wake anyone up, but not a flicker … he was deeply unconscious. This meant he was due for the Resus' room.

We rolled him (rather quickly) into the Resus' room and were met by a rather angry nurse – she wanted to know why we hadn't pre-alerted the hospital. I explained that he had just lost consciousness outside the department. She then asked me why he didn't have oxygen on him. Again, I repeated that he had collapsed when we were outside the hospital. We got him onto one of their Resus' trolleys while the doctors in the department ran into the room.

For the third time I explained what had happened, and that I had no vital sign observations; this time they paid attention, and accepted what had happened.

To be honest I don't blame them, the A&E department rarely has any surprises – the hospital is normally forewarned about any 'nasty job' we are bringing them, and to suddenly have a seriously sick patient turn up without any warning is always a bit of a jolt.

Now the patient was unconscious the nurses were able to do those vital observations that I was unable to do – and they were all normal. His pulse, blood pressure and blood oxygen levels were all better than mine, his blood sugar was also well within normal limits. There was no obvious reason why he was in such a deep state of unconsciousness.

He was quickly intubated, and we left the department. I've spent some time wondering if I missed anything – if there was anything I would have done differently – but to be honest I don't think there was. Even if I had managed to get a full set of vital sign observations, they would have all been normal and there was nothing that indicated his condition changing so quickly. I can't 'assault' a patient who has refused a procedure (such as observation taking), and all I could do was exactly what I did do – watch him while we took him to hospital.

The current idea is that he had taken an overdose of some sort along with the alcohol, and that it had started to work. Because the patient hadn't spoken to me, I had no way of knowing if he had taken an overdose.

I never did find out what had happened with the patient – it's one of the poor things about this job, that you can't always follow them up.

Protecting Little Old Men from the Police?

We were asked go to the local police station to help with arresting someone. The arrestee (is that a real word?) was an 80 (or more)-year-old male who was accused of recently committing a crime that I would suggest required some amount of physical strength. We were to follow along because the person had heart and breathing problems – so much so that he had bottled oxygen in his house.

We met with the police officers (nine in total, and all rather scary looking plain-clothes types) at the police station, before following them to the address in question.

Once the police had made their entrance we were called forward to give the patient a clean bill of health. We watched as this frail man slowly dressed, needing help from his son to tie his shoelaces; we watched as he struggled around the house and wondered how he could possibly be guilty of any crime that needed any form of physical exertion.

The patient's son was also a bit put out by the allegations, and promised to have a good laugh at the police's expense when the truth came out.

Throughout the arrest the police were polite, helpful and behaved in a thoroughly professional manner at all times.

The patient/arrestee was also calm throughout and the whole thing went, as far as I could see, very smoothly, and our ambulance followed the car in which he was taken, until it entered the police station and the FME (Forensic Medical Examiner – a doctor that the police use) took over.

The next job we went to was to outside the same address: a woman had been mugged and the police who were searching the address had called us as she had a rather large bump on her head. Unfortunately, the mugger managed to get away. It surprises me that you can get mugged outside a house full of police and the mugger can still escape.

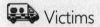 Victims

Imagine, if you will, getting sent to a job where a 15-year-old boy is threatening suicide. You turn up at the address and discover that it is a care home. Meeting with one of his carers she hands you a list of the boy's medications and it reads like a 'Who's who' of psychiatric drugs. You talk to the boy, and he seems calm, collected and very polite. He explains that he wants to jump out of a window and kill himself, and agrees that he would like to go to hospital. You take him into the paediatric department of a local hospital. As this does not feel like the normal 'Teenager wants to kill themselves' you have a chat with the children's nurse and you ask them to let you know what happens to the patient. You leave, and continue with your shift. The next day you ask the children's nurse about the patient and she tells you 'The boy wanted to die because he wants to have sex with, and kill, small children – and that he knows that it is wrong'.

I hate paedophiles as much as any other member of society, but in front of me that day, I saw a victim.

Behind Locked Doors

One of the jobs that I both enjoy and hate is for a 'Collapse behind locked doors'. This is when a (normally elderly) patient has not answered the front door or the telephone, and is presumed to be in some trouble. What we often get is someone who has died during the night. Although I hate having people die, the one good thing about this type of job is that I get to use my size 12 boots to kick down a door.

There is a skill to kicking down a door, and I was taught by the best – a policeman. The police also have a huge ram that they can use when their boots aren't enough. These are very heavy, but also lots of fun to use.

We got called to a house where the daughter could see her elderly mother lying on the floor; shouting through the door and banging on windows didn't get any response, so we assumed the worst. The daughter was (understandably) crying, so I had an attempt at kicking the door down.

Unfortunately for me, the woman had been burgled earlier in the year, and so had two locks, and a bolt holding the door shut, so it took a couple of minutes of prolonged (and eventually painful) kicking to get the door open. I also managed to wake up all the neighbours, and it's always fun to be the centre of attention . . .

Finally, the door gave and we gained access, we were greeted by the elderly woman sitting on the floor smiling at us – earlier in the morning she had fallen and couldn't get up. When we had tried banging on her windows she had been asleep, and it was only the repeated bashing of my foot against her door that had caused her to wake up.

This was a good job in a number of ways: the lady was happy and healthy, and just needed a hand to get up off of the floor; I got to kick in a door and get away with not causing any serious damage; and finally we looked like heroes to the two daughters of our patient. There were smiles all round and we left the job feeling that we had really been of some use today.

🚐 Substitute

I know that the ambulance service is being used as a substitute GP service these days, but it really takes the biscuit sometimes. Take, for example, the job I was sent on last night. It came down to our ambulance as 'Patient wants to kill his doctor'.

I immediately called up Control on the radio and asked if we were being sent because they couldn't find the patient's GP? Although I was half joking, I wondered what good we could do for the patient. Control got back to us, and let us know that they were sending the police, and that we should wait until they turn up. However, when we arrived at the address we knew who the patient was – so we cancelled the police and sorted out the patient's problem.

I mention this if only because, when I got back on station and read the local newspaper, I found a story about a coroner's investigation into the death of a 55-year-old female who had taken a fatal overdose of bloodpressure medication. When Control asked if she was violent, they were told that yes, the patient was violent. The police were called and the crew waited at a rendezvous point for half an hour until the police turned up. By then it was too late, and the patient died. Once more, the paper blames the ambulance crew. It doesn't blame the psychiatric services who discharged her a few weeks earlier after a failed suicide attempt, neither does it blame the person who made the phone call that said that the patient was violent. It blames the crew who, quite rightly, waited for the police. If one of the crew had been stabbed to death, it might be a more sympathetic headline. We are expected to go into people's houses, where we have been told that the patient is violent, where we could get assaulted or even killed – but as soon as we start thinking about our own safety, *we* are the ones to blame for anything that goes wrong with that patient.

Violence from the drunks, druggies and criminals doesn't worry me – the job that worries me is the little old lady who has become confused.

and is sitting in her living room with her husband's service revolver, or her favourite kitchen knife, desperate to stop the strange men in green from stealing her away in the night.

As normal the ambulance service has investigated, but in a show of support for its road staff, has stated that the policy of waiting for the police at a rendezvous point is the correct thing to do.

We are not cowards, but neither are we stupid/paid enough to wander into dangerous situations.

Nicked

I've just gotten on station for the start of my shift, only to find out that some scrote had broken into the station last night and nicked the video recorder and DVD player.

I mean, it's not like we are ever on station long enough to use them, but it's the principle …

These are the sort of people that we serve, these are the sort of people we are polite, professional and caring towards – and this is how we are repaid …

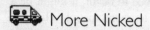 More Nicked

It's getting so you have to tie things down now …

Yesterday a 'Decontamination POD' truck was stolen; this is an unmarked truck that we use to carry around chemical incident equipment. The current word is that this truck was carrying a load of atropine, which is the treatment for nerve agents.

If people were to start injecting this into themselves, they could get serious (as in fatal) effects.

I leave it as an exercise for the reader to decide if this is a good or a bad thing ...

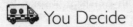 You Decide

Still no drunks, but the weekend starts today and my shift ends at 2 a.m. ...

I'm going to describe a job I went to last night.

The patient is female and 30 years old. She is married and is attempting to get pregnant. The only medicine she is taking is fertility treatment, and she is (obviously) having unprotected sex; she is normally fit and healthy and has no allergies. Her normal menstrual period is regular, but her period is over 2 weeks late this time around. She has been having nausea and vomiting for the past 3 days. She has no abdominal pain, and is not tender or guarding. She has no pain or increased frequency of passing urine. All vital signs are within normal limits.

So ... given this information ...

(a) What do you think is 'wrong' with her?
(b) Does she need a trip to hospital in an ambulance?
(c) Why do you think she hasn't done a pregnancy test?

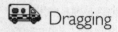 Dragging

Sometimes a day can just drag along. Today, due to rather unusual circumstances, the day really dragged. Here is the time-line of today:

10:00 Turn up for work, brew a cup of tea.

10:01 First job of the day, taking someone from Newham hospital to Barts hospital.

10:02 Cut my finger on my locker door, try to stop bleeding, look for plaster.

10:23 Give up search for a plaster – there are none on the station – leave for Newham hospital.

10:26 Arrive at Newham hospital, ask for plaster; they also don't have a plaster so I now have a huge dressing on my finger.

10:28 Meet with patient, pleasant woman – meet nurse who will be accompanying patient, barely understand nurse because of her inability to speak English.

10:30 Get patient's notes and read them – they make more sense.

10:32 Ask nurse in charge why this patient (who is having cardiac monitoring and a blood transfusion) is going to an outpatient department. Get told that the patient 'just is'.

10:54 After packaging the patient on a stretcher, loading them on the back of the ambulance, we set off for Barts hospital.

10:55 Nurse escort tells me that she gets travel sick.

10:55 and 20 seconds Give nurse a vomit bag.

11:37 Arrive at Barts hospital.

11:38 Enter outpatients' department. Reception seem rather surprised to see patient on stretcher appear in front of them.

11:40 Problem is referred to the sister in charge, she also looks befuddled.

12:00 We wait while sister in charge phones around the hospital trying to work out why this patient is in her outpatient department.

12:30 Still waiting … We let Control know why we are waiting – there is no stretcher/bed to put the patient on.

13:00 Still waiting.

13:30 Still waiting – we let Control know that we still have the patient on our stretcher while they work out what they are going to do with our patient.

14:00 Still waiting.

14:30 Still waiting – we let Control know that we haven't gone to sleep, we are told by sister in charge that patient will be admitted soon.

14:45 We place patient on an examination bed so that we can go back to answering emergency calls; patient will hopefully be in a hospital bed soon. We leave the nurse escort with the patient.

14:48 We are finally available for another job.

14:49 We realise we have nearly no fuel, and no fuel card to pay for fuel. We decide to return to station to borrow a fuel card off an unused ambulance.

15:20 We arrive back on station to look for fuel card (and have a cup of tea).

15:30 We leave to get fuel. Take infusion pump back to hospital – the ward seem surprised that the patient has been admitted to Barts.

15:48 We have fuel, we are now ready for another job.

16:00 We get a call, out of area Matern-a-taxi.

16:09 Arrive at Matern-a-taxi, contractions (genuinely) every 2 minutes, previous baby born in 3 *hours*, drive rather quickly towards her booked hospital.

16:12 Patient's waters break – start swimming in back of ambulance.

16:20 Arrive at hospital.

16:24 Throw patient at midwife, run back to ambulance.

16:30 Tell Control that we need to return to station to mop out the back of the ambulance.

17:20 Get back to station, mop out.

17:45 Crew to relieve us are already on station; await ambulance to dry out.

18:00 Leave for home.

18:37 Get home, collapse into sofa, start writing this post.

- Fin -

This is how you get to work an 8-hour shift, yet only do two jobs …

After this post I got given a box of plasters by a fellow blogger. No more searching around ambulance stations for sticking plasters.

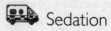 Sedation

I should be working today, but (and I want loads of sympathy here folks) I'm off sick with a work-related injury. Thankfully, it's nothing too serious, certainly nothing as serious as last time when I swallowed HIV-positive blood.

On Thursday we got called to a big conference centre in town for a (possibly) suspended/dead/fitting male. We rushed over there and were met by their security who had rather cleverly staked out both entrances to this place so that they could lead us to the patient. Parking up we had to climb a couple of flights of stairs carrying nearly all the equipment from the ambulance. Our first-response bag, oxygen and associated kit, defibrillator, suction and carry-chair are quite heavy and, as we were in a rush to get up the stairs, we were a bit out of breath when we reached the patient.

The first thing that we saw (and were *very* happy about) was that the patient had not suspended, and was instead thrashing around on the floor with some security guards and the centre's medic sitting on top of him. Approaching closer we saw that he wasn't fitting, but was instead very combative, trying to fight off the people who were holding him down in a very confused nature. 'Aha!' we thought, 'he's post-ictal'.

During the post-ictal phase of a seizure, the fitting has stopped, but the patient is often disorientated, sleepy or aggressive. In this case it appeared that the patient was both confused and aggressive – he was not responding to anyone trying to talk to him to calm him down, and he could only make guttural sounds. Normally, these episodes last less than half an hour, so we stay with the patient until we can get them into the ambulance.

Sometimes the aggression can come from physically being held down – the patient is confused and frightened, and all they can feel is people holding them down, so they struggle. I suggested that the security guards let him go, which resulted in the patient trying to stand up, only to fall over again (don't worry, we caught him) and unfortunately the centre medic got a head butt for his trouble. I managed to get a blood glucose reading, which was normal, and a work colleague phoned the patient's mother, so I could get a bit of history. The patient is normally fit and healthy, not diagnosed with epilepsy, but has had 2 fits in the past 2 years. All during this phone conversation the mother could hear her son shouting in the background. He had never been violent before.

We resigned ourselves to a bit of a wait, so we managed to get him over to a leather couch, and held him down there. After 10 minutes there was no change in the patient's condition – normally they get a bit tired or they start to have a change in their condition. So we started to think about other ways in which we could help the patient at the scene. We couldn't get him to the ambulance while he was so combative, and so we thought he might need some form of sedation. I ran back to the ambulance and asked Control to get us a BASICS doctor, or at least someone who could give some form of sedation.

Instead after about 10–15 minutes we got the PRU (Physician Response Unit), which is a new service where a doctor from the Royal London Hospital covers medical emergency calls – it's a bit like HEMS, only without the helicopter, and instead of going to trauma they mainly deal with medical emergencies.

The doctor (who is a very nice man) and paramedic crew with him took one look at the patient, listened to the history and decided that sedation was a very good idea.

Cut forward 40 minutes' worth of trying to sedate the patient with increasing amounts of medication. For the medically trained out there, the patient needed 10 mg haloperidol and 17 mg of midazolam. At one point the doctor was thinking about knocking the patient completely out and intubating him. Luckily the patient was sedated enough for us to get him out of the conference centre and into out ambulance, where we 'blued' him into Newham hospital just in time for him to wake up (the sedation lasting only around 15 minutes) where the doctors there did paralyse and intubate him.

We have few ideas why the patient was so violent and so deeply confused – it's something that will be investigated in hospital. We were considering epilepsy, head trauma (from when his head hit the floor), meningitis (so antibiotics were given on scene) or some form of brain insult. I'm asking my crewmate to find out what happened to the patient.

The reason why I am off sick? Well after holding the patient down for an hour and 10 minutes, I managed to sprain my thumb. Since I can't be considered safe to carry a patient downstairs, I'm taking today off (plus 2 days of leave) so that my thumb can heal and I can get back to saving lives picking up drunks again on Monday. Oh, and it's my birthday tomorrow – 33 is such a young age don't you think?

I did manage to see the patient again ... see the next entry.

 ## Patient Gets Better!!!

I went to visit our patient from the last post. This morning I'd put my hand in my pocket and found that I had £2.66 of his money that had spilled out of his pocket during our struggle and I'd put it in my fleece for safe keeping – given the saga of the job, I'd forgotten to hand it in when we reached the hospital. I thought it would be best if I returned it to him, so I had a chat with the lovely receptionists at the hospital, and they told me what ward he was on.

I went to the ward to find him sitting there, seemingly none the worse for wear. He did have a bit of a black eye (not my fault ... honest), and when I spoke to him he told me that the doctors suspected that he had fainted, and when he had hit his head had suffered a form of concussion. His CT scan and blood tests were all normal, although I suspect that they will be running EEGs (electroencephalograms) and other more detailed tests a little later. He told me that he was feeling pretty much normal and I suspect that they are keeping him in hospital to continue to run their tests.

He was very pleased to see me, and we had a little chat. I offered him his money but he refused and suggested that I get myself a pint with it.

It's the first time I've actively gone to look for a patient after bringing them into hospital – and it is a weird experience going into a ward to see a patient whom I last saw trying to fight me. Yet another new thing I've done because of writing this blog.

 Safety Net

I've mentioned before how the ambulance service and the A&E department are often seen as a 'safety net' by other health-care providers. Both yesterday and today we had perfect examples of this.

Yesterday we were called by a 70-year-old man with a urinary catheter which had blocked. This is a fairly simple thing to solve as it just needs a flush of water up the catheter to clear the blockage. It's a 5-minute job that we, as ambulance crews, aren't allowed to do. However it is the sort of job that district nurses are supposed to do.

So why hadn't a district nurse been to see the patient so that she could flush the catheter and prevent the patient from having to attend A&E? Why was the patient, who had phoned up the nurse himself, and told her exactly what he needed doing, forced to call an ambulance?

Because the nurse didn't have any water to actually flush the catheter. It's a bit like if I turned up to someone having an asthma attack, and didn't have any oxygen to give them.

So the district nurse told the patient to dial 999 for an ambulance. We arrived and found him with a bladder so full it was causing him severe pain. We took him into Newham hospital, who, within minutes, had cleared his catheter, and eased his pain. They gave him a 'takeaway' bottle of water so that the district nurse wouldn't have an excuse the next time she needed to visit him.

Today, we were called to a patient who needed his anti-Parkinson's disease medication. He had a carer, who was supposed to visit him once a day to clean and arrange his medication. But for the last 2 days, because the 'carer' couldn't get in touch with the patient's GP, she'd just left him without his medication. We turned up, not knowing what we could do to help. The flat in which the patient was living is brand new, and yet was already very untidy. The patient told me that he was lucky if the carer spent longer than 5 minutes with him (the carer is contracted to work with him for an hour a day).

This poor man was left, alone and shaking, with a carer who seemed to think that if she ignored this 'problem' it would soon go away. So, we did the only thing that we could: we took him to hospital, so that they could sort out his medication for him. Meanwhile I filled in an 'LA260' which is a 'vulnerable adults' form and allows the LAS to bring situations of abuse, and potential abuse, to the attention of the local social services. They now have the name of the care agency, and this problem can be solved before it repeats itself in a month's time.

Hopefully, someone will get a bollocking, and our patient will get a carer who actually cares for him.

It often feels that we, and the local A&E departments, are left to do the jobs that other people should be doing, but because we are there, these other agencies don't seem to care about doing a competent job. I'm aware that there are probably loads of health visitors/social workers/

district nurse/CPNs and GPs who do actually give a damn about their patients – it's just that we never seem to meet them.

I never did get any feedback from the LA260 that I filled in – normally you get a little note sent to you explaining what has been done to resolve the situation.

A Hidden Pregnancy

Our 'interesting' call of last night was a Matern-a-taxi. What, I hear you ask could be interesting about taking a pregnant woman 1.2 miles into the local maternity department?

Well, apart from the patient, no-one else knew that she was pregnant – she had been hiding the pregnancy from everyone. She hadn't seen a doctor; neither had she booked into a maternity department. Her family suspected nothing. It's not as if she were a 'large' woman, who could perhaps hide the tell-tale bump under the pretence of fat. She was actually rather slender, which leads me to ask how she could hide her rather obvious pregnancy from everyone.

When my crewmate spoke to her (I was driving), she told him that she had hoped that the pregnancy would 'go away'.

We tried to prewarn the maternity department that we were coming (because she was quite close to actually delivering the baby), but they hung up the phone twice on our Control. The problem is that the entrance to the maternity department is locked at night, and we need someone to come down and open it for us. So … we were left standing around outside the department waiting for the midwives to phone for a porter to traipse the length of the hospital to come and open the door for us (as opposed to one of the midwives walking down the stairs and opening the door).

By the time we got in the patient was starting to bleed, and we were getting more irate at the apparent ignorance of the midwives.

So, tonight we are going to put in a 'clinical incident report' to highlight the danger that standing outside the maternity department for 10 minutes while they arrange a porter puts the patient in.

One of the people on complex has had to deliver a baby in the back of their ambulance while they were waiting for the doors to be opened, so something needs to be done.

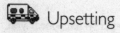 Upsetting

Three of our jobs today had the potential to be upsetting, and while they were all sad, only one seriously upset me, and did so in a way I consider rather out of character for myself.

The first job of the day was to an 86-year-old female in a nursing home with a 'blocked nose': we raced around there because … well … it was a Category 'A' call and those are the top-priority 'get there in 8 minutes to please the government target' calls.

Just as we pulled up outside Control let us know that the patient was upgraded to a 'Suspended' (no pulse, no breathing), and sure enough we ran into the home to be greeting by a FRU who was doing CPR. I jumped down and did a round of chest compressions, which cracked her ribs (a recognised side-effect of effective CPR), and then noticed that on the cardiac monitoring machine her heart rhythm had changed. She had a pulse! … People don't normally get a pulse back from cardiac arrests of her particular type. We rushed her to the hospital, where a full cardiac arrest team was assembled. Her pulse was lost, and then returned. Unfortunately, her prognosis was poor, but she stayed alive long enough for her daughter to reach the hospital. She died with her daughter there, which is a small victory, but one that we are getting more used to.

The second potentially upsetting job was to a 1-year-old boy who had pulled some boiling milk on top of him. We turned up to find about 20 police officers on scene, and the HEMS helicopter circling above. The same FRU responder was there and the child had around 10% partial thickness burns to parts of the neck and chest. While nasty, this wasn't immediately life-threatening, but the HEMS doctor who turned up decided that it would be best to take the patient to the Paediatric Burns Unit at Chelsea and Westminster Hospital by helicopter. As the helicopter could get the child there in under 20 minutes it seemed like the right plan of action. My job during this call was to (1) hold onto the other two toddlers in the house, (2) mix up some paracetamol for the child, and (3) drive child and doctor to the helicopter, which was around 300 yards away. The job was interesting because she was the type of parent who thought it was a good idea to wedge a settee into the hallway to stop her children from falling down the stairs …

The final job was a lot simpler – we were called to an 18- to 22-year-old female who was 'unresponsive' in a bus. The bus had reached the end of its route and the driver couldn't wake up the patient. (Possibly interesting aside – bus drivers cannot touch any of their customers to wake them up.) We turned up and soon managed to wake up the very sleepy girl. She remained drowsy but agreed to let us take her to the place where she lived, but after talking to her a bit, we soon realised that she was homeless. This, coupled with the way she would fall asleep as soon as we stopped talking to her, made us think that it would not be safe to leave her on the street. We decided instead that we would take her to hospital. When we reached the hospital she refused to go in, and instead pulled out a 'crack' pipe and started to light up. We told her that she couldn't do that … So she jumped up, pushed my crewmate and ran off. As there was nothing physically wrong with her we couldn't chase after her; instead we returned to our station to fill in the necessary paperwork.

So why was it that this last job was the most upsetting, not only for myself but also for my crewmate? Well it wasn't because she was pretty (she wasn't, and she had a remarkably nasal voice), and it wasn't because she was ill, neither was it because my crewmate got shoved.

With our first job, the woman was at the end of her life, and until she died, had enjoyed fairly good health. She didn't die a painful, protracted death, and she died with her daughter next to her. With the scalded child, he would forget the pain, and will receive excellent care from the hospital he went to, he would return home to his loving (if ever so slightly dense) mother. With this girl, it was as if she were lost; at some point in her life her potential future had unravelled. Instead of getting an education, holding down a job, finding someone special and living a long and happy life, she is homeless, a drug addict, and her future is probably painful and short. What is so depressing is that no-one was able to turn around this descent, and this is perhaps why I despair at society – that so many people are prevented from reaching their full potential. I understand that she has made her own choices, but how much power did she have to make those choices? I wanted to help her, but there was no way I could do this.

And it's that which annoyed and upset me.

I keep getting upset and annoyed at the same things – the waste of a life is a terrible thing to see. That, and the knowledge that I am helpless to do anything to change it. I imagine that this is why I dislike alcoholics so much.

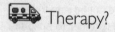 Therapy?

We got sent to a job of a 6-month-old baby not breathing. While this often means that baby has a cold, it could also be one of the worst jobs you can get. We sped to the address and entered a house where the whole family was distraught. It was an Indian household, so there were a lot of people there, and most of them were crying. Once more, I heard the type of crying that can only mean that something awful has happened – entering the living room I instantly saw a baby lying dead on the settee, father crouched over it crying and the mother standing and wailing, shouting out that her baby was dead.

There is only one thing that you can do in a situation like this, which is to scoop up the baby and run to hospital as quickly as possible. I reached down and picked up the baby; I was shocked to find that it was as stiff as a board and very purple, indicating that it had been dead for some time. It looked more like a doll than anything that had once been alive. We could have recognised the child as dead on the scene, but taking the child to hospital would mean that the parents would see that everything that could be done was being done and, more importantly, they would be in a hospital with all the support that the hospital could provide.

I ran out to the ambulance with mother in tow, and told my crewmate to get us to hospital as quickly as possible. The father and grandmother followed behind us in another ambulance who had heard this call go out and had turned up to see if there was anything that they could do to help. On the way to hospital I did the CPR that I knew was ultimately pointless and spoke to the mother. She had last seen the child alive at 3 a.m., and he had been fine then. It looked like it may have been a case of sudden infant death syndrome, and I did all that I could to prepare the mother for the worst.

We pulled up at hospital and handed the baby into the care of the hospital. I spoke a little more with the mother and grandmother, but there is nothing that you can say to people who have had such a tragedy. Our station officer met us at the hospital and asked us if we were alright, then he booked us off the road so that we could go back to station and have a cup of tea and 'decompress'. If we needed more support I think it would have been there, but I just wanted to get away from the hospital.

I'm not often affected by jobs, and this isn't the first dead baby that I've had to deal with, but it is the first dead baby I've had since joining the ambulance service and it is very different from dealing with them in hospital. Going into someone's house to take away a dead child is very different from having the child and parents turn up at hospital, which is your safe territory.

At the hospital all the other crews were asking if I was alright and, to be honest, I wasn't really alright – I was upset that while I was doing CPR on the baby its legs were seesawing into the air, and it looked too much like a doll. There was a point after the job where I thought I was going to start crying, but a moment outside the Resus' room and I was back to functioning as I normally do. I'm not weak, and when in the midst of something I can deal with anything – it was only after the doctors and nurses at the hospital had taken over that I started to feel anything.

We returned to station, where the therapy of talking about anal surgery with another crew, and a cup of tea, soon had me feeling better. It used to be that you would return to work straight after a job like this, but then I think they realised that if we got our normal inappropriate call (belly-ache for 2 weeks sort of thing) we might say something to the patient that we might later regret.

Well, an hour on station later and I feel fully prepared to deal with that sort of thing again – but I think that I'll be haunted by the image of that child lying dead on my trolley.

I had loads of people commenting on this post, loads of support, which was very much appreciated. The title is a reference to the fact that I have found my blog to be 'therapy' for some of the things that I've seen and done in the ambulance service ... and it's cheaper than hitting the bottle.

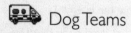 Dog Teams

I've often mentioned that the ambulance service and the police tend to get on rather well together; this is at least in part due to us both being called to the same jobs, and probably because we share the same view of the 'Great British Public'.

An example: we got called to a drunk who was being verbally abusive to a bus driver – we were called because the drunk had fallen over, while the police were called because of the abuse. The drunk man was obnoxious, and well known to both of our services, and because of the lack of an injury was left in the care of the police. If he had been injured then the police would have left the matter in our hands.

So, when we co-respond, the ambulance crew pray that the patient is uninjured, so the police have to deal with them, while I suspect that the police hope that the patient is injured so they don't have to arrest them.

However, there are a lot of specialist teams in the police service that we tend not to come into contact with that often; we mainly get to meet the normal 'beat' coppers. Thankfully, we rarely see the murder, child abuse, drugs or dog teams. This isn't to say we never see them (and our station did get a Christmas card from the local murder squad telling us to 'keep up the good work'), it's just that it is fairly rare.

So, it was rather surprising that I met with the dog-handling team twice last week. On the first occasion, we were called to a known schizophrenic who had threatened to kill herself. The patient herself (a regular attender at the local A&E) was a bit of a pain to deal with, she wanted to stay at home and kill herself and couldn't see why we wouldn't let her do that. Her dog, on the other hand, was a real pleasure – happy to see us, interested in smelling all our equipment and extremely friendly. As the police were already there, they got the dog squad to look after the animal until the patient was discharged from hospital.

In case you think I am being harsh on the mentally ill, the patient attends A&E every day with the same complaint of wanting to kill themselves ... she hasn't managed it yet.

The second time I saw the dog-handling team was when we had to gain access to a house where the patient was unable to come to the front door and let us in. The interesting part in this story is that there were five dogs of unknown temperament in the house. For half an hour the police unsuccessfully tried to gain access, mainly by climbing up a ladder and trying to open a bathroom window. We were able to talk to the patient, and so we knew that they were not badly hurt, otherwise we would have had to kick the door down. Then the dog team turned up and, using a top secret criminal technique, managed to get the front door open in about 10 seconds, thus putting to shame the half-hour everyone else had spent trying to gain entry.

All five dogs were really lovely, although energetic, and at the end of the job I had to spend 20 minutes brushing the dog hair off my uniform.

There is a joke we have about dogs. When we ask a patient if the dog is friendly, the patient *always* answers that they won't bite; the reply to this from the ambulance crew is to add the unspoken 'They only bite people dressed all in green.'

I've only had one dog take a dislike to me. But I managed to pull my hands away from his gnashing teeth before he could catch me.

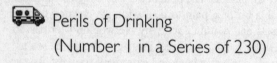 Perils of Drinking
(Number 1 in a Series of 230)

It was the usual type of busy last night – we heard rumours that there is such a thing as an 'ambulance station', a mythical building where one might use the toilet or partake of the life-giving 'cup of tea'. It must be a myth, as we never saw it at all.

As I have mentioned, we get our calls sent down to a computer screen in the ambulance cab; sometimes you wonder how the Control crew have entered it while keeping from laughing down the phone at the patient. A case in point was one of our calls last night which was given as '53-year-old male, taken 3 × crack cocaine, cold and lonely, needs to be put back together'.

Avoiding the rather obvious 'Humpty Dumpty' jokes, we soon realised that the complaint, and the location he was calling from, fitted one of our semi-regular callers. By the time we got there he had left the phone box and neither us nor the police could find him after a search of the area. Obviously I was distraught …

Our other stand-out job of the night was a 57-year-old male fitting. We quickly made our way to the location, to be met by a block of low-rise flats that often sneak up on you in our area. These are three or four floors high, and have no lifts. Also there was one of our First Responders. We entered the block, and immediately made our way to the stairs (it is a little known law of physics that in flats with no lifts, people on the ground floor are never ill … only those on the top floor).

Entering the flat, the general state of disrepair, mess and the 3-litre bottle of strong cider I tripped over tended to give the impression that it was owned by an alcoholic. We got into the living room to find a large man lying senseless on the floor, while his daughter was sat over him stroking his hand, trying to reassure him. A quick check over, some oxygen and a chat with his daughter revealed a history of alcoholism (surprise!) and the occasional alcoholic fit. He was a big man, so we packaged him up in our carry-chair and carried him down three flights of stairs. All the time his daughter was saying how strong the nice ambulance men were – which only goes to show that she wasn't paying attention to my reddening face and struggles for breath …

We got the patient into the back of the ambulance where he started to fit again, this time lasting about 2 minutes. He also decided to bite his tongue and vomit, which meant that the back of the ambulance (and myself in some part) was covered in bloody, cider-smelling vomit. I think I've mentioned before how I can't smell alcohol on someone's breath, yet I can smell cider when it has been vomited all over my ambulance … and it turns my stomach. We packaged him up and 'blued' him into Newham, where he had another two fits (despite some rather strong sedation) and by the end of our shift he was still in Resus' having infusions of phenytoin and Pabrinex.

So, a busy night without the chance to see our station, with at least one mopping out of the ambulance … pretty standard really.

The vomit in the ambulance took place at the end of our shift, so we couldn't even get back to station to use the mop. Unfortunately, with the increased number of calls we have, getting back to station is becoming rarer than ever.

 Security

Yes, I know I've written before about kicking down doors. However, in this post I offer people advice in making the beating down of their door as hard as possible. So please excuse the repetition. Like all good health-care professionals I regularly ignore my own advice.

There is a visceral pleasure in kicking down a door. Once or twice I've managed to see someone who is really ill trapped behind a locked door, occasionally there has been someone who has just been unable to open the door. And just the once I have kicked down a door that the patient refused to open because they were schizophrenic and didn't want to open the door – not that I knew that at the time.

I've even been surprised at the ease in which I can kick down the doors of the flats that I live in. Actually, it would be more accurate to say that I am *scared* with the ease in which the doors can be broken. Oh well, it's not as if I have a lot to steal anyway …

My experience of kicking down doors has taught me which security features are useful when trying to prevent someone from stealing your TV and video.

If you have a deadlock-type lock, then use it – always. The skill of kicking down a door relies on breaking either the lock, or the wood holding the lock; deadbolt-type locks are a lot more secure than the normal Yale type lock.

If you are in the house and have a bolt on the door, then use it. It takes a lot longer to kick down a door when there is a bolt in the way. Another trick behind kicking down a door relies on applying the force of your kick to the (hopefully) single point of resistance. If there is a bolt at the top or the bottom of the door it makes it a lot trickier to break that door.

Windows in the door are a bad idea – they are a weak point that can be easily broken, and then a skinny hand can reach through and unlock the door.

If you really want to be safe then have a bar across the door. I've seen it once or twice, and if someone has a bar across the door then there is no way I'd be able to break that door down. Just make sure you don't collapse behind it.

 ## Major Incident Cover

One of the perks of this job is the need to cover football games. Well … it's a perk if you enjoy seeing your local team play. Personally, I can't stand football but overtime is overtime, and it does make a nice change from the usual jobs I go to. So, this Sunday I got to see West Ham play against Derby.

The LAS provide 'Major Incident' cover for these games, we don't look at sprained ankles or minor injuries (that is the job of the St John's ambulance). We also don't look after the players who get hacked down and are unable to walk, only to watch them turning somersaults a scant 5 minutes later when their team scores a goal (that is a job for the private medical firms).

So, unless a stand collapses, there is a major fire, a bomb goes off or someone drops dead in front of us, there is very little we have to do. At the West Ham ground (my local football club), there are four 'road crew' present, along with at least one major incident support vehicle, one radio operator and an officer. The road crew sit down near the pitch, while the officer and radio operator sit in a VIP box overlooking the whole ground.

Today I was given the role of 'safety officer', which doesn't mean I've been promoted, it just means that in the event of a major incident, I'm supposed to watch out for the safety of the ambulance crews present, liaise with the police and fire service about any hazards that might be a problem, and to make sure that any crews that attend the incident are not getting too stressed. I also have to talk to the person in overall control at the incident about any issues within this sphere that may occur.

We were warned that there was an increased chance of violence at this match because some hooligan 'supporters' were appearing before the magistrate tomorrow, and that some of their 'crew' might want to cause some trouble. Luckily for us, that did not happen, despite a 2–1 loss.

It was really cold down there in the stands, I had my undershirt, shirt, body armour, fleece and hi-visibility all-weather jacket on, but I was still freezing. Anyone listening carefully as I walked around trying to keep warm would have heard a clink-clink-clink-clink sound as my frozen balls knocked together.

As I've mentioned before, I'm not a huge fan of football (overpaid idiots, getting more money in a week than I get paid in a year for booting around a plastic ball), so I spent most of the match listening to music (The Magnetic Fields) on my smart-phone, while stamping around trying to get some sensation back in my toes.

As a quick aside, who needs an iPod Shuffle? My smart-phone can do the same thing and more – it can even make phone calls …

Half-time came and went so we joined the St John's Ambulance for a cup of tea and a sandwich, rather than watch a bunch of scantily clad young women prance about. Then we were back in the cold, where I tried to stay awake while West Ham, perhaps predictably, lost …

With the exception of someone having a crafty cigarette and setting off a fire alarm, it all went rather smoothly. I did find it funny that the people in the stadium knew what the 'Inspector Sands' announcement meant, and did nothing but laugh quietly at it.

At the end of the match we have to stay around until we are 'stood down' as the last few supporters leave, so we sat in the ambulance, with the heater going, wrapped in our own blankets (remember, we know what those blankets have been wrapped around, yet we still used them – that is how cold it was).

We then started making our way back to station …

… to come across a policeman who had tried to stop a car – only to have them speed up (possibly accidentally) and hit him. He wasn't especially badly hurt, but we took all precautions as we transported him to hospital. He'll need a few X-rays, but I suspect that he will be fine.

'Inspector Sands' is a codeword for use over a public address system. It is used to let the staff know that a fire alarm has gone off without alerting the public and possibly panicking them.

Phonetic

I'm aware that because I am my own self-publicist I may come across as trying to sound 'perfect'. I will however blog about my mistakes … or at least the mistakes that won't lose me my job …

Part of our job involves using a radio to talk to Control, so part of our training is in the use of the radio. The training is about 3 hours long, and you spend it pretending to talk on a radio passing jobs back and forth (this is before the computer terminals were introduced).

One of the things we are taught is the phonetic alphabet, which I am sure you have all seen in film and TV. Normally, it sounds something like 'Foxtrot Alpha Sierra Tango Charlie Alpha Romeo', and is designed to make the spelling out of words over an unreliable radio transmission clearer and less likely to have errors.

One other thing that you should be aware of, is that our radio has an open broadcast: this means that everyone in the sector can hear you talking on it. You can recognise your friends' voices, and this radio chatter gives you a general idea of what they are doing. Of course, this means that should you make a mistake, everyone knows about it.

Why was it, when spelling out a name, I suddenly forgot the phonetic for 'M' (Mike), and instead, in a moment of panic, decided that the new phonetic for 'M' would be …

… Mango?

It's not as if I have mangoes on the mind – I can't remember the last time I ate one – but for some reason it was the first thing that came into my mind.

I bless the radio operator for not bursting into laughter and calling me a twit.

Odds and Ends

Today was typical, in that the jobs we did veered from interesting to dull, and from heartwarming to heartbreaking.

As an example of how one job can be different from another, we found ourselves attending an elderly man who was looked after by his daughter and son-in-law. They lived in Portugal, but when he had become ill they had moved back to England to look after him. The house was spotlessly clean, as was our patient; there was real love in the house and they obviously cared deeply for him. He was generally a bit poorly after a fall earlier in the day, so we took him to hospital for a check-up. Straight after that job, we ended up going to a pair of alcoholics living in squalor, where one of the pair had fallen over while drunk and had cut their ear. The patient later said that his partner had punched him, and that is why he had a cut ear, that and she had also kicked him in the stomach.

This is the fun bit of this job, we go from loving families to quarrelling drunken couples.

We had a bit of a 'trauma' with a victim of a hit-and-run. The patient was crossing the road when he got hit by a car, bounced up onto the bonnet and ended up in the middle of the road. Luckily, he wasn't hurt in a life-threatening way, but he did have a broken arm (for the medics in the audience, or those who can use Google, the patient had a simple transverse fracture of the mid-shaft humerus). He didn't have any other injuries, which in my book makes him rather lucky, especially considering the speed that cars can get up to down that particular road.

What was particularly interesting was that, although the man was lying in the middle of the very busy road, only a bus and one bystander had stopped – the bystander was making sure that he didn't get hit by any other cars. People were so unbothered that at one point I had buses rushing past my head as I treated him. You'd think people might slow their driving a little when swerving around an ambulance parked in the middle of the road with all its lights flashing …

But not around here they don't.

We also went to a 'Fire job', where a mother had left a 7-year-old, a 5-year-old and a 2-year-old locked alone in a house while she popped out for some fruit. A small fire had started, and the children had only been saved when a neighbour walked past and saw the kids crying at the window, and the orange flicker of flames in the background. He broke the window and saved the children. The mother was, perhaps unsurprisingly, distraught. A moment of carelessness nearly cost her children their lives. The quick thinking of the neighbour had meant that the children were completely unharmed, so I hope he gets a nice write-up in the local papers.

The final job of the day was to a 'nursing' home. The patient had apparently developed a bony lump under her hip. The staff thought that she might have broken her hip, but as the patient is bed-bound and as no-one admitted dropping her it would be a very suspicious fracture. I had a look at the supposed 'fracture' and couldn't see anything unusual, the patient was just extremely frail. The patient was suffering from dementia, and when I further examined her was also rather dehydrated. So we took her into hospital – along with a 'carer' from the home. All throughout the transport the patient was scared, so I did my best to look after her, hold her hand, talk to her, that sort of thing. During the journey the 'carer' stared out the window of the ambulance and didn't say a word apart from worrying that she would have trouble being relieved when her shift was finished.

When we left the patient at the hospital I told the 'carer' (can you see why I put 'carer' in quotes?) that her job now was to 'hold her hand, talk to her and reassure her because she would be scared in this unusual place. In fact, it gives you a chance to do that *caring* thing that you don't have time to do normally'.

I think she knew I was a bit angry at her but she did as I said, so maybe she got the point.

Another 12-hour shift tomorrow – then (hopefully) I'll have a day or two off, when I can sleep and perhaps manage to fix my laptop.

If the above post doesn't make any sense then tough, I'm knackered and all the Red Bull in the world can't make me into a Hemingway.

The man who saved the children did indeed get mentioned in glowing terms in the local paper. Once more I mention a lack of sleep and computer troubles, which along with a constant search for a nice cup of tea are the two constants in my life.

A Changed Role (the Secret is Out)

So, after some time (arranging things with work, battering my computer into submission and having a day of doing nothing except 'chilling out') I think I can finally reveal the 'big secret' that I have been using to keep you coming back to read this blog …

I'm still in the London Ambulance Service, and I've not been promoted; however, the vehicle that I drive, and the role that I play, will change.

I'm no longer going to be driving one of these …

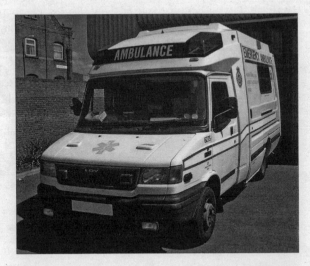

Or even one of these …

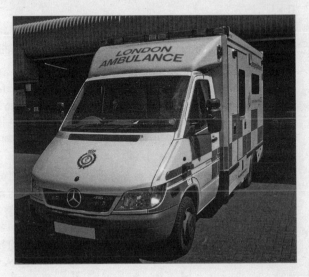

But one of these …

For the foreseeable future I am going to be on the Fast Response Unit (FRU).

The role of the FRU is to get to emergency calls within 8 minutes, thereby pleasing the government, and by extension, pleasing management.

I am to get to calls as quickly as possible, get a history off a patient and start treatment until an ambulance can arrive, then leave the patient in the care of the ambulance crew and drive off looking for another emergency call. When I don't have a call to go on, I am to spend at least some time driving around the area in the hope that I will be closer than an ambulance when a call does come in.

This means that I have even more autonomy than working on an ambulance, because I am working on my own – there is no crewmate to bounce ideas off. There is also a better chance of things going horribly wrong – imagine having to deal with a cardiac arrest on your own, with distraught relatives knowing that there isn't going to be an ambulance for 30 minutes …

Still … it should be fun, especially considering that I'm starting this new rota with a Friday, Saturday and Sunday night.

I stuck it for nearly a year before returning to an ambulance. Too much time spent on your own is bad for your mental health methinks. From here on in the posts are all about being an FRU pilot.

First Night

My first shift on 'the car' went fairly well. There are lots of things that are different between working from the car and working on a truck that I think you may be interested reading about, which means I'll have a series of postings about FRU work to write about when I next get some days off.

While others were dealing with stabbings and shootings (at least two in the area last night) I, who am supposed to go to the most serious calls, had two patients who actually needed hospital treatment, a crying baby, and five cases of 'D&V' (diarrhoea and vomiting). I was not alone in dealing with this sudden increase of D&V, Newham hospital was very busy with an epidemic of similar illness, and it seemed that crews were persuading a lot of them to stay at home and nurse themselves …

If you live in the area I work then I'd stay away from the kebab shops in Romford Road (Manor Park end) if I were you, as at least 12 cases were tied to one kebab shop, with perhaps as many as 27 people eventually falling ill with the same symptoms after eating from the same shop.

Now … can I name the shop involved? Legally and ethically, am I on firm ground?

Maybe I should study journalism at night school …

I may have something more interesting tomorrow, but for the first night it was really pleasant to be eased into this entirely new way of working.

Now to sleep …

🚑 Major Food Poisoning Incident
   – D&V Part 2

It turns out that Newham General Hospital had at least 70 people through their doors with the food poisoning epidemic. Some patients also had gone to King George's hospital or to Whipps Cross hospital, which, if you add in the number of people who are suffering in silence at home, makes a lot of rather sick people.

The kebab place has duly been closed and the various public/environmental health bodies are looking closely at the situation. I have heard an unconfirmed rumour that the cause of the sickness was *Salmonella*.

At least one person is very ill, and at least eight people were admitted to Newham hospital. This has stretched the resources in the area to near breaking point, Newham hospital and King George's hospital were both closed on Sunday night because the A&Es were full, and there were no beds left in the hospitals. It got so bad that Newham hospital declared an internal 'major incident' – a wise choice I think, as it means that the resources needed to deal with the situation are pointed in the right direction.

Unfortunately, with our local hospitals closed, patients have needed to go further to get to a hospital. Some are quite happy, such as those who get taken to the Royal London (in most people's eyes the Royal London is *the* hospital to go to). Meanwhile others have been less happy (such as those who have been taken to Whipps Cross).

It is my belief that a terrorist network doesn't need bombs to bring London to its knees, it just needs to spread a little *Salmonella* around, and then watch the NHS collapse.

It was a month or so later that the national news caught up on the story. Apparently the meat was contaminated at source and the kebab shop was blameless. Just one more example of how bloggers can move more quickly than more traditional media.

🚐 Shopping

I went out today and saw an alcoholic, a COPD (chronic obstructive pulmonary disease), a couple of heart failures, a handful of kids with chest infections and at least three anosmias (anosmia is a lack of a sense of smell).

The anosmia patients are those teenage girls who think that the best way to attract a slack-jawed mate is to empty half a bottle of cheap perfume over their heads – do they not know what they smell like?

However, I wasn't in an ambulance, and I wasn't on the FRU – in fact I wasn't working at all

The answer is fairly simple – I just went shopping.

The problem with being surrounded by patients for 12 hours a day (first as a nurse, then to a lesser extent as an EMT), is that your eye is automatically drawn towards people with obvious symptoms. It's not just your eye – a trained ear can hear the cough of a child with a chest infection, or the puff and wheeze of a chronic bronchitis.

I suspect doctors have the same problem, the constant inspection of clubbing in the fingers, the subliminal inspection of the eyes and the unconscious appraisal of someone's gait.

In some part, it's because you are trained to look for what is wrong with people – but equally, there is that desire not to be around the person who is most likely to have a heart attack in front of you. At least when you are not on duty. This is why, when the 80-year-old female with ankles the size of tree trunks and blue lips decides to hit the pavement, there won't be a medical professional to be seen for miles.

It's not that we are lazy, or that we have no love for our fellow man when we are not getting paid for it, its just that without any of our 'kit', there is very little we can do to look busy, or effective. Without equipment, the options are CPR (if their heart has stopped), the recovery position (if they are unconscious) or a 'there, there', with a bit of hand holding, if it is a grazed knee.

Of course, the first thing to do is to call for an ambulance.

🚑 Mobile Phones

We often have problems with mobile phones in the ambulance service – we find ourselves trying to talk to a patient, while they are more intent on talking to their friend/mum/cousin/dealer on the phone.

I've had to pull people out of the way of incoming traffic because they are so focused on photographing the damage to their car with their mobile phone that they neglect to realise that they are standing in the middle of a busy dual carriageway.

I've been trying to resuscitate dead patients when their mobile phone has rung – I look at the screen and see that the person trying to call them is 'MUM'.

I've been in the middle of what can best be described as a 'public order situation', and while trying to deal with the injured (and prevent any more injuries), half the crowd are on the phone telling their 'posse' to get to that location as quickly as they can.

I've even had a patient and a relative fist-fighting in the back of my ambulance over an overheard phone call, made while the patient was pretending to be unconscious.

Standby

As the LAS doesn't have an ambulance station on every street, and given the state of London's roads and traffic, we find ourselves going out on 'Standby'.

Essentially ambulance crews and FRU cars are told to drive away from the station (with its heating, toilets and tea-making facilities) and sit in public roads to help cover a wider area. The idea is that because the 'resources' are spread out over a wider area you will be able to get to calls quicker, thus improving our all-important response time.

Crews don't like going out on standby, but I doubt anyone would like sitting in an ambulance cab waiting for someone to be ill/injured/drunk. Management like to have crews put out on standby because it apparently improves response times; this in turn pleases the government. I am yet to see some proper scientific evidence to back up this claim.

The standby points are chosen to be reasonably far away from station, around three miles in my case, and in an area where there is a reasonable expectation for there to be a high number of calls.

They also try to place you where a number of major road routes meet, so you can rapidly make your way out of your area to cover the shortfall in other sectors …

There are limits to how standby can be used. You can only be put on standby for 20 minutes at a time, and you can only be put on standby between the hours of 8 a.m. and 8 p.m., so while it is unpleasant to be put on standby, it isn't the complete torture that it could be.

On the FRU there is another ruling – that they can't spend longer than 30 minutes on station, so although I had five jobs over the space of 12 hours yesterday, I spent very little time actually on station. Most of my time was spent sitting behind Stratford shopping centre with the engine running so that I didn't freeze to death. When I got bored with that, I would roam the area, essentially looking for some trouble.

It is a fair assumption that it takes half an hour to do one job, from activation to being ready for the next job, so I was only actually working for two and a half hours since for an hour and a half I was on station, leaving me sitting in the car for 8 hours.

As I neared the end of my time on the FRU, one of my main problems was that I was getting severe back pain from sitting in a car for long periods of time. Management also wanted to change the times they could send the FRU on standby to 24 hours a day. Too dangerous for my liking.

Worthwhile (For a Change)

Yesterday I felt that my role as a FRU was justified and this, coupled with the better weather, means that I am in a much better mood.

The unfortunate thing is that it was a tragedy that made me feel better.

The first job of the day came 2 hours into my shift, the call was 'Woman fell out of bed, not breathing'. I got to the house in 2 minutes and climbed the narrow stairs to find a 55-year-old woman lying in the lap of her daughter; also on the bed were two small children (perhaps 1 and 2 years old). The younger woman was crying and my patient wasn't breathing.

I had to pull her out from the side of the bed so I could get my resuscitation attempt started – not very dignified, and probably not that nice to watch either, as a stranger in green pulls your mother across the floor.

I connected her to my heart monitor/defibrillator, and saw that she was in PEA (pulseless electrical activity – a heart rhythm that means your heart isn't moving blood around your body and which is ultimately fatal), so I started chest compressions, and ventilating her with my Ambu-bag.

While doing this I was trying to get some form of medical history: none of her relatives could speak English that well, but I managed to gather that she had just rolled out of bed, and besides tablet-controlled diabetes she was otherwise healthy.

I was just about to finish the first round of CPR when I heard the ambulance crew turn up – I shouted down the stairs that the call was indeed a 'Suspended', and when they entered the room they started to intubate and try to gain venous access. Venous access means that we can give potentially life-saving drugs, but in this case the woman's veins were so small that after two attempts we realised that it wouldn't be possible. Instead, we were able to give her the drugs via the ET tube, which is the breathing tube we use to protect the patient's airway.

We then saw a change in her cardiac rhythm: from PEA she entered VF so we 'shocked' her with my defibrillator. She then went from PEA to VF and back again every time we shocked her.

At one point during transport to the hospital we got a pulse back, but this soon degenerated into VF.

The hospital worked on her for an hour, and at one point she had both a pulse and a blood pressure, but unfortunately she later died.

The memory of the job that I have is of cleaning her hair from where it had gotten stuck to the Ambu-bag, just after she had died in the hospital, hoping that the son-in-law wouldn't then choose that moment to look in the back of the ambulance.

At least I felt justified in my role. All too often you get used to being called to jobs that are, frankly, crap. This was a 'proper' job, and although we didn't save her, we gave her the best chance we could. If we hadn't been there then she wouldn't have had even that chance.

This is a strange job – people who aren't sick annoy you, and yet the really sick people are 'good jobs'. We are only happy when someone is suffering.

This feeling of only wanting 'good jobs' is one I keep wrestling with. It's not right to want people to suffer serious injury just so that I can have an 'interesting' day at work.

☕ Happiness is a Warm Pizza

An excerpt from a conversation I just had with Control:

Control: 'Hello, EC50, we have a job for you'.
Me: 'Ah, you rotten buggers! I've just got myself a pizza'.
Control: 'Hold on a sec … OK, stand down (Other Callsign) is closer'.
Me: 'I love you like I have loved none other'.
Control: '… giggle, enjoy your pizza'.

Control can be nice sometimes … (*and if you want to do that again, I won't be complaining*).

☕ How to Blog and Not Lose Your Job

Listen to Uncle Reynolds as he sits you on his knee and explains these simple facts to stop you losing your job over blogging. These points relate mainly to work-blogs, but with a bit of thought will translate pretty well to anything that you write on the Internet. Most of this is just common-sense stuff, but there are people out there who falsely think that bloggers should be elevated over non-blogging employees.

Disclaimer – I am not an expert in employee law, I just have my opinions. Seek professional or union advice if you feel your job is under threat. At the end of the day, my company is trying to get fewer customers, not more. So my ideas may be a little screwed up. Don't come crying to me if you lose your job following my advice. Also don't come crying to me when I'm sitting on station trying to have a cup of tea.

How to blog, and not lose your job – version 1.0

You are not anonymous. In today's world of easy investigation (via the Internet of course) it is normally a matter of an hour's work to find out who a blogger is. It's really easy if the person who is doing the investigation works for the same company you do. Sure, you might use a pseudonym and reduce your boss and fellow workers to nicknames, but it only takes one mention of some uncommon point to blow the whole thing open. For me, it was when I wrote about swallowing some HIV-positive blood; the news spread around 'in real life' and it didn't take a genius to work out who was writing my blog. In some places your company might be able to force your blog hosting company or ISP (Internet Service Provider) to reveal your details. *So write as if you are writing under your own name, or be honest and don't bother with a pseudonym.*

In a related note, you will probably be read by people who know you. It's probably inevitable, but folks who move in the same social circles as you will have similar interests. Your interest in blogging about your job in sheep shearing may well mean that when your colleague does a search for websites about sheep shearing for promotional interview reasons, your page may well turn up. If you are going to be publicising your blog, then there is a large chance that your target demographic will include some of your friends. Actually, if it doesn't then either your blog or your friendships are not very honest. *So blog as if everyone you know reads every word.*

You are not immune to the rule of law – really, you aren't. Blogging may be a great new thing, it may well have expanded quicker than any other medium in the history of humanity, but the laws of Libel, Slander and Defamation of Character (your country's laws may vary) still apply to you. Sure, the Internet fosters a sense of anonymity, and of free speech – but that only goes so far. A lot of bloggers who have been fired from their jobs have found out the hard way that you *can't* breach your company's rules/country's laws and expect the defence of 'But it was on the Internet' to hold much water. If I write something that defames someone, then they are fully within their rights to sue me, whether I'm published in a paper, a book or on the Internet. You have to follow civil and criminal laws online as well as offline. These will vary depending on where you live. For the Americans in the audience the whole 'Free Speech' bit in your constitution concerns your government making laws to curtail free speech, it says nothing about companies.

The truth will find you out – if you lie on your blog and there are any number of people reading then you will be found out. I'm not suggesting that there are a multitude of fact checkers out there, but it only needs one falsehood to completely blow any reputation you may have built up. If you lie about people then once again you are laying yourself open to a juicy bit of court action, which might bump up your pagehits, but not in a good way. If you aren't sure about a bit of information that you are writing about *mark such inconclusive evidence as being just that – inconclusive.*

If you think you will get in trouble with your blogging – ASK. I know that it may be easier to ask forgiveness than permission. But your company might be all out of forgiveness. If you think that your blogging might cause friction, or lead to you being disciplined, then ask your boss first. Go in prepared, with all the opinions and evidence that blogging is a good thing. Do a good enough job convincing them, and they might start paying you to blog. If they refuse flat out to let you blog, then consider whether this is a company you want to be working for, or if you want to blog strongly enough to risk losing your job. Do this, and don't be surprised when you get the sack.

Companies as well as people have secrets, and they will be mightily annoyed if those secrets are aired for everyone to look at. Companies have bigger secrets than individuals: they have to protect their profits, enjoy the support of their stockholders and maintain patent pending secrets. If you blab about 'Secret Project X', then the company will find some way to fire you. You might not think that revealing that chip X will be used in the new graphics card you are working on is proprietary information but it never hurts to check first. Just think before posting *'Who will this revealing secret hurt?'*: if you are not prepared to deal with the consequences, then don't post. Of course, if it is in the public interest to post about something, then you need to weigh up the possibility of being disciplined.

Companies, and people, have a reputation to protect: if you want to shout about how working in company X is like slavery (complete with whipping and a bread-and-water lunch programme), then that company might take a dislike to you doing so on the Internet. Actually, this is one of those things that is made worse because of the nature of the Internet. If you tell your wife that your job is awful, your company is unlikely to find out. Tell the same thing to a bunch of your friends down the pub and, if found out, the company may discipline you. Paint it in 6-foot high letters on the side of their building and you would expect to get the sack. Writing something on the Internet is much like painting it across the face of the moon. *If you are that unhappy, then find another job.* If you can't get another job, then at least be fairly subtle about your moaning. Your employers love you, and want what is best for you: if you are really that unhappy at work they will help you with some tough love by forcing you to choose other career options. You'll have to clear out your own desk though.

A lot of people won't like being written about – I mean, the Internet is full of freaks and weirdos right? Who'd want any details of their life on the 'inter-web super-info-highway' so just about anyone can read intimate details about them? If you are going to write about other people, then *anonymise them.* How you do this depends on the style of your blog; do you give them all nicknames, refer to them as initials or call them 'one of my workmates'? If you do give people nicknames, remember – they may well find out about it, and while calling your boss 'SmellyGit' may not be a sackable offence, it may well have a negative effect on your chances of a future promotion.

If work has a problem with your blog, find out exactly what the problem is, and work with them to correct it. Some workplaces won't let people blog at all, some have no policy for blogging, while others (perhaps most) have no idea what blogging is. Work with them to get a policy written, be helpful, be cooperative and be evangelical. Telling your company that 'it isn't fair' when they ask you to stop your blog will work about as well as it did on your mother when you wanted to get that tattoo. Let them know how blogging 'humanises' the company, talk about how 'branding is a conversation'; let them know that you are performing 'grassroots, viral marketing'. If that doesn't work, let them know that people are going to start asking questions about why the blog has stopped, and that they will draw their own conclusions. This isn't a threat, but a reality. Get them to let you continue the blog but allow them to clear any information that you post about.

Can you blog on company time? Most companies have a policy about Internet usage. Your work might well have a policy that covers blogging without actually mentioning the word 'blog': probably something about using the Internet on company time. I suggest that if you are going to be posting during working hours you take a good long look at those policies. Remember, they are paying for you to work, not to write your diary (no matter how many people read it). Obviously, this doesn't apply to people whose job description is to blog. *If blogging is encroaching on your work or personal time in a negative way, then stop blogging – it's just not worth it.*

Sometimes blogging is just an excuse to get you fired. Sure, you might roll into work drunk, do very little work, backchat to your boss and fall asleep during the afternoon – but the reason they sacked you is because they found out you have a blog! I'm no expert on how easy it is to sack people, but I suspect that 'gross misconduct', 'failure to follow Internet policy', 'bringing the company into disrepute' and 'revealing company secrets' are fairly easy things to get past an industrial appeal board. I would imagine that some of the people who have been fired or disciplined have comforted themselves with the thought that 'it's because I have a blog, that's the only reason'. So be a good worker, then they won't be so quick to sack you.

Just because you blog, it doesn't make you special. Sure, you might have 10 000 page-hits a day, you are 'Slashdotted'.[*] This occasionally results in overwhelming levels of traffic, capable of knocking your website over on a regular basis, and you have Dave Weiner's[**] home phone number – but that means nothing to your boss. Blogging doesn't bring with it a 'Get Out Of Jail Free' card, you have no 'Freedom of the Press', and just because thousands of people hang on your every word it doesn't mean that they will help you keep your job. Blogging grants you no immunity to normal disciplinary procedures. Sorry about that.

Does this emasculate your blog? Well, perhaps a little, but if you are posting inflammatory lies about people, revealing industrial secrets and whining about how much your job both 'sucks' and 'blows', then be fully prepared to be fired. If you are writing things that are really that negative, ask yourself if you are in the right job. Journalists working in countries under a dictator need to be careful about what they write – and while you might not get thrown in prison, or worse, just be aware that bad things happen to people who rock the boat. *It's not fair, but it's the way the world works*.

Finally, if you do lose your job, you have a whole audience of people finding out about it, any of which might help you get a job. I know at least two people (people I've met, not including people I've read about), who have gotten jobs based on their blogging. In most cases people are happier with their new jobs than their old, if only because their new company understands and supports their blogging.

[*] Slashdotted (verb): to have your website linked to by the incredibly popular technology news website www.Slashdot.org.

[**] Don't ask!

Fit

Yesterday was busy, but busy in a good way in that most of the calls that I got actually warranted an ambulance. Actually, if I had been dropped on my head repeatedly as a child leading to me believing in the supernatural, I would have thought that there was something strange going on. The majority of my jobs, and a lot of the jobs that I heard being given out over the radio, were for people having seizures.

The first call of the day was to a known epileptic who had been fitting while in the bath. Luckily, his father heard him thrashing against the side of the bath and pulled him out before he could drown. He was still quite drowsy, confused and a bit 'punchy' – normal for people who have just finished having a fit. The ambulance crew got there and as the patient was a known epileptic, and was feeling better, he was left at home with the instruction that should he have another fit, then he should go to hospital.

I then bounced from that job to another young male who was having recurrent epileptic fits: in over an hour he hadn't managed to recover from a fit. He had three fits and was still extremely 'floppy'. The crew asked for my help in controlling him in the back of the ambulance, so I left the car and helped keep his airway clear while we 'blued' him into the local hospital. He had one more fit in the back of the ambulance, which I never like dealing with, as there are a few too many hard surfaces in the back of an ambulance that you can injure yourself on.

The ambulance crew then returned me to my car, and I was pleasantly surprised to discover that it was still there, and that the wheels were still attached.

I then ended up going back to my first epileptic, as he had suffered another seizure. This time the ambulance crew took him to hospital for a check-up. There are a couple of things that can reduce the effectiveness of anti-epileptic medication, and while the patient's family believed that he had been drinking recently, it is always a good idea to rule out the other causes for an increase in seizure frequency.

Then there was a hoax call for a 'pedestrian versus car', which had me, the HEMS doctors, an ambulance and the police trying in vain to find a victim. Great …

Next was a middle-aged man, who was having his first heart attack. The call was given as a chest pain. When I walked in the room and saw how ashen he was, I immediately broke out the oxygen and medication. He gave a classic history and description of a heart attack; luckily, the ambulance was quick in turning up and the job went like clockwork, with the patient getting transported to hospital very quickly.

Then I went to a patient with cancer of the bowel who had abdominal pain; an easy job in one way, but rather shocking in another because the patient was the same age as me …

My final (late) job was to a 1-year-old child who had been … wait for it … fitting – the very common febrile fit (when a child has a temperature that rises quickly they can often have a seizure). While it is a medical emergency, it's something that because we deal with them a lot we find an 'easy job'. Essentially, you cool the child down, and give them oxygen.

In more general news, the sat-nav screen on one of our ambulances was stolen the other night. Someone broke into the ambulance to steal a bit of equipment that helps the community. It says it all for some of the people in this area really …

 45+

Yesterday was fairly busy, but the two remarkable jobs of the day were caused by what we in the trade call 'Tricky extrication'.

The first job was to a young male collapsed in a bookmaker's toilet. I've been to a couple of these, and for some reason bookmakers' toilets are favoured places for junkies to 'shoot up' in. I've been to more junkies in bookmakers than I have drunks in pub toilets. Do not ask me why.

The toilet itself was 3 feet by 5 feet, and in it was a heavily drunken Lithuanian, covered in vomit, urine and the drink of champions – 'White Lightning', about 3 litres' worth. He was, to all intents, unconscious – unable to talk, stand, walk or do anything except drool … and he drooled a lot.

Because of the size of the toilet (barely enough room for one person, let alone me as well), the slippery floor (vomit, urine and cheap, nasty cider) and the state of the patient (big, thickset, heavy and completely unable to help) I had to grab him by his belt buckles, and with the aid of the crew manhandle him out to the ambulance.

I followed the crew to the hospital, so that I could wash some of the 'stuff' I had all over my arms – the hospital knew the patient, because he had been there yesterday, for exactly the same thing …

The last job of the day was to a 45-stone male (285 kilograms for the metrically minded) with difficulty in breathing. He was up one flight of stairs, found it very difficult to walk, and was in a flat full of cardboard boxes. It took us an hour to get him out of the house, down the stairs and into the ambulance and at the hospital it took another half an hour to get him inside. Our trolley-bed (and these are the new trolley-beds – fairly strong things) was buckling under his weight, and there was a moment or two when I thought it would collapse under the weight.

It took so long to get him out of the house that I got an hour's worth of overtime – which, for my mercenary nature, was rather nice.

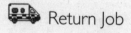 Return Job

I could hardly believe it, the first job of my shift was to the 45+ stone patient who was my last job on my last shift.

It only took 45 minutes to get him out of his flat this time, which just goes to prove that practice does indeed make perfect.

I've been back to him twice more. He's a nice enough person, but I still dread the call to his flat.

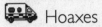 Hoaxes

One of my regular readers is someone from an Ambulance Control: they left the following in my comments section about why we on the road tend not to see too many hoax calls.

We do get a fair number of hoax calls in Control. Most of them can be spotted a mile off, however, and consist of someone under the age of 16 requesting police, fire and ambulance for some unfeasible event. They usually hang up when you read them back the address they are calling from or, if they are in a call box (which they usually are), tell them to 'look up at the security camera in the box so I can see your face' or 'the doors of the phone box will now lock automatically – the police are on their way to catch you for making NAUGHTY HOAX CALLS'. Obviously, you have to be 100% sure that it is a hoax before you do this, otherwise someone will die and then you will get the sack.

I also spend a fair deal of time when working on the dispatch desks calling back suspected hoaxes from call boxes until a member of the public answers and confirms there are no dying individuals lying around that we ought to be attending to.

One or two do slip through the net, though. There was an almighty ruckus when some really 'funny' people decided to tell us that someone had fallen down the stairs and then given birth to her sixth baby on the spot. A whole fleet of ambulances and midwives turned up to find a bunch of sniggering teenagers on the doorstep and no sign of any woman or baby. They didn't even have the sense to give a false address. One of the midwives rang up and shouted at me for half an hour.

So, thanks to the folks up in Control around the country for dealing with the obvious hoax calls.

Masking Histories

Sometimes patients can be awkward buggers: all their signs and symptoms point to one illness, and it is only a bit later, with a bit more investigation, that you find out what is actually wrong with them.

Today was a case in point: I got called to a 42-year-old male who had been suffering from chest pain for the past 2 hours. I turned up and started my examination of him. He had fallen down the stairs the day before, his chest was painful when I pushed on it and he had no symptoms leading me to believe that the problem was anything to do with his heart. I immediately thought that the pain was muscular in nature, rather than a more serious cardiac problem.

The only thing was that his pulse felt 'funny', a strange little 'thrumming' sensation that was a little like a double heartbeat. I thought that if I hooked him up to my cardiac monitor I'd have a better idea what was going on. However, the leads on the monitor weren't working so I would have to wait until the ambulance turned up.

It was a little embarrassing because the patient and his wife were both doctors (probably working in research). Both were happy with their treatment and the ambulance soon turned up. The patient was connected to their monitor and we found out that he was in SVT (supraventricular tachycardia) which is a rhythm problem with the heart, causing it to beat too quickly.

The actual 'chest pain' was probably related to the fall, being either a bruise or a muscle strain, while the patient's real problem was hidden from a cursory examination. It is only because we have the capability to electrically examine the heart that the patient was sped into hospital rather than taken in normally.

I'm wondering if the fall somehow caused the arrhythmia, it's probably not outside the realms of possibility.

Knowing what the patient's problem was also meant that the ambulance crew didn't look embarrassed after handing the patient over to the nurses at the hospital.

Tomorrow I have a special learning day – learning how to 'maintain personal safety', how to defuse aggressive situations and how to escape from grapples and the like …

I went to this patient about 9 months later. He'd had a sudden cardiac arrest and, despite our best efforts, he died.

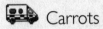 Carrots

As promised, the quality of this blog is about to nosedive, as I discuss some of the things I have personally witnessed up a patient's rectum.

I've not seen a FBUA (foreign body up arse) while in the ambulance service – I think most people are so embarrassed that they tend to make their own way to hospital rather than risk being laughed at by two hairy-armed ambulance people.

The one that sticks most in my mind was the first one I ever came across. I was working in A&E at the time, and I think I'd only been there a year or so, when I saw a load of doctors crouched around an abdominal X-ray.

'You can see it there', said one.

'Don't be daft, but you *can* see the bowel being pushed out of shape', another said dismissively.

'Of course you can't see it', said another, 'It's organic …'

Being a nosey nurse I asked what they were looking at, and was told that the patient had a carrot up their rectum. Looking closely at the X-ray I could see where the lower part of the bowel was *stretched* upward by a large amount. There was no sign of the alleged carrot, but then it wouldn't show up in a normal X-ray film anyway, it being as organic as the flesh that X-rays go through unimpeded.

The story I was told was that the patient was a 72-year-old male who had gotten his groceries and was taking a short-cut across the local park when he was 'caught short'. Desperate to open his bowels, he had dropped his trousers and crouched behind a tree to – cough – 'have a poo'. However, two 15-year-old boys ran up behind him, grabbed a carrot from the bag and inserted it rectally.

The patient didn't want the police involved because he 'didn't want to be any trouble'.

Us professionally trained staff were of course sympathetic to his plight, and obviously believed every word of his tale.

Who am I kidding … we didn't believe a word of it. The patient went to have the carrot surgically removed and all was well in the world.

Carrots are a popular thing for FBUA – it was a year or two later, when I had become much more cynical, that I came across another 'carrot insertion incident'. The patient was a young male who fully admitted having taken some 'Ecstasy', and had been fooling around with a carrot when it had become stuck.

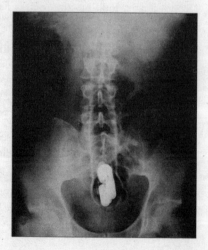

The patient himself wasn't too bothered because, ever mindful of disease, he had put a condom on the carrot.

So, I think the government is giving our youths the wrong message when it tries to dissuade drug use. Instead of the dangers of overdose, heart attacks and reduced sexual function, they should just show a picture of someone putting a condom-wrapped carrot up their arse while thinking it's a good idea.

It's not all carrots, as some people have already mentioned in the comments section, sometimes it can be things that are 'supposed' (sort of) to be used in such ways.

I was working in triage in A&E at the time, where my role was to do the initial patient assessment to see how urgently they needed to be seen. A young man and his girlfriend walked in, the male was in obvious distress and I soon found out why.

The pair had been indulging in 'sex games' and they had been using a vibrator. Unfortunately for the male, his girlfriend had gotten a bit vigorous in inserting it into her boyfriend's rectum, and it had been sucked into his body.

What people need to realise is that there can often be a 'suction effect', which means that things will just shoot up there and refuse to come out.

Well, being the kind of nurse I once was – I had to have a listen. So the stethoscope came out, and after being gently applied to his abdomen I could hear a loud buzzing noise. I wondered how long the batteries would last.

The patient, while worried about his health, was more concerned that his mum would find out that he was at the hospital, and would turn up demanding to know what had happened to her son. Not wanting to be the nurse who had to explain to an irate mother that her son had a vibrator stuck up his arse, I got him seen as quickly as possible.

We got an X-ray taken – you could see the circuitry really well, but the 'body' of the vibrator was a lot harder to see.

He was booked for surgery, and just before he was about to go the theatres his mum turned up.

He started off by trying to tell her that he had a generic abdominal pain, but she questioned why he needed to go to surgery for a belly ache. So he sat her down in a private room (provided by me, I may be cruel, but I'm not *that* cruel) and explained exactly what happened.

To be fair, his mum took it quite well, there was no shouting, ranting, arguing or even sniggering. Instead she was supportive, if a little bemused.

If it was me I think my mum would disown me …

The vibrator was removed under anaesthetic, and the patient made a full recovery.

I don't know what happened to the vibrator though …

I posted a couple of other stories about FBUA. It was all I wrote about for a week. Lots of people liked the stories. As I have mentioned earlier these are the sorts of stories you tell down the pub and people will end up buying you drinks.

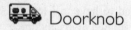 Doorknob

For the final post about FBUA (for I am on night shifts from tonight), I'd like to relate the tale of the doorknob.

A 45-year-old male came into A&E with a doorknob inserted where the sun doesn't shine.

His story was less than original. Apparently he enjoyed vacuuming his house while naked. While doing this he had backed up against his living room door, only to have the doorknob disappear up his rectum. Unfortunately, the doorknob was loose, and when he tried to remove himself, the doorknob gave way and thus became trapped up his bum. Thankfully, he got dressed *before* making his way to hospital.

Cue surgery, and removal of said object, when asked if it caused much damage, the surgeon replied '*It rect'um*'.

… Bad joke, I know, but that's surgeons for you – she probably spent the entire surgery thinking that one up.

I vaguely remember two other stories: one of a woman who came to our hospital with a bed-knob inserted anally. The other is of a person who shaves doll heads, swallows them and then gains sexual gratification from passing them in his stool. This may not be true (I read it on the Internet), but it wouldn't surprise me if it were.

Short-Term Memory Loss

I've just come back from a 'Matern-a-taxi', and it always amuses me when I turn up *5 minutes* after they have called for an ambulance. Then, when I knock on the door, they look out the window, take in the uniform, the ambulance parked outside, and the big bag of medical equipment and ask …

'Who is it?'

Liars

I'm kind of prosaic about our regular callers, they have chronic conditions (normally brought on by drinking), but they are normally easy to deal with and, if you keep friendly with them, they are seldom trouble.

… Until they start being incontinent on the back of your ambulance. But that is a subject for another day.

What I do dislike are the regulars who feel the need to lie to our call-takers.

Take regular patient number one: she calls for an ambulance, claiming that she has had a fit. When I turn up (I get mobilised for patients having fits a lot), she tells us that she hasn't had a fit, but her legs hurt, so can we take her to the hospital. Repeat this once or twice a day and you wonder why some of us won't be too upset when we eventually find her dead in the gutter.

Tonight I went to regular patient number two: he is an alcoholic, who tonight told our Control that he had been assaulted 20 minutes earlier and had had a seizure as a result of this assault. I get sent the job, and speed 3 miles to get to the patient, only to find him drunk; he hadn't been assaulted and there was no evidence that he had been fitting.

It isn't the actual going to the patient that bothers me, as I mentioned earlier, it's an easy job. What does annoy me is that I rush to these calls, putting myself and other road users at risk, only to find the patient not undergoing a life-threatening event. I get very cynical about these jobs.

I've tried telling them that if they call for an ambulance and say they have a painful leg, then they will still get an ambulance, but that they won't be putting other people's lives at risk by having me drive on blue lights and sirens (at risk of hitting a pedestrian), or by taking an ambulance away from someone who urgently needs an ambulance at that time.

But still they insist on calling with phantom illnesses for an ambulance.

The woman that I mention as regular caller number one, has been found a place to live in a nunnery. We haven't heard from her since.

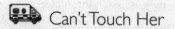 Can't Touch Her

My shift ends at 6:30 in the morning, so I was very happy to be left alone from 11 p.m.

Except that at *6:20* I get a job (I ask them if they are joking – they aren't). The job is a chest pain on a bus, in a bus garage.

It is also so far out my normal area that I have to study the map for some time before I can work out how to get there.

I turn up to find out that the 'patient' is an alcoholic who is asleep in one of the buses. She denies any chest pain, injury or illness and after some persuasion she leaves the bus under her own power and leaves the scene.

If I were being cynical, I would be thinking that the bus company, unable to actually touch her for fear of assault, has called for an ambulance purely so that someone else is responsible for getting her off the bus.

Previous experience would suggest that this is indeed the case.

Why would they say she had chest pain – perhaps they know that this gets the quickest response from us …

Oh well … it's all overtime.

 HAI

One of the bugbears that each political party is addressing for the upcoming election is the concept of HAIs (hospital-acquired infections). So far, the politicians have been mainly concentrating on MRSA (methicillin-resistant *Staphylococcus aureus*), but this is not the only thing that you can catch in hospital.

I've just come from a job where a 95-year-old female, who had spent a week in hospital for a blood clot on the leg, was suffering from some difficulty in breathing.

The patient had been discharged from the local hospital yesterday, and during the night had developed laboured breathing, a cough and a feeling of tightness in the chest.

Upon examination it seemed that the pain was not related to any cardiac cause. The tightness was worse when she breathed in, she had a slight temperature and, coupled with the cough and no history of heart problems, it seemed like a simple chest infection.

The patient and her daughter were happy with this provisional diagnosis, but were glad that she would be going to hospital for some more tests.

… But then the daughter asked me where her mother could have caught her chest infection … and I really didn't want to say 'from the hospital'.

I imagine that the ward from which the patient had been discharged had one or more people with a chest infection. Having worked in a hospital I know that a lot of patients, and their visitors, don't cover their mouths when they cough, and it seems completely reasonable that this is where the patient caught this infection.

It is probably unrelated to nurse or doctor hygiene (as these sorts of infection are often airborne) but instead caused by something as simple as someone not covering their mouth when coughing. It might not have been another patient – hospital wards see a lot of visitors, including small children who are constantly exposed to, and incubating, infections.

It seems to me that a lot of hospital infections could be cut if patient visitors didn't treat the ward like some form of hotel, tracking their infections in and out of the community, and generally acting as if the rules of hygiene don't apply to them. I'm a big fan of restricted visiting for the majority of cases – and is there really any reason for children to be dragged around a hospital at all hours of the day?

It used to drive me barmy when I was running a ward.

However, medical staff do indeed need to improve their hand washing.

Flat

So there I was, pulling up to a job (male fitting in street), the ambulance was already there (having been dispatched from the same station as me, only 2 minutes earlier).

Then I heard a loud bang, and thought the bottom had dropped off the car – the crew on scene and the police who were there all looked in my direction.

My front tyre had burst as I had ridden up the kerb a little too forcefully.

There I was, stuck by the side of the road waiting for the tyre fitter to come and change my tyre. I may well have a spare tyre in the back of the car, but if I fit it, and it later falls off, then I'm to blame.

I returned to station to find a new wallpaper on the station computer …

'*Brand new tyre required for Vauxhall Astra FRU, All enquiries to J2 station c/o Tom Reynolds*'.

I love my workmates …

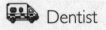 Dentist

I often moan about GPs that leave their patients who are seriously ill alone in their waiting rooms, or outside in the street having a cigarette. But until today I'd never been to a dentist (which might explain the state of my teeth – *ho-ho*).

The patient was a 42-year-old female who was 'shaking' on the dentist's chair. I arrived and the patient was still in the chair, and was being given oxygen and reassurance by the dentist.

The patient had a long history of these episodes, and the dentist gave me a complete handover, including the social history of the patient, and while I was assessing the patient was still spending time reassuring her. The patient was not suffering from anything serious, but she agreed to go to the hospital for a quick check-up.

I must admit I was really impressed by this dentist for actually caring for their patient. It is only as I sit writing this that I realise that I'm impressed at a health-care professional that is *actually doing their job*.

Isn't that sad …

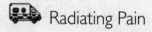 Radiating Pain

Sometimes you are really glad the patient isn't facing you.

I went to an elderly male with 'chest pain'; the ambulance crew turned up at pretty much the same time, so I found myself standing behind the patient as they got a history from him.

'Where is the pain?' the ambulance attendant asked.

'Here', he replied pointing to the top of his chest.

'What does the pain feel like?'

'Kind of a burning pain'.

'Does the pain go anywhere else?'

'Well, it didn't go with me to my friend's house …'

… Cue me trying (thankfully successfully) to stop from laughing out loud. Instead, I managed to restrain myself to just some silent sniggering.

For those that aren't aware, chest pain which is related to the heart often radiates to the jaw or arm.

Bless him, I love this job.

I've just spoken to the crew, and the pain was related to his heart.

 Values

I was called to a 39-year-old male, possibly dead. As I entered the house I saw his relatives crying, and sitting on a kitchen chair was my patient. He looked dead and wasn't breathing.

I felt for a pulse, didn't feel one, so I hooked up the heart monitor and there was no electrical activity at all.

I turned around to his relatives and told them that there was nothing that I could do for him, and that an ambulance crew would turn up shortly to help them out.

It took 10 minutes for the crew to turn up, and I didn't recognise them at all – they must have come from outside our area.

Suddenly, one of the crew said they had felt a pulse!

The patient was also breathing. Oxygen was given and he was rushed out to the ambulance. All that was running through my head was how I had 'starved' him of oxygen, and how much trouble I was going to be in.

One of the crew told me to fake my paperwork, and say that I'd given the patient oxygen. But I knew I was going to get into trouble.

I felt sick for the patient, and sick for myself. This is the sort of mistake that can cost you your job …

… Then the postman rang my doorbell, and I woke up from the nightmare I was having.

It's funny how this job can play on your mind – the things that I've seen and dealt with on this job and as an A&E nurse. Yet, it seems that the fear of making a mistake with a patient is still the thing that scares me most.

I've dealt with murders, mutilations and miscarriages. I've seen death in the faces of 3-month-old children, 14-year-old girls and 22-year-old men. I've dealt with limbs hanging off, distraught relatives and people vomiting blood until they die.

But the only thing that haunts my dreams is the fear of doing something wrong.

Shouldn't the patient have more of a place in my mind?

 Rough

Today is one of those days where I really need to be careful, otherwise the disjunction between what the public expects of us and what we actually do will get me in trouble.

At the moment my body is feeling ready to give up, a troublesome changeover from night to day work doesn't help; neither does the sore throat or the feeling that my soul is still on holiday in Seattle and waiting for a flight back to my body in London.

This means that the chances of me having a 'sense of humour' failure are greater than normal.

I noticed it yesterday with my last job – I was called to a '60-year-old male, collapsed in park'. Now there are of course many reasons why someone collapses in the park, and while I keep an open mind the chances are very high that it is alcohol related.

So I got there, and there was a concerned member of the public fussing over a drunk alcoholic. All power to him, he had spotted someone in distress and was trying to help out as best he could, and I'd much rather have people like that compared with the calls we get of 'Man lying in street, poss. dead. Caller cannot stay on scene', which *always* seems to be a drunk.

The care I gave was the same as the care I would normally give, but I wasn't as 'warm' as I normally am. I was polite, but there was something deep down in me that really couldn't be bothered with dealing with yet another alcoholic.

The ambulance turned up about a minute later, and took care of the patient – but I was aware that the bystander was probably not happy with my apparent lack of empathy.

This is that disjunction that I mentioned: the public expects us to be constantly caring people, dealing with what they see as a serious emergency, while to us it is a regular alcoholic, with very little newly wrong with them. While we often hide our apathy behind our professionalism, it can sometimes slip.

It's that sort of job that will earn you a complaint from someone for being 'not caring enough'.

The fact that I feel rough (through no fault of my own) might just mean that the mask of caring might slip – and while I have no problem with people who are actually ill, if I get the usual rubbish, I'll have to be very, very careful.

I never did get a complaint about this job and it shouldn't surprise people that us ambulance staff are human too, and that we have our 'off' days as well.

Whether the Weather

One of my commenters asked if it was true that the full moon affected people so much that the local hospital had to hire extra night staff every month. There have been scientific studies to disprove this, and I have never worked in a hospital that hired extra staff on the basis of the phases of the moon.

But it did get me thinking about the effects that the weather has upon people, because in my experience this *does* have an appreciable effect.

When I was teaching children, we would dread days when it was windy, because we knew that the children would be more active and more prone to be disobedient. Another of my commenters said exactly the same thing, so I know it wasn't a local phenomenon.

It works for adults too. I'm much busier on windy days, and while this is just my impression, I always seem to think that there are also many more assaults.

If the weather is grey and overcast, we tend to go to more old folk who are sitting indoors, or more commonly, falling over indoors. Sometimes you get the impression that they just want someone to talk to – or to not be alone. There also seem to be more suicide attempts as well, and it is fairly well known that suicide rates go up in springtime. So, on those rainy spring days you end up seeing a lot of paracetamol overdoses.

Spring and autumn rains (and in England, summer rains) bring with them car-versus-car collisions, as an infrequent rain lifts off the layer of rubber and pollution left on the road by passing cars and the roads become a skid pan. Fallen leaves on the road don't help, and neither do the effects of the rapidly changing hours of daylight on a driver's body clock.

Ice on the streets means that we will be going to plenty of 'Nan Down!' calls – little old ladies falling over. When working in the hospitals I remember one icy day where I personally dealt with **23** elderly people with broken wrists caused by falling on the ice.

When the weather is sunny there can also be chaos on the streets – this Sunday had really nice, sunny weather, the kind of weather you only seem to remember from your childhood. East London has a lot of narrow residential streets, with cars parked nose to tail on both sides of the road. If these streets are 'quiet' then children tend to forget that cars do occasionally travel down them (thankfully not often at any speed).

So, this Sunday there were more than the usual number of children being hit by cars. I went to one where a 6-year-old had run out between two parked cars and been struck. He had a minor head wound, and complained of neck pain, so I put a hard collar on him and when the ambulance crew turned up we did a full restraint. He was an excellent patient – normally I can't stand kids, but he was exceptionally brave, and when I explained about the collar, he was happy to have it on because he had seen them in use on the television.

There was also a (well behaved) crowd of about 30 people standing around, and when the police turned up they got the people out the way by saying 'I know it's a cliché but, please move along there is nothing to see …'

It's a good job I don't get performance anxiety.

The hot weather also brings out the people who start drinking at lunchtime and continue throughout the day; tie this in with a lot of sporting fixtures and we find ourselves going to a lot of fights in a lot of pubs.

 Recognised

A strange thing happened tonight.

For the first time ever, I was 'recognised'.

The job itself was simple enough, genuine illness that had become worse. I walked into the house had a quick assessment of the situation, and then said my usual bit which goes something like …

'OK, I'm the fast car, so I turn up to make sure everyone is still breathing. There will be an ambulance along in a bit to actually take you to hospital'.

I *wasn't* expecting one of the relatives to then say:

'You also blog about it as well – I recognise your face'.

Sudden panic, followed by an admission that I was indeed that particular ambulance person.

It's strange, I suppose I've always thought that this might happen one day, although given the amount of alcoholics I see, and the way that they don't tend to read blogs, I thought that it might take longer than it has.

It's not as if I altered my treatment in any way, and if anything it made the treatment easier, as he knew that I wasn't some fly-by-night cowboy.

I hope …

The person who recognised me left a comment on the blog saying that they were happy with the treatment they received. Apparently I have been recognised at least once more, but that the person involved didn't want to admit it to me. Apart from these two times I remain blissfully anonymous.

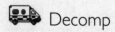 Decomp

For the first time in ages I got sent to a decomposing body. The social housing people had been around the elderly gentleman's flat a week earlier, noticed a bit of a smell, but ignored it. When they came back a week later and the smell was still there they decided to talk to the caretakers. The caretakers beat down the door – looked at what was in the bedroom and called the police.

The police then passed the job on to us, so that we could confirm death.

The first thing that you notice when dealing with a 'decomp' is the smell, it's quite unlike anything else – it settles in the back of the throat and stays there for some time. I was sucking mints and drinking tea for some time after leaving the flat to try and get the *taste* out of my mouth.

The other thing is the flies. You find yourself in a room with flies that have grown and fed on the tissues of a dead person. Sometimes they land on you. For hours afterwards you can feel them crawling on your skin (I can still feel them now, about 8 hours later). It doesn't make me feel dirty, but it does make me scratch.

The sight of the corpse isn't too bad after all that. The eyes are gone, and the skin is either dark brown or black. The thing that makes you realise that the thing in front of you was once alive is the hair. The hair is the same as when the person died, in this case it was white, clean and neatly brushed. The entry points to the body (the eyes, the nose and mouth) are crawling with flies and maggots, and this is the only movement you'll see.

The patient looked to have died in his sleep. He was lying in his bed and it looked as if he had simply passed away without waking. Not a bad way to go.

I can see this being my end, as I plan to outlive all my relatives, I don't talk to my neighbours at the moment (because, in part, they don't speak English) and at the rate I'm going I doubt I'll be married.

I hope I make a *really* stinky corpse. Perhaps making a young trainee EMT vomit in disgust, so that everyone at their station can have a good laugh at their expense.

Yes, since you ask, us ambulance people tend to have a strange sense of humour.

Matern-a-water-taxis

The other interesting job yesterday (for, with one exception, today was a day full of maternities and elderly chest pains) was a maternity with a difference. The patient was supposed to have a home delivery, but the delivery was taking too long, the mother was getting tired and the baby had meconium-stained amniotic fluid. Meconium is babies' first poo. It's a sign of a baby being in some distress.

The midwives decided that it would be better if the baby was delivered in hospital, so called for an ambulance to transport the mother.

What was different was that the patient lived on a houseboat.

… Cue myself, carrying a load of heavy, expensive equipment down narrow docks, narrower walkways and unbelievably narrow boat walkway, then out again carrying even more of the midwife's equipment.

Little Things

First off, there is an emergency GP doing the rounds who seems to have some strange ideas. Examples of his work are the elderly woman who is dizzy and has jaundice, a man with all-over muscle pain for 2 weeks and an elderly man with 'fluid on the lungs'. All these were prescribed antibiotics and were told, 'It's probably an infection, but I don't know where'. I'm not sure if it's the same GP, but if it is, then they really are clueless.

This is probably why the Primary Care Trusts like the ambulance service – because we don't faff around, but take everyone who is ill to hospital, and leave the well ones at home.

I went to a little old lady who had fainted. Absolute darling (if only because she laughed at my 'you should take more water with your gin if it makes you dizzy' joke), but who didn't want to go to hospital because she cares for her disabled husband. They lived in a warden-controlled flat, but the wardens in those places are not supposed to do any 'caring' work. Our patient wouldn't go to hospital and leave her husband, so, falling back on my nursing experience, I got Control to call the social services that look after that family. After promising that everything would be fine, she agreed to go to hospital.

Why did I go through Control to contact the social workers, rather than phone them myself? Well ... (*as mentioned previously*) Control record all the phone calls they make, so if someone promises to do something, then we have the proof ...

... *Not that I have a lot of experience dealing with social workers at all* ...

I got a job as a '15-year-old Suspended at school' (suspended is a polite way of saying 'dead'), I don't think my foot lifted off the accelerator pedal at all to the school, and I suspect that a lot of rubber was left on the pavement as I power-slid around the corners (who says computer racing games are no use?). I hit the school at about the same time as the ambulance crew (who had also driven like maniacs), and we ran up three flights of stairs, across the school, and down three flights of stairs. I saw the girl lying on her side, rolled her over, and had a huge sigh of relief as she recoiled in horror from my ugly face staring down at her.

The patient had very little wrong with her, much to our relief.

We were all understandably happy, but then the adrenaline crash hit us pretty hard, and coupled with the physical exertion of running, I felt like crap for half an hour, until a nice cup of tea worked its magic.

However ...

Tomorrow, I shall be on the hunt: I shall be hunting for a specific lollipop man (or whatever they are called these days). When I find him, I shall be shoving his stick where the sun doesn't shine.

The reason?

Picture the scene – I'm racing down the road on lights and sirens, and since I think that I'm going to a dead 15-year-old, I'm driving, as previously mentioned, at a stupidly fast speed.

… So what does this bloody idiot do to a kid waiting on the other side of the road? He tries to get the kid to run across the road before I get there!

This sort of thing makes me want to go stabby …

Lots of things make me want to go stabby, but this guy took the prize for sheer stupidity. Despite looking for him for the rest of the week I never did find him.

A Happy Job (For a Change)

Barely 2 days since moaning about Matern-a-taxis, than I get sent to another one.

'We have a job for you', said Control.

'Of course you do, I was just about to have a cup of tea', I replied, 'so … what is it'.

I looked at the display terminal in the car.

'It's a bloody maternity'. I was outraged. 'One-minute contractions – I bet they'll be 10 minutes apart when I get there'.

'I reckon they will as well', replied Control.

So I dutifully shot down there, to a place fairly well known to me – it's a large housing unit for teenagers; they all have social workers and are looked after pretty well. To be honest I think it's a pretty good place, I've never had any trouble there and the residents get a fair bit of support.

I entered the accommodation, to find a young woman having a contraction while standing in a puddle of fluid.

No problem, I thought, the waters have just broken.

'I really want to go a poo', she said.

'Oh bugger', thought me.

It's one of the guides as to how close you are to delivering the baby – if you want to go poo, then birth probably isn't too far away.

Then she had another strong contraction, then another – they were 1 minute apart …

So I turned on my breezy, 'relax, everything is fine, nothing to worry about' personality and quickly phoned Control to see where the ambulance was. I was told it was on its way and they turned up pretty quickly, but by then birth was too close, so we decided to 'stay and play'.

A midwife was called for, and she told Control she would make her way there in her own car. I do have a slight problem with this. If an ambulance crew needs a midwife, it's generally as an emergency, otherwise we transport the patient to hospital. If it's an emergency then shouldn't we pick up the midwife and get her to the job on blue lights and sirens?

The ambulance paramedic and I let the ambulance EMT do most of the mucky work. Not because we are (particularly) cruel, but because it was his first ambulance delivery … and it's a good experience.

A lovely baby girl was born at 10:29, and we let the father cut the umbilical cord.

Then, after all the screaming, poo, blood, fluid and pain, the midwife turned up.

Luckily for us the birth was uncomplicated. It took maybe a shade longer than I like, and apparently the birth fluid was stained green (to my eyes it looked normal, but then I do have strong prescription glasses). The fluid being green means that the baby may have pooed while being born, and that could be a sign of distress.

I also managed to use all my bad jokes during the delivery, which is a sign of how long the delivery took, because I have a lot of bad jokes.

It's always good to be involved in the birth of a baby: everyone is happy, you hopefully end up with a pretty little baby, and dad normally bounds around taking photos of everything. It always feels like a 'job well done'.

We don't get much training with birthing, and when we do deliver it's normally in an awkward place, with poor lighting and loads of people panicking. It would be nice if our training encompassed a little time in a maternity unit, rather than sitting in a classroom for a morning.

However, in an uncomplicated birth, it really is a case of just catching them as they pop out.

Anyway, it gave me a big grin on my face for the next few hours.

Physician Response Unit

The PRU is a doctor and paramedic team who run from the Royal London Hospital. Their role is see patients who might not need a trip to hospital, and to treat them at home – thus saving the patient having to wait around in A&E for a couple of hours, and freeing up emergency services for more serious cases. They also provide support for more serious incidents where a doctor on scene is a really good idea.

I've had a couple of jobs with them; normally it's something simple like a patient with a chest infection or other minor illness. A lot of patients in our area don't have a GP to see them, and so A&E and the ambulance service is their first, and only, port of call.

The PRU is manned by a doctor and a paramedic; they drive around in a blue Subaru that was donated by a firm of solicitors.

The last time I saw their statistics, they managed to treat a patient at home without needing an ambulance, or a hospital visit, 30–40% of the time.

(They also wear the orange HEMS jumpsuits for some strange reason ...)

I mention them because I had a job with them the other day. I was called to a little old lady who had collapsed in the street. I got there first, and started my assessment – she was frail-looking, but fully aware of what was happening to her. Her pulse was on the low side of normal, and her blood pressure felt a little low (just off the pulse), then, just as I'm about to check her blood pressure using our normal tools, the PRU rolled up behind me and two orange-clad people jumped out.

I gave a quick handover to the doctor, and he continued assessing the patient while I measured her blood sugar. Her blood sugar was normal, but her blood pressure was pretty low; a quick look at her heart rhythm didn't show anything unusual, and neither did a further physical examination.

Meanwhile we were waiting for an ambulance.

I was asked if I wanted to cannulate the patient (put a needle in a vein so that drugs or fluids could be given), but as it's been 3 years since I last cannulated someone, and she was a nice little old lady (instead of some stinky obnoxious drunk), I declined – I'm not *that* cruel to inflict my rusty skills on someone who is actually nice for a change ...

There was still no ambulance to send, so it was decided to take the patient to the hospital in the back of the Subaru as the patient wasn't getting the investigations she needed lying around the local market. All I can say, is that she looked a lot healthier sitting in the back of the car, than lying on a market bench.

The PRU (when it is running, manning the vehicle is apparently a bit of a nightmare) is a quality addition to the local NHS, and someone has definitely taught the doctors how to be nice to ambulance crews. It's just a shame that the Royal London doesn't get any extra money to run this service, which covers the gaps in local GP provisioning.

Just one more bit of the NHS being run on goodwill and charity ...

Nowt

No jobs yet. I have a suspicion that although I have told Control that I am working, they may have forgotten to put me on the main computer.

So my options are as follows …

(1) Sit on station, have something to eat, have a sleep and if they continue to ignore me, have a restful night.
(2) Let guilt get the better of me, give Control a ring and then spend the rest of my night actually working …

Guess I'm going to be phoning Control then …

This happened a couple of times, and each time I reminded them that I was working. It only took 4 months for them to start remembering me.

Tesco

I've just gotten some milk for the station, and chocolate (and some other, healthier foodstuffs) to see me through the night.

I've got to say, I love the way people doing their shopping stare as I walk past them in my uniform, clutching a shopping basket.

Not that I enjoy being the centre of attention, but the looks I get make me think that people are *disappointed* that us medical emergency types actually eat.

Try working a 12-hour shift without eating and I think you'd find yourself a bit less able to deal with the stresses of the job.

A happy belly equals a happy EMT.

Seriously. Keep us fed and watered and we'll be quite happy to tackle anything you can throw at us. Starving ambulance crews get a bit … 'testy'.

Scum

So a crew (not me, I'm relaxing on station) get called to a woman who is 38 weeks pregnant and has been mugged.

Her mobile phone was demanded from her, and after she gave it over, the attacker then punched her so hard in the stomach that her waters broke. He only stopped from kicking her in the stomach because someone came out of a nearby house.

… I try not to swear on this blog …

The crew turned up, and took the patient to the local hospital to the maternity department.

They pre-warned the unit to meet them, as they keep their doors locked at night.

So why, when they turned up, were the doors still locked? The excuse from the '*idiot*' midwife?

'I forgot to tell anyone'.

Followed by:

'We haven't got any beds'.

It's not bad enough that some scumbag deliberately attacked a pregnant woman, but then the people who are supposed to help her don't seem to give a damn.

The crew involved have put in a report about it, as this isn't the first time this has happened. Sometimes it seems that we are the only people doing our job properly.

Quite rightly the crew are spitting mad about the whole thing and are determined to do something about it.

I later found out from the crew that the patient later gave birth to a healthy child. Thankfully, a happy ending.

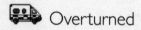 Overturned

'Can you pop along to Westferry Road', asks Control, 'the fire brigade have reported an overturned car'.

'Of course', I replied, thinking there would be something interesting to blog about.

I raced down there, and indeed there was a car on its side, but the driver had run off.

Bugger.

On more than one occasion I've gone to a car crash where I would have immobilised the patient and 'blued' them into hospital, yet the patient has run off (normally because the car turns out to be stolen, not insured, or the driver is drunk). Damn them for spoiling my fun.

A New Definition

My last patient gives me a new definition of unconscious …

'refusing to move or talk after having argument with girlfriend'.

To be fair, I think there is some form of underlying psychiatric problem.

But at this time of the night, you aren't going to get a mental health assessment.

🚑 An Hour to Go

I've just spent the last 50 minutes with a little old lady (93), who has been vomiting since 3 a.m. An emergency GP was called, but decided not to come, instead telling the warden of the patient's flat to dial 999 for an ambulance.

The patient was a little darling, she wasn't confused, she got around on her own and generally looked after herself, and was a real pleasure to talk to. Then I looked down her nursing notes and saw that she had just finished palliative therapy for cancer.

At 5 a.m. in the morning that'll choke me up every time.

So we sat and chatted about all manner of nonsense until an ambulance was free to take her to hospital.

Why did I have to wait so long for an ambulance? Well there was another sick person at that building, and an ambulance was required about 10 doors down the road.

Coincidence?

Once more (midwives, NHS Direct and now an emergency GP) it seems that the ambulance service are the only people who actually try to do our job these days. We, and the A&E, seem to be the 'safety net' that all the other services rely on to get out of doing any actual work.

It's a quarter to six in the morning; perhaps I should stop moaning and instead start thinking about my lovely warm, comfortable bed.

Palliative care means that we are treating the symptoms, rather than the incurable disease itself. Often this means that the treatment is designed to ease the patient's pain until they die.

Get Them When They Are Young

A couple of nights ago I got sent on a job to a 16-year-old male. He was complaining of chest pain. That makes it a high-priority call which warrants a Fast Response Unit, and therefore my attendance.

The location was in the street, so I made my way there, and met a thin looking boy. Throughout the night I had been waiting a long time for ambulances, so I was aware that I would have to make small talk.

A quick examination and history from the patient revealed a cough, and that this was the cause of his chest pain. I then started chatting to him and found out his real problem.

He had left his familial home sometime last year, and was living with a friend of the family. Then, two nights ago, he had been thrown out of that house. Too scared to go back to his mother and father, he was sleeping rough.

Skin and bone, with rotten teeth and poor skin, he had obviously been neglecting himself even before he was made homeless. I asked him about his diet, and he told me that it was junk food and a vitamin tablet. I suspect that he was living on cola and cigarettes, if not something stronger.

All while I was talking to him, he was polite, pleasant and respectful – something I don't often get from people his age.

He told me how he had fallen in with the wrong sort of people, and I realised that his chest pain was a call for help.

I decided that we needn't wait for the ambulance, and so loaded him into the car (Shhh … don't tell anyone, I'm not really supposed to do it), cancelled the ambulance and took him to the local hospital.

There are two types of nurses in the local hospital: those I trust to do the right thing, and those who seem to be marking the days until they can get out of there.

So I spoke to one of the nurses I trust; I told her all that I've just written and we both agreed that there was a serious need for some social services input. Thankfully, the department didn't seem too busy, so I was happy that he wouldn't get forgotten. She is also the sort of nurse who will quite happily annoy the social services until they do something.

On the way out, the young man shook my hand and thanked me.

I don't often get thanked, especially by teenagers.

Sure, he didn't need an ambulance for his physical problems. His chest pain was nothing, and while he had a poor diet, it wasn't a medical emergency, but what he did need was access to people who would care for him, and would get him on the first steps of something that I hope will lead him away from trouble.

I go to a hell of a lot of alcoholics and drug addicts, they tend to start when they are young; cruising the streets I see the men and women in their 30s who are spending the day drinking cheap cider, sitting on street corners and collecting their dole. It upsets me because they are ruining their lives.

I'm kind of hoping that we have managed to 'catch' this kid before he becomes one of them, and then becomes yet another of our 'regulars'.

Here's hoping.

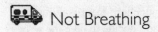 Not Breathing

The call was to someone who was not breathing.

I threw myself into the car – a quick look at the address, and I knew where I was going. I knew the best route, I knew how to avoid the worst of the traffic and I knew I could make good time.

If she wasn't breathing, then my speed could save her life.

Blue lights were turned on, car was put into 'sport' mode (for better acceleration), trip counter zeroed and seatbelt fastened; I was ready to go.

I pulled out of the station; a quick look left and right, then left again – no traffic. A couple of kids were standing outside the chicken shop on the corner – none of them were standing in the road (for once) so I made the sharp turn onto the road.

The first junction. Traffic here is forced into a single line, and drivers often don't see the blue lights as they concentrate on not hitting the parked cars. Thankfully, there was no-one else on the road, so I turn right and accelerate away.

The first hazard is the humpback bridge – visibility is poor, and while there is a crossing on top, kids sometimes cross just under the brow of the hill. The car hugs the road, which means that I can't see over the bridge until I'm already on top of it.

I ease off the accelerator, all clear – I gun the engine.

… 20, 30, 40 m.p.h. I can see the next hazard, some shops leading up to the traffic lights at the junction. I slow down, right foot covering the brake pedal. A quick check, no-one is looking to cross the road, the car heading towards me has pulled over, and I have a free run to the junction …

… and the red lights.

The siren goes on; it's loud, but the closed windows take away some of the sound. Light braking as I approach the junction; there is a queue of cars waiting for the lights (there always is) so I decide to take the wrong side of the road. I'm braking some more; it's a wide junction, so I can see what the other cars are doing. They are all waiting at the lights – the way is clear.

I swing the wheel round into a tight left turn, my folder and my bag shift in the passenger seat. The equipment in the back slides slightly, but is held in place by safety straps.

A good clear road, long and wide, just how I like them. I keep the siren going. It's sunny, and people might not see the lights. I pass the police station and a copper waves as he gets into his car. I wave back.

My eyes defocus, I don't know what I'm looking at, I try to take in the whole of the road and the pavement at once. Two kids on the right side of the road, but they are walking along, unlikely to interfere with me, one looks around at the sound of the siren.

A car ahead pulls out in front of me – can he not see me? He pulls over and lets me past as soon as he clears his turning. No matter, I had to bleed off some speed because I didn't know if he would pull out completely in front of me.

A slight hill. Visibility is less of a problem here, but I still can't go as fast as I'd like. I clear the hill – nothing – the road is clear and I power down towards the next junction.

More shops, more cars; the lights are with me, but I know this junction well – cars will often 'jump' the lights, so again, I'm forced to slow down.

I change the sound of the siren, it becomes more insistent, shriller. My eyes are still unfocused. I note the hazards: the woman with the pram looking to cross the road, the bus in front of me looking to pull away from the bus stop, the car waiting to turn right at the junction, the bike rider (is he weaving around a bit?).

Once more, my foot covers the brake, nothing changes, the woman waits on the kerb (good girl), the bus sits there (thanks mate), the car moves over slightly, clearing my way (good boy), the bike rider straightens up (excellent).

I'm through the junction, but the traffic gets heavier, I need people to pull over and let me pass. I have a choice: I can go down the bus lane – it's clear – but people can get confused and can pull in front of me. My other option, and the one I choose in a heartbeat, is the middle of the road, forcing those on my side to pull into the bus lane, and those who can see me oncoming to pull over a little to let me pass.

I hear Obi-Wan Kenobi tell me to 'Use the Force'.

I go wide, trying to make myself as big and noticeable as possible. Lights and sirens, yellow and green livery – I should be easy to see. Some people don't pull over, I *make* them pull over. Oncoming traffic gets out of my way, they can see me from all the way down the road. One man, however, thinks it clever to flash his headlights at me and try to play 'chicken'. Obviously I don't realise I'm driving down *his* side of the road.

I swear. I swear at him loudly – he can't hear me, but it makes me feel better.

He is making me slow down. He gets out of the way, he has no choice – I give him no choice.

I continue down the road and gradually pick up speed as the traffic gets lighter. I'm constantly looking to see if any silly pedestrian wants to run out in front of me. If people weren't so daft I could drive faster.

Now for the problem road. I swing into the High Street; traffic is extremely heavy, shoppers are crossing the road. There is barely room for two lines of traffic, let alone that magical third lane I need.

I change the siren, then change it again, then again. It's a strange sound, and it gets everyone's attention. Cars slowly try to get out of the way, a bus holds its distance. Someone decides that they can run across the road before I reach them. They are wrong, I have to jump on the brake – luckily I'm not going too fast. I swear some more, then start off again. My speed is slow; my driving has gone from speed to squeezing through gaps.

Don't look at the cars or you'll hit them I think to myself. I concentrate on the gaps between cars, some are very small. On an instinctive level I know which gaps I can make, and which ones I need to sit behind the cars, lights flashing, sirens blaring, until they make the gap wider.

How did I get here? I'm turning into the street I need – it's one way and the way ahead is clear. I'm glad, once more the parked cars make it barely wide enough for a single car.

I'm counting the door numbers – I'm looking for number 112. Odd numbers on the left, evens on the right …

... 288 ... I speed up then slam on the brakes for a speed bump.

Again, again, again. I curse the people who think speed bumps are a good idea ...

... 186 ... more bumps – I pray no children are hiding between the cars ...

... 172, 162, 128 ...

I slow down. I'm trying to see the numbers, but some are small, and some are missing; while I'm doing this I'm trying not to drive into a parked car ...

... 112 ...

The door is open.

I stop. There is nowhere to park, so I'm blocking the road; it can't be helped.

I grab my bags and run into the house.

'Where is she', I ask. My eyes are taking in the house, is there anyone lying on the floor?

'It's me', comes the reply.

I breathe a sigh of relief.

'I've had a cough for the past week and it hasn't gone yet', she tells me.

Another normal job for me then.

Not reflective of any one job, more a reflection on all my jobs.

Knife Time (Well, Actually a Sword, But You Know What I Mean …)

This is one of a series of posts I wrote one week about the scourge of knives being used for violence.

I tend to walk the mean streets of London alone and unbothered by the thoughts of being attacked – I know that most violence is committed by people who know each other, and that truly random violence is rarer than most people think.

It was nearly three in the morning, we had all been busy that shift, so Control asked if I could attend an 'amber' call because there were no ambulances to send. I'm only supposed to go to the highest-priority 'red' calls but, to be honest, it doesn't bother me if they send me to a little old lady who has scraped her knee, and this particular job sounded fairly interesting.

It only took me a minute to find the minicab office, it is only 300 yards away from the ambulance station; it was surrounded by police cars. None of the police looked particularly panicked, so I realised that my patients probably were not seriously hurt.

The story I got was this …

At 1 a.m., patient one got a phone call to talk to his friend, the manager of the minicab office. Patient one collected his friend, patient two (who has only been in the country from Pakistan for a few months), and they both went to the minicab office. At the office, they were met by the manager and four other people. They were then pistol whipped, and a sword was poked into them. They were tied up and robbed of their mobile phones and £400 that one of the men was carrying. Injuries were minor, and it took them a little time to escape and call for help.

I quickly assessed both patients, and although they had been knocked around a bit, all their injuries were fairly minor, and as they were giving their statements to the police the Sergeant turned up.

(At least I think he was a sergeant, he had some stripes on his shoulders.)

He immediately voiced the thoughts that we were all having, that there was something 'dodgy' going on. Why would you go to a cab office for a chat at one in the morning? Why would you be carrying £400 at one in the morning to a cab office? Why were my patients being reluctant to give too many details to the police? Why would four people who you know want to torture you?

The Sergeant was polite, but firm with the men, even when they were being evasive with their answers. I was particularly impressed when he told both the men to stop talking to each other in their native language every time he asked them a question. It's a brave man who does that today, and doesn't worry about being called racist.

I left the patients with the police – their injuries were such that the FME could deal with them, and I suspect that the police would be happy to have the patients in their presence for a while.

While these people were 'victims', it's likely that the attack wasn't random in the truest sense of the word, although the use of a pistol and a sword is unfortunately getting more and more common.

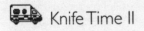 Knife Time II

I got sent to 'Male, stabbed in street, police present'. Luckily, I was pretty close, so I got there in 3 minutes. Lying in the street was a young male who was bleeding from the stomach.

Why?

Well, he'd run out of a shop to stop a traffic warden from putting a ticket on his car and bumped into someone, who had then pulled a knife and slashed him.

There were loads of police on scene, they'd put a dressing on him but it was soaking through with blood. I examined the wound to be sure that it wasn't a stab, and seeing that the wound wasn't that serious I cancelled the HEMS helicopter.

He refused to stop bleeding, so I spent most of my time on scene pressing on his belly with a dressing trying to stop the bleeding. It did stop eventually, and I had plenty of time to stay on scene and 'play' as the nearest ambulance was in Dagenham …

… It took *40 minutes* for the ambulance to turn up – not their fault, and to be fair it is to be expected because we have been so busy, and undermanned.

The one good thing about the job is that it is sunny today. While I had those 40 minutes kneeling in the street, pressing on a bleeding abdomen I was simultaneously working on my suntan.

You have to look on the bright side of these jobs. Thankfully, the patient was fine. There was a bystander who was convinced that the reason the ambulance was taking so long was because the patient was black. Racism would explain the FRU and 20 police at the scene of course …

Knife Time III

'Male, cut to arm, threatening to slice up neighbour, known psychiatric patient, wants London Fire Brigade for fun'.

That is how the job came down the computer terminal to me. Now, normally I'm not too bothered about going into potentially dangerous situations (I can run really fast if someone is chasing me), but this job rang warning bells.

(1) He has a cut to his arm; did he do it himself? If he did do it himself, then he'll probably still have the knife.

(2) Why does he want to 'slice up' his neighbour? Is he angry with them? Neighbour arguments tend to be rather nasty.

(3) What is his psychiatric history? Does he have a history of violence? Does he have a pathological hatred of the colour green? (*Our uniforms are green ...*)

I decided that for this job I would wait for the police to arrive.

So, I'm sitting in my car around the corner; there is an ambulance with me and we are waiting for the police to come and protect us.

My mind starts to wander. How bad is the cut to his arm? He could be lying on the floor bleeding to death if an artery has been cut. What about the neighbour? In the time I'm waiting, has he stabbed them? When I finally go around there, will I come across a bloodbath?

I consider having a look myself. I have a stabproof vest, but my arms, legs and head are still vulnerable to having 8 inches of sharp metal shoved into them. If I did go around and get stabbed there are 2 things that would happen:

(1) I wouldn't get any attention until after the police turned up.
(2) I also wouldn't get any sympathy from work as they've already told me not to go near the place.

So we sit there, members of the public stare at us, and I try to chill out by listening to the latest Coldplay album (*verdict: rather good actually*).

Why haven't the fire service turned up yet? He did ask for them, and I'm sure they, like us, can't refuse a call.

They never turned up though.

The police turn up. We go around to the address and the patient is as nice as they come. He'd been (allegedly) pushed over by the neighbour and had a graze to his arm.

So, while I could have completed the job in minutes, to do so *safely* took a lot longer.

This is the sort of thing we have to think about as we go to each and every job … and that's just sad.

The confusion came from the patient himself as he had some mental health problems. Yet another case for being careful how you talk to our Control when you call us up.

 Flat

This time it isn't my fault. It was a slow leak, rather than me mounting the kerb a bit too vigorously.

I heard a 'flapflapflap' sound coming from the car, but I thought that I needed something to eat first. So I pulled up outside McDonalds and two community police officers pointed out the flat tyre.

The plan is that we are supposed to wait around until the RAC (Royal Automobile Club) come out and change the tyre. Unfortunately, they would be between 3 and 4 hours in coming.

So I got my hands dirty and changed the tyre myself. If you were in the Stratford area this morning you may have seen me scrabbling around on the floor trying to work out how to use the car jack.

I changed the tyre, but I don't trust my hand-tightened nuts to hold together when I screech round corners. So I am now sitting on station while our fitters change and check the tyre.

For some reason the phrase 'I need to get my hand-tightened nuts checked' made the woman in Control laugh.

What little I can remember about my father is that he was/is a tyre fitter – so maybe it's in the blood?

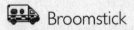 ## Broomstick

It started off as 'hit with a broomstick', but ended up resembling a cross between a riot and a carnival.

In a small road, perhaps 20 households, down on the Isle of Dogs, a family feud had finally spilled over into violence: one woman had been hit with a plastic broom, another had hurt her leg and a 10-year-old child had brandished a knife.

One of the injured parties had knocked on every front door in sight looking for witnesses, so there were around 50 people (mainly children) milling around. It was a beautiful day and people were enjoying the spectacle in the afternoon sun. Children were running around, ice-creams were being sold, and teenagers were staring at the scene, smoking, snogging, and getting in the way.

The police had come in a van, and no-one was listening to what they said. They couldn't arrest the 10-year-old: there were no witnesses, the child was under-age and, yes, if he *had* stabbed someone then they could arrest him.

There were half a dozen languages being spoken, and people were angry that the police and I aren't fluent in Urdu, Hindi, Somali, Turkish and Twi. They didn't realise that running up to a policeman, waving their hands around and shouting what sounded to me like gibberish, when there is someone who can translate standing next to you isn't the best way to go about things.

'She hit me', 'All three of them hit me', 'I was kicked', 'I have a broken leg' (*No … you don't*), 'My mum is going to have a heart attack', 'I want them arrested', 'I want this written down', 'It's been going on for ages, why haven't you done something?', 'Why are we waiting so long for the ambulance?', 'What are you going to do about them?', 'My mother has fainted', 'My leg is still broken'.

I suggested that the police get the riot squad down. A good idea, but they were all on day-release having a picnic.

The police were starting to lose their temper; no-one was listening and no-one cared for what the police could or couldn't do, they just wanted the attackers punished, locked up, or evicted.

People started to filter away when they realised that no-one was going to get handcuffed and thrown in the police van.

I finally managed to get to one of the 'patients'. Her family were pouring water over her head. There is a section of our community that believes that water being poured over the afflicted area will help, so I get sent to people with difficulty in breathing and chest pains who are being soaked with flannels or are dripping wet.

I'm used to strange beliefs, my mother thinks inanimate objects have feelings …

The water was running clear from her head, no blood. No loss of consciousness either. Looking at the 'broomstick', a light plastic pole, I'd be surprised if it even left a bruise.

The ambulances came – crews looking confused as I gave them the shortest version of the respective stories I could come up with.

The other 'patient' was complaining of a broken leg. She was still convinced she had a broken leg as she climbed up the steps into the ambulance.

Two patients, two different hospitals (we like to keep people separated in cases like this) and half a dozen police officers.

Slowly the street returned to normal and I settled down next to the Thames to do double the normal paperwork.

'*No obvious serious injury*'.

🚑 Apologies to All Police

Medical stuff is easy, I know exactly what to do when someone is having a heart attack, has a broken leg, or has driven their car at speed into a wall.

It's the 'social' stuff that is really tricky.

Its 3 a.m. in the morning, and I find myself going to a call, 'Female, fell down stairs'. On arriving outside the flats I heard two people arguing, and initially the female wouldn't let me into the flat. Then, a young-looking boy (he looked and sounded about 13 to me) buzzed me into the flat.

The patient had a black eye and a possible broken nose. She was covered in blood and was extremely upset.

She also refused to go to hospital, because she had her young daughter asleep upstairs.

The patient maintained that she had been out drinking, while the young-looking lad had been looking after her daughter – she didn't want to go to hospital because she didn't want to leave her daughter with the lad any more.

I confronted her over being happy leaving her daughter to go drinking, but not to go to the hospital – she was still determined not to go to hospital.

I also asked her if she was telling the truth, and that she hadn't been assaulted. She stuck to her story that she had simply fallen down the stairs.

Unfortunately, I can't drag people off to hospital, and even if I could, I'd have to arrange care for the young daughter.

I asked the young man how old he was, and he told me he was 22.

If he is 22 then he has some serious hormone imbalance problems, as his voice hadn't broken.

So, I had a woman who looked to me as if she had been punched, refusing to go to hospital. I had a 13-year-old boy (or thereabouts) looking after her and her daughter ... and I had heard them both arguing loudly from the street about something.

I couldn't just leave them like that, but what to do?

At 3 a.m., there is only really one thing to do, although I hated doing it ...

... Call the police.

Contacting social services would have taken weeks to sort out the problem, and there was nothing us ambulance folk could do, so that left the police.

I know that they are busy, I know that they don't like attending this sort of thing, and I know that their hands are tied as much as mine. But I lived in hope that they could do something about this situation – at the very least get it calmed down.

I'm still not 100% sure that I did the right thing, but compared with ignoring the problem I think that getting the police involved is 'the path of least evil'.

For all I know they have a huge file on this woman.

So, to all the police who read this blog – Sorry.

 Tongue

This post is completely egotistical – but sod it, I can blow my own trumpet sometimes ...

I think I just saved someone's life, but only because I'm honest.

It was 6:20 a.m., and I had 10 minutes to go until the end of the shift.

I'd just finished a Matern-a-taxi at the other end of my patch, so I considered sitting there for the 10 minutes of my shift before 'greening up'. That way I wouldn't get another job; I could get back to station near enough in time, and by extension be safe and warm in bed before 7 a.m.

'Sod it', I thought, 'what are the chances of me getting a job in these 10 minutes'. So I 'greened up', and started heading back to station.

6:28 a.m. My computer display started buzzing, '58-year-old Male, swollen tongue'.

'Bugger'.

It's at the other end of my area, on go the lights, on goes the siren, and I key the mike to ask Control if there is anyone nearer, or anyone that finishes at 7 a.m. who could take the job. There isn't.

The problem with getting a job at 6:30 a.m. is that pretty much every other ambulance and FRU in the area finishes their shift at 7 a.m. So if they have all been on jobs, they'll sit out the last 20 minutes of the shift at hospital. Or they could all be genuinely busy.

If Control are holding a job, then they'll broadcast it over the radio and hope that someone will take it, which, to be honest, someone normally does.

So I race around there, getting there in 9 minutes. Damn, the job is a failure … I need to get to every job in under 8 minutes.

The patient has a swollen tongue alright, so much so it's nearly falling out of his head. Apparently it started swelling up from last night, and has just been getting worse.

It looks to me that he is suffering an allergic reaction, quite a serious one at that, although he has no idea what he might be allergic to.

OK, I think, if it's taken that long he has plenty of breathing time; we can wait for the ambulance, and the hospital can treat him with the nice drugs. The only drug I have in this situation is adrenaline, which can have some fairly nasty side-effects (nothing serious, just it's not a pleasant drug to have injected into you).

So we wait, have a bit of a chat, and I manage to calm him down.

'It's still getting bigger', he says. So I have a look, and it is indeed getting to a dangerously large size. If it swells much more his airway will obstruct and he won't be able to breathe.

'Alright then', I say, 'time for that injection I told you about' …

… 500 mcg of adrenaline, straight in the muscle.

… 4 minutes later, and he tells me that 'It's getting smaller'.

… 10 minutes later and it is noticeably smaller, and he is able to talk in a much more normal voice.

His mum, 86 years old, and dressed in a little checked work pinny, comes down and offers a cup of tea.

Fifty minutes after arriving on scene, and after having a good chat about the state of English rugby, the weather and the good the NHS does, an ambulance rolls up outside.

The ambulance has also 'greened up' with 10 minutes to go on the end of their shift. Bless them.

I get back to station and finish my paperwork – it's now 8 a.m., one and a half hours' overtime then. Back in 10 hours to do the same again.

Then I start thinking … If I hadn't been honest, then I wouldn't have gotten the job, the patient's tongue would have swollen, and he could have choked to death.

All those little random decisions came together to help this patient …

… and I managed to go home with a warm glow inside, rather than the sickness of fatigue, and the dejection of yet another drunk/assault/drunken assault.

Multiple Explosions in London
– July 7, 2005

There are a number of dead bodies from the bus bomb being stored in the BMA (British Medical Association) building. There is blood up the windows. This comes from a friend who was there when the bomb went off.

 Today – July 7, 2005

A bit 'stream of consciousness' I'm afraid.

I found out about the terrorist bombs in London only because I was told by an electrician who was fitting some new wall sockets in my new flat. I rushed to plug in my small television, and found out about the bombs.

I phoned up our resource centre, as I was on my day off, and they told me that I should come in and go to Newham station.

I then covered the Newham area along with others who had volunteered to come in and cover for the ambulances that were dealing with the aftermath of the attacks.

I think we had a lot less calls than we normally have; I was sitting on station for longer than normal until I, and another, manned an ambulance and took a Matern-a-taxi to an Essex maternity department.

Once the shock had settled, I started to feel immense pride that the LAS, the other emergency services, the hospitals, and all the other support groups and organisations were all doing such an excellent job. To my eyes it seemed that the Major Incident planning was going smoothly, turning chaos into order.

What you need to remember is that this wasn't a major incident, but instead *four* major incidents, all happening at once.

I think everyone involved, from the experts, to the members of the public who helped each other, should feel pride that they performed so well in this crisis.

London will not be beaten, we spent 20 years under the shadow of the IRA, and are used to terrorists.

The medical staff at the BMA building did their best to save their 'civilian' staff from looking at the carnage that was left from the bomb on the bus.

The mobile phone networks appeared to be shut down – a good plan for potentially stopping more bombs from being triggered, but bad if you are trying to get into contact with relatives.

My brother considers himself very lucky: yesterday he took 40 schoolchildren to the Science Museum – right through the affected area.

I'm back to 'normal' work tomorrow, I wonder what it'll be like.

It took a year before the police admitted to closing down the mobile phone networks. Even now I hear stories about the blasts that contradict what eyewitnesses were telling me during and just after the attack. It's strange to be 'inside' such an important story, and yet still want to write about it.

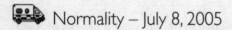 ## Normality – July 8, 2005

It seems that the LAS is back to normal. No hospitals are closed, the Underground is recovering and the buses are pretty much back to normal.

London isn't in fear, and we don't seem to be hanging Muslims from lampposts. Instead, we are dealing with it and getting back to normal. This shows the resilience of Londoners no matter the faith, ethnicity or class.

I think Mayor Livingstone summed it up best when he said,

'I want to say one thing: This was not a terrorist attack against the mighty or the powerful, it is not aimed at presidents or prime ministers, it was aimed at ordinary working-class Londoners. That isn't an ideology, it isn't even a perverted faith, it's mass murder. We know what the objective is. They seek to divide London.'

Now it is up to the nurses, physiotherapists, radiographers, medical applications, therapists and all the other allied services to take over the long-term and continuing healing process. These people are often forgotten but have a vital role in saving life and function.

Once more the blogsphere provided up-to-date news as well as reporting on what the mainstream media was saying.

We have a *highly* unofficial message board; there have been a lot of messages of support. Here are a few excerpts (all unedited).

The LAS and its sister services did a stupendous job today. I doubt if any city in the world could have mounted a similar response. The press talk about heroism. I'd rather talk about professionalism, organisation and effectiveness.

The street level emergency may have wound down, but a lot of our health-care friends and colleagues are still working hard to save the lives and assure the recovery of the many victims.

I was involved in the incidents from start to finish and can honestly say no matter how much we moan and whine, it all came together today, be it the LAS, the LFB, the Voluntary services, hospitals, the DSOs and AOMs' we slag off, the Met', the MOD plod, BTP, private amb services helped out, Miat teams, medical teams, HEMS, London buses who conveyed walking wounded, the GPs and district nurses who set up treatment centres in schools, Joe Public who gave out food to 999 personnel, the outer county services who responded to assist and anyone else I may have missed.

I might regret this, but I can actually say I was proud to work for the LAS today. I've been on duty all day out in the 'burbs in south London. We've been listening in on channel 9 most of the time. To those involved you have my total admiration for a job superbly done, you're all a credit to this service.

I have to say I have never seen a service as organised as the LAS were today. I offered to go to work and when I arrived there was absolute calm and professionalism amongst every rank.

To be honest I thought it would be a nightmare but I was proved wrong. How well everyone did was astounding and a credit to the service.

Well done all involved and especially well done to all in CAC and gold control for organising what can only be described as a massive operation.

Also, well done for all the Techs, paras, ECPs and TQATs. You can feel very proud, all of you.

Thanks also to all the outer counties that assisted. Cheers boys and girls. Your efforts will not be forgotten.

Just got home. It was a bit of a bugger out there today.

Drink. Shower. Drink. Sleep.

Talk to you all later …

Well done folks – went as well as could be expected.

Well done all those who attended today, and well done to CAC on channel 9.

Was listening in, and communication was second to none. Fantastic job.

Phone link went down to one of the receiving hospitals, CAC put out GB for any crew at hospital to relay blue call info. Fantastic.

I am proud today for the Service I work for.

We all moan, we have gripes about what now seem trivial matters.

Many of us came together for what was a horrendous and cowardly act of lunacy. Everyone deserves a large pat on the back safe in the knowledge you all did a fantastic job.

The thing that has annoyed us ambulance staff is that various awards have been handed out, but none of them found their way to the road crews first on scene, or to the dispatcher(s) in Control who did an excellent job and held it all together.

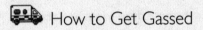 How to Get Gassed

You may be amused to know that at the moment I am being quarantined as a potential poison gas victim. I do have a funny taste in my mouth. More when I know myself …

And so what is the first thing I do? Start composing blog posts using my mobile phone. Do I have strange priorities? This post was a day after the London bombings, so people were a little nervous.

Contaminated

Later that day, after I'd been given the all clear, I gave the reason why I was quarantined …

I finish a job, and start to roll back to station for a nice relaxing cup of tea. As I pass one of the roads on my route I see a *lot* of firefighters, loads of police and a Duty Officer's car.

'Hmmm', I think. 'Something interesting there'.

Then I notice a strong smell of gas.

'A-ha, that's what they are there for, someone has left the cooker on'.

So I continue on my way, with a bad taste in my mouth, and roll up to the station …

… Only to find a load of officers, strange ambulance crews (well, I say strange, but what I mean is crews from out of our sector) and some St John's people.

'Something happening?' I ask.

'Yes', says one of my friends. 'We are roaming London ready to deal with anything out of the usual'.

'In fact', she continues, 'we are here because there might be a chemical incident in Lucas Avenue'.

'Oh bugger', I think.

So I let them know that I drove past it, and they tell me to sit in my car so that I don't contaminate anyone. Apparently, one of the tests for nasty chemical stuff came back positive.

I'm not too worried, if it was anything that nasty I'd already be dead.

They retest their samples, and it's negative. The team are stood down, and I'm allowed out of the car and back to work.

Still it's nice to know that our people are still on the ball.

8:30

8:30 this morning. I'm trying to explain something to an (understandably) hysterical woman, and her two children (4 and 7 years old).

I'm trying to explain that her 37-year-old husband, and their father, is dead, and that there is nothing I can do for him.

There is nothing I can do to stop her crying. The children are in disbelief and I don't know what to say to them either.

Sometimes this job is really shitty.

Sometimes it makes you feel really shitty when you can't help someone.

Street Resus'

My last call for yesterday was to a '65-year-old female, fall in street, possible head injury', I was only 2 minutes away, and I was happy to do a nice simple job.

Falls in the street are often minor injuries, where I have to do little other than minor treatments, and give a bit of the old Reynolds chat.

I pulled up on scene and saw a crowd of people standing around, looking fairly relaxed, and in the middle of them a woman lying on the floor. Someone was stroking her hand.

I walked up, looked down at my patient and said, 'Hello, what seems to be the problem'.

There was no answer, and her eyes kept staring ahead.

I checked her pulse, she didn't have one, nor was she breathing.

'Oh … bollocks', I thought.

I quickly started our treatment for this condition. Connecting my defibrillator to her (a box that monitors heart rhythm and can 'shock' the heart), I saw that she was in 'VF'. This is what is called a 'shockable rhythm', which means that I can give her heart an electric shock in an effort to restart her pulse.

When you see doctors on the telly shouting 'clear!' and then the patient's body jumping, this is what is happening.

So I 'shocked' her three times; when I wasn't shocking her, I was doing CPR (pushing on her chest to keep the blood flowing to her vital organs) and breathing for her with my Ambu-bag. I had to cut her clothes off (so I could attach the pads through which to deliver these shocks to her chest).

All the time I was fully aware of the crowd around me, and I was hoping that none of them had a cameraphone. None of the bystanders had seen anything, and none of them knew the woman (it looked to me as if she was just popping down the local shops).

The crowd were thankfully no trouble; actually they tried to be helpful – one person offered to help me with her breathing (I refused, because in reality it's trickier than it looks). There was another person who helped me, by running into their house and getting me some paper towels.

Why paper towels?

Well, I tend not to wear gloves, and while trying to resuscitate her, the patient had vomited up her last meal. So my hands were covered in her vomit. The paper towels were so I could wipe my hands before belatedly putting some gloves on.

So the crowd were, as we say in this part of London, 'as good as gold'. They didn't get in the way, they didn't annoy me by asking awkward questions while I was busy, and even the little kids who were watching were well behaved.

It took a long 9 minutes for the ambulance to arrive, it wasn't their fault, they were a long way away, and the traffic at that time of the day is pretty heavy.

We continued to attempt resuscitation, and at two points we managed to restore the patient's pulse. Unfortunately, she later died in hospital.

Once more I was left thinking about the relatives, who would be sitting indoors wondering why mum/gran was taking so long to get back from the shops.

Also, a resuscitation attempt is not the most dignified thing to have happen to you. That this woman had to have me cutting her clothes off, me jumping up and down on her chest and her vomiting over herself, all in full view of the crowd, is not the best way in which to leave this world.

I'm hoping I have nothing but minor calls today …

The family wrote to the ambulance service to find out what had happened to their mother. Thankfully, I'd written everything down in a detailed fashion that day, so it was fairly easy to give them a full reply.

Things to Do When Hit By a Car …

Or … 'The reason why Barking Road will be closed for an hour or two'

(1) If you have broken your arm and leg, please don't wave them around, as the sight of your bones trying to protrude through the skin is not a pretty one.
(2) If the nice ambulance man puts your neck in a hard C-spine collar and tells you to stop waving your head around, listen to him. Broken bones heal, broken necks can be a bit more … final.
(3) Do try to get hit down a side road. If you get hit in a main road, then the disruption to traffic will be a lot worse.
(4) If your 'friends' say that they saw everything and will be at the hospital, try to have the sort of friends who will actually turn up

there, and not just think better of it then bugger off to whatever hole they crawled out from.

(5) Yes, I know your arm and leg are broken, but seriously, keep your neck still.

(6) If you don't want me to know your name that's OK. Just make sure you carry some identification in your wallet.

(7) Having a shaven head makes it really easy to spot a head injury, thanks for that.

(8) Loose clothing is really easy to cut off. Please dress appropriately.

(9) Keep … Your … Bloody … Head … Still!

Why the flippancy? Lets just say that he and his friends are 'well known' to the local police, and to the odd ambulance crew. Also, you want to know how we deal with nasty trauma? Dark humour …

The patient was a drug dealer – which explains why his 'friends' disappeared when the police turned up.

🚐 Handbags

There is a special diagnostic procedure that us seasoned medical professionals use – 'Handbag medicine'.

To the lay bystander it may seem that we are standing over the unconscious (or merely uncooperative) patient, rooting through their belongings, looking for something expensive to steal. For women this is normally a handbag, for men you will find us going through their wallet.

However, it is not true that we are seeking to boost our wages (meagre though they are): instead, dear reader, we are trying to help the patient.

If the patient is unconscious then we need to get as much information as possible, and one way of doing this is to go through their possessions.

The best thing that we can find is a card that is big, bright and hard to overlook with 'I have epilepsy' written on the front (with the patient's name, date of birth and next of kin contact details written on the back).

The next best thing is often an address book/diary, it's especially helpful if the patient has filled in the front 'personal details' bit.

At a pinch we can use our detective skills with envelopes (opened and unopened), credit cards, GP slips, prescription forms (often very helpful), immigration or asylum documents (popular in this area) and (also popular in this area) court summons.

So, an East Anglian paramedic Bob Brotchie has come up with a rather good idea, given that people today (myself included) seem wedded to our mobile phones ...

... ICE

You put the details of the person you would like contacted 'In Case of Emergency' into your phone under the name 'ICE'.

It's a good idea, and the drawbacks (the phone might be broken or separated from the patient) are the same drawbacks as anything that you would write on a piece of paper ...

So, do it today!

True, if you are seriously injured enough, then we won't be rooting around your mobile phone (we'd be actually treating you), but it would help the staff in the hospital when they get a quiet moment.

There have been hoax emails going around saying that if you put ICE into your phone then you get your phone credits drained away. This is absolutely a hoax.

This has been a public service announcement.

I've only ever seen one mobile phone with ICE on it – but it was very helpful in that circumstance.

Again?

Looks like it might be kicking off in London again. An FRU has been sent to Warren Street station, smoke has been seen. Decon Officer on station hasn't heard anything yet.

 ## Decon

The Decontamination Officer has been told to get ready for a potential incident.

 ## Raised

Our Decontamination Officer has just been told that he has to come off the road and be ready on standby. This means that our level of threat has been raised a bit.

Could it be because they are worried that there may be a chemical component to an unexploded bomb?

Apparently there are chemical-suited people going down into Warren Street station.

(*Probably just making sure that everything is 'clean'*).

No-one on station has had a 'normal' call for the past 40 minutes.

🚐 Shifting Resources

One of our crews has been told to 'blue light' down to Headquarters in order to provide cover for the area affected.

Decontamination officer is still on standby.

Everyone here is fairly relaxed about the whole thing, but we are quite a way away from everything.

🚐 And … Relax …

So, it seems that there isn't anything chemical/biological to worry about – so no doubt the decontamination team are all disappointed …

The Police Commissioner has told all us Londoners to carry on as normal, but to avoid the affected areas.

The last I heard was that some of the team were looking at a 'white powder' incident – we get a couple of them a week, so it's unlikely to be anything serious.

Once more, most Londoners will look at what happened today, shrug their shoulders and make a cup of tea.

(*Something I'm going to do now …*)

The previous five posts were made 'live' during the failed bomb attacks on the tube and bus services a fortnight after the first terrorist bombs. Thankfully no-one was hurt, but it did put us all on a higher state of alertness.

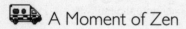 A Moment of Zen

Dark street.

A man who has been beaten unconscious.

I kneel down, and use my hand to steady me.

Under my palm I find two of his teeth.

Saturday night in East London.

If I were a cleverer person than I am, I'd have made this a haiku.

Bit of a Surprise

I got a call at about 5:30 in the morning to a 'Collapsed female' with 'shouting in the background', not normally a problem, so I took advantage of the empty streets and raced there.

I narrowly avoided crashing into the ambulance also coming to the job from another direction, and so we both arrived at the house at the same time.

The patient was a middle-aged woman who had been drinking with her family, then had been some sort of argument and she was feigning unconsciousness.

Nothing unusual there.

Still no problem – the family, while concerned, were happy to agree that the patient was indeed 'faking it'.

I went out to my car to pick up a bit of kit, just in order to rule out anything medically wrong with the patient, and on the way back two men in a car parked outside asked me what was going on.

'Nothing serious', I replied, and went back into the building.

It was then that the sole male of the house cried out, 'Who's shouting outside my house', and went outside.

I ignored him and we finished checking over the patient. As suspected there was nothing medically wrong with her.

Then the male came storming back into the house, grabbed two kitchen knives and ran outside again. The ambulance crew and I thought that this would be a good time to call for the police.

We sneaked out of the house, and stood by the ambulance – meanwhile the six women who had just left the house looked as if they were (a) arguing amongst themselves and (b) about to tear the men in the car to pieces.

The final result of the arguing, holding people back, pushing and shoving, and shrieking at the top of their lungs, was that the car drove off at high speed, missing me by about half a yard. Meanwhile, the argument continued between the sisters/cousins/whoever.

The police did turn up (and to their credit, turned up very quickly), and while they went about collecting statements there was various talk about samurai swords and the like being waved around (which isn't too surprising in this particular part of East London). We left the police dealing with what seemed to be some form of family feud.

Returning to station, we were all stood down by the duty station officer, so that we could fill in the relevant paperwork.

On reflection three things spring to mind:

(1) None of us were wearing our stab vests – and probably wouldn't have felt safe even if we had.
(2) Why, when I had my own mobile phone, my FRU phone and my work emergency phone, did I use the household landline phone when calling the police?

(3) Finally, is it wrong to think 'With the paperwork we now need to do, this job'll see me to the end of my shift'?

The 'phone' thing was probably because my brain saw it there, and thought 'I can dial 999 on that', rather than taking longer on wondering which pocket of many my mobile phones were in. Thus, my brain was able to concentrate on the whole 'not getting stabbed' thing.

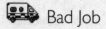 Bad Job

This is a tricky post to write. Normally I would write something to emphasise how I feel, or to try and get my readers to understand what happened, or to highlight some point.

But I can't do that in this post.

All I can do right now is tell you what happened.

I got sent to a call near the edge of my 'patch', given to me as a '12-year-old female, collapse'. The navigation point wasn't accurate though, so while I could get into the right general area, it wasn't directing me right to the door. I got there fairly fast, because I always drive fast to my jobs, even if I suspect that the illness is a panic attack, a faint ... or a broken fingernail.

I met up with the ambulance crew coming from the other direction while I was checking my map, and talking to Control so as to get a better location on the patient. Control called back and gave me better directions and I told the ambulance crew to follow me.

The location was down a private road, which had huge, unmarked black speed-bumps. I hit the first one at about 30 m.p.h., and had to check my mirror to make sure that I hadn't left important parts of my vehicle behind in the road.

The patient was lying in the road ahead of me, with her family standing around her. I parked my car next to her and got out to see what was happening.

The family were quite calm, and they told me that their daughter was travelling in the family car and told her parents that she felt unwell. They stopped, she got out, shook a bit and then fell onto the floor.

The parents had laid her into the recovery position and, while worried, were not screaming and crying.

Examining the patient, I saw there was a small bit of vomit in her mouth.

She then grunted.

I then saw that she had stopped breathing.

I am lucky that the ambulance was right behind me.

By now the medic on the ambulance was with me, and I told him that she had stopped breathing. I threw him my bag with the Ambu-bag in it (the bit of kit which we use to breathe for the patient), and while he started breathing for her, I cut off her clothes and connected our defibrillator.

She was in fine VF, which is a rhythm that is 'incompatible with life', meaning that her heart isn't pumping blood around her body. It is also a rhythm that we can 'shock' to try and bring her back.

I shocked her.

The monitor on the defibrillator showed asystole, which is where the heart isn't moving at all, but this can be 'normal' after giving a shock.

It was about now that the parents realised that their daughter was more ill than they thought. They asked us what was happening – all we could tell them was that their daughter was 'very ill'. You can't tell people that their daughter is dead while you are in the middle of the road, in case they mob you and the patient, and prevent you from doing your job.

By now I was doing CPR (pumping on her chest to keep the blood circulating), and she had vomited a large amount everywhere. Normally we care about getting vomit on our clothes, but in this case we weren't thinking of that.

By now the driver of the ambulance had gotten the trolley off the back of the ambulance, so we decided to 'load and go' – this girl needed to be in hospital as quickly as possible.

Her heart changed into fine VF again, so I shocked her another two times – once more she was in asystole.

We loaded the trolley onto the tail lift of the ambulance – and it wouldn't lift!

We gave everything a kick (because there is sometimes a loose connection) and it still wouldn't lift, so I ran around and got the handle that we use to manually raise the lift, but then the tail lift started up.

We got the patient, and the father, on board the ambulance; I jumped on to continue chest compressions, while the medic was trying to clear the airway and continue breathing for her.

The driver then put in a priority call to the nearest hospital, and started driving.

We sometimes drive fast in this job, but if there is one thing that will have us driving like a maniac it's for a nearly dead child.

While weaving our way through traffic at high speed I was keeping up the chest compressions while telling her father what we were doing.

It is hard to stand up in the back of a Mercedes Sprinter when weaving through traffic at high speed, and it is really hard to do so when some idiot in front of you decides to brake suddenly.

The vehicle lurched, there was swearing from our driver, and I grabbed a handrail. It was then I felt something 'go' in my wrist and hip.

We reached the hospital in one piece, and a nurse took care of the father, while we wheeled the patient into the Resus' room, where a team of specialists were waiting for us.

The good thing about the local hospital is that they let the parents watch the resuscitation attempt if they want. There is loads of research that shows that this is good for the family to let them know that everything was tried for their child.

I was in the reception area when the rest of the family arrived. I showed them to the relatives' room, and took the mother into the Resus' area where they were still trying to save the patient.

I was outside in the ambulance bay when I heard the family start crying, and I knew that they were crying because they had just been told that their daughter/sister/granddaughter had died.

The ambulance crew and I had a little de-stress in the nurses' messroom, and then the crew took me back to my car.

There was a small amount of vomit and a bottle of water still on the scene.

I went back to station, filled in an injury report form, completed the rest of my paperwork, and spoke to Control and told them that I would be sick for the rest of the night, because by now my wrist and hip were really starting to hurt.

All throughout I wasn't 'feeling' anything, instead I was 'blank', and not because of 'shock'.

I think that it's because, by my fourth night shift, the ability to care about anything leaves me.

I was contacted by a Duty Officer, to check on me – he was one of the nicest officers I've spoken to. He wanted to make sure that I was psychologically alright (*I was*), and he told me that he would sort out the injury part with my station officers so that they would know what was happening.

I then went to bed.

This morning, while telling my mum what had happened, I started to feel sorry for the girl – so I know I'm not a monster.

Sometimes this job is really shitty. Everything went right with the resuscitation attempt, yet the patient still died. I'm left thinking that while I will continue, and will forget about this job (until the Coroner's office asks for a statement), that family may never recover.

I've left this post much how it is in my blog.

Multiple Trauma and Floppy Children

One of the 'problems' with working on the Fast Response Unit is, because you are so 'fast', you can often find yourself first, and only, responder on a job where you would much rather have a large number of ambulance crews.

I'm thinking specifically of the FRU who was the first, and only, paramedic on the scene of the recent London bombings.

I got sent on a job to one of our main roads, given as 'Car vs. bus'. I thought that it couldn't be too bad, as the speed of traffic on that stretch of road is about 4 m.p.h.

The police had already gotten the area taped off, and there was minor damage to the front of the bus.

Sitting some way away, nudged up against a shop, was a blue car. The first thing that hits me is that there is no way that an impact that does such little damage to a bus, spins a car through 180 degrees and throws it against a shop.

(*I later realised that what had probably happened, was that that the bus clipped the car – the driver then hit the accelerator and drove over the kerb, ending up ramming the shop.*)

'Hi', said a friendly policewoman, 'there is a full-term pregnant adult female with a head injury, a baby that she was carrying on her lap and six other children, none of whom had seatbelts on'.

'Gaa!' I mumbled.

I got onto Control, 'I'm going to need at least three ambulances'.

I went to check on the woman – she is indeed pregnant, not wearing her seatbelt and she had 'bullseyed'* the windscreen. She had the world's tiniest cut to her head, and minor stomach cramps.

… A quick examination, and I'm happy she hasn't broken her neck, and is not actually that badly injured. There is nothing much to do with her.

A very quick look over the multitude of children standing around showed a swollen lip on one of them, but probably nothing serious.

A female police officer was holding the 18-month-old baby, 'I keep stroking his cheek and he keeps waking up and crying', she tells me.

I took a closer look … seems a bit pale.

He also looked a bit 'floppy'.

I stroked his cheek.

Not a flicker …

… Shit.

My salvation then came around the corner. An ambulance. A lovely big, yellow, blue flashing lights and sirens ambulance. An ambulance that can take this child away from me and into hospital where he needs to be.

The police officer and I jogged over to the ambulance and I gave the quickest handover to a crew ever.** They took one look at the child and

---

* To 'bullseye' a windscreen, the head hits the glass and causes a distinctive ringed crack pattern. There is often hair left in the glass.

** Apart from the time my handover was a disdainful, 'the patient has a verruca' (incidentally, also the shortest triage note I ever wrote when an A&E nurse).

215

'blued' it into the hospital. (I later found out that the child was faking it all, and was absolutely fine.)

I then had to examine each of the kids to make sure that they were not hiding any serious injuries, which thankfully they were not. I then rechecked the mother of the toddler, explained why her child had gone to hospital without her, and tried to keep her calm. While doing this I was also trying to chat up one of the female police officers (*but she's having none of it*).

So I'm kept a bit busy.

I'm was also being watched by an increasing crowd of people, who were not impressed by the power of police tape, and so wanted to wander over and offer advice. The police did a good job of shooing these people away, but it was a bit like Canute trying to hold back the sea.

Thankfully, there were no serious injuries (although if I had the kit, I'd have liked to have immobilised everyone involved), and the other ambulances soon turned up to ferry away the patients.

My paperwork consisted of one report form with 'Multiple patients' written on it, and a description of what I'd seen and done.

Then I went back to station, had a cup of tea and then got sent on a job on the edge of my patch, described as '12-year-old female, collapse' …

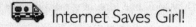 Internet Saves Girl!

I was going to moan.

I *was* going to tell you about the driver who tried to play 'chicken' with me. I would have told you about the brain-dead idiot who ran out, without looking, from behind a bus, causing me to leave 20-feet long skidmarks (on the road, not in my pants). Maybe I would have mentioned the kid who thought it would be a fun thing to pretend to jump out in front of my car. All while on blue lights and sirens.

I might even have complained about the maternity department who told their patient to 'phone for an ambulance' (which she plainly didn't need).

I definitely would have told you about the two drivers who couldn't wait for 5 seconds before swearing at the ambulance crew and myself for 'blocking the road'. Didn't matter that we wanted to see if the guy lying on the pavement was dead or not. They only stopped shouting when two policemen sauntered over to them in their 'I can't believe you are that stupid' way, cultivated by long hours in Newham.

I would have moaned, but I've had two Chinese takeaways, so I am now feeling content and will therefore tell you about how the Internet saved the day.

I got called to a 12-year-old female who had collapsed in a block of flats.

Nothing particularly interesting about the actual collapse, but what was interesting was how the ambulance was called.

The patient was talking to a friend via a web cam.

Her friend saw her collapse (well … slide down under the view of the web cam). The friend then phoned the patient's house, where the phone was picked up by the patient's gran.

Gran then rushed into the patient's room where she saw the patient collapsed on the floor. Gran then phoned for an ambulance.

We turn up.

We save the day.

Yay for us.

So all hail the Internet, saviour of teenage girls!

Sheer Bloody Terror

Very little scares me: violent drunks, dark alleys, terrorist bombs, careering around corners at silly speeds – none of these things bother me. But I do have one completely irrational fear ... and today I faced that fear.

Terror is often depicted as happening at night, in the middle of a thunderstorm, but for me terror happened on a sunny Monday morning.

The first job of the day was nice and simple, a little old lady with a leg infection who needed some antibiotics that can only be given at hospital.

Just don't ask me why this was a high-priority call, and therefore needed a Rapid Response Unit.

I spent some time chatting with the patient and her relative – nice enough folks just feeling let down by their GP. Little did I know the trauma that would soon be inflicted on me ...

The ambulance crew turned up, and put the carry-chair next to the patient. The patient was having severe pain on standing, so one of the crew and the patient's daughter grabbed an arm each and gave her some help standing.

During this I was standing in the kitchen door, and the other crew was standing in the hallway door.

Then I saw it.

I have big hands, and the spider that ran up the back of the patient was just a shade smaller. I was standing some way away and even with my poor eyesight, I could see its huge fangs, its hairy legs, and an evil glint in its eyes.

I froze.

'I'm not f**king wrestling with that monster', was the first thing that sprang to mind.

Sprinting onto the patient's head it sat there for a moment, no doubt deciding which of us would make the tastiest meal.

The daughter screamed, the (female) crew helping the patient screamed, the (male) crew standing in the doorway swore, screamed, and ran out into the hallway to hide.

'Get it off! Get it off' the daughter screamed.

The spider decided to sit on the face of the patient, its legs gripping the patient's ears like a facehugger from the 'Alien' films.

'Eeek!' screamed the patient.

The daughter then smacked her mother right in the face, and the spider went flying across the room. I had visions of it smashing into a vase, bringing it crashing to the floor.

(*Did I mention that this spider was fairly large?*)

I stood there like a lemon, my long-dormant arachnophobia flaring into action – I was petrified.

I don't like killing ~~things~~ animals – I even rescue the silverfish from my bath before washing my hair – but if this thing came near me it would be a fight to the death.

The patient sat alone in the room in the carry-chair, breathing heavily from her daughter's assault.

Neither of the crew wanted to go near the patient in case the spider was merely lurking … biding its time until it could attack. My bags were taken off me and I was told in no uncertain terms that it would be me who would approach the corner in order to actually collect the patient.

A deep breath, a muttered Litany against fear, and I scooted across the room and, keeping my eyes on the many dark corners, swiftly bundled the patient up and got her out of the house.

'Don't worry', said the daughter as we left the house, 'Mum's dog will soon eat it'.

Depends how big the dog is, I thought …

I was left a comment on my website by the (male) crewmember who screamed like a little girl (I only refrained from screaming because I didn't want to attract its attention). He told me that he thought he heard the doorbell and was going to see who it was. This is a blatant lie.

The Benefits of Lovely Weather

It's funny how the nice weather we are having at the moment makes you look at everything in a different, happier light.

Take today for example, I was sent to a 'Life status questionable' in the street. Now a 'life status questionable' is supposed to mean that the person who called us doesn't know if the person is alive or not.

What it means in reality is that the caller has either driven past in a car without stopping, or the patient has such an offensive smell that the caller dare not get close to them.

So, I rush to the scene and find an alcoholic sitting in the street. Around him are his four alcoholic friends.

The person who made the call is nowhere to be seen.

'He's just tired', I'm told by one of his friends.

'Why's that?' I ask.

'Well, he's just walked from Whitechapel' (Whitechapel is about 6 miles away).

'Oh', I say, 'No wonder he is having a bit of a sit down'.

'This'll help him out', says one of his friends giving him a can of Special Brew.

The ambulance crew turn up, and we all have a little chat on the corner of the street; everyone is as nice as pie, and no-one is really injured.

I know that I should be annoyed (waste of ambulance time and resources, waste of lives on the part of our alcoholic friends), but it wasn't really their fault that an ambulance was called.

And the sunny weather just put everyone in a nice mood.

Long may it last ...

Of course, saying that, nice weather means that young men drink long into the night, and then beat each other up.

The counter to this is that when the nights are long and the days are short and dark I find myself stomping around in a foul mood. I'm very fickle.

☕ Waitrose

Good karma is due for the duty manager of Waitrose who gave the ambulance crew (and, more importantly, me) some free doughnuts for helping one of their shopgirls.

Yummy.

Sorry

I spent an absolute age trying to get this post right. Eventually I just threw up my hands in surrender and posted it in the format below. I hated it, but a lot of my readers liked it.

Dear patient,

I'm sorry.

I know you thought that you were going to die peacefully, but we have to try and save lives, even though you were terminally ill. Your husband didn't want you to die yet, neither did your daughter.

I'm sorry that when I reached you, you were breathing your last. It meant that I had to lift you off your bed onto the hard floor.

I'm sorry that I had to do that, but it is the only way I could do effective chest compressions. I'm sorry I had to do the chest compressions; I know I broke some of your ribs, but please understand that it is a known side-effect of trying to keep your heart pumping.

I'm sorry that we had to put those needles in your veins, but you needed the fluid. You also needed the drugs that helped your heart beat, but it was probably painful.

I'm sorry that we had to pump air into your lungs; it can't have been nice for you, but we needed to keep your vital organs supplied with oxygen.

I'm sorry that because of the air in your pleural space we had to push two large needles into your chest. I don't know if you felt it, but it did help reinflate your lungs.

I'm sorry that your husband didn't quite understand what was going on – we tried to explain, and I think that at the end he did realise that you probably weren't going to wake up.

I hope you didn't mind when we had to keep passing a couple of hundred joules through your body. It made your body jump, but it's not your fault.

I don't know if it hurts. I hope that it didn't.

I know that the journey into hospital wasn't the smoothest ride, and the sirens were loud, but we did need to get you into hospital quickly.

I did remember to wrap the blanket around you so that anyone standing outside the hospital doors wouldn't see that you were naked.

But ...

... I'm *not* sorry that we, and the hospital, were able to keep you alive long enough for your family to arrive and gather around you.

I hope that there was a part of you that was still aware of what was happening, and was able to hear their words of love.

I hope that it was worth the pain so that you could hear those words, and feel their presence.

When I left you at the hospital your heart was beating and you were breathing. I hope that your end was without pain.

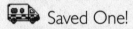 Saved One!

I know it's a rare thing, but we actually managed to save the life of someone! It was bloody hard work mind you, so I wouldn't want to do it too often ...

I got sent on a job with very few details; all I got was 'Male, unknown age, unconscious, unknown cause'. I knew roughly where the address was so I rushed around there, and saw the ambulance pulling up at the same time.

I quickly checked my computer screen and saw that I had gotten to the location in under 8 minutes. Whatever happened now the government would consider this job a success.

There was something about the family member who let us through the security doors that set my 'spider sense' tingling. That 'something' was confirmed when the ambulance crew and myself walked into a bedroom and saw a rather dead-looking 30-year-old male lying on the lower part of a bunk bed.

I must admit that my first thought was 'I wonder how long he has been dead?', because if he had been dead for a while, we wouldn't have to attempt a resuscitation. We quickly pulled him from the bed and laid him on the hard wooden floor.

'*Grrrooooooollll*' was the noise he made.

I'm very used to dead people making unusual noises: it's normally as a result of their last breath leaving their body.

We quickly hooked up our heart monitor and checked for a pulse.

His heart was beating!

He took a shuddering breath.

The patient wasn't breathing often enough to maintain life, so we would have to take over breathing for him, which we did using a bag and mask.

One of the crew lay on the floor and peered down his throat. Would we be able to intubate him? (Intubate = stick a breathing tube down the patient's throat in order to protect their airway.)

'Nope', she told me, 'his airway is too tight'.

We picked up the (heavy) patient and wheeled him out of the house and into the ambulance.

Another attempt at securing his airway …

'No chance', she said, 'his airway is the size of a pencil'.

This explained why I was finding it hard work to force air into his lungs.

'Perhaps it's his asthma', I suggested, 'shall we get some salbutamol into him?' (Salbutamol is an asthma medicine that is inhaled – we can use various complicated connecting tubes to give this drug while I continue to 'bag' him).

'Let's give some adrenaline as well', I said; seconds later it had been drawn up and given (giving adrenaline is another treatment for asthma).

(Why was I the one making all the suggestions? Well the crew were busy connecting monitoring equipment, gaining intravenous access and doing other tricky things – I had the simple job of breathing for him, so I had plenty of time to think about our next step of treatment.)

Then it was time for the run to hospital. By now the patient's chest was getting harder and harder to inflate. The levels of oxygen in his blood were lower than I would have liked, but it was pretty understandable considering how incredibly close he was to death.

His chest got so tight that it ended up with two of us 'bagging' him – one of the crew would hold the mask to his face, while I was using both hands to squeeze the breathing bag. I can still feel the pain in my arms where I was using all my strength to squeeze the bag in order to force air down his tiny airway and into his spasming lungs.

Then he vomited blood – well, 'vomit' is an understatement, he actually went off like a geyser – bloody vomit flew up to the ceiling of the ambulance, on the walls, over my arms, onto my trousers and covered my face and glasses.

I have learned, however, to keep my mouth closed when this happens …

We got to hospital and, as we were entering the Resus' bay, the patient was starting to breathe for himself – and by the time we had cleaned up the ambulance (and my face) the patient was sitting upright and was talking.

He had made such a recovery that the staff at the hospital had trouble believing that he was as ill as we told them he had been.

(Until they checked his blood levels, and on getting the results ended up sending him to intensive care.)

A quick round of pats on our collective backs, and it was back to work … where my next job was a 30-year-old with a painful foot for the past week.

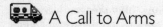 A Call to Arms

An attempt to show my political leanings.

It's that special time of the year again, when death-dealers descend on Newham to enjoy the 'Defence Systems and Equipment International Exhibition'.

It's an arms fair.

In *Newham* of all places.

I'm always worried that the local gangs are going to storm the fair and loot it of some 'interesting' souvenirs. Then, for the next couple of months, I'll find myself dodging cruise missiles and landmines rather than the usual broken bottles, knives and dog turds …

Both the mayor of Newham and the mayor of London want the exhibition to stop coming here, but it still comes, bringing with it massive disruption for the people of Newham.

So there will be lots of demonstrations (some have already taken place, such as a street party), but as the exhibition starts tomorrow we are expecting things to start warming up a bit. I haven't seen any ~~soap-dodgers~~ protesters yet, but I'm guessing that tomorrow will see the banner-wielding population of Newham increase a thousand-fold. At the moment it seems that a lot of their tactics involve blocking various roads that control entry to the exhibition.

So far I have seen a veritable army of police arriving, shields at the ready (4 000 police taken from other duties to cover the event). Obviously, this leaves the rest of London a bit short on policing. I've seen convoys of riot police making their way to the area, and this morning there appeared to be random vehicle checks. For the police it must be nice to have so much overtime available.

On our part, the LAS have manned an extra ambulance or two for the duration of the exhibition. Sitting in the sun watching people shouting seems like an easy way of getting some overtime. We are also doing other things, but it's probably not a good idea to tell the world and his wife about it. I just hope that the exhibition organisers are paying for our services, after all, it's not like they are short of money.

It might be interesting to print out a spotter's card of dictators, warlords and despots just to see how many you can catch turning up in unmarked limousines.

I must admit I'm torn. I like the police, they are always helpful; they do a job that is remarkably difficult and when I've needed help they've always turned up and been very useful.

But …

I really sympathise with the protesters, and if I wasn't working, then I'd probably be there amongst them waving a banner and trying not to get stood on by a police horse.

So I'll sit on the fence and say that they are both going to be a huge pain in the backside because they are both going to block roads, probably injure each other, and will cause traffic jams when I'm planning on going home.

The Philosophy of Reynolds – *'balance through the dislike of everyone'*.

Mercy! MRSA!

The media has reported a fair bit about MRSA in ambulances of late; one of my commenters has asked how the London Ambulance Service deals with patients who are MRSA positive.

(*Note: I'm also writing this to avoid losing my job by posting about a family who have called an ambulance more than seven times in the past week for the same illness.*)

Primarily the problem is that we just don't know who is MRSA positive. MRSA is prevalent in the community, and I would suggest that most nursing homes have plenty of colonised residents. I remember working in hospital, having to swab everyone coming in from a 'high-risk' environment, which meant anyone from a nursing home, or another hospital.

It takes time to swab and grow a culture (3 days if I remember correctly), and each test costs a not inconsiderable amount of money.

If a patient is MRSA positive, then our infection control booklet tells us that we should use our 'personal protective equipment' (our uniforms) plus what are known as 'universal precautions' – essentially latex gloves.

To clean an ambulance after transporting an MRSA-positive patient we use 'System 1' and 'System 2 or 3'.

System 1: Detergent.
System 2: Chlorine spray.
System 3: Alcohol.

Anything the patient has come in contact with is wiped with detergent, and then we either spray it with chlorine solution, or wipe down with alcohol wipes.

The other problem that we have is that we are so chronically overworked that we often only have a little time to clean the ambulances. If you are having a heart attack, then you won't be impressed if all the ambulances on duty are off the road waiting to dry.

When the LAS do something, we often do it right. Our boss realised that the ambulances aren't as clean as they should be, and that road staff didn't have time to 'deep clean' ambulances every shift. The solution was to contract an outside firm who now cleans and stocks our ambulances for us and from what I have seen, they do a pretty good job.

So, every night a gang of underpaid workers clean as many ambulances as possible. This 'make-ready' crew are paid a frankly pitiful £6 an hour, working from 1 a.m. to 6 a.m. They can clean around 16 ambulances a night using industrial cleaning materials. Every month they are quality controlled by random swabbing. So far they have only had good results.

So, I personally think that the LAS is doing something positive and effective against the spread of MRSA.

It will never be eradicated, unless we force everyone at gunpoint to use alcohol gel after every physical contact (and this includes 'civilians') and enforce daily antibacterial showers for the entire population of the world. However, we can do our best to prevent the spread of MRSA (and other, nastier diseases).

 80/50

A strange day; it wasn't that hot, but all I seemed to be doing was going to young women that had fainted.

A *lot* of women who had fainted.

It started off on the 30th floor of a skyscraper in Docklands, which had a lovely view. People were having meetings around tables in the expensively furnished corridors, and all the office walls were made of glass … which made me glad that I didn't have to undress the woman who had fainted.

Then it was across the road to another woman who had fainted in another (less well furnished) office.

Then a bit of a run north to yet another woman who had fainted.

Then a gentleman who had fainted on the bus.

Then a woman who had fainted in the local shopping centre.

It seemed like people were dropping like flies.

The *really* unusual thing was that the blood pressure of all the patients was 80/50, which is really rather low.

It also struck me as interesting that the first of my fainters was near the arms fair, and then got progressively further and further away ... I didn't think to check the direction of the wind ...

Thirteen jobs today, I am, as they say, bloody tired.

Unconscious? (Tricks of the Trade)

Some people seem to think that faking unconsciousness is a good idea: either they are mentally ill, drunk or, more commonly, have had some form of argument and have decided to 'go unconscious'.

For some reason, benefit offices and rent payment offices are popular places, as are police cells, magistrates' courts and the checkouts of supermarkets.

The easiest and quickest way to see if someone is faking unconsciousness is to lightly brush your finger against their eyelashes. If their eyes flicker, then they are almost certainly faking it. Also, if they try to keep their eyes closed when you try to open them, they are definitely faking it. Another way of checking is to hold their hand over their face, and let it drop. People tend to be reluctant to let their hand hit them on the nose, and so the hand will instead magically drop to one side.

The other giveaway is that they open their eyes to look at you when they think you aren't watching them ...

But what happens if someone is able to wake up, yet is refusing to?

Let me quickly explain an important part of measuring someone's 'Glasgow Coma Scale'. The Glasgow Coma Scale is a way of measuring how deep someone's level of unconsciousness is. Part of this process of assessment is how they respond to pain.

The official method of applying this pain is to push hard against the upper part of the eye socket. This does no damage but is apparently painful.

… Not to me it isn't, and not if you are deeply drunk.

So there are other painful stimuli, one of which (my favourite) is the 'sternal rub', where you rub the knuckles of your hand against the patient's breast-bone. Some lily-livered people think that this assessment is too close to assault, but I would ask them to consider that if we didn't get drunks to wake up, we would be forced to undertake invasive medical procedures on them in order to ensure that their airway is clear. If you can tolerate my sternal rub then there is something seriously wrong with you, and you need emergency treatment – if you wake up then I have effectively 'cured' you.

Either way the assessment is complete.

Of course I did get a broken rib for my troubles when 'curing' an unconscious drunk who had sexually assaulted a female pedestrian. I also can't see how one way of causing pain may be assault, but another isn't.

The moral of this story is simple: don't pretend you are unconscious, because we will know, and don't pretend to be unconscious when you are drunk, because it can get painful for you.

My favourite tale of how to uncover a pretender in a hospital setting was a doctor, who would loudly ask for the 'brain needle', to draw off some brain fluid from the unconscious patient via the ear. Of course, he would continue, the patient needed to be unconscious because otherwise they might flinch and the needle go into the brain itself. This was normally followed by the patient 'waking up' and asking, 'Doctor, where am I?'

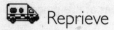 Reprieve

Four miles away 'Bob' was about to stop breathing.

Bob's friends had seen him come out of rehab' earlier that day; they had then invited him around to their flat where they then saw him inject some heroin.

Bob's friends had then watched him pass out for half an hour, and then his breathing had slowed and he had gone a funny shade of blue.

His friends decided that now might be a good time to call for an ambulance.

I arrived at the same time as the police, who were there to make sure that I was safe.

One of the residents held open the main door to the tower block.

'Another fucking junkie?' she asked. 'It's a fucking crack house up there'.

We got in the lift, carefully avoiding the nasty-smelling puddle in the middle of it, and I hit the button with my gloved finger.

Sure enough, if you worked in film making and were asked to create a set based on a crack house this is probably what you would come up with. Actually, as crack houses go, it wasn't too bad – there were no human faeces spread around for a start. No carpets either, which is a good thing because it's easier to spot the wet patches on lino.

To give Bob's friends some credit, they had managed to put him into the recovery position in the middle of the kitchen. Bob had either vomited, or his friends had poured some water on him. Either way there was something sticky on the floor around him.

For the second time on this job I was really glad I was wearing gloves.

His friends were both clutching cans of cheap, but strong lager. One of them was so skinny he would have made Iggy Pop look like Pavarotti. I left the police talking to them.

Bob had decided that breathing four times a minute was quite enough for him but the blue pallor of his skin, and my training, would tend to disagree with him. Bob was very nearly dead; I suspected that he would soon break the first habit of his life – the habit of breathing. I put an airway down his throat, pulled out my Ambu-bag and started breathing for him.

He soon pinked up and perked up, and his breathing got better, so I could stop 'bagging' him. I could relax a bit, and watch him while I waited for the ambulance to arrive – which wasn't long.

We moved him into the carry-chair, being careful not to stab ourselves with any needles that might be lying around him (or in his clothing, his pockets, or lying underneath him). It was about now that he started to wake up.

Another life saved, although no doubt his habit will kill him one day.

It strikes me as ever so annoying that for some reason I can manage to save heroin addicts, but not 12-year-old girls.

 More

At least three people in my area have called an ambulance because of being in the early stages of labour.

Something else that upsets/annoys me is that a family bought in their dead toddler by private car, and never thought to call an ambulance.

Make of that what you will.

I was particularly annoyed that evening. Most of my calls were to people wanting to give birth, yet were so far away from actually giving birth they could have walked to the hospital. Then I hear about the dead toddler who needed an ambulance and, because of the way they died, might still have been alive today if an ambulance had been called when they started to get sick.

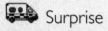 Surprise

I walked in through the door and there she was, standing stark naked in a pool of her own blood.

Heavily pregnant, she was sobbing while blood ran down her legs. Her neighbours were making an attempt at comforting her, all the while trying to clean the blood away. Meanwhile, between great sobs of tears, the patient was trying to fit a sanitary pad to herself.

As I write this I can still smell the blood.

The ambulance was 10 minutes away.

Someone in my comments box made an off-colour remark and was berated by my regular commenters. I remember this job because while the patient was black, the neighbours who helped her were two white 'granny' types. It was nice to see people being helpful across supposed cultural barriers.

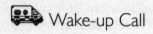 Wake-up Call

I walked into work at 6:15 a.m., I'd been awake since half past five. Well, I say awake – what I actually mean is that although I was somehow moving around, and managed to drive to work, my mind was still comfortably asleep in bed back home.

I start to check the equipment in my FRU; most of it is there, but I'm missing a few pieces of kit – expensive pieces of kit, probably sitting on a vehicle elsewhere in our complex.

Then my phone went off. 'Hello', said Control, 'we've got a cardiac arrest for you'.

I jumped in the car, checked the address, then saw the age of the patient …

… 42.

Control also sent a message that the patient's wife is doing CPR. This meant that he might just have a chance of surviving this …

I raced towards the address; it didn't take long, although because of recent rainfall, I was sliding all over the road.

It's only when I turned onto the road that I realised that I'd been to this address before. I'd spoken to this man previously; he seemed like a decent person. I *know* him.

I ran in through the door; the hallway was clean but I could not see anyone, so I shouted out.

'Up here', came the cry of an obviously distressed woman.

'Sounds genuine', I thought.

So I bounded up two flights of stairs and into the bedroom, where I saw the wife performing pretty effective CPR on her dead husband.

She was crying.

I took over. Connecting the patient to my monitor/defibrillator I saw that the patient's cardiac rhythm was asystole – there is no activity in his heart at all.

Now came the tricky part. I was on my own, and there are a lot of things that I had to do very quickly.

I did 15 chest compressions – this would hopefully get some oxygen to his essential internal organs. But to continue doing this I needed to get his lungs full of air. So the next thing I did was is connect up the 'Ambu-bag' to my oxygen cylinder.

I tilted his head back and used the Ambu-bag to inflate his lungs twice.

I started another 15 chest compressions.

Downstairs I heard the crew entering the house.

'Top floor mate', I shouted. 'Job is as given'.

When I say the 'job is as given', I mean that it was given to us as a cardiac arrest, and that it is indeed a cardiac arrest and not a faint/panic attack/cough or bellyache.

It seemed like ages, but when I later checked the times, the crew were less than 2 minutes behind me.

Three people came bounding up the stairs. The FRU from another station had jumped into the back of the ambulance – he was waiting on station for the previous shift to return when the crew got the call.

I continued the chest compressions. One medic put a breathing tube down the patient's windpipe, the other gained access to a vein, so that we could give essential medications. The last crewmember was doing the very important (*but often underrated*) job of looking after the wife.

After about 9 minutes of this treatment, the rhythm on the heart monitor changed. It looked suspiciously like a decent heart beat.

I checked for a pulse.

I found one!

The patient then spent the next couple of minutes (while we were preparing to move him) slipping in an out of either having a pulse, or having a 'shockable rhythm', which needs an electric shock to revert this back into a heart rhythm 'compatible with life'.

He ended up getting defibrillated twice before we could load him onto the carry-chair, lug him down two flights of stairs and into the back of the ambulance.

We then found a member of the public upset that we were blocking his parking space. He was blocking the only exit that the ambulance had.

One of the crew had a word with him. She is much more polite than I would have been.

He moved out of the way rather quickly.

As there were three crew in the ambulance, they didn't need my help, so I followed behind them so that I could get my equipment back. By the time I reached the hospital the patient was being prepared for transport to the intensive care unit.

The wife gave the crew a hug, and sobbed how grateful she was. Even the doctor at the hospital complimented us on a job well done.

But, failing a miracle, the patient will die – he was without oxygen for too long.

Once more it seems that we are just making time for the relatives to say goodbye. But for us it still seems like a success.

This is the patient I mentioned earlier who was having a 'thrumming' heartbeat. It was a damn shame.

🚑 'Care' Home

I usually only tend to see the bad nursing homes. I'm not talking about nursing homes where the patients are abused in the traditional sense, but rather where they seem to have simply been … left.

I went to one the other day, run by a large prestigious private health-care company, it is clean and looks very pretty … but I'd rather die than spend my final days there.

The patient was 90 or more years old and had been bleeding from her vagina since 9 a.m. that morning. I was called at nearly noon. They had left her bleeding for 3 hours.

I found her lying on a towel on a plastic bed; there was no sheet and the only bedclothes she had was a single sheet across her body.

Her room was clean, but was empty of anything personal – there were no pictures, no letters, no ornaments … nothing.

I looked at her drug chart. She was on two types of painkiller, but for the past 5 days, those, and her other medications, were marked as having been 'spat out'. I'm guessing that this was because of her advanced dementia, rather than an informed refusal.

If she was spitting out her medicines, I wonder if she was also spitting out her food and drink. There was a bottle of drink next to her bed, but there was no way that she would be able to reach it. Looking at her skin, she did look dehydrated.

The 'nurses' all walked with the speed of arthritic turtles, and I had to struggle to find one that knew anything about the previous visit the patient had made to the hospital. Actually, I struggled to find a nurse that knew much about anything.

'I don't know this drug', I said to one of the nurses testing her, 'what is it for?'

I knew what the drug was for, but the nurse didn't …

One of the care assistants sat on the end of the patient's bed. The patient seemed a bit distressed at this, but it was hard to tell as she was staring at the ceiling. The carer suddenly got off the bed, and this obviously caused the patient pain as she cried out.

The care assistant left the room, and I was left trying to comfort the patient, holding her hand and apologising.

I wondered what this woman had seen, what she had lived through. I could imagine her dancing in the 1930s, being married and having children (her daughter was on the way to the hospital already), raising her children while living through the war, maybe working as part of the Land Army. I thought about her husband, probably long dead, and the friends she had also probably outlived.

It always depresses me to think that some people end up in homes like this, where the care is slipshod, and her life is now just an accumulation of numerous small acts of omission.

Epileptic Fit

We got called to a 'Female – epileptic fit' in the street. This was a call that was sent to us by the police. Now, I may be accused of being overly cynical, but when the police call us to an 'epileptic fit' it is normally because they are arresting someone, and in order to avoid going to the police station the person fakes a fit. There are ways and means of detecting when this is the case, some of which I have mentioned previously. Even though this was the likely explanation for this job, we still rushed down there, fully prepared for it to be genuine.

We turned up to see a car being towed away, and the police that met us had a slight smirk about them. The finely tuned sixth sense I have made me suspect that the police were hiding something from me. We were led to the patient, who was lying in a darkened alleyway, with her boyfriend standing over her.

As is my normal approach, I said something along the lines of 'Hello love, can you open your eyes for me', I brushed the thick, long hair from out of her eyes, and, being unable to see the patient properly, pulled out my torch and shone it in her face. At first I thought it was just a very unattractive woman, then I brushed the hair back a bit further and that caused the wig to slip …

This female was born a man.

239

Now, I have no problem with transsexuals. I know a couple in a social situation, and apart from the time I caught one of them going to the bathroom in a pink dressing gown and pink bunny slippers, their gender doesn't pay any part in what I think of them (*as with gay men, I just think, 'Great! More women for me!' Of course it doesn't work out like that, but I live in hope*).

The hardest bit is working out whether to call the patient 'he' or 'she'. So I asked the boyfriend.

It looked as if the patient had had a genuine epileptic fit, and so we got 'her' onto the ambulance and started our treatment. I managed to get a lot of the details off of her boyfriend. We got her into hospital, where we found out that she was not unknown to the hospital. By now she was starting to come around.

As she and the boyfriend didn't live in the area that we found them in, I asked what she was doing there. Apparently, she had parked the car on the estate, then someone had stolen the keys. Given what she was wearing (pink furry moon-boots, tight leather miniskirt, tight pink top, and a leather/furry frock jacket), and what I saw when I peeked at her previous medical history, I wonder if she was one of those 'ladies of the night' that we often drive past.

I mean, most of them look a bit rough, but having been born a man might explain a lot …

Yet another 'dinner party' story.

🚑 Community Relations

(WARNING: It has been a while since I was in education, so I don't know the current ideas on political correctness, so if the post below is insulting, I'm sorry. You should know by now that I treat everyone the same. If you think I'm racist, then check out my archives. However, it's not against the law (yet) for me to say that I think religion is a generally silly idea.)

Written by the Ambulance Service Association, the *Community Handbook* (pocket edition) is an easy reference guide to many of the ethnic groups that we may come across. Of course, in London there are around 200 different ethnic groups, so any 'comprehensive' handbook would weigh a ton – we get a two-page spread of some of the commoner ethnic groups in the UK.

POCKET EDITION
Community
Handbook

A guide to
understanding the
diverse faith and ethnic
communities in the UK.

AN ASA PUBLICATION

It's very pretty, and I can imagine it possibly being useful for ambulance trusts who do not have a large 'ethnic' population. But I work in Newham, where the 'ethnics' outnumber the WASPs, and I've found that you tend to pick up on other people's culture pretty quickly, as in a week or two, on the job.

One amusing point of the book is that for a lot of cultures, it says that you should remove your shoes on entering the house. Yet one of the main things we were told in ambulance school was that you never take your boots off, as it's just too dangerous. I've only once been asked to remove my boots before, when I was entering a mosque. I explained that I couldn't and the head bloke there told me not to worry, as the sick person was more important (he was as well – he was having a heart attack).

For a number of cultures, the book tells us that we should speak through the head male family member. Again, in practice I've never come across this. What I do tend to come across is a 7-year-old girl doing the translating for the whole family, which is why I think you have a lot of very 'grown-up' Asian girls. Language is always a problem, but I've found that although people tell me that they can't speak English, it is more probable that they don't have the confidence to try. I always try to talk to the patient, and then the relatives will translate the odd tricky word.

Various cultures also apparently have a taboo about men dealing with women. Again, something I have very little trouble with, as I'm not about to perform gynaecological examinations on my patients. The only time I've found that it might be an issue is with delivering babies, but if there isn't a woman around then I've found that people are just plain happy that there is someone around who knows what to do.

Although, having seen some of the ethnic grannies, and their attitudes to their granddaughter having a baby (something along the lines of, 'Stop being a wimp, and push it out') – I suspect that they have more idea about delivering babies than I do.

I can't see any culture being happy about having their women undress alone in front of strange men.

The book also has little sections on 'Customs around Death'. I'd like to think that we are so successful at treating people that we don't have to deal with it that often …

To be honest, a lot of the book is trying to teach us to suck eggs. As long as you have some semblance of common sense, and are polite and respectful to everyone (*except maybe drunks* …), then you shouldn't have any problems. If in doubt, ask, is my motto and I've learned quite a bit about other cultures just by asking the patient. I'm guessing that a lot of ethnic people have come across a fair bit of unconscious culture clash, and have developed their own strategies for dealing with it.

Please note how Reynolds has made a special effort to make everything positive in the above post. Note how he hasn't mentioned that some people have a huge chip on their shoulder about their culture, or how one culture seeks to emulate the worst qualities of another culture, or how a lot of non-drunken violence seems to be 'ethnic' vs. 'ethnic' violence. Just remember, I dislike everyone equally – I'm an equal opportunities cynic.

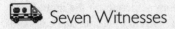 Seven Witnesses

I got sent to a job 'Female 14, collapse in back of police van'. Nothing suspicious about that – we often get people collapsing when they are being arrested/evicted/given final notice/have the repossession people around.

So there they were, in a side turning just off a main road. I parked up and could tell from the relaxed attitude of the police that it was probably nothing too serious. One look at the patient confirmed this – she would have to go to hospital (to protect everyone against being sued), but she was fine. I examined her vital signs and everything seemed to be normal.

The ambulance turns up and I'm just handing over the information about the patient when a woman in an SUV turns down the (now blocked) side turning. Realising that she was not going to fit between ambulance and police van, she started to reverse.

The ambulance crew, the four police officers and myself could all see what was going to happen next.

'STOP!' shouted the policeman.

'Stop!' shouted (slightly less loud) one of the ambulance crew.

'Oh dear …', I whispered under my breath.

CRUNCH ... went the (slightly battered) SUV against an absolutely pristine vintage Jaguar.

'FUCK!', went the driver of the Jaguar (quite understandably I feel).

'You *muppet*', muttered the police officer.

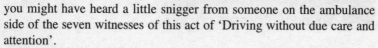

If you listened carefully you might have heard a little snigger from someone on the ambulance side of the seven witnesses of this act of 'Driving without due care and attention'.

Not from me ... obviously.

The patient went into the back of the ambulance, and I was left chatting to one of the policemen.

'I bet', I said, 'she doesn't have any insurance ...'

'Well', he replied, 'it seems that half the people around here seem to think it's optional'.

So, I have a little eavesdrop, and sure enough, she had no insurance. The driver tried to get angry at the police, but this soon vanished when she realised exactly how much trouble she was in.

(*In the great scheme of things, not that much, but enough to cause her some serious anguish.*)

The police officer spent the next 10 minutes rolling his eyes as he contemplated the paperwork he would have to do.

I tried to cheer him up by telling him that he had personally successfully detected two crimes.

I don't think it worked ...

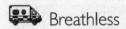 Breathless

The first of my two nights wasn't too bad, I didn't have to wait too long for the ambulances to turn up.

Shame about the second night ...

My first call was to a 71-year-old female with 'Difficulty in breathing'.

I turned up, and was met by loads of small children. Making my way to the patient, she was using her own home medication to try and ease her asthma.

It wasn't working.

A quick check of her oxygen levels showed 71%. It should be above 95% – anything below 85% makes me rather worried. You might guess that 71% really put the wind up me.

I spoke to the son while preparing my treatment. He'd obviously seen this before, as he gave as good a description of the patient and her problems as I would have expected from a medical professional. The patient had been in intensive care twice for her asthma. If an asthmatic ever ends up in ITU, then it shows how rapidly the patient's condition can deteriorate. At the very least, it makes me rather nervous that the patient will 'go off on me', and suddenly it turns into a respiratory arrest.

The medication was given to the patient, salbutamol – a nebulised drug administered straight into the lungs in the form of a gas. I was also giving her a large amount of pure oxygen in an effort to raise her blood oxygen levels.

Then I turned around and nearly fell over three rows of seven children, quietly sitting cross legged and staring up at me with big brown eyes.

'Don't mind them', said the patient's son, 'It's Eid, so the whole family are celebrating'.

'She', he said indicating the patient, 'has 21 grandchildren'.

I nearly suggested that this might be why she was breathless …

So now it was time to wait for the ambulance to take this very sick patient out of my responsibility and off to the hospital. I could see her getting more and more tired, although her oxygen levels were more normal (if only because I was blasting plenty of oxygen down her face-mask).

'Would you please leave the room', asked her son after talking to the patient, 'she needs to use the commode'.

Now, ask any medical professional when is the most dangerous time for your patient, and I would think that 99% of them would say that it's when they go to the toilet.

'Hmmm … alright', I said, 'but someone stays with her'.

I was standing right outside the room, waiting for a shout for help and then for me to bound into the room to resuscitate her in front of 21 small children.

Luckily for all involved she survived her encounter with the commode and we settled down to wait again.

While I was waiting, I was constantly reassessing the patient. I really wasn't happy to have her waiting so long because while my treatment was improving her condition somewhat, she needed better care than I could give.

The son offered me a cup of tea.

He knew how serious it was. He knew that the ambulances in the area were probably picking up drunks, and yet he understood my apologies and offered me a cup of tea.

Thankfully, the ambulance arrived and because of my earlier treatment, the patient had become a little more stable. She still needed urgent hospital care, but I wasn't worried that she would die on the back of the ambulance.

It had taken 45 minutes to get an ambulance to the patient. Sometimes I like it that when I'm on the FRU then I can get to a patient in time to actually make a difference.

I also love the drugs I carry – I don't need to use them much, but when I need them, they really do come in handy.

I hope everything turned out alright, because, as I followed the crew and the patient out to the ambulance, the son shook my hand and said, 'Thank you'.

… Waiting 45 minutes for his critically ill mum to get a proper ambulance, and still he thanked me.

 ## Soft, Wet Snooker Ball

The first job of the morning has stayed with me for the rest of the day.

– Warning: not for the faint of heart –

I was sent to a 'Male, 59, fitting – locked in empty bathroom'. I got there quickly, within 8 minutes, so already it was a 'successful' job.

As the person who met me opened the door to the flat I was overwhelmed with an intense and incredibly disgusting smell. At first I thought that it was the person opening the door (he was rather dishevelled and I've smelt breath that bad before), but no, the smell got stronger as I entered the flat.

There were four people there, all of them looked like the man who opened the door, and the state of the flat made me think that everyone in there was an alcoholic.

Sitting, or rather propped up, on the sofa was the man who had been fitting. His friends had managed to undo the door to the bathroom, and had manhandled him into the living room.

'He's been drinking – we were both drinking heavily yesterday', I was told.

'Fair enough', I said. 'Is he epileptic, or does he have alcoholic fits?'

'Both, I think', replied his friend.

Then I looked down.

Something the size of a snooker ball had rolled down the inside of his jeans and was sitting in front of him. It was brown, it was wet, and was rather horrible looking.

A pile of poo … his poo. A poo done after a night of heavy drinking.

Suddenly I realised where the smell was coming from …

I'm sure that most people realise that after a night on the town, the first poo you do can stink to high heaven. This was that epic poo. I imagine that there was a lot more of it smeared over the inside of his jeans. This is the sort of poo that would issue forth from the arse of Satan himself. It was the sort of poo that shouldn't be flushed away, but instead sealed in a barrel and buried in a place that has lots of warning signs pinned to the barbed wire fence surrounding it.

It really did smell that bad.

His friend (who actually didn't know him that well), picked up the poo with a bit of newspaper and ran it into the toilet.

I could hear him gagging from his new-found proximity to the toxic poo. When he came back into the room his face was an interesting shade of pale green, and there was a thin film of sweat upon his brow.

I treated the patient – actually quite a simple job. Then the ambulance crew turned up, and I pointed out that the patient's shoe was covered in his own sticky poo.

Carrying the patient down the stairs, the poo managed to get transferred from the shoe onto the shirt of one of the crew. He wasn't happy.

I stopped myself from laughing …

… *almost*.

The only problem is that I can still, several hours later, smell the rank stench of that demonic poo from hell. Actually, I can still taste the poo in the air.

I almost feel sorry for the nurses at the hospital …

The Humanity of Bystanders

Well that's the last time I say that I haven't had an interesting job all shift …

My final job of the day was to a 'Collapsed male in the street'. Unfortunately, Control were having a bit of a computer failure, so the job was given to me the 'old fashioned' way, by someone at Control telling me where to go.

'Collapsed in the street … he'll be drunk then', I joked.

No matter, I still raced to the scene as quickly as possible (I've mentioned this before, that what I get called for and what is actually wrong with the patient are often two very different things – so I always try to get to the job as quickly as possible).

The location wasn't exact, so I spent a bit longer than I would have liked peering down dark streets, looking for a man collapsed on the ground. Some people driving towards me told me that the patient was a bit further down the road.

My heart sank when I saw a huge crowd of people standing around a man lying flat on his back. My heart sank even more when I saw a man doing CPR on the patient.

I jumped out of my car, grabbed my bag and trauma shears and started cutting the patient's clothes off. A quick look at his face, and I didn't hold much hope for him.

'He was jogging, and just collapsed', said one of the men who had been performing CPR, 'he hit his head, we've been doing CPR at 100 compressions a minute'.

'Are you medically trained?' I asked.

'No', he replied, 'I'm a teacher, but I've done a first-aid course'.

'Well', I said, after glancing at the monitor, and noting that there was no activity in the heart at all, 'you were doing really good CPR, so you have given him the best chance he has for survival'.

I just wanted them to know that they were doing the right thing. I knew the patient had pretty much no chance of surviving this event, but that these strangers were trying their best renewed a bit of my faith in human nature.

The ambulance arrived only a few moments after I did, and as I looked at the driver, I could see by the expression on his face that he also realised how serious the situation was.

There was no time for any playing around, so we loaded the patient on the back of the ambulance, and took off for the hospital. I was 'bagging' the patient, while the ambulance attendant was continuing the CPR.

We arrived at the hospital, but there was nothing that they could do.

As he was out jogging, he didn't have any identification at all. We had also taken him to a different hospital than would be expected – it was not the closest hospital by distance, but it was the hospital that we could get to the quickest.

… So somewhere, there was probably a family wondering why their husband, or their father, or their brother, or their lover had not come home. They'll ring the local hospital, and they won't have heard of him, and it will only be when they go to the police that they will find out the truth.

I'm also aware that the bystanders who were doing CPR would probably have this event haunting them – I deal with sudden death a lot, but for these people, it was probably the first time they ever had someone die in front of them. I wish there was some way told them that I could have stayed and made sure that they were alright, and told them that I was proud of them and that they should be happy that they did the best that they could.

So, a traumatic event for everyone except for us ambulance and hospital staff. And to think that people ask us how we deal with jobs like this …

We later found out who he was. Seems like he was a really nice man, which makes his sudden death all the more sad. His family only found out after they went to the police when he didn't return home.

 ## Crying

'Two-month-old child – not waking up'.

'Shit!' I thought (*actually I may have said it*).

'Not waking up' could mean that the child was dead. There was something about the way the job was written up on the terminal screen that made me fear the worst.

I raced around there, brakepads burning, and swearing loudly at bus drivers who thought that it might be a good idea to pull out in front of me.

Two minutes thirty seconds later I screeched to a halt outside the house, bounding from the car, grabbing my kit and running into the house.

The baby was crying.

The ambulance crew turned up about 30 seconds later.

I was smiling, the crew were smiling, the mother was smiling. The only person not smiling was the crying baby.

But I was happy at that.

I like children who cry when they see me, it normally means that they aren't seriously ill. It's the quiet ones you have to watch out for.

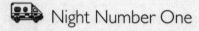 Night Number One

Bit of a busy night, partly I think due to the frost on the roads. I know that I was not able to drive too fast, as I was occasionally fishtailing across the road. The first job, aptly enough, was a man who had driven his car into a bus. The car was an utter mess, and I would have wanted to immobilise him in the car and have the fire service cut him out. I say *would have wanted* because once the crash was over, he'd run off ...

So I'm guessing that the car was either stolen, or more likely he just didn't have any insurance, road tax or a driving licence.

A couple of 'nothing' jobs, then another car accident. Some bright spark had decided to borrow his friend's car, and then lose control of it on our main 'A' road. The car, yet again was a write-off, and the driver kept telling me that he was going to 'get done', because he didn't have any insurance ... or a driving licence.

Can you see a pattern in the drivers from my area?

I then had to go to a 13-year-old child with a progressive and ultimately fatal disease. He was having difficulty in breathing because of a chest infection, and when I got there his breathing was incredibly irregular, and his oxygen levels were only 67% of what they should be. Even with high-flow oxygen his oxygen levels were only just adequate.

There was a bit of worry about what I was going to do if he stopped breathing, as he had a 'Do not resuscitate' order, but it was a year out of date.

Thankfully it never came to it, and I was very happy when the crew arrived to take the child to hospital.

My final job was a bit of a nasty one. A young man (a cleaner) was found not breathing in a local supermarket. The call woke me from a light sleep and, as I mentioned, I couldn't drive too quickly to the call. I got there as the ambulance crew arrived, and we were led through the warren of the supermarket by the cleaning supervisor.

The patient was large, covered in blood and vomit, and was not breathing. We attached our heart monitor and it showed no activity in the heart at all. In the process of doing CPR, everything got covered in bloody vomit. As I type this, my jacket is in a plastic bag, waiting to be taken home and washed.

We got him to hospital, but they were unable to save him.

Once more it was a patient who no-one seemed to know (no-one there knew his name, although they had been working with him for a couple of days), and I don't think he had any identification on him.

A tricky job for the police.

A busy night, but as my mum would say, 'At least it made the time go fast'.

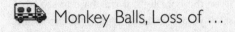 Monkey Balls, Loss of …

It is, to put it bluntly, cold enough to freeze the balls off a brass monkey, which is *really* cold.

No matter, it keeps the drunks off the street … well, it *mainly* keeps the drunks off the street …

I got sent to a '50-year-old man, fallen in street. Blood from ear'. The location was given as 'Outside Red Lion Public House'. I could guess what had happened.

I pulled up, leaving the headlights pointed at the patient, lying on the ground, covered by a blanket borrowed from the pub.

Surrounding him were:

A lot of police (about five or six officers).
Two sons, both of which were crying and worrying about their dad dying.
Some bystanders, most of them had come from the pub, and …
One off-duty fireman, who was clutching the patient's hand.

'Fair enough', I thought, 'best get to work'.

The lighting in the street was bad, but my headlights and some police torches made it a little better. The patient had been celebrating in the pub and had tripped over a kerb while trying to walk home. He had possibly been knocked out, and there was some blood coming out of his left ear.

The first thing that you think of when someone who has fallen has blood coming out their ear is that they may have fractured their skull. With a fractured skull you will sometimes get cerebrospinal fluid coming from their ear (cerebrospinal fluid is the liquid that your brain and spinal column float in, and should not be outside the body at all).

The standard test is that blood and CS fluid don't mix, so you'll see yellow streaks in the blood. Given the poor light it was hard to see, so I fell back on an old trick. You stick your (gloved) finger in the blood and if there is CS fluid in it, the blood will feel 'slick'.

The side-effect is that your gloves get covered in blood. It was cold. I wanted to wipe my nose. My gloves were right out, and I wouldn't like to wipe my nose on the cuff of my jacket because it's a disgusting thing to do, and also (mainly) because my jacket is horribly unclean.

The patient also had a large swelling on the back of his head and, because of the way that he had fallen, I couldn't rule out an injury to his neck. In a perfect world I would have liked to have put a cervical collar on him to immobilise his neck, but this is far from a perfect world. A cervical collar only really immobilises a patient if they want to be immobilised, in a drunken or combative patient this will often make them thrash around trying to get it off. So, often a better course of action is to tell them to lie nice and still and leave the collar off until you need to move them.

The off-duty fireman had obviously had a bit of first-aid training, because he was keeping the patient constantly talking. This was fine, as it meant I didn't have to talk to the patient too much, apart from assessing him, and getting his details.

The crowd were pretty well behaved; I kept hearing one of them moaning that the disabled ramp to the kerb was the reason behind the fall, and that they were 'bloody dangerous'. I didn't want to mention that walking while drunk was perhaps more of a contributing factor …

I threw another blanket over the patient because there was little else I could do until the ambulance turned up. Unfortunately, I'd been waiting a long time for ambulances all night, and I suspected that this would be the same.

My nose still threatened to drip on the patient.

Suddenly behind me was a flash of a high-visibility jacket, 'Excellent', I thought, 'the ambulance has turned up'.

But, no, it was one of our duty managers come to see how I was doing. They knew the ambulance would be some time, and wanted to make sure I was alright.

'Ah', he said, 'I can see you have everything under control', and left.

He could have wiped my nose for me …

By now I was losing sensation in various small, but important bits of my anatomy. I looked at my watch and saw that I'd been with the patient for over 30 minutes. I was cold, but at least I wasn't lying on the cold wet floor.

Finally the ambulance arrived; they had travelled from out of their area to attend this call, and I was very grateful for them turning up when they did. We put the collar on the patient, strapped him to a stretcher and loaded him into the back of the ambulance where it was much warmer, and I could remove my gloves and wipe my nose.

Can you see what was uppermost on my mind?

The patient was swiftly taken to hospital, and as I prepared to face the crowd of people and explain exactly why the ambulance took so long to arrive, I was instead mobbed by people who wanted to shake my hand and thank me. None of them were bothered by the 40 minutes it had taken the ambulance to arrive, and they were actually happy that we had done our jobs, accepting that as it was a Friday night we might be a bit busy.

It was only later that I found out that there had been another shooting in the area (some drunk men had been apparently thrown out of a pub, they then returned and fired a pistol through the pub windows, hitting a barman).

 Sickle Cell

I'd just done a job with a lovely patient suffering from a sickle cell crisis, but I was shocked when I heard from another crew how the hospital chose to treat her.

This post is one that I've been thinking about writing for at least a year, but I've always been a bit shy of writing it because it touches on possible racism. Just remember, I hate everyone, not just one type of person.

Sickle cell disease is a horrible illness; it results in massive pain, and because of the blood cells 'clumping' it can cause stroke, blindness, kidney failure, heart attacks and numerous other complications. The pain these patients feel is unbelievable.

The thing is, most of these patients are black.

Here is the problem that I have. There are a number of sufferers who are banned from certain emergency departments. There are legal orders that say a patient should not go to a specific A&E when they get a crisis. It's normally because the patient has caused trouble while waiting to be treated; I was an A&E nurse in North London for long enough to realise that some sickle cell disease patients are not saints, but …

In my personal experience, sickle cell disease patients are the only patients who get banned from departments. Drunks can be much more violent, yet they never seem to get banned. Some patients are 'Frequent flyers': they attend every day, use up more time and resources than those with sickle cell disease, yet they never seem to get banned. I've also personally witnessed nurses being hit, yet the patient still receives treatment, and is not banned.

While I understand that sickle cell disease patients can be demanding, they are in a huge amount of pain. Some are indeed opioid addicts, but my thoughts on the matter are that it isn't hurting me to give them painkillers, and that the stresses of withdrawal can cause a sickling crisis. However, it does seem that sickle cell patients are being discriminated against.

This affects the ambulance service in the following way: we might pick up a patient 200 yards from the local hospital, he has chest pain, and is in a lot of general all-over pain. If he is banned from that local hospital, we might have to travel miles to get him to a hospital that will accept him. If he has a heart attack or stroke in the back of the ambulance, is it our fault for bypassing a nearby hospital?

These patients often have a 'treatment protocol' at their hospital – this states the type of pain relief that they get, and who should be contacted to continue their treatment. These patients are often concerned that if they are not taken to their specialist centre (always miles away …) then the hospital that we do take them to will not have their treatment protocol.

Also, will we be called more because we are now carrying morphine and will maybe give it to patients, when their personalised treatment protocol states that they shouldn't have morphine at all?

In my opinion, sickle cell disease patients are treated poorly in A&E departments, and I don't think that it can be just that they are 'demanding' for their pain relief, or that they are personally 'annoying'. While a lot of these patients can be annoying, I think it's only because they are treated poorly to start with.

Disclaimer – I used to work in an A&E department with a huge population of sickle cell disease patients.

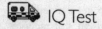 IQ Test

General practitioners (family doctors) are supposed to be intelligent … right?

So here is a question for you all, answers to the usual address on the back of a £10 note …

An elderly patient enters your surgery. She is asthmatic and is having real trouble in breathing. Do you?

(a) Start treating the asthma attack, giving the correct amount of treatment, then when she doesn't improve, call for an ambulance, keeping the patient on oxygen. You then take her vital signs, and observe her closely until the ambulance arrives. You even manage to phone the hospital to refer her to the correct speciality. Or …

(b) Give her the paediatric dose of the medicine (the dose you give to under-12s). When she doesn't get any better, you call an ambulance and sit her (without oxygen) out in the waiting room where her wheezing can entertain the toddlers playing there. You write a letter to the hospital, but as you haven't written any vital signs on it, you can't have even taken her pulse in the first place.

Warning, if you answer (b), you then might have to put up with a slightly miffed FRU person explaining that you might have just been a bit silly ...

There is a scarily large number of GPs who just cannot deal with anyone who might be seriously ill.

Still that's what the LAS are for, and also why we still rush on blue lights and sirens to patients who are being looked after at their GPs.

I could write an entire book about the silly things I've seen doctors do. But I'm of the opinion that I only ever see the results of poor workmanship. The good GPs must be better able to deal with patients without the need for regular ambulance attendance. The next post provided a balancing experience.

 ## How It Should Be Done

It was as if my prayers had been answered, a GP who today managed to balance the poor skills of yesterday's doctor.

I was sent to a 74-year-old male with difficulty in breathing and chest pain. My computer display told that me that the GP was going to remain with the patient.

I got there and was met by an apologetic GP who thought that the patient just had a chest infection, but while she was talking to him, the patient developed a possibly heart-related pain. She had tried treating him herself, but thought that the best thing was for him to have some further tests in hospital.

My assessment and treatment of the patient went without a hitch, and I agreed that although I also thought the pain was a consequence of his chest infection, it would be best for the patient to be assessed in the local A&E department.

As was the case yesterday the ambulance was 40 or more minutes in arriving, so I had a bit of a chat with the GP (who was rather pretty ...) and the patient (not so pretty). As there was nothing else the doctor could do with this patient, I let her leave the house to see her other patients.

A nice job, made easier by another health-care professional.

Just how it should be.

One day I'll have to start counting the number of good GP experiences along with the number of bad GP experiences just so I can get some empirical evidence to prove that there are plenty of good GPs out there.

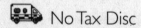 No Tax Disc

I was miles out of my area, but this was not a worry, as the sun was shining, the scenery was pretty (well ... prettier than Newham, not that that this is difficult) and there was some nice music on the radio.

Then the call came down my terminal. 'Male ?Suspended in car'. I consider it a personal strength that I was thinking 'Excellent! I can use my big trauma shears to break a window'.

I soon reached the car and was dismayed to find the passenger door open, and two bystanders watching the man intently.

'He's breathing', they said.

I tried to hide the disappointment that I wouldn't be smashing any windows.

Checking the patient, who was slumped over the passenger seat drooling like a baby, I immediately thought that it would be one of three things: he was either having a diabetic crisis, had just had a stroke or was just incredibly drunk.

A quick test of his blood sugar showed that he wasn't diabetic, a neurological assessment showed that he probably hadn't had a stroke (he was also younger than me, so a stroke would have been rather surprising). This left the last option … he was drunk.

Once more I found myself cursing my own particular disability – that I can't smell alcohol. Thankfully, the ambulance crew turned up and let me know that he did indeed stink of booze.

The crew loaded him onto the ambulance, which was tricky as he could hardly walk, while I turned off the engine to his car, amazed that he had driven as far as he had without crashing into something. He was also lucky he'd stopped when he did, as less than 100 metres away was a main road with a speed limit of 50 m.p.h.

We called the police, who duly arrested him. Meanwhile he kept saying that all he wanted to do was die …

… I would think that his desire to die would only increase as his hangover hits him in the police cell. I got the impression that the reason he was drunk was because he had had an argument with his family.

Somehow I don't think that getting arrested for drink driving (oh, and his tax disc was out of date as well) will do him any good with his family.

See, I keep telling people that getting pissed solves nothing. But do they listen to me? Do they buggery …

I had to make a police statement before going back to work, returning just in time to get called to a Bed and Breakfast where an alcoholic was having a panic attack.

Gah!

Forty stone patient.

On the floor.

3 hours on scene.

Tears, swearing, pain and blood.

Up to 9 staff on scene at once.

I am f*****g knackered. Maybe a more detailed post tomorrow, maybe not.

Gah …

I never did write a longer post about that job. So now is my chance.

The patient weighed around 42 stone and was stuck on the toilet – this is when I arrived. In an effort to get her up she managed to slip onto the floor, which was better for her as the blood flow to her legs returned. An ambulance crew turned up and we had a little conference about what to do. The fire service were asked to attend, but they decided not to, as it's now against their policy to help us lift heavy patients. By now the family were starting to get angry at the patient.

Our control suggested a 'Mangar Elk' which is a lifting aid that uses compressed air to raise patients off the floor. So along came a Duty Officer and a Training Officer with the bit of kit and the expertise to use it.

Our complex boss turned up and fed the patient some chocolate biscuits – we looked at him in a most stern manner and he left.

We phoned the local hospital to pre-warn them and they tried to refuse the patient. Our Duty Officer had a chat with them on the phone and after much to'ing and fro'ing they agreed to accept her.

The patient was frightened about leaving the house. The family were getting more and more annoyed at the patient …

... Then the patient's drunk partner turned up.

After several attempts we managed to get the patient out of the house and into the ambulance.

Just.

 Tickets

I've checked with my sources, and the story is true.

At Poplar ambulance station there is no room to park. The station itself is tiny, barely bigger than a Portakabin. There is a big metal fence and electric gate around it. There is minimal parking.

So the ambulances park out on the street – if they didn't then every emergency call would be delayed by minutes as the crews wait for the gate to open and then manoeuvre the ambulances out. This would be very bad for the patients (and more importantly, extremely bad for our ORCON times).

There is nowhere else to park.

So ... a couple of days ago the ambulances all got parking tickets.

Apparently there is a man who lives in one of the nearby tower blocks who keeps complaining because his daughter nearly had an accident pulling out of the turning.

So a nice man from the council (or a parking warden) came around and put tickets on the ambulances. In his defence he did try to not ticket them by telling the crews to drive around the block ...

The ambulance crews find this all very amusing.

(*We are, by our driving exemptions, allowed to park where we like as long as it's not 'dangerous'; we are guessing that this man has complained so much the council has been spurred into action.*)

It's not the first time this has happened, and it won't be the last. I feel sorry for the warden who has to give the tickets — it can't do much for the reputation of ticket wardens to be seen sticking one on an ambulance.

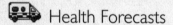 ## Health Forecasts

Did you know that the Meteorological Office offers 'health forecasts'? We got a memo from them (via our office) about a predicted increase in paediatric respiratory infections.

No kidding! For 2 days all I attended were patients with chest infections.

Then on Friday all but two of my 13 calls were faints, or epileptic fits. I'm left wondering if it is something in the weather that caused that little spike.

Oh, I also attended three schools on Friday (one epileptic and two fainters), while normally I wouldn't see that many schools in a month.

A strange day.

Is it any wonder us ambulance folk are a superstitious lot?

We Sometimes Do Good Work

We deal with a lot of crap jobs on a day to day basis, but when we are really needed I think we do a bloody good job.

One of the people injured in the London bombings is getting married this weekend.

The thing that gets me is this quote.

'As well as losing both feet in the bombing, Ms Hicks lost 75 per cent of her blood and her heart stopped twice on the way to the hospital.'

That means that an ambulance crew successfully resuscitated her twice – long enough to get her to hospital – and that because of that unnamed crew she is now alive and getting married. Its stories like that which make me happy to do the work that I do; sometimes we can make a difference.

I was talking about this story with one of my station-mates. He'd seen the report on the television and was astounded – not only because he had been the one to run her into hospital, but also because he thought that she would have died. So congratulations to the crew involved, Brian Robinson and Lisa Isaacs – you did us all proud.

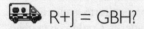 R+J = GBH?

'Warning: Assailant may still be on scene, wait for police' had apparently flashed up on my computer screen. Unfortunately, it had done so silently, so the first I saw it I was pulling up outside the house. Luckily, I was pulling up to the house which had a police car outside it.

I entered a house that was full of four generations of Bangladeshi people who were mainly shouting at each other and the two beleaguered police officers. Quite rightly, so I thought as I looked at the 15-year-old boy, I had been called to treat. He had been hit around the head with a metal bar. Thankfully, his injuries were fairly minor, although there was a possibility that he had broken his elbow.

Unfortunately, this was one of those nights where ambulances were a bit thin on the ground, so I was waiting for some time. At least this meant I was able to get the reasoning behind what had been happening.

There were two families, one with a daughter, the other had a son (my patient). He had apparently offered her a place to sleep after she had been in an argument with her family. This had then turned into a feud that had dragged on via school bullying. The police had just told everyone present that they would be going around the other family's house to arrest people when the father of this family turned up.

To say there was a lot of shouting would be an understatement. There was also a procession of stern young men in the garden having a bit of a war council, mobile phones clamped to ears as they called in reinforcements. The atmosphere was getting a trifle warm for my liking.

Luckily the police were able to calm the situation down somewhat, a bit tricky when the father was shouting about how he was going to burn the other family's house down if they didn't do anything. Meanwhile, large numbers of youths were appearing and disappearing into the night. I thought that there was a real chance of things turning nasty.

'Sir', said one of the policemen, 'I don't wish to insult, or cause offence, but normally with this kind of trouble it is one cultural group against another, but in this case both parties are Bangladeshi. Could you explain that to me?'

One of the calmer young men replied, 'That's how it *used* to be, now everyone is fighting everyone else, and race doesn't matter'.

By now I had the real impression of angry villagers with pitchforks and flaming torches gathering. Thankfully, I was rescued by both police backup and an ambulance to take the injured party away to hospital.

'Control', I called up on my radio, 'just to make you aware, if there are any assaults in this part of my patch, don't let crews go in without police escort, because it might kick off big time'.

'Roger that EC50, I'll make a note'.

I don't think that there was any trouble that night, but it is a little hard to lynch someone if you (or they) have been arrested …

🚑 The Friday Before Christmas

It's the busiest night of the year for us, as everyone goes out and gets drunk at their work Christmas party. I don't know what's going on at the moment, but it's barely 21:00 and already we are at 3 500 or more calls.

We normally do 3 500 calls in a day, so how many more will we squeeze in over the next 3 hours?

My first job was to an alcoholic having had a fit. A common symptom of being an alcoholic is having fits. I'd say that of the two types of fits that we go to, I tend to see more alcoholic fits than epileptic fits. I don't have any numbers to prove it, but it just seems right in my experience.

This job was typical. I had to step over the detritus on the carpet, the packets of tobacco, the trainers and the half-eaten takeaway container. I saw my patient sitting on a chair, being sick. He was vomiting directly onto the living room floor, his wife didn't see fit to put a bucket under the stream of vomit.

Lovely.

Like a lot of our regular alcoholic customers, he was topless, while his tracksuit bottoms were stained with … well I wouldn't like to guess, but they were stained with something. Homemade tattoos covered his chest, arms and hands, and in between bouts of vomiting he would continue making a roll-up cigarette.

'Can I turn the living room light on?' I asked the wife.

'Don't work', she said back to me in a voice that I guessed had been arguing with her husband just before I'd arrived.

I guessed this because she then started arguing with him again.

While the living room had a nice stereo, a reasonable television (satellite included) and a gaming console, they didn't have a light bulb.

He didn't want to go to hospital, but I always think of the potential headlines in the paper the next day 'Ambulance leave patient to die', so the crew and I persuaded him to go to hospital for a 'check-up'.

You know why? No-one ever lost their job by taking a patient to hospital.

'I don't want to waste their time', he mumbled, 'I'm just an alcoholic'.

'It's alright mate', I replied, 'we look after everyone, even alcoholics'.

There were around 5 200 jobs that day up to midnight and over 1 000 calls before 3 a.m. the following morning.

 Panic on the Streets of London

When I'm at a 'job' I don't panic, it's part of my job description to keep control of a situation and to stop other people from running around like headless chickens. Sometimes I will have to be forceful, or act quickly, but I *never* panic.

I got a job, '14-month-old child, floppy and lifeless'.

'Fuck', I thought.

It was in a part of my patch I'm not very familiar with – new buildings on the Isle of Dogs. The address was given as 'Flat 1, Rose House, Starling Road'.

This is obviously not the address I was given, I do respect patient confidentiality after all.

I rushed to Starling Road, a new estate with loads of buildings, none of which seemed to be marked.

'Fuck', I thought.

If a child is floppy or lifeless, then the chances are it is either *very* ill, or is dead.

I sped up and down the road. I spotted some of the names of the flats in tiny writing, on little blue plaques, many of them pointing away from the road. My pulse started to race. It had taken me 4 minutes to reach the area, but how much longer would it take me to locate the potentially very sick child?

I found 'Lilac House', 'Lily House' and 'Tulip House', but I couldn't find 'Rose House'.

Now I was starting to panic. Was I being stupid? Had I driven past it? Was the baby dead, and if it was, was it because I couldn't find the fucking house?

I could feel the sweat soaking my back, without being able to get to the patient there was nothing I could do. I cursed the council, the builders, the architects – everyone who had thought that putting pretty but bloody useless signs on the buildings was a good idea.

I got Control to ring the parents back, the mother came out to meet me. 'Rose House' was behind another block of flats, behind a road barrier. The name plaque had text around an inch high, pointing away from the road.

Luckily the baby only had a runny nose.

I hated it though, the utter feeling of helplessness that comes with being unable to find a patient – the sweating, the raised pulse and the vaguely sick feeling in the bottom of the stomach as you race up and down a street in the dark trying to find the right location.

Please. If any architects, builders, council planners or sign writers read this, make the signs bigger. Make them so I can read them at night. Make them so that if it is *your* relative that is critically ill, I can find them before it is too late.

I got a comment from an architect explaining that they get no say in the marking of the houses they design – so I'd like to apologise for including them in this rant. However, can I then take the opportunity to shout at architects who think that spiral staircases are a good idea? If you ever

269

try to carry a patient down a spiral staircase you'll find that it's bloody hard work, if not impossible.

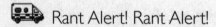 Rant Alert! Rant Alert!

The past couple of nights I've gone to calls where I've wanted to grab some parents and shake some common sense into them. Instead, I have to be polite, if only for the quiet life.

Apologies – judgemental post ahoy!

'Madam', I hear myself say, 'the reason that your four children have asthma may well have something to do with the four packs of cigarettes I see sitting on the sofa. When you were at the antenatal classes, and they told you the effects of smoking on your children, did you think that they just liked to hear the sound of their own voices? Or, did you in an uncharacteristic spark of intelligence, think that they may just be the agents of some vast conspiracy financed by the companies who make nicotine patches?

'You might also consider that the reason all your children have runny noses, is because smoking makes them less likely to fight off respiratory infections. You might not know this, but asthma kills people, and that includes children. You are condemning them to a shortened life of ill health and hospital visits, all so that you can feed your oral fixation.'

To other parents I might say …

'So, when you got an electric shock from the uninsulated wire poking from that hole in the wall, you didn't think of … I don't know … let's say … protecting your children by having it fixed? Sure, it might cost you a bit of money, but at least your toddler wouldn't now be in hospital to make sure that being electrocuted by mains electricity didn't do any permanent harm'.

'I like that toy', I'd say to another mother of two, 'I particularly like the little bite-sized bits of plastic that are strewn over the floor. Yes, I understand that your oldest child is a mite untidy … but when your 18-month-old is choking to death on a toy soldier, some might consider it too late to tidy up. I know it's hard to teach 6-year-olds to clean up after themselves, especially one who seems to be happier peeling your wallpaper off the wall while you shout at him to "stop fuckin' doin' that!" Perhaps you might try a different approach? In answer to your question, no you can't smoke in the back of the ambulance'.

To one angry parent I might say …

'So your baby stopped breathing for 5 minutes … and I took over half an hour to come? Well, I'd like to show you the time you called, and how it took me only 2 minutes to get here, but I think the computer display in my car might confuse you. Besides, I'm not delivering your pizza, you don't get your money back if I'm longer than 30 minutes. Still, back to the baby – she's breathing alright now, perhaps I could interest you in employment in the ambulance service, as you seem to have a Christ-like ability to get children breathing again. Oh, sorry, baby is a 'he' not a 'she'? Sorry, I was confused at the two hoop earrings, the three necklaces, and the rings – all at under 6 months. Why stop there? Maybe they would like their belly button pierced as well? Still I suppose Shayne is a manly name – funny way of spelling it though. Never mind, we're off to hospital now, don't forget your fags'.

And don't forget those who may have strange priorities …

'JESUS CHRIST! Aren't the 6-foot Santas and inflatable snowmen supposed to be outside the house? I thought I was going to get mugged by a madman in red. Nice television though, if you could just turn the volume down a little so I can hear what you are saying to me. Yes Tyler is an adorable 8-year-old, even if he did injure himself smashing his neighbour's windows. Why, might I ask are his hands that colour? Ah, how silly of me, paint from his self-expression in the fine art of graffiti. Did you consider a taxi to take you the 400 yards to hospital? You can't afford one? Ever think of selling the TV? Or maybe the Santa? Yes, yes, you can bring your cigarettes'.

And breathe … and relax …

It was supposed to end at the first paragraph, but I just kept rolling … Oops.

I'm not normally so hateful … Honest.

Why I Hate Smoking Parents

This followed a bit of a naughty post about mothers smoking in front of their children – while pregnant. In it I try to explain why I'm a bit of a health Nazi about smoking in front of children.

From my nursing days – a reason why I hate people who smoke around children.

Eight-year-old girls don't look like they are sleeping when they are dead. At least not after over an hour of trying to save her life from an ultimately fatal asthma attack.

We were all distressed, she had been gasping for breath when the ambulance crew had 'blued' her straight into Resus'. Asthma nebulisers hadn't worked, and all anyone could fixate on was her chest desperately trying to pull air into her lungs.

She died a frightening and painful death.

The doctor and I went to tell her parents. They were in the relatives' room; I could barely see them as I walked in – clouds of smoke filled the air.

They cried, of course they cried.

Then they went outside and had a cigarette.

Then they came back inside the Resus' room and sat with her body.

The father lit up another cigarette.

This is why I hate asthma; this is why I hate people who smoke when they are pregnant; this is why I hate people who smoke around children. Kill yourself if you want to, but don't kill your kids.

There are jobs that haunt you. This was one of them. Try calming down an 8-year-old girl who is dying in front of you because they can't breathe. Then try and forget about it. I did a cot death once, beside the cot was a full ashtray. Sure, the parents are punished by the death of their child. But it doesn't help the child …

… As I typed this I realised that I was clenching my teeth.

 Can't be Bothered

I've just come from a call to one of my semi-regulars. He's alcoholic, has a stomach ulcer and is as thin as a rake. He is sitting in a filthy kitchen surrounded by empty bottles of cheap booze.

He's 26 years old.

His friend, of the same age, is also an alcoholic. He has pancreatitis.

Asked if they want to try a rehab' programme, I was told that they weren't interested.

I've got to confess, it made me angry. Two lives being washed away with bottles of cheap cider.

'So you want to die?' I asked.

They didn't have an answer.

Now I just want to hit something.

Anger for all the usual reasons – that I hate to see people throwing their lives away.

273

 Spaces

Sleep deprivation does funny things to my mind.

I'm having a bit of an insomnia moment, so I turn on the television and randomly tune it to various stations. I come across the 'extreme sports' channel, and watch a film about skateboarders and parkour runners. As I'm watching them using steps, guard rails, benches, ramps, statues and other street furniture to make their way across town in an interesting way, I start to wonder if they see the city in a different way to the rest of us. Do they see jumps, 'grinds' and the like on an almost unconscious level?

Then I start thinking about how I see the place where I work. I see it on three different levels. I see the streets as a map. Main roads to use in order to get to the different areas of town, the junctions that I always seem to be taking, turning left to get to the police station, turning right to head towards Forest Gate. Turning right here to get to Leyton, or straight on towards Stratford. It's all there in my head in the white and yellow of the A to Z. This is the way I think of Newham as I'm going to a job.

The other way that I think of the streets is as I'm trying to make my way through the traffic. I stop seeing cars and lorries as vehicles. Instead, I'm watching the spaces that they make. I'm watching the patterns they make in the road ahead. I'm unconsciously aware of where the drivers are looking: have they seen me or not? The way the vehicles move is also in my mind. Are they hesitant? If they are then there is a good chance that they will stop suddenly. Are they speeding? In that case they may overtake the car that has seen me and has pulled over. I spend my time seeing, and aiming for the spaces.

Finally, I see Newham in terms of the patients I have treated. Over there was the 34-year-old who dropped dead playing football. Across the road is one of our regulars, a lovely old lady with a list of ailments as long as your arm. That street I'm about to pull into had the drunk who didn't notice that he had a broken hand. Now I'm cruising past the road that a 12-year-old died in. A hundred yards from where I'm eating my McBagel is where the teenager got stabbed after the Notting Hill carnival. Every street has a story, and some memories are always triggered as I drive past them. For me, Newham is full of ghosts.

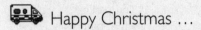 Happy Christmas …

Just been to a young woman in her late 20s.

Deceased.

Leaves behind two children.

Happy Christmas.

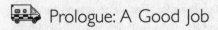

Two a.m. and we are standing on the side of the road waiting for the fire service to take the top off the car in front of us. The wind whistles across the flats making us all shiver despite our fleeces and jackets.

Two cars have been involved in a high-speed road traffic accident (RTA), the parked car that was hit has been shunted forward leaving ten-yard-long skid marks. The cars aren't too damaged but the seats inside have shifted around, trapping the occupants.

There are seven ambulances here, four fire trucks, half a dozen police and three ambulance officers with clipboards. There are eight patients, all but one need cutting from the cars and collaring and boarding. The only woman involved is 'walking wounded'.

The reason that it is taking so long for our car to get its lid removed by the fire service is because of the position of one of the patients inside. He looks rather unwell and the crew looking after him really would like to get to him sooner rather than later.

Our ambulance was fourth on scene. When I arrived I spoke to a stationmate to see what he wanted us to do, who he wanted us to look after. Normally he is the station clown, now he's all serious and professional, no fake beards or silly glasses.

Everyone gets checked over, all the ambulance crews are calm, it's serious but it doesn't look like anyone is about to die; more a case of being careful moving the patients 'just in case'.

The roof comes off the car and with the help of another crew and some firefighters we get our patient out safely and strapped to a board. He is freezing cold. He is not wearing warm clothing so the delay in getting him out and the terrible weather have us concerned for his body temperature.

We are in a new ambulance so the heater works. Turning it up to full we are soon sweating as we assess the patient and prepare for transport.

I get on the radio to pre-alert the hospital. For some reason the radio isn't working properly and our Control can't hear me, so I use my phone instead. Thankfully it works.

I travel a mile over speed-bumps to get to the hospital; there is no other route and every bump makes me aware of my patient in the back being jostled around. It's not the first time that I curse the council.

After all our patients are safe at the hospital we stand outside and laugh and joke. We reconstruct the accident, we talk about the more injured ones and we mock the driving skills of one of the officers.

We occasionally help people.

It's a good job sometimes.

PART 2

Introduction

I'm not special. All I am is one of the faceless people who work for an ambulance service. If you are lucky you'll never meet me in a professional capacity. Most of the time you won't even think about us; perhaps only occasionally sparing a thought for our work when an ambulance whizzes past you on the street, lights flashing and sirens sounding.

This book is a series of snapshots from the life of one ambulance worker. For the past few years I have been writing about ambulance work on the internet, regularly updating my website. From around the world people have come to read, and comment on, the sorts of jobs that I go to on a daily basis.

This book is not special – there are no tales of heroics, no exciting derring-do, nothing to compare with what the dramas on TV and film would have us believe. This is what ambulance staff the world over deal with day in and day out.

This is a book that lets you understand some of the situations that ambulance staff encounter every day, some of the pressures, and some of the humour that we use to let off steam.

Every time I talk about a patient in this book that situation has happened for real, to a real person.

Taxi

The staffing of ambulances at the moment is ... to put it bluntly ... poor.

Working on the fast response unit (FRU – a car that is designed to get to the sickest patients quickly) means that I often get to an emergency call within minutes of it being made. Unfortunately, with so few ambulances on the road, the patient and I are often left staring at each other for long periods of time; in a couple of cases up to an hour.

I was sent to a young man having an asthma attack. It was late at night, and he had been queuing to get into a nightclub when he had started to feel his breathing getting tight, the sign of an asthma attack, so had headed to a taxi office in order to go home. Unfortunately, his asthma progressed and so an ambulance was called. What he got was me, on my own, in a car.

After dealing with the drunken group of teenage girls that had taken time out of waiting for a cab to start loudly 'caring' for my patient, I started my assessment. It was a cold night so I sat the young man in the taxi office and listened to his chest. I could hear a nice loud wheezing from his lungs so I started him on the first dose of our asthma medication. I got his details and checked his vital signs, and waited for the ambulance to turn up.

It takes between five and ten minutes for the asthma medication to finish, and by the end of it there was still no ambulance.

I listened to his chest again, still an audible wheeze, so I gave him a second dose of the medication. So there he was, sitting in a cab office at three in the morning with a mask over his face, 'smoke' pouring from it, and all around us were intoxicated people getting cabs home.

It was not very dignified.

We started chatting, and I was impressed by this polite young man with good manners and common sense. The second medication finished and so we continued to wait, and wait, and wait for the ambulance. I phoned up my Control and asked if there was an ambulance assigned.

'Sorry EC50, we are still holding calls in that area.'

I was on my own with this patient for the foreseeable future.

Sometimes I can transport a patient myself to hospital, but it's not *technically* allowed. Actually, we've been told that we shouldn't do it at all, but in some cases I think I'm doing the right thing for the patient. So I will load them into the car (which only has the front passenger seat, the rest of the car is taken up by equipment) and nip into the nearest hospital. Control is often happy for me to do this, as it means one less job that it needs to send a proper ambulance to.

I couldn't transport this patient, though, because he wanted to go to his local hospital, which would mean driving past two other emergency departments and out of my area. I couldn't see Control, or my bosses, being too happy with that.

So the patient, at his insistence, got a *cab* to hospital. The double dose of medicine had cleared his lungs up nicely, but he would probably need some short-term steroid treatment. I rechecked my assessment of him, and was happy that his physical condition was good enough for him to get a cab to hospital. I wasn't happy, though, that there was no ambulance for this patient who actually warranted one.

As I write this I wonder what would have happened if he hadn't responded to the medication that I gave him.

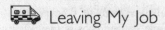 Leaving My Job

I think I'm going to be leaving my job soon.

I went to a six-month-old baby with possible meningitis. The baby had the right sort of rash (although it was only on the back of the knee and, after checking, nowhere else). It had a temperature, but was one of the happiest, most alert children I've ever had the pleasure of meeting. It just didn't *seem* as if it had meningitis, and trust me, I've seen a fair few children and adults with it so I have a pretty good idea what it looks like.

Then, as in the past, I was left waiting for an ambulance.

For around 45 minutes.

There was no way I was going to be able to transport the patient in my car. It's just not equipped to carry such a small child. We don't have baby seats and as the family didn't have a car they didn't have one either.

So the family ended up phoning a friend to take them to the hospital. The ambulance turned up just as they were getting into their friend's car.

All I had going through my head was the potential newspaper headline 'No Ambulance For Baby Dying Of Killer Bug!'

Later that night I went to a woman who was having an extremely painful miscarriage. There is nothing I can do for that on scene, the patient needs to be in hospital. Thankfully the ambulance wasn't too far behind me, but if I had been waiting on scene then it would have been a very awkward and distressing wait (again, because of the pain, it would have been impossible to transport her in my car).

More and more I'm looking at my watch as an ambulance fails to arrive. It's only a matter of time before I have someone die in front of me while waiting for an ambulance.

So, I'm seriously considering leaving the FRU and going back to work on an ambulance. That way I can pick up sick people, and take them to where they need to be: a hospital.

So after the holiday season, I think I'll be sending a memo up to the office asking to return to my ambulance role.

Zafira

I'm not perfect.

I arrived at work to find that my FRU car was nowhere to be seen. There was no one on the early shift, so where had *my* car got to?

The week before a friend of mine had had an accident in the Newham FRU car (in front of a load of police officers, which had given them some amusement I would imagine). So the car that I would normally use was being borrowed by Newham station.

So the plan was for me to get picked up at my station by a station officer, go to Newham, get the keys to the brand-new Vauxhall Zafira, return to my station with the car and start working.

The station officer met me and drove me down to Newham station. He asked me, because I was leaving my secondment on the FRU, if I could write up my thoughts on what was good, bad and what could be improved about it.

I told him that I'd be more than happy to point him in the direction of where my thoughts lay.

The brand-new Zafira was parked in the garage at Newham so I hopped behind the wheel and, after some struggling with the new design of handbrake, managed to reverse it out and into the parking area.

Where to the absolute horror of the station officer I drove into another car.

Oops.

Luckily there was no damage to the Zafira (which had less than 600 miles on the clock) and very slight, if any, damage to the other car.

The first accident I had in over 18 months and it was in front of a station officer ...

Not a good start to the shift.

My thoughts on the Zafira are these: if you wanted a *rapid* response vehicle, the Zafira shouldn't have been chosen. It is too top heavy and wallows like a hippo in thick mud. The acceleration is awful, you hit the pedal and it takes one and a half seconds before the diesel engine gives you any sort of power. It is comfortable to pootle around town in, and the high-up viewing position is quite nice.

But there is no way that it could be considered a 'Fast' car.

I think the reason why we have them is because they are able to carry patients, and I imagine that soon FRU drivers will be asked to take the coughs and colds that we see so much of to hospital.

☕ NYE Night

New Year's night was a busy one for the London Ambulance Service. There were *38* stabbings over the course of the night. I spoke to my workmate who was on the FRU that night; he attended four stabbings one after another.

By 5 a.m. there had been in excess of 2000 calls (we normally do a shade under 4000 calls over 24 hours).

On the television one of our top-ranking management people described the night as 'horrific', which I would say is a pretty fair assessment.

I am extremely glad I wasn't working that shift.

🚑 Ten Deep Breaths

The call details appeared on the computer terminal in the FRU:

'Nineteen-year-old male – Patient has lump on ribs – difficulty in breathing.'

Halfway to the address, a private house, my screen was updated:

'Patient has taken cocaine.'

I was met at the front door by a young male, stripped to the waist and obviously agitated.

'Comein, myribsfeelfunny, andmyshoulderbladesdon'tfeelright.'

'Slow down,' I said, taking his pulse – 110, a bit on the high side, but he was bouncing off the walls.

'My ribs man! They don't feel right! Have a feel.' He then started running his hands up and down his chest.

'Have you fallen over? Been hit? Anything unusual happened?' I asked.

'No man – just feel them ... FEEL THEM!'

'Look, you need to calm down,' I replied. 'I can't do anything while you are hopping all over the place.'

He started shouting, 'FEEL THEM! JUST FUCKIN' FEEL THEM!'

He turned his back to me, indicating that I should feel his normal-looking ribs.

A sudden wave of anger passed over me – it was all I could do to not punch him in the back. I examined his ribs; they felt perfectly normal to me.

'There,' I said, 'your ribs are fine.'

'What about my shoulder blades man?'

'Look, you've taken cocaine right? You are feeling paranoid, it's normal, just try to relax a little.'

'WHAT ... ABOUT ... MY ... FUCKIN' ... SHOULDER BLADES!'

He turned his back on me again. I gritted my teeth and grabbed his shoulder blades. 'They are fine. Now. Sit. Down.'

He sat down. Then he stood up, then he paced around the kitchen, then he did a few circuits of the sofa, then he sat down again, then he stood up and hopped around a bit. I was getting tired just watching him.

'Look,' I said trying to calm him, and me, down, 'is this the first time you've taken cocaine?'

'No man!'

'OK, well if you want we can take you to the hospital, get you checked out if you'd like?'

'NO!' he shouted. 'I'm not going to hospital.'

Fine, I thought, not that the hospital will thank me.

'OK mate, then are you alone in the house?'

'Nah, my dad's asleep upstairs.'

'Well, I'd like to have a chat with him, so he can keep an eye on you.'

'NO! Get out of my house.' He started advancing towards me. 'No hospital, no waking my dad up, just get the fuck out of my house!'

I left the house. While a fight with the patient would have done absolute wonders for my stress levels, it certainly wasn't worth the hassle, the risk of injury and, most importantly, the paperwork.

But what should I do now? If a patient isn't transported then we should leave a copy of our patient report form with them. Should I post it through the letterbox? The problem with that was if his father saw the report I'd be breaching patient confidentiality. I guessed that the police wouldn't be too interested in paying him a visit either. So I left the form sitting in my car – there was little else I could do for him, as he didn't want help.

I sat in my car, filled out my forms and took a couple of deep breaths. It would be a long Christmas ...

 Taxi?

I've had a couple of people send me a story that appeared in the newspapers.

Nursing staff from a Telford hospital have been accused of using an ambulance as a taxi after a night out.

It was claimed some of the nursing staff got into an ambulance outside The Swan in Ironbridge on Sunday.

The ambulance service has found a crew did provide unauthorised transport to staff but said it was not in operation and returning to base at the time.

To be honest this tends to happen a bit with nurses asking if you can give them a lift to the train station and the like. You tell the nurse 'Hop in the back, we'll give you a lift – if we get a call you'll have to hop out again.' It helps keep relations good between the hospital staff and ourselves. It doesn't hurt anyone and it definitely doesn't remove an ambulance from service.

In fact, it can do good. A crew I know was giving a nurse a lift to the train station after her shift finished when they then got a call to a cardiac arrest and the nurse was able to help out. As long as the crew wasn't refusing calls then I can't see the harm in it. In London I'd imagine that our Control would love it as it would mean we are out roaming rather than sitting on station, something our management is eager for us to do.

And if I'm going to spend all shift taxiing drunks around, I don't see why we can't sometimes help out the poor buggers who work their fingers to the bone looking after those same drunks.

I wonder if the person who complained is the sort who expects an ambulance to turn up seconds after they've cut their finger?

 Chickenpox

I went to two cases of adult chickenpox last night. The hospital says that there was another adult with chickenpox the day before that. It seems like we have a little outbreak here.

As both my patients were Nigerian, I have a sneaky feeling that the big (mainly Nigerian) church in Newham may be where the disease was spread and the timing of the symptoms would support this.

As one of the families had school-age children with the disease, I'm going to guess that a lot of children will be ill over the next few days.

Off the top of my head, I can't remember if I have been vaccinated against chickenpox – but I do know that I had it twice when I was a child, both times at Christmas.

 Rough

It was cold, it was dark and it was raining the sort of thin greasy rain that soaks straight through your clothes. I was making my way to one of the Docklands Light Railway stations for a 'Male – collapsed, caller not willing to approach patient.' I'd been to this station in the last week for a hoax call and I wasn't sure if this was a repeat performance.

At the bottom of the stairs just sheltered from the rain was a young man in his twenties, dirty, dressed in filthy clothes and curled up next to a plastic bag. Standing over him was another man, this one dressed in a suit, looking a bit concerned.

(The London borough of Tower Hamlets has both the richest and the poorest population in London.)

'He's just laying there, not talking,' the smartly dressed man said. 'I didn't really know what to do ...'

I let him know that I'd take care of the patient, and that he had done the right thing and could go home.

It was just me and the patient. Given the way he looked it was a reasonable assumption that he was homeless. If he was homeless then there was a reasonable assumption that he was drunk and given that he was in such a public place there was a chance that there was something physically wrong with him.

I attempted to wake him up – he was keeping his eyes closed when I tried to open them, so I knew that he wasn't really unconscious.

'Look mate,' I said, 'if you don't open your eyes, I'll have to check your blood sugar, which means poking a needle into your finger. If you open your eyes then I won't have to do that.'

No response.

So I checked his blood sugar along with the rest of his vital signs; everything was fine.

I crouched down opposite him.

'Look, you can open your eyes and talk to me you know – we'll still take you to hospital. To be honest, I can't blame you, an A&E waiting room has got to be a pretty good option on a crappy night like this.'

Some commuters walked between us; they didn't look at us. I looked in his plastic bag; there was a sociology textbook.

'Sociology? I could never enjoy reading that sort of thing.'

He opened his eyes. ''S'all right.'

Excellent. He was talking to me, which meant that the paranoid voice in the back of my head telling me that he might be seriously ill could shut up. It is something that always worries me – that despite my experience I'd miss something serious on a drunk or homeless guy.

We had a little chat while I was waiting for the ambulance to arrive. He'd been a rough sleeper for two years; he admitted to drinking too much. He seemed a nice enough person.

'Bloody freezing tonight,' I said to him. 'I reckon the hospital has got to be a fair bit warmer and drier tonight.'

'I don't want to go to hospital,' he said back to me.

I was surprised. 'Are you sure mate? It's no skin off my nose if we take you in.'

'Yeah, I'm sure. I've just had too much to drink.' He mentioned a hostel nearby. 'Which way is it from here?'

I pointed him in the direction of the hostel and he wandered off down the road.

I've got to admit that I felt sorry for him. I didn't know why he was homeless, and I'm not a strong believer that all homeless people are victims, but because I'd sat and spoken to him, because he hadn't tried to hit me and because he seemed like a reasonable person I felt some sympathy for him. He must have made some sort of impression on me as I can still remember the job six weeks after it happened.

Maybe I'm just getting soft in my old age.

The Black Dog Has Been Taken Outside and Shot

I left work this morning with a song in my heart and joy in my step; last night was my final shift on the FRU car.

No longer will I be standing around with my hands in my pockets for 45 minutes while a six-month-old child lies in front of me with possible meningitis. No more will I be told by Control to go and drive around and look busy when there is something good on telly, and no longer will my only conversation with people consist mainly of 'Where does it hurt?' for twelve hours straight.

The letter that I wrote my boss telling her that I wanted to come off the FRU takes effect from Friday. I'll soon be back to working on a 'truck', a nice big person-carrying medical-taxi truck.

Lovely!

I was hoping that this last shift would fly by in an exciting cascade of trauma, life-saving and dramatic illness.

Ahem.

It was actually a fairly quiet night. I did seven jobs, four of them being people with coughs (one cough having lasted three weeks before the patient decided to call an ambulance at five in the morning). My last call was to an elderly gentleman with emphysema (and a cough) who actually needed hospital treatment.

However, my first two calls were to drunks.

My second job was a 'classic' – 'Male collapsed in street, unknown life status – caller refusing to go near patient or answer any questions.' So I rushed there and found two female police officers standing over a drunk male who was asleep in the street. I did all my normal checks to make sure that he was only drunk (as opposed to being drunk and in a diabetic coma, drunk and has had a stroke, or drunk and has been stabbed). Everything pointed to him being just drunk.

We woke him up and were prepared to send him on his way. He stood up – took one look at me, and smacked me in the mouth.

I 'assisted' him onto the floor. The police officers and I then stopped him from injuring himself by sitting on him in a professional manner.

The police have been trained in restraint – they are all careful because they don't want people dying of positional asphyxia. I haven't been trained in restraint (well, not in the ambulance service) but I'm guessing that someone isn't going to die because I'm kneeling over their arm while holding their wrist.

So we carefully restrained him (for around 25 minutes), while he explained how he was either going to kick my head in or sue me. By then the police had tracked down a, now mortified, relative who came and took him away.

No damage done to me, although I would think that as he wakes up this morning he'll have a number of bruises. I hopped in my car and told Control that I had been assaulted twice in two jobs, so I asked if I could head back to the station for a calming cup of tea, which they allowed. They also made sure that I was all right and didn't need any other help.

When my mother found out about my being assaulted, did she ask how I was? Did she ask if I had been hurt or damaged?

No.

Her comment was, 'At least you'll have something interesting to blog about.'

Bloody lovely that is ...

🚐 Complaint

It is a constant danger in this job that a patient, or more likely a patient's relative, will make a complaint against you. While a member of the public can moan about a perceived insult (and half of the complaints against the ambulance service are due to 'attitude'), there is little that we can do about a patient who is generally acting like a twit.

I have been pretty lucky in my career in that I've only had two complaints made against me: once while a nurse and once while working on the ambulances.

The nursing complaint was that I checked the correct dosage of a drug with another nurse before giving it to a child. For some reason this person had decided to complain about me for following the sensible rules laid down by my superiors. My boss at the time called me into the office, patted me on the head and told me I was a good boy and should keep up the excellent work.

The ambulance complaint went to a local investigation.

I was called into the office and asked if I remembered calling a patient a 'bitch'. As I have a poor memory I didn't remember until the ambulance officer gave me the paperwork for the job.

We had been called to a patient who had been arguing with his family, he'd drunk a bottle of wine and pretended to be unconscious. As he didn't want to 'wake up', we decided to take him to hospital. While in the back of the ambulance he slapped my leg.

I told him that he 'slapped like a bitch' and that he really shouldn't do it again or I might get upset.

I know, not the best insult in the world. He'd surprised me and I had to come up with something witty on the spur of the moment. If he'd hurt me then I would have thrown him off the ambulance, but as it was such an ineffectual strike I found it more amusing than anything else.

The officer had to investigate the allegation so he interviewed the other staff present and they supported my side of the story. He then had to travel to the patient's home and interview him there. Luckily the officer saw the character of the patient and convinced him not to go any further with the complaint.

If I'd complained to the police it would no doubt have been considered 'not worth prosecuting' by the CPS, but if the patient had continued to complain I could have been seriously disciplined.

All of which only makes me think that I shouldn't leave any witnesses alive ...

🚑 Snapshots

... We get the call to the RTA, a car has crashed into a bus; normally these things are 'nothing' jobs. We put on the blue lights and head towards the crash ...

... The radio bursts into life, there is an officer who 'lucked' onto the scene – he tells Control that he needs a lot of ambulances, the fire service and the police. The injuries are all serious. We wonder if he is talking about the same crash we are going to ...

... We crest the hill, with one look at the car and the bus we know it's going to be serious ...

... I jump out of the ambulance and head to the car; I ask the officer what he wants us to do. He tells me that we can't wait for the fire service to arrive to cut out the first patient as his breathing is so ragged. We agree that he needs to be out of the car immediately and that a possible neck injury is a low priority ...

... We get him out and I watch as he takes his last breath ...

... We work on him; he is so young we have to make the attempt. The DSO (duty station officer) and other FRUs work on the other people in the car ...

... He is lying lifeless in my ambulance and the BASICS doctor declares him dead – then we rush off to the next casualty ...

... This one gets sedation. I write the dose and time on his chest so that the information doesn't get lost in the chaos. Another ambulance crew speeds him to hospital ...

... The next one is declared dead as the firefighters cut him out ...

... The other dead man is left in the car, there is nothing to do for him, it will be some time before the firefighters are able to free him ...

... I check on the people in the bus, there are some injuries that will need hospital treatment. I'm trying to keep them calm and relaxed. My crewmate and I move from our 'all-business' personalities to our 'reassurance' ones in the time it takes us to walk to the bus. I deal with the multiple casualties one at a time, my crewmate helps me out ...

... My ambulance becomes a mobile mortuary; the police are checking for identification. The blood is pooling on the floor ...

... I'm sitting on the back step of the ambulance, two of the dead are in my ambulance; one, wrapped in a sheet, is at my feet. We are waiting for the undertaker ...

... The police investigation team is chalking the outlines of vehicles and taking photographs of the scene ...

... My paperwork is done. It seems like such a little bit of writing for such a serious call where three men have been killed ...

... Medical equipment and wrappers mix with the debris of the accident. There is the familiar 'tick-tick-tick' of our blue lights revolving in their housings ...

... Back at the station I have a face mask on as I clean the floor and trolley of the ambulance with the jet spray we normally use on the outside of the vehicles. My crewmate is doing the gentler job of cleaning the equipment. The blood comes off eventually ...

... It's time for our next job.

🚐 Repeat Offender

On Saturday one of the first jobs was to go to someone whose name my crewmate recognised.

'He's a nice old boy,' he told me. 'When his wife was alive she'd call us every time he coughed. He's deaf and blind. He used to be a British champion boxer. He's a big fella so I hope we don't have to carry him downstairs. We don't see him much now; he hasn't called us out in ages.'

The patient was sitting alone in his flat, scattered around him were books that he could no longer read. In the corner was a television that probably hadn't been turned on in years. He was just a frail man sitting quietly in his chair marking time. On the table next to his chair were the remains of some 'meals on wheels'. I could see that he had once been a 'solid' man, like the old men still living in our area who used to work on the docks – tall and thick with muscle. He wasn't that man any more. He was frail, shaking, and seemed nervous of everything, not something that you'd expect from an ex-boxer.

It was hard getting his history as I needed to lean close to his ear and shout. At one point he let out a hacking cough just as I was up close to him so we took him to hospital with a possible chest infection.

Our last job of the day was back to the same address – he'd been discharged from hospital and just wanted someone to 'check his pulse'.

We didn't mind.

🚑 Algesia

Seven-hour shifts are really easy to do, especially when you have spent the last year doing only twelve-hour shifts.

The jobs tonight were pretty easy – even easier for me as I was driving the ambulance rather than treating the patients. We had a 16-year-old girl with a sore throat, a pair of drunks, one of whom had a twisted ankle, a little old lady who'd fallen over indoors and had a nasty scrape to her arm, and a young woman, twelve weeks pregnant, who had been assaulted at work and struck in the stomach.

The real standout job for me shows just how daft some people are.

The patient was a twelve-year-old boy. We got the job as 'child banging head on walls and floor' and when we turned up the child was indeed clutching his head and hitting it against a wall. The parents and child spoke poor English, but we easily managed to learn that the child was suffering from an earache, and that this was the cause of the head-hitting.

'How long has he had the pain?' asked my crewmate for the night.

'Five years then, three hours now,' replied the father.

We understood what he meant – the child had an earache five years ago, but this current episode, and the reason why we were called out, had lasted three hours.

'Have you given him any painkillers?'

'No,' the father looked confused.

'Do you have any painkillers?' my crewmate asked.

'Yes, but we haven't given him any,' said the father.

So the family could see their child rolling around the floor, screaming in pain and banging his head against the walls, and didn't consider that a painkiller might have – oh, I don't know – helped with the pain.

I can imagine the scene in the hospital when the nurses give the child some pain relief – the parents looking at each other, slapping their foreheads and saying, 'Doh! We could have done that!'

There are a lot of daft people out there – and I get to meet most of them.

🚐 Back on the Car …

There is a slight problem I have with returning to the ambulances, and that is my new partner is currently on sick leave, and has been for some time. No one knows when she will be fit to return – so I often find myself 'single' with nobody to work with.

When you are single you can be teamed up with another single pretty much anywhere in London.

At the moment our sector is having trouble reaching our government targets (which are calculated at the end of February). Of particular concern is Poplar ambulance station which, because of atrocious manning, is struggling to meet them. To counter this management have made it known that any shortfall in manning Poplar must be corrected as a priority.

So, when I'm single I'm often going to find myself making my way over to the Poplar area.

Last night, however, there was no one for me to work with at Poplar so they asked me to work on the FRU.

Fear of being asked to travel over to the other side of London if I refused meant that last night I was once more a solo responder.

This meant I had the right hump.

Thankfully it wasn't too busy; the usual complaints of 'my child hasn't eaten properly for two days', 'I'm having an angina attack' and 'I'm drunk' were quite enough. There was one interesting job though – a policeman hit a pedestrian with his car.

Thankfully he wasn't travelling on blue lights, nor going too fast for the road. The woman apparently ran out into the road without looking, which given some of the pedestrian activities I normally see wasn't out of the ordinary. Luckily for the woman involved there was an anaesthetist walking past, and he managed the immediate need to keep her neck still. After our examination our main concerns were that she was concussed and that she was cold from lying in the road – thankfully the ambulance was pretty quick, and she was soon in the warm, where our further examination showed no immediate injuries.

The area was cordoned off and as the woman was being looked after by the crew I went to make sure that the policeman who had been driving was all right. He was quite shaken up by the event, and I hope he gets support from his work.

 Wee-Wee

The plan was perfect – we'd just taken a drunk to hospital and the patient (a 45-year-old man, married, father of two) had decided to urinate in the back of our ambulance. Both my crewmate and I were happy at this as we would have to return to our station to mop out, and on the way my crewmate could grab a chicken takeaway meal.

And I could get a cup of tea.

This apparently flawless plan was spoilt when we stopped for the food and a man came running out of a pub to tell me that a friend had 'a fuckin' big gash in his head' from when he had fallen over.

So I dutifully entered the pub, to find a 50-year-old man with a cut down to the skull running from his hairline to his eyebrow. Most impressive.

Less impressive was his friend telling me that the patient had taken some speed earlier.

I don't know about you, but I consider myself too old to be taking that stuff, let alone someone old enough to be my father.

Not that I've ever taken speed myself. I like my brain cells exactly how they are, thankyouverymuch.

Luckily another ambulance turned up and took the patient off our hands, and so we returned to the station where I completed the job of mopping out the urine that had been washing backwards and forwards on the floor as we drove along.

I just wish I could be a fly on the wall when our original drunken patient tries to explain to his wife *exactly* why he has pissed his trousers.

 Swagger

'He'll end up in the bush,' I said.

'Nope – the road,' replied my crewmate.

'Bush.'

'Road.'

The man we were watching dropped to the floor – in the road.

It was the last call of the night – a police CCTV camera had seen a man sitting in the middle of the road in what can only be described as a 'dangerous' part of town.

We arrived to find our patient rather drunk and sitting in the road under a CCTV camera. Circling him was a hungry pack of feral children who scattered when they saw us arrive.

We had a pleasant little chat with him – he had scraped his face when he had fallen over, and had no desire to get out of the road.

We spent 20 minutes trying to persuade him to get out of the road. We tried being nice, we tried reverse psychology and we even tried explaining that the police would soon be here and they would make him move on. He refused to move, and he refused to go to hospital – he was a very stationary object.

We got back into the ambulance, where it was warm, to await the police. We'd already parked in a 'fend off' position so that a passing car wouldn't hit our patient.

I don't believe in making work for myself.

'Control, have we got an ETA for the police please?'

Control replied, 'I can only tell you what they have told me – there are no policemen in the big policemen storage box, as they are all out dealing with other things.'

Great.

Right, I thought, time to try a little trick I learnt while reading a book about how the human brain works. Certain gestures and objects have 'hard-coded' responses in your brain. So if you walk up to someone who is sitting in the road and give them your hand (as if you were about to shake theirs), they will often take it, and from there it is fairly easy to get someone standing.

Success! Our patient was now standing (well ... swaying) and indicated that he wanted to go home. His home was about 400 yards away in one of the tower blocks that surrounded us.

He took two steps and started to fall – he grabbed at my crewmate's jacket, spun himself around her and by some miracle remained upright.

'I'm fine,' he said. 'I don't want you helping me walk home.' He pulled his arms out of our grasp and started to stagger home.

We got into the ambulance and slowly followed behind him.

A message from the police (via our Control) appeared on our display terminal. 'Are you all right? Does the man have any warning signs?'

Warning signs?

'Control,' I was back on the radio, 'I've got this message about "warning signs". Well, I don't think he has any signal flares, or any of those reflective red triangles you put behind your car when it breaks down.' Yes, I know ... I was being silly.

While trying not to laugh Control replied, 'I wondered what the police meant by that as well.'

What I think had happened was that the CCTV operator had seen what looked like my crewmate being attacked by the patient when he was just stumbling around.

We kept following the patient.

He started to swagger.

He started to sway.

He swaggered some more.

We quickly laid bets on him falling into some bushes by the road.

I chose the bushes.

I lost.

We got out of the ambulance and picked him up again. This time we decided that 'technically' breaking the law and frogmarching him home would be in the patient's best interest. So we grabbed an arm each and in a jolly fashion walked him home.

With the three of us all with linked arms making our way down a deserted street, it was inevitable that I'd start whistling 'We're off to see the wizard'.

The patient got home safely, although I'd guess that the family member who answered the doorbell wasn't too pleased with him.

Scent

Way back in my past I trained to be a teacher (of small to medium-sized children). Rather thankfully I've managed to block out much of the trauma from those days. My poor memory does have some positive sides.

However, I've just done a job in a primary school, and all those memories came flooding back.

To be honest I think it was the smell that did it. Smell is strongly tied to memory, which is why certain odours can transport you back in time, say to helping your mum bake a cake, or to painting a shed with your father.

In this case it was the smell of the floor polish coupled with the scent of the powder paints in the air that flung me back to my days of trying to control 33 mini-disaster machines (or as they are known to the general public 'children').

I'm sure that new parents must have the same experience when they first visit their child's school.

The job itself was quite an easy one, one of the teachers was having a panic attack, which is fair enough really – I know that if I were still trying to teach, I'd be in a constant state of panic attack.

Betting Shops

I know I've written about having a wager with my crewmate about which way a drunk would fall, but I don't want to give you the wrong idea.

I think betting is silly.

I have no idea how to work out any odds. Terms like 'odds of 11/7', 'each way', 'accumulators' and 'handicap' make no sense to me at all. Since childhood the betting shop has always seemed to me to be a seedy place where hard-drinking, and hard-smoking, men flush their money down the toilet. Not somewhere I would ever visit.

Occasionally I do find myself, because of the duties of my job, frequenting these dens of vice. And to be honest most of them aren't that bad. The most common reason why I am sent to these places is because someone has passed out in the toilets due to drugs, or less commonly, drink. For some reason betting-shop toilets seem to be really popular places to take drugs.

Don't ask me why.

These jobs are fairly rare, so I was surprised to find myself called to betting shops on two separate jobs in one day. Even more surprising was that neither of these jobs was junkie related.

The first job was to a 50-year-old male who had collapsed, and when we arrived the FRU driver was looking a bit concerned. The patient was as white as a sheet and not talking. We were all worried that he was going to die while in the shop, so we quickly loaded him into our carry chair and removed him to the ambulance.

While trying to do this, every other user of the betting shop continued around us without batting an eyelid. Normally we'd get a bit of an audience, but not so in this case. At one point a man 'tutted' me because I was standing between him and some vitally important bit of paper on the wall.

I'll leave it to you, dear reader, to guess my reply to that.

As soon as the patient was in the ambulance he started to come round. All of our investigations showed nothing unusual, so we concluded that it was just a 'simple' faint. As it was a slightly prolonged one we took him to hospital for a few more tests.

The second job to a betting shop was for a 60-year-old male who was having a critically low blood sugar. He was a diabetic, and when we arrived he was rooted to his stool watching the horses racing on the TV screens. His wife was starting to get frantic at his refusal to talk.

On checking his blood sugar we discovered that it was very low, and this would explain his strange behaviour.

We tried to persuade him to drink a can of Coke but he refused so we made the decision to give him an injection of glucagon. This drug, when injected into a muscle, is often good enough to reverse a low blood sugar for a short period of time. The plan was to get his blood sugar high enough for him to come out of his confusion for long enough so that we could get some sugar in him.

That was the plan at least.

Instead, we just gave him enough strength to start fighting us, his wife and the betting-shop lady who threatened to ban him if he didn't do what the 'nice' ambulance people told him to do.

In an effort to get him into the ambulance, we ended up wrestling with him in the street. It was a bit strange to be physically restraining a pensioner while trying to (a) not hurt him, and (b) not look like a bully, even though he was a good couple of inches taller than me.

Then a police car drove past us.

It did a U-turn in the middle of the road and pulled up in front of our ambulance.

A couple of police officers got out and helped us persuade the patient to get into the ambulance where we could finally get him to drink the can of Coke we gave him. Sometimes it just needs a couple of big men in black and white uniforms to get a patient to do what you want.

This is one of many reasons why we like the police.

What didn't help was the wife who would alternately berate her husband for poorly controlling his diabetes, and then spend time telling us that she was a devout Christian.

Thankfully the Coke did the trick and the patient made a full recovery – we left him and his wife in the nearby café getting something more substantial than a can of Coke and a Mars Bar.

Two good jobs, and not a trace of drink or drugs on them.

Makes a nice change.

It Says 'London' on the Side

Last night was a bit strange, which for a change had nothing to do with the patients I was seeing.

Newham hospital was packed to the gills with patients, there were no beds available there, so a lot of my workmates ended up transferring patients from Newham to other hospitals around the area. At one point it got so bad that for two hours Newham 'diverted', or closed to non-'blue light' ambulance jobs. Hospitals don't like doing this as they get fined for restricting their services, but when the situation is dangerous it's actually in the best interests of the patients.

But my crewmate and I had to be that little bit different.

We had managed to return to station for three minutes when the phone went. Control wanted us to transfer a patient from a hospital out of our area to another one on the other side of London. We were told that there were no ambulances available in the originating hospital's sector.

The patient was a young lady who might have been in premature labour with a pregnancy of 30 weeks. The nearest SCBU (specialist care baby unit) with an empty bed was in Hammersmith. Hammersmith is on the other side of London. I suppose we should have counted ourselves lucky that it wasn't in Brighton.

So I drove through our sector, into another sector to pick up the patient and the midwife. We then drove 30 miles through the centre of London to get her to Hammersmith hospital. I don't drive through London very often – I don't need to, London Underground is cheaper and easier than trying to find a parking space. Thankfully all our ambulances now have GPS navigation systems installed – so it's a simple case of following the arrows on the little screen and avoiding the cars that insist on trying to crash into you. I had a strange feeling of pride that I managed to find the hospital without getting lost or crashing. I then cruised around the hospital looking for the maternity entrance, and managed to find it by sheer luck and good fortune.

The hospital itself was completely different from the hospitals in our area – it was clean, it had comfy chairs, and the doctor who met the patient showed us the staff kitchen so we could get a cup of tea.

The only thing the same as the hospitals 'back home' was the angry glare from the midwife as we entered the unit.

On our way back to Newham we managed to get a job.

'Aha!' we thought, 'this might be an interesting one.'

But no – it was exactly the same sort of patient/job that we get in Newham: an elderly Bangladeshi gentleman with all over body ache and a heavy head.

Still, he was a very pleasant man so we didn't mind.

This patient went to St Mary's hospital by request, and I'll admit that on my first attempt at getting him to the hospital I drove past the obviously well-hidden entrance ramp. So I had to enter the one-way system, adding an extra mile on our journey. St Mary's have a 'welcome mat' outside their A&E department. You don't get welcome mats at Newham. At Newham you have to force open the ambulance bay doors ...

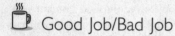 Good Job/Bad Job

Good Job

Any time where a patient actually needs an ambulance.

People having an acute flare-up of a chronic condition (diabetes, asthma, heart disease).

People who can't walk, but who live on the ground floor.

People who make an effort towards managing their chronic conditions.

Maternal emergencies.

Nice people.

Old people.

Children who don't cry.

Any time a patient, or their relative, says a simple 'Thank you' at the end of their trip.

Bad Job

Runny noses, coughs and colds. Verrucas.

People who have had an argument with a family member.

People who can't walk, but live at the top of a block of flats with no lifts. And are heavy.

People who abuse their bodies with drink or drugs.

5 a.m. matern-a-taxis.

Gangsters crying because they have been stabbed for dealing drugs on the wrong street.

Awful nursing homes.

Parents who weep over their child's cut finger causing them to have hysterical screaming.

Mr 'I know my rights'.

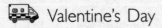 Valentine's Day

First off ...

... Bah humbug.

(It's not just for Christmas.)

I've just finished with a job that makes me question this whole 'love' idea.

I had been sent to an alcoholic who had just had an epileptic fit and I arrived to find his fiancée looking very worried.

She told me, 'I've known him for ten months and I've only seen him fit once, so I'm afraid I got scared and called for an ambulance.'

I reassured her that this wasn't a problem and that she had done the right thing.

I looked after the patient, it was an easy job, and I spent some time waiting for the ambulance to arrive. (I was 'single', so I had been asked to work on the FRU again; the alternative was to work out of Waterloo station.)

I looked around the room they were staying in. It was not what you would call 'homely'; it was the typical house of a young alcoholic (he was the same age as me). Cans of cheap cider were lying around the place, there was no furniture apart from a settee and a TV, empty cigarette packets littered the floor and the pictures hadn't been mounted on the walls.

There was an axe leaning against the fireplace.

His fiancée was young and not obviously unattractive, she didn't seem particularly stupid and she didn't look like a fellow alcoholic. So I was confused as to why she would want to marry an alcoholic.

I'm afraid it just befuddles me as to how you can love someone who loves their next drink more than you. In any partnership you will come second to an open bottle of cider.

I just don't understand.

Tagged

We help the people of Newham.

One of these people has seen fit to 'tag' one of our ambulances with graffiti.

This means that the ambulance will be taken off the road so that it can be cleaned.

This will cost money.

It will also remove an ambulance from the road.

This means an ambulance might get delayed coming to a call.

I hope it is a call to the 'tagger', and I hope that they are in a great deal of pain.

In the past we've had people break into our ambulance station to steal radios from the cars parked there as well as steal the station's TV. When you are working yourself into an early grave on a cold and wet night shift it makes you want to pack the whole job in.

🚑 Lost Words

Canary Wharf has a skating rink at the moment and my crewmate and I were sent there to attend to a 'fall, head injury'.

'Excellent,' we thought, 'a nice simple job – nothing complicated.'

We were met by a worried-looking ice rink worker who wobbled across the pavement on his skates to meet us.

'We wouldn't normally bother you guys, but we think it might be serious.'

Grabbing my bags I was led to a woman sitting in the changing area with two youngsters, both of whom were looking a little concerned.

'Hello there. I'm with the ambulance, what seems to be the problem?' I normally start with a version of this as a conversational opening gambit.

The patient replied, 'Well, I had a bit of a fall—' She paused. 'I—' She paused again. 'Head ... hit ... migraine—'

She seemed to be having trouble finding the right words to use. I quickly examined her, and was happy that she hadn't hurt her neck and the small lump on the back of her head didn't look serious either. So why was she acting so strangely?

'I get migraines,' she told me. 'I ... lose ... um ... er ... um ... words, and I ... eyes ... eyes ... go blind.'

This is a pretty rare presentation of migraines, but not unheard of.

We got her into the back of the ambulance and all my examinations there were normal. She was complaining of 'losing her words' (expressive dysphasia) and of going blind in her right eye. She didn't seem too upset by this and had already taken her normal migraine medication, although I'm not sure how paracetamol and metoclopramide would help with these symptoms as I'm not an expert on migraine treatment although I know that triptans can sometimes be used.

Her symptoms started to get worse, she couldn't find any of the words

313

that she wanted to use, and so I needed to get a more thorough history from the two youngsters. They were her nephews and she had been treating them to a trip to London. Although young, they were both very mature and helpful and after some prompting from the patient ('Laptop ... look ... laptop') we found a patient information card in her purse. The card let us know that all the symptoms that she was experiencing were indeed part of the presentation of her migraine.

It was a short trip to the hospital, during which she started to make a slight recovery and we left her in the capable hands of the A&E nurses. Unfortunately for the patient, the hospital was extremely busy, so I'm guessing that she had to wait a little while for any treatment.

The three of them had come from Surrey, so they didn't know the area well, although we were able to give them directions home from the hospital. We had chosen this one over another slightly closer so that it would be easier for them to get home after any treatment.

A day out in London turning into a trip to the hospital – it happens more often than you would think.

 Bleurgh

For the past five nights the majority of my patients have been sick with one or more of the following:

High temperature,

Runny nose,

Vomiting,

Night sweats,

Lethargy,

Cough,

'Generally unwell'.

So there must be at least one highly infectious disease epidemic in the area. While you or I might want to curl up in bed with some Lemsip and paracetamol, it would seem that a large number of Newham's population would rather sit for hours in an A&E waiting room.

Madness.

Which leads me to the point. Ambulance crews spend a lot of time around these infectious patients, who have often never been taught the good manners of putting their hand over their mouth when they cough.

So is it any wonder that I've got painful eyes, a streaming nose, a constant mild headache and a feeling that I'm suffering from a mild hangover.

But:

Ambulance crews mustn't have more than three periods of sick leave in an 18-month period.

So I'm having to drag my potentially infectious body into work – where maybe I can infect some more people ...

So in conclusion:

Send me nurses – pretty female ones with plenty of drugs.

☕ Free-Market Oxygen

Some patients with chronic lung disease need oxygen, and rather than keep them in hospital, these patients often have cylinders of oxygen delivered to them at their home.

Until recently it was the pharmacist who supplied these cylinders, but the government in its infinite wisdom has decided to privatise the supply of oxygen. This means more paperwork.

And now a patient has died, possibly because of a delay getting her oxygen delivered. It drives me crazy that I spend my time in my ambulance going to 23-year-old men with coughs, yet apparently no ambulance was called for this woman.

It all comes down to the government wishing to run the health service like a business.

I know that some people believe that the free market will constantly provide superior service to anything run by the government. Unfortunately healthcare isn't a 'market' and this market view of the NHS leads towards some very silly initiatives. It's why 'failing' hospitals get less money than 'successful' hospitals. Who would want to throw money into a failing business?

Why are hospitals so dirty? It's because of the free-market contracting of cleaning to the cheapest supplier – regardless of the quality.

It's also why, despite increasing numbers of patients, more calls, very few new staff and all the other reasons why we may not meet our government ORCON target this year, we'll get less money to be spent on improving our service.

But what do I know – I'm a van driver not an economist.

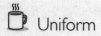 Uniform

The thing about wearing a uniform – it really changes your behaviour.

I'm guessing that a lot of you are aware of the Milgram experiment, where members of the public more willingly follow instructions if the giver is wearing a uniform or other symbol of authority. (Go to the internet for a more complete explanation. If you've never heard of this experiment, it and the Stanford prison experiment make scary reading.)

So when I am wearing my uniform I am more confident and can order people around. The police, firefighters and members of the public tend to do what I tell them if there is someone sick around. Obviously I only use these powers for the force of good, but without my uniform I am a much shyer person.

I noticed this when I went to a recent gathering of internet people. When I arrived I knew one person there, and once I'd stopped talking to her I became an instant wallflower.

But there is a flip side to wearing an ambulance uniform, you also become more passive.

Out of uniform, if I was in the street and some drunk tried to hit me – I'd punch them on the nose. If I was verbally abused – I'd soon be in their face shouting and ranting along with the best of them.

Yes, I know three paragraphs before I said I was a wallflower, but this is in a social situation. When my temper is roused it is a terrible thing to behold.

But in uniform I'll gently restrain the drunk trying to hit me and I'll ignore any verbal abuse that is thrown at me. Unfortunately the anger that I feel is then turned inward, which I am guessing is not a healthy thing to do.

I wonder if it is the uniform, or the risk of having a complaint put in about me, that turns me into such a wimp. It might just be that I spend so much time trying to keep patients calm, that I'm feeling very mellow when people abuse me.

Abuse Your Ambulance Crew

I was racially abused on Friday night, and it meant I spent the rest of my shift gritting my teeth and wanting to punch someone.

We were sent to a 'standard' abdominal pain with vomiting. The patient, a black woman, had vomited ten times that day and had lower abdominal pain. As always I treated the patient with respect and compassion (as that is my 'default setting'). All her observations were within the normal limits. Talking to the patient was a bit tricky as she insisted on having me ask every question at least twice before answering.

So we took her to hospital, where I handed over the patient to the triage nurse. She was happy to have another nurse perform a further assessment (for example, an analysis of the patient's urine). Unfortunately the place for this assessment was physically full, so we were asked to take the patient into the waiting room until some space could be made. My crewmate did this, while I booked the patient in with the reception staff.

My crewmate told me that when the patient saw she was going to be put in the waiting room, she let out a loud 'Tut!'

My crewmate then joined me in the reception area which overlooks the waiting room.

The patient then threw herself on the floor and pretended to be unconscious (trust me, when you've seen people *really* pass out in a chair, you can tell when they are faking it).

The waiting room erupted with two people jumping to her aid. The security guards went to get a nurse. Then a lot of the people in the room started shouting at us to come and help. Never mind the half-inch-thick glass between us and them.

We told them that a nurse was on the way.

'Look at her! Look what's happened to her!' shouted one man.

'Yes mate,' replied my colleague, 'there's nothing wrong with her – all she's trying to do is get seen before you.'

The patient was loaded onto a trolley and taken into the main area of the A&E.

The crowd in the waiting room then started moaning *at us*.

Then both my crewmate and I heard the comment that would have us angry for the rest of the shift.

'You wouldn't treat her like that if she were white.'

My crewmate stormed out of the department – he was, quite rightly, fuming.

All I could do was laugh loudly at the black teenager who had said this. 'Well, if you are that stupid, you've just opted out of talking to me,' I said to her.

I left the hospital.

Here is the thing that made my crewmate and me so angry. We like our job – we both like helping people and we'll help anyone, we don't care what colour their skin is, which religion they believe in, or if they can speak English or not. I don't even care if they are an illegal immigrant. We sure as hell don't do this work for the pay. My crewmate is a trained plumber so he could be earning much more money installing radiators.

We don't need to work in this area – I could put in for a transfer to a more 'white' area tomorrow. But I enjoy working in east London – it's a challenge – and I enjoy working with all the different cultures that make up our 'demographic'. For me, a predominantly white area would be incredibly boring.

But that comment: 'You wouldn't treat her like that if she were white.' It made me despair as to how we are seen by the non-white population. Are we all seen as being racist? Does the assumption that I would treat a patient better if they were white sit in the minds of the people I treat? Is this why I get so few thank yous? When I walk into a household, do the people there think 'I won't get good treatment from these two, they are both white'?

I wish I'd gone around to the person who had made the comment and challenged her. I wish I'd gone into the waiting room and explained exactly what had happened. But as I've mentioned earlier, the uniform that I wear makes me more passive than I would normally be. So I turned the other cheek and walked away.

I'm still fuming.

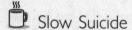 Slow Suicide

Imagine that you are 23 years old.

You are also a 'brittle' asthmatic. This means that you can have asthma attacks that can rapidly progress to life-threatening status. You have been intubated in ITU a couple of times – this is a last ditch treatment to keep you alive.

So why, whenever you get taken to hospital, would you treat your disease as a mere annoyance?

Also, why would you smoke 20–40 cigarettes a day, knowing that it will make your asthma worse?

And why would you self-discharge yourself from the resuscitation room against medical advice only to require a blue light return straight back to the resuscitation room?

It's just a form of slow suicide.

I Wouldn't Trust Them with My Dog

I have another example of why I don't think that the free-market system is particularly good for the health service, or at least not good for the patients who use it.

I was working in another area a little while ago, and while there got sent to a private nursing home. The patient was given to us as '80-year-old female with difficulty in breathing'. We arrived and saw what looked to be two nurses having an animated discussion in the main foyer.

Grabbing our equipment we followed one of the nurses into the depths of the home, and were shown to the patient's room.

The patient was very much dead.

Also in the room were four nurses. They were standing around and they weren't doing CPR, they weren't breathing for the patient. They looked at me for guidance.

I immediately switched into commanding mode. 'Why isn't anyone doing CPR?' I asked.

'We were,' one of the nurses replied, 'but I saw you coming in the mirror and stopped.'

The mirror was positioned so that if she had been doing CPR, she would have had to have eyes in the back of her head to see me coming.

When someone isn't breathing you have to breathe for them – this is the 'ambu-bag' that TV doctors put over someone's face and operate by squeezing it. It forces oxygen into your lungs. Unfortunately the patient had a normal oxygen mask on her, which would just bathe her face with oxygen, but it wouldn't get it into the lungs where it needed to be.

The patient was also lying on an air mattress, which would have meant that any CPR which may have been done would have been ineffectual because you need the patient on something hard so you have something to push against.

I felt the jaw of the patient – rigor mortis had already set in, so there was no point in attempting to continue any resuscitation attempt.

Someone had tried to take the patient's blood pressure, as there was still a BP cuff around her arm.

As is usual in these cases where we know or suspect that care has been – shall we say – lacking, we offer the services of the London Ambulance

Service (LAS) to teach the nursing staff more effective resuscitation skills. However, they should have these skills anyway as *qualified* nurses. Talking to one of the people who teaches these courses, it seems that many of these nurses have forgotten how to do this. It's free to them although I don't think we get any extra money from the government to run it.

The nurse in charge, who was busy photocopying in the office while all this was happening, refused.

So, in a world of competition between privately owned care homes, it would seem that the care has not improved. Instead you get poorly skilled nurses, managed by staff who don't want them to improve. This despite a number of suppliers who are all in competition with each other – it's a lucrative market providing elderly care.

Laughing Policeman

You've got to laugh when an 'old salt' police sergeant tells you that he'd like to meet the person who assaulted my patient ...

... And shake their hand ...

... And you agree with him even though you've only known the patient for 20 seconds.

Structural Collapse

The radio sparked into life, 'General Broadcast, General Broadcast – are there any crews able to deal with a ceiling collapsed on a mother and her two-year-old child?'

We were just finishing up the paperwork on our previous job so we asked for it to be sent down to us. I was driving and we were soon at the house. From the outside everything looked normal.

However, inside the house it was pure chaos.

There were seven children running around the house, all of them under the age of twelve. A single mother was clutching her two-year-old to her chest. At first glance they looked unharmed. The mother seemed more frightened and angry than injured.

We soon got the full story: the mother and her child were having a nap in the bedroom when the ceiling had fallen on them. We entered the bedroom expecting a few scraps of plaster. Instead we were met with the sight of one-and-a-half-foot plaster and lath ceiling, a huge chunk of which had fallen six foot onto the bed.

The hole in the ceiling was about five feet in diameter; there was a lot of heavy debris spread across the bed and floor.

Rather understandably the woman was a bit upset – the individual pieces of plaster that had dropped on her were about the size of my hand and were over an inch thick. I couldn't estimate the total weight of the plaster, but each lump was very heavy.

It was about now that the headache I'd thought I'd got rid of earlier in the evening started to return.

As a single parent who had just moved into the area she had no other relatives to help look after the children so she was refusing to go to hospital. My crewmate took her and the toddler into the ambulance so that he could examine her more fully. If he found nothing too serious then we could leave her at home to look after her children.

So off they went to the ambulance.

Which left me looking after six anklebiters.

I don't like children.

While he was in the ambulance my crewmate phoned the patient's GP and arranged for them to come and visit the patient. He then arranged for the police to turn up and give the patient some legal advice. Rather obviously the patient was a trifle annoyed at the landlord who had assured her that the house was fit to be lived in.

Meanwhile I was doing my best to entertain the children. My best wasn't enough.

I was relieved when the children's older brother arrived with some takeaway chicken meals. Yes – there were now eight children in the house of this 36-year-old woman. This older brother was more like a father to the others and he soon had these apparently feral children under control.

Luckily for the woman and her child our initial guess was correct – neither she nor her child was seriously injured.

My crewmate and I escaped from the scene as soon as the police arrived.

Shorn

An ideal invention for the blogger in your family would be a pair of video-recording glasses – wear them all day, and should something interesting happen the wearer presses a button to save the last 30 seconds of video to a small storage device.

If that were possible I'd now be showing you a video of a lovely young man.

I was driving along on blue lights and sirens (to an 'intoxicated – feeling unwell') just heading past the Underground station when from the pavement I could hear someone shouting: 'Wanker ... Wanker ... Wanker.' He was also making the traditional hand gestures.

A quick look at him led me to believe that he was either homeless or an alcoholic, or both. I could see that he had no front teeth and he only looked around 30 years old.

I slowed the ambulance so that my crewmate and I could laugh loudly in his general direction.

He turned his back on us.

He bent over.

He pulled his trousers down.

Suddenly we were confronted with a skinny white arse, and dangling between his legs were equally white and skinny testicles.

They looked *shaved*.

Just then a police car came over the hill.

I wound down my window and spoke to the police driver, 'See that fellow with no teeth? He just exposed himself to me.'

'The one calling you a wanker?' asked the policeman.

'That's the one ... Have fun!'

We continued on the way to the call as best we could between tears of laughter.

It's strange the things that make your day.

12th November 2046

The young man breathed a sigh of relief as he finally sighted his quarry of the past four days. The old man was sitting on the park bench enjoying the sun and feeding the ducks.

'Hello fella,' the young man said as he sat down on the bench. 'You said that you'd be able to tell me about the old days? About 2006? About the blankets?'

The old man tore off another piece of bread and threw it in the pond and watched a small crowd of ducks hungrily fight over it. 'Sure, if you want to hear about that sort of stuff.'

The young man started a mini-recorder and placed it on the bench between them while the old man continued to talk.

'It was back in o-six, about the middle of February, and if you believe the reports it was the first winter of the "big freeze". I remember the years that followed, OAPs dropping dead in the road, cats frozen stiff in the streets ... Happy days.'

Before continuing the old man took a swig from a bottle of something, probably illegal, which he'd concealed in a brown paper bag.

'As you know I was working in London for the ambulance service, it was a pretty good job, but back then the health service was run and funded by the government. So a lot of things went wrong.'

The young man interrupted, 'That was when Blair the Deceiver was in power? Just before the Party started to dissolve parliament?'

The old man looked sullen. 'That's right, bad days, very bad days.'

Sensing that the old man was about to enter a fit of depression, the young man decided to prompt him, 'But about the blankets ...?'

'Yes,' replied the old man, eyes suddenly snapping into focus, 'we used to say back then that the only equipment we *really* needed was a chair and a blanket, but on that day there were no blankets to be found. We searched the stores, we even tried ransacking disused ambulances in case they had some – but there were none to be found.'

'What did you do?' asked the young man.

'Well, we got onto our Control – they tried to contact someone in management, but no one seemed to be around. So Control spoke to their overseers – the people who had the job to look after these emergencies. They were no help.'

'Was the management ever any good?' the young man asked.

The old man was quiet for a moment before continuing, 'In this case it turned out that there were no blankets at our central stores. Normally the blankets would be stored there before being delivered to individual stations by a tender driver. But the warehouse that washed and packed the blankets hadn't delivered any to the stores.'

'With no blankets, how could you help patients?'

'Well, after talking with Control they suggested that we "liberate" some blankets from the hospitals in the area – so some of us went on stealth missions. We'd take in a drunk and while the nurses' backs were turned your crewmate would sneak out with an armful of blankets.'

The old man threw another chunk of bread to the anxiously waiting ducks. 'We didn't call it stealing. Besides, the hospitals had more than enough.'

'Of course,' the old man continued, 'back then we'd share a blanket among a couple of patients – there wasn't enough for one blanket each. This was before the H5N1-MRSA cross-breed became epidemic. You'd never get away with it these days. But back then if there wasn't filth on the blanket, you would use it again. We had to or there would have been blanket shortages every day of the year.

'In this case the shortage lasted for a couple of days. It turned out that nearly everyone in the blanket warehouse had applied for annual leave at once, so there was hardly any staff working. In those days you had to use up most of your annual leave before April. That year they prevented the ambulances from collapsing by letting us carry over more leave to the next financial year than normal, but they forgot about some of the support workers.

'We were lucky that year ... we didn't know it was about to get worse –'

The youngster clicked off his recorder before the old man could continue. 'Yes, but we all know what happened in twenty-o-nine. I'm just researching the precursors to the health collapse and I was thinking that this might be of some use.'

'Well, I hope I was of some help,' the old man said standing up from the bench with a groan. 'I'm off to stretch these worn bones. If I can be of any more help, just let me know.'

'Will do Mr Reynolds,' said the young man, 'will do.'

Yes, we did have a ~~shortage~~ absence of blankets a couple of days ago. So far there is no official reason, but the tender driver told me the theory that I used in this story. It's also true that we have to reuse blankets for different patients. There was a manager around, but he was in a meeting. I don't know what the 'overseers' suggested.

There is no H5N1-MRSA cross-breed. I'm keeping my fingers crossed that I'm still alive in 2046.

Yes, I wrote this because I have too much time on my hands.

Sorry.

On the Power of Blankets

I have mentioned that the blanket is one of the more important and versatile bits of kit that the modern ambulance can have. In the good old days of horse-drawn ambulances the proto-EMT would refer to his equipment as 'one and one', meaning one carry chair and one blanket.

Even today, with our increasingly technologically based healthcare system, the humble blanket has a multitude of uses. For those of a 'hitchhiker' mindset think of a blanket as a towel writ large.

Primarily it is used to stop little old ladies (LOLs) from getting cold when you drag them out of their nice warm house into the often freezing conditions of the ambulance.

Said little old ladies don't like being wheeled around in our carry chair – it has no handrests and feels very unsafe. LOLs will often try to grab out at things to steady themselves – this is dangerous, especially if we are carrying them down stairs. So we wrap the patient in a blanket, and make sure that their hands are gently restrained.

You can use the blanket as a sliding/carry sheet when transferring a patient from a bed to a stretcher, or from the ambulance stretcher to the hospital trolley. The ambulance blanket is thick and strong with a close weave. While I wouldn't like to try using it to lift someone off the floor, I would imagine that it is strong enough to do so.

When in the ambulance we can use the blanket to protect modesty. Some of the things we do to people require them to bare their chest, for females this can be troubling. We can use the blanket to cover the patient as much as possible.

If the patient has been incontinent while wrapped in the blanket, we can 'gift' the blanket to the hospital – it's what nurses are for (and we don't carry warm soapy water and wipes in the back of our ambulances). Nurses soon learn to unwrap carefully the patient who has been left in the ambulance blanket.

Because of the thickness of the blanket, and the difficulty of carrying vomit bowls into houses, the blanket can catch any vomitus the patient may produce while leaving the house. Reassuring the patient that it is fine to vomit on the blanket is important in case they become embarrassed.

When moving a dead body from a location, two blankets in the 'T-wrap' will disguise the lack of life from bystanders. It's also good for wrapping up very frail LOLs when it is freezing outside.

With the addition of two triangular bandages the ambulance blanket can be converted into a pelvic splint. This helps stabilise pelvic fractures which can become life threatening if allowed to wobble. As an aside, the next time I see a trauma surgeon flex the pelvis in a suspected fracture, I'm going to find their car and let down their tyres.

If you don't have the head blocks that go either side of the head to protect a possibly broken neck, then by the correct folding of the blanket

329

you can form a snug-fitting c-spine restraint. I prefer the use of blankets to the specialist kit here because the blanket is better able to form itself to the patient's head and neck.

Our blankets are red – this makes them ideal for hiding blood.

If you have a nasty trauma in a public place the blankets are large enough to be used as screens. This requires the use of two firefighters to hold each end. Don't worry, they were probably standing around doing nothing anyway.

The blanket also works well as an 'NHS special' pillow. We don't carry pillows on our ambulances and many hospitals are short of them. So roll up your blanket and place under the patient's head. LOLs with a curvature of the spine will be especially grateful, as in a moving ambulance without a pillow their heads tend to roll around like a nodding dog.

If folded correctly, you can put it on your trolley bed and have 'AMBULANCE' written down each side. This not only looks good but also makes it really easy to wrap patients up in it.

If you have a patient who might become aggressive then the blanket – if tucked in tightly – can provide a mild restraint.

Doing CPR on the floor for an extended period of time can be wearing on your knees – a folded blanket makes a nice cushion to rest on while pounding away on some dead person's chest.

If someone decides to have an epileptic fit in the back of your ambulance, the blanket can be used to protect the head (or other part of the body) from hitting the ambulance wall or other hard surface.

Have you had a huge spillage of some noxious fluid? Are you worried that as you return to your station to mop out the back of the ambulance the fluid will run through the door into the driver's cab and thus contaminate your packed lunch? Simply mop it up with a blanket.

If someone tries to attack you, throw it at them like a net – it may distract them long enough for you to run away.

There are probably a hundred more uses for the ambulance blanket – and no doubt as soon as I publish this I'll think of another 20. Still, I think that you will see that the humble blanket has many more uses than our defibrillators and ECG machines.

Friday Night's All Right for Fighting

The first job of our Friday night was to a little old lady (actually, she wasn't *that* little). She had been standing on her bed with her daughter to fix the curtains when she'd felt dizzy and fell down. She then bounced off the bed and landed on the floor. Unfortunately for her, she had landed on her neck and head.

One of the first things that I do in a case like this is to make sure that there isn't an injury to the neck. I'll do this by gently feeling the neck while the patient tells me if it is sore. If there is soreness to one side of the neck then this will normally be a muscular injury while if the pain is in the middle of the neck then there is a chance that the injury is more serious. Like a broken neck.

This woman nearly leapt from her bed when I gently touched her neck – she had a potentially serious neck injury.

So we needed to be extremely careful in order to make sure that if the patient had broken her neck, we wouldn't make her injury worse by bouncing her down the stairs from her flat to the ambulance. Unfortunately, everything we had to tell the patient had to be translated by the daughter. I *need* to learn Bengali; it's a real shame I have no head for languages.

The patient had to be moved down the bed so that our scoop stretcher could go under her then she needed to be securely strapped onto it ready to be carried downstairs. In this case I used a blanket roll to secure her head rather than the more expensive and less effective head blocks. We called for another crew to give us a hand because in a case like this it is better to be safe than sorry, and you need to be careful carrying a potentially unstable neck fracture down two flights of stairs.

We were all really impressed with the neatness and effectiveness of the strapping. I wanted to take a photo of it because it doesn't often look as good as it did with that job.

As mentioned, she wasn't too light, and it's really tricky to manoeuvre a six-foot-long orthopaedic stretcher out onto a balcony, around half the building and down two flights of stairs. At one point we had to suspend the poor woman's head over the balcony in order to get her around the awkward architecture of her building – pretty lucky that she wasn't looking down at that point.

The job itself went like clockwork.

My back, however, was starting to hurt from the less-than-safe lifting that we needed to do to get the woman out her flat and into the ambulance.

We then had a couple of 'nothing' jobs – coughs, colds and bellyaches.

We got to around midnight when we were sent on a call for a '17-year-old male, has a knife, cutting wrist, suicidal'. As it was in the street I thought that we'd go and have a look – if he was violent then we could soon drive off and await the arrival of the police.

The young man was lying on the floor, his left hand was covered in blood and there were already two policemen there. They looked happy to see us.

A quick assessment later and it turned out that the patient had nearly severed his left little finger. He was covered in blood and refusing to say anything except that he wanted to die. I managed to get a 'quick and nasty' bandage on his hand while the police and I wrestled with him. He wasn't very happy with being put into the ambulance and once inside fought with us like a man possessed. Blood was everywhere, he was trying to bite us and the police had to handcuff him (which for some reason, probably paperwork, they really didn't like doing). It took the three of us struggling with him to get him to hospital and when he reached the department there needed to be six police guarding him in the psychiatric room.

He was, to use an ambulance service technical medical phrase, '*proper* mad'.

I felt sorry for the fellow – he didn't ask to go out of his gourd.

I also felt pain.

Pain in my back.

While fighting with the patient in the back of the ambulance I had somehow wrenched my back and the whole right side of my body was in pain.

So we went back to station, I filled out the required paperwork and went home. I stayed home for the next two nights, partly due to the pain and partly due to a desire on my part to avoid exacerbating the injury.

Gassed and Splinted

I often bemoan the fact that I tend not to get sent to many jobs involving 'trauma'. If you've been stabbed, I'll be down the road picking up a matern-a-taxi. If you've fallen out of a second-floor window, I'll be one street over dealing with the sleeping drunk. And if you've thrown yourself under a tube train, I'll be one stop down dealing with the twisted ankle.

It's not that I like people to be badly hurt, it's just that I occasionally like to have a job that I have to think about. So the smallest little traumatic injury makes me happy.

We were sent to a 50-year-old man who had fallen. We made our way up the stairs to the gentleman's bedroom and saw him lying on his bed;

with him was a woman in a nursing uniform crying her eyes out. The patient had indeed fallen; his foot was the main injury.

The patient normally wore a caliper on his foot because of nerve damage from having polio as a child. He had fallen and the caliper had caused the toes of his right foot to bend upwards. He had split the skin on the underside of his foot where the toes meet the body of it, and he had probably broken something.

The woman in the nursing uniform (who turned out to be the patient's wife) told us that at least one toe had been dislocated and that the patient had twisted it back into shape himself.

He was, unsurprisingly, in a lot of pain.

First, we gave the patient pain relief, some Entonox. The paramedic I was with was going to give him something stronger, but the patient's pain completely disappeared with the 'gas and air'.

We then bandaged his foot and placed it in a vacuum splint. This is pretty much a sand-filled bag that becomes rigid when you suck the air out of it. They are *very* handy when dealing with injuries in awkward areas. I don't get to use them often, but when I've needed one, they are perfect.

We then had to very carefully carry the patient down the stairs.

All the time the patient was thanking us for looking after his pain and for helping him get to hospital. He was a genuinely nice man, and his wife was nice as well. It was a *good* job. We were able to aid someone who needed help and while we needed to put on our thinking caps as to how best to get the patient out of the house the job went smoothly.

I spoke to him later in hospital – he'd managed to break three toes and one of the bones in his foot; his wife was still with him and once again they thanked us (and let us know that the Entonox was a better painkiller than anything the hospital gave them).

It put me in a good frame of mind for the rest of the day.

🚐 More Crap GP Work

I was working on the FRU again for a shift; I'd turned up to work on an ambulance, but there was no one else to crew up with me.

One of my first calls was to a possible heart attack in a GP surgery.

Once again I found the patient (a very pleasant lady) sitting out in the waiting room. There are a number of treatments that should happen with someone who is having a heart attack. First they should have a full set of vitals, then oxygen should be given along with an aspirin and, if the blood pressure is good enough, a squirt of glyceryl trinitrate (GTN). It's pretty standard stuff and does a world of good for the patient (aspirin alone increases your chance of surviving a heart attack by around 25 per cent).

So, how many of these things had the GP done?

Well, he'd taken some vitals but they were *very* different to what we got in the back of the ambulance. However, vitals can change and I wouldn't want to call the GP a liar.

At no point had the GP given aspirin, GTN or even waved some oxygen under the patient's nose. The receptionist was helpful, and she led the patient from the waiting room into her office so that I could better assess her without everyone in the waiting room listening in.

I checked the patient's blood pressure, gave her some GTN, an aspirin and put her on oxygen; all things that should have already been done by the GP.

Thankfully, the ambulance was pretty quick in turning up, and the patient went off to hospital.

I had a chat with the GP – it's one that I've had a couple of times now. It's a chat about how possible heart attacks shouldn't be sat out in the waiting room, about how ISIS-2 and NICE say that an aspirin should be given. How GTN is a good thing to give such a patient, and that oxygen can really help with the pain and anxiety.

'I don't care about that,' said the GP, 'I just want her to get TROP-I.'

(TROP-I is a special blood test to determine a heart attack.)

He then didn't want to hear that sitting a woman out in the waiting room with a potentially life-threatening condition was, on reflection, a bad idea. I know GPs are busy, but is a two-year-old with an ear infection really more important?

I'm left in awe of GPs who don't seem to want to *treat* anyone. Like nursing homes I'm sure I only meet/remember the rubbish ones. But if my mum was having a heart attack and went to the GP I'd be fuming if they sat her in the waiting room for an ambulance to arrive. It's not hard to give someone an aspirin, it's not hard to give them oxygen and it's definitely not hard to keep an eye on them in your examining room while you wait the (less than) eight minutes it takes for an ambulance to arrive.

I've mentioned before how the LAS will visit and help train rubbish care homes – I'm beginning to wonder if we should also go to GPs and let them know what the ambulance service (and by extension the local A&E departments) expect.

Wasting the Time of a GP

I'm not aiming to annoy GPs, but the day after the 'heart attack in the waiting room' I went to another case where the GP was less than helpful.

It sounded like one of our 'crap' calls: 'six-year-old female, losing weight, tired', not what you'd mark down as needing an emergency service.

The ill child was *very* thin, and her concerned parents told us that she had been losing weight for the past couple of weeks. She was lethargic, wasn't eating well (she was mainly drinking a lot of fizzy drinks) and had been having spells of dizziness. To my eye the child did look rather unwell.

The father had taken her to the GP earlier in the week, and the GP had told him that he was 'wasting his time' and that the child would soon put the weight back on. The father asked for the child to be sent to the hospital, and the GP refused this.

We got the child into the ambulance and starting running our tests.

Her pulse was normal, as were her blood pressure and oxygen levels.

Her blood sugar was not normal. It was above 33 mmols (which is, I think, around 660 dg/l). The normal value is around 5 mmols.

The child was (almost certainly) an undiagnosed diabetic.

In my 'big book of how to tell what might be wrong with someone' there are six probable causes for severe long-term weight loss. They are Malignancy, Depression, Thyrotoxicosis, Uncontrolled Diabetes, Infection and Addison's Disease. Within minutes of meeting this child for the first time, we had a provisional diagnosis.

It's not hard to do a blood sugar test in a GP surgery; it takes less than 30 seconds.

So why did the GP tell the parent to go away? Was it because the GP was so busy trying to fill the government's targets? Or was it the case that the GP considers severe weight loss in six-year-old girls a 'phase' that they will grow out of?

However, now I realise why the ambulance service is doing diabetes screening.

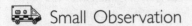 Small Observation

When the weather is nice, a polite 90-year-old woman who has drunk a bit too much wine and has fallen over can be a very endearing patient.

🚑 (Another) Nan Down

Since I am feeling (and to be more honest *looking*) fat I've decided to take up cycling again. I'm sure that I gave a great amount of joy to anyone who saw this particular tubby man puffing and panting against the wind while cycling along at 1 mph. Still, if I want to stop from looking six months pregnant I need to start some exercise. Another reason is a job I did yesterday.

We were sent to a strange call. It was given as 'Elderly woman lying on the green as you enter Kellett Road. Woman may have got up.'

Rushing to the green we found it empty. So we decamped from the ambulance, grabbed our bags and went for a little wander to see if the patient was hiding in a dip in the ground. Across the green, near some houses, some people started waving at us so we trotted over.

The patient was a *very* elderly woman. She was wearing a nightdress, a threadbare cardigan and nothing on her legs. She was also barefoot – I was surprised that the thin skin on her feet hadn't been torn apart by the pavement.

The temperature, not taking into account the strong windchill factor, was around 1° Celsius.

She was – unsurprisingly – a bit blue and she felt like a block of ice.

We only had our medical equipment with us; we didn't have a blanket so I took off my fleece and wrapped it around her before running back to the ambulance to bring it closer to the patient.

I was shocked by how out of breath I was after jogging about 150 yards. Twenty-four hours later and my ankles were still in pain.

I brought the ambulance closer and we bundled the patient into the back, turned the heating on full and wrapped her in our blankets. The patient was one of those little old ladies that you would want to give a good cuddle to if she were your gran. We had a short and uneventful trip to the hospital where she was soon receiving the attention of the nursing staff.

My crewmate filled in a 'vulnerable adult' form, which means that the social services will get involved so that the patient will (hopefully) get any long-term care that she needs.

I managed to get my fleece back.

It now smells of granny wee.

It's in the washing machine as I type this.

More Madness in East London

We were called to a fourth-floor flat in one of the many housing blocks in the east of London where we found an unkempt man in his forties pacing back and forth along the access balcony to his flat.

He wasn't wearing any shoes, socks or a shirt, and his trousers and pants were falling off him.

While he paced he was muttering about God and the Devil.

The patient obviously had mental health issues, but we also suspected something else was causing this behaviour. At one point he made to throw himself over the balcony. We stood in his way to prevent him doing this, and more importantly to stop him making us go through the, frankly hard, work of trying to save his life in the face of major trauma.

As we led him back into his flat to get some shoes/clothes we realised that the reason why he was behaving so strangely might have been exacerbated by drug use. We nearly tripped over an empty bottle of methadone.

The flat was – as I've mentioned before – exactly how you would expect a drug den to look. There was drug paraphernalia strewn around the place, mattresses on the floor and the heavy curtains looked like they had never been drawn.

The patient continued to pace around while occasionally becoming quite agitated. While we didn't think that he would become violent we were still rather wary of getting too close to him or letting our guard down.

After half an hour we had managed to get him dressed and were able to lead him downstairs where we 'ahem' 'gently' got him into the ambulance.

While I drove us to the hospital my crewmate did his best to keep the patient calm. We pre-warned the hospital that they would need security and the secure room ready for us. Unfortunately, the hospital switchboard wasn't picking up the phone so there was no one there to meet us when we rolled up outside the A&E doors.

At one point he exposed his genitals to my crewmate.

A bit of a struggle began where the patient wanted to jump off the ambulance and run away, so my crewmate and I ended up restraining him until security arrived to help drag him into the department's 'padded room'.

I had a similar job the day before, another job where I ended up wrestling with a mentally disturbed patient.

What struck me as amusing was that on consecutive days the first job of the shift was to someone with an altered mental state who was blaming their God and the Devil, and who would later go on to show us their genitals.

I wonder if it's something in the water?

I also sometimes wonder what the mentally disturbed would rant and rave about if we hadn't thought up the idea of religion.

🚑 Ethnic Relations

After two days of struggling with people, it was nice to go back to the simple jobs that are a joy to do. It's also good to see a sense of community.

In this case it was a little old lady who had tripped over a wobbly pavement in one of our local markets. She was surrounded by people of all backgrounds. There was a black market warden who had put cones over the offending paving stones. A Bangladeshi man was chatting to her and two Greek-looking men met me at the ambulance and led me to the patient. A Sikh stall keeper also pointed me in her direction.

The patient herself was one of the dying breed of 'traditional' English east Londoner. Normally an extremely healthy 80-year-old, she had a graze to her nose that refused to stop oozing blood. A real pleasure to talk to, we chatted about how the east of London has changed in her lifetime and how she still enjoyed living here.

'I'm an ethnic minority now,' she told me, 'but there are still a lot of people around who'll help you out.'

And she was right – as an ambulance person I tend only to see the worst of people. I go to the assaults and the arguments. I hear about the murders and the abuse, the neglect and the trouble. Just as this woman was, for me, an unusual patient in that she was a healthy 80-year-old, so it was that I saw the unusual event of people helping someone in distress.

It was one of those jobs that leaves you with a smile on your face for the rest of the day.

🚑 Lying to Patients

Here is the thing – I'm a pretty poor liar. I don't get much practice, I don't like doing it and as part of my personality flaws I love sharing things that I know with anyone who'll listen. Unfortunately, in this business you need to try to keep some things to yourself.

I was called to a place of work where a 55-year-old woman was complaining of constant headaches. When I arrived on the scene a work colleague was comforting her as she had obviously just been crying.

I got a verbal history from the patient – the headache had been coming and going for two weeks and normal painkillers weren't touching the pain. There was no other history of ill health, she hadn't been to the doctor for years and she had no allergies. She told me that on that morning she had woken up with the headache and also a feeling of 'not being connected to the world'. Once more, her painkillers hadn't even touched the pain.

A quick 'n' dirty neurological examination didn't reveal anything particularly scary and her observations were all normal apart from a moderately raised blood pressure. I discounted the blood pressure as her being scared and sitting in the back of an ambulance looking at my ugly face.

So we had a drive over to the hospital.

All through the trip I could see that her main fear was that she had grown a brain tumour. The words were never mentioned but her fear was of such intensity and direction that I knew that this is what she was thinking. I would have loved to lie to her. I would have given a lot to be able to put my arm around her and tell her that there was no chance of the headaches being caused by a brain tumour.

But I couldn't.

I had to sit there and explain about all my 'negative findings'. I could tell her that her pulse was fine, that she hadn't had a stroke, that her blood sugar was better than mine and that her short neurological exam didn't show anything unusual.

But I couldn't tell her what she wanted to hear.

We reached the hospital, and while I handed over to the nurse one side of her face started to become numb ...

A little later, while returning to the hospital with another patient, I saw our woman in the resuscitation room. She was sitting up and talking to her work colleague who had accompanied her in the ambulance. I wondered why she was in there but was too busy to ask the resuscitation nurse.

Towards the end of my shift I saw our patient walking back from the toilet (with colleague still in tow). I asked her what the doctors had found.

'They are keeping me in,' she told me and my heart sank, 'apparently I have a really high blood pressure, and that's what's been causing it.'

'Oh superb!' I said. 'They can cure that!'

You could see that she was a lot more relaxed, and that her main concern was that she was now going to be in hospital while the doctors treated her blood pressure.

Hardly a concern at all.

The thing that I didn't tell her was that her blood pressure had been so high, our machine for recording it hadn't been able to measure it correctly. Which is a little troubling.

Patientside

Let's imagine that you are old and need a bit of care in your home – simple stuff, nothing too taxing, just a bit of a hand to help you wash when you wake up. Maybe you need help with some of the fiddly little tablets you have to take. Perhaps you just need someone who'll help you keep your flat tidy.

Then, for the sake of argument, let's say you've had a bit of a fall – nothing too serious, it's just that your legs are starting to get a bit weak, and you don't want to use the walking frame the hospital has given you. You are lying by your front door. You press the community alarm button you are wearing and when your carer arrives she lets herself in and then the ambulance people.

The ambulance people quickly check you over while you are on the floor – they let you know that they don't want to pick you up if you've broken your leg. So you let them examine you, and when they find nothing, you ask them if they can just put you in your normal chair by the television. You wonder why the ambulance crew are tutting at your carer for not at least putting a pillow behind your head while you were stuck on the floor.

The ambulance crew help you up and put you into your favourite chair. As you aren't hurt by the fall you don't want to go to the hospital – you'll only sit in the department for several hours before some young doctor tells you that you should be using your walking frame. It's easier to sit in your own flat. The ambulance people seem pretty nice, though, and they want to give you a full physical check-up to make sure that there is nothing obvious that would cause you to fall.

You tell the ambulance people that you've been having a few falls as your legs have been getting a bit weaker recently, but that you get around all right and that you have the community alarm button around your neck should you get into any trouble. The ambulance people try to persuade you to go to hospital, but you refuse again. One of the ambulance people checks various pulses and pressures and sugars and heart tracings before agreeing that you can refuse to go with them.

The ambulance man is looking around your flat and tutting at the carer again. He doesn't like it that as he walks around he is making a crunching noise as he crushes your tablets which are strewn all over the carpet. It's not your fault that you sometimes drop them. It's not the carer's job to make sure that you can take your pills.

The ambulance man then asks you that as you don't want to go to hospital, would you mind if he got your GP out to see you? You agree and the ambulance man says that your GP might be able to arrange to have handrails put on your walls – it sounds like a good idea as you really don't like using the walking frame. You tell the ambulance man your GP's phone number but he doesn't want to borrow your phone. He tells you that if his Controller phones the GP then the call is recorded so if the GP promises to come out then they darn well better. You wonder why the ambulance man is so distrusting of GPs.

The ambulance man then disappears for a bit into the kitchen, he's talking to the carer before she leaves. You can't hear what he says, but his voice seems a little forceful.

The ambulance man comes back and asks you one last time if you'd like to go to hospital, you refuse and the ambulance man reminds you to use the walking frame for getting around – and also to make sure that you have your emergency button on you at all times. He tells you that he is only a phone call away. He picks up his equipment and prepares to leave.

You've enjoyed chatting to him and his partner, so you try to keep up a conversation – the only person you regularly see is your carer, and she doesn't talk to you much – she hasn't said a word to you while the ambulance people have been here. The ambulance people stay and have a chat with you, but they can only stay ten minutes. But at least those ten minutes are ten minutes of conversation you wouldn't have had otherwise.

The ambulance people wave goodbye to your carer as she walks out the door without saying a word.

Ten minutes later you wave goodbye to the ambulance people, and you are left on your own until the evening carer comes.

Downstairs in the ambulance, an ambulance man's heart breaks just a little.

🚑 Hit and Run

We were sent out of our area for a 'Pedestrian vs Car'. Often these are 'nothing' jobs, the person isn't badly injured simply because there are very few roads where a car can get up the sort of speed to cause serious injury. Then I had a look on our mapping terminal and which road it was.

'Bugger,' I said to my crewmate, 'could be a nasty one.'

Despite the general low speed of traffic in London, there are still some roads where cars can build up a dangerous speed. This was one of them.

We got there quickly and found an FRU already on scene along with some police, one of whom was holding the patient's neck as still as possible. The patient was writhing around on the ground in a mixture of fear and agony. The FRU paramedic looked rather relieved to see us.

As I jumped out of the ambulance he came over and told me that it was a hit and run, that the patient had been thrown some distance and that she had an open fracture of her arm.

An 'open fracture' is where a bone has been broken and is sticking out of the skin. There is always a worry about infection in this sort of injury; we also worry about nerve and blood vessel damage – it is a serious one.

My first concern, however, was to protect her from any other injuries – specifically any neck or back ones – and then to get her off the cold dark road and into the warm and well-lit ambulance. Then we would 'scoop and run' to the hospital which was less than three minutes down the road.

First things first – I told my crewmate to get our scoop stretcher and trolley bed off the back of the ambulance, then I grabbed a cervical collar and, taking control of the patient's head, placed it around her neck. It is here that I'm glad of my hospital experience as she was wearing a necklace that I took off before putting on the collar – you

346

can't X-ray a neck that has one on it, and once the collar is on then any necklace is that much harder to remove.

While I was doing this the paramedic was putting a temporary dressing on the patient's fracture, so while I was holding the patient's head I started to talk to her. She didn't remember anything about the accident and she kept repeating herself. While this can be normal after a traumatic event, it made me consider, as always, whether she might have received a brain injury as a result of either hitting the car or the ground.

I was certain that we weren't going to 'stay and play' at all.

We strapped her to our scoop, lifted her onto the trolley and then put the trolley in the back of the ambulance. We could have put needles into her, filled her with fluid, given her pain relief – but with the closeness of the hospital I thought that the best thing for her would be to be out of my ambulance as quickly as possible.

In her confused state the patient kept wanting to poke at her broken arm, so the journey to hospital was mainly taken up by my holding her (working) hand while standing over her so I could talk to her in a vain effort to try to keep her calm.

Soon we were relaxing at the hospital having handed the patient over to the resus team. The FRU paramedic told me he had been returning to his station after an equipment failure when someone had jumped out at him and shouted that the patient had been hit by a car. As he put it, 'Four months on the FRU and the most interesting job I have is the one I get waved down for when I have no kit in the motor.'

My crewmate asked me later if I missed A&E nursing. While generally I don't, I do miss a 'nice' trauma sometimes – my first thought is to get the patient into hospital so I don't often get the chance to use my trauma nursing skills.

But then again – I do now get to drive the wrong way down the road.

Rereading this writing from three years ago I have absolutely no recollection of this job, which is strange as I don't get that many trauma calls.

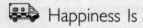 Happiness Is

Happiness is ...

Driving over a crowded Tower Bridge on blue lights and sirens, sometimes on the wrong side of the road.

Despair is ...

Doing all that to get to a drunk who then tries to assault you and ends up crushing your hand against a door handle.

Offering the Chance

There were two police officers standing over the crying woman. From 50 yards you could tell she was an alcoholic, blood matted her hair and she held her head in her hands.

We walked her onto the ambulance, it was warmer than the night air, and we had more comfy seats than the wall she was sitting on.

The policewoman joined us to get the woman's initial statement – as the woman was drunk, another statement would have to be taken after she had sobered up.

The woman told us how she had been drinking all day in the park with her partner and his sister – then her partner's sister had kicked and beaten her before stealing her handbag.

She told us how her partner continually bullied her and how she lived in fear of him. Her partner's name was known to both the police and me and it wasn't known to us for him being a paragon of virtue.

The police officer was friendly and supportive – she called on the specialist team for domestic violence and started the process of getting her referred.

348

I took her to the hospital; while her wounds weren't serious she would need some sort of social services input before she could be discharged – her home wouldn't be a safe place to go.

'This time,' she told me, 'this time, I'll press charges and get out from him.'

When she sobered up she'd probably go back to him, but we had to offer her all the chances we could – just in case, this time, she was right.

Sometimes, life is like a bad TV programme.

Shaken Baby

We were called by the police to a child of a few months old. The father of the child had allegedly got into an argument with its mother. He had then shaken the baby in an attempt to silence its crying.

The police had already arrested the father and taken him away. The child seemed unhurt by the assault. However, we took the child to the hospital for a check-up.

What strikes me (besides the obvious bastardy of shaking a baby) is that even if he becomes the best father in the world, should his child, when grown, ever look at their medical notes the words that will leap out at them will be, 'Patient violently shaken by father.'

Imagine if you were to find something like that in your medical notes. How do you think that would make you feel?

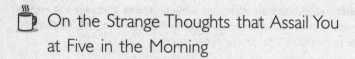 On the Strange Thoughts that Assail You at Five in the Morning

I have two ideas. One is more serious than the other.

I'll leave you to decide which one is serious.

Idea One

The LAS should have business cards printed up which state something along the lines of 'Due to your inability to control your drinking of alcohol you have wasted the time and resources of an emergency ambulance and staff (including dispatchers and call takers), an A&E department along with nurses, doctors, radiographers and other NHS staff. Please think on this.' We could then leave these in the pockets of the drunk patients we pick up so that they could reflect on their behaviour when sober.

We might have to get it printed up in a few languages, though ...

Idea Two

Concerning matern-a-taxis at 5 a.m. Can I beat one of them to death please? Just as a warning to the others.

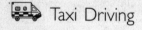 Taxi Driving

Matern-a-taxi!

Ten minute contractions!

Treated as a large yellow taxi by the whole family!

The family never said thank you to their highly skilled medical crew!

Treated to a free pram, carry cot and car seat by my taxes!

(If they have a car seat then they must have a car.)

Total distance travelled: 0.8 miles!

Unhappiness of this particular ambulance crew for being used as taxi drivers: 7/10!

An Upsetting Job

She was 31 years old and I was kneeling next to her forcing air into her lungs because she had stopped breathing.

I was sent the call as a '31-year-old suspended' and to be honest I didn't think that it was going to be as given. 'Suspended' means no signs of life, and that tends not to happen to young people. I was working solo on the FRU at the time, and I sped to the address, reaching the place at the same time as the ambulance. It was an ambulance with two trainees working it. While one of the trainees and I went to the patient the other one and their supervisor turned the vehicle around so that they could leave the scene quickly if needed.

I rang the bell to the block of flats. Whoever answered the entryphone seemed to be a bit disorientated, but we soon got in.

'Probably a psychiatric patient,' I said to the trainee as we stood in the lift.

'I hope so,' replied the trainee, 'I've not done a suspended before.'

'Don't worry about it,' I said. 'Just remember that you need to try to keep calm. I'm there to run it until your supervisor gets there.'

The doors to the lift opened and we made our way to the flat. I walked in through the door and all hopes of the call not being a suspended were dashed.

The patient, a deep shade of blue, was lying flat on the floor. Over her was a man I took to be her partner; he had one ear on the phone, listening to instruction from one of our call takers. Tears were running down his face as with his free hand he pushed on the woman's chest in an effort at CPR.

On the sofa was the daughter of the patient – she was around five or six years old. She was also crying. I realised that it was this little child who had opened the flat door for us.

The trainee and I fell into our roles – I managed the patient's airway and breathing while the trainee connected the defibrillator. The patient had had a pulse but had suddenly stopped breathing. There was nothing in the patient's history to suggest what had caused this sudden stopping of breathing. The mother had overcome a serious illness a few years earlier, but that wouldn't account for what was happening today.

The job itself went pretty well; while the patient didn't start breathing again on her own, we did manage to 'pink her up' a lot. The transport to hospital went well and we handed the patient over to the hospital staff with a real hope that she would make a recovery.

I went back to the hospital a while later.

The patient had suffered a sudden huge and unrecoverable bleed into the brain. She would never wake up.

For some reason this really upset me. I don't normally get upset at people dying, but for some reason this one really did.

I don't know if it was because she had left a small child behind – a small child who saw her mother die in front of her. I don't know if it was because the mother overcame a serious illness six years ago for the sake of her child. I didn't know what would happen to the child as the mother's current partner wasn't the biological father.

I suspect that it was because, for once, I thought that in giving the patient the best chance possible, she might have survived. I'm guessing that I was disappointed that the patient died despite doing our best work.

Whatever the reason, I was at my most upset over a dead patient since I'd attended the death of a 13-year-old a year ago.

If there is a slight upside to the story it's that because we kept her organs protected by breathing for her, those same organs were used to give a new lease of life for a number of other very sick patients. I only hope that this fact gave some comfort to her family.

Yes, I'm a registered organ donor.

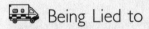 Being Lied to

The patient said that he had been kidnapped.

He hadn't.

He said that the people who had kidnapped him were Serbian.

He then said that they were Bosnians, then that they were 'Pakis'.

He said that the keys to his car had been stolen.

When the police searched him, they found his car keys.

He said he didn't know where the damage to the side of his car came from.

There was a matching damaged skip just down the road.

He said he had been walking home.

Other people had seen him driving; they were the ones who had called the ambulance.

He said he had only had a drink or two.

He was so drunk, he could barely walk.

He said that he didn't want any trouble.

He had previous convictions for assaulting both the police and ambulance crews.

He told the police that he didn't want them involved.

He got arrested for drink-driving.

He told us to 'fuck off'.

So we did. Then he spat at the police.

We put one of our face masks on him to stop him spitting at anyone else.

He smashed his head against the floor in temper.

His hand was causing him pain, but the injury wouldn't cause any lasting damage.

We were quite happy that he refused the ambulance. The police doctor would probably arrange an X-ray and treatment of his hand.

I hate drunk drivers with a passion. I particularly hate abusive drunk drivers who could have killed someone and who have been flagged as being violent towards anyone in a uniform. When he told us to 'fuck off', I was more than happy to open the door to the ambulance and have the police remove him.

For some reason I find it difficult to care about his painful hand.

🚑 Clockwatching

It's 3 a.m. in the lonely hours of the morning and I'm nervous.

We are in the bedroom of a six-year-old boy. His mother found him having trouble in breathing half an hour ago.

His airways are so tight that every breath that he takes turns his chest inside out. He is trying to breathe so hard that I'm waiting for his breastbone to snap under the strain.

From across the room I can hear the air whistling through a tiny airway. He has the classic posture of the asthmatic trying to force air into their lungs – he's sitting upright, hands on knees.

He can't cry, he hasn't the breath for it.

I want him in the ambulance. No, I want him in *hospital*.

But we can't go just yet. The single mother has two other children, both under the age of five, and they can't be left alone in the house. They need to be woken up and dressed. One needs to be thrown, still sleeping, into a pushchair.

I'm counting the seconds; I'm waiting for the boy to start turning blue.

I'm eyeing the kit in our bag, how much experience has my crewmate had in intubating a closed-down airway?

We are already giving him all the drugs that we can. He's so sick that he quietly accepts the noisy nebuliser mask.

I help the mother dress one of her children – socks and shoes slipped onto sleepy feet.

Then it's time to go. Like all parents she worries about our insistence that we leave the child topless as we walk out into the cold air. It's because of his high temperature I tell her. I don't tell her that it's also so we can easily see that he's still breathing.

For once my big fear isn't a complaint from the mother – it's that the child will die in the back of our ambulance.

I pass the 'blue' call over the radio to pre-alert the hospital; the radio isn't working too well so I have to repeat some of it. I don't think that the radio operator understands one of the medical terms that I use; it's not their fault as it's pretty obscure. The broken radio means that I can't be sure of the read back.

I don't care, as long as they have the paediatric doctor waiting for us there I'll be happy.

We are 1.9 miles from one hospital, 2.4 from another. I go for the further hospital, the drive is straighter and I can use the A13 which at this time of the night is clear. The other hospital has too many speed-bumps and side turnings on the route.

I'm listening to what is going on in the back of the ambulance. My crewmate sounds relaxed and over the sound of the engine is the reassuring noise of the child's breathing.

I glance at the speedometer – I'm hitting 80 mph; I didn't know that these ambulances reached that kind of speed. I'm thankful that the road is clear and empty and that there are no hazards.

I spot the patient's young sister looking at my face in the rear-view mirror, her eyes wide open now.

We pull up to the hospital and I take care of our patient's siblings; I bed them down in the relatives' room while the doctors and nurses and mother look after their brother.

It's only half an hour later that I'm talking with the paediatric nurses. While it looked touch and go for a bit, our patient responded well to the medications that we can't give. His breathing is back to normal.

I love the paediatric A&E nurses at this hospital; they are experts at what they do and despite the cynicism that is endemic in the NHS, they really do care for their patients.

We are chatting and laughing at the memory of our fear. We have fought back against death, and this laughter is our victory cheer.

The family are reunited.

I still have that memory of fear, though.

Thank You Taxpayers

If you pay UK taxes, I'd like to take a moment to thank you. You have helped me out quite a bit.

We got a call as 'Two people in collapsed state', so we rattled around to the house only to find the two 'patients' having a nice (for them) drug trip. They were boyfriend and girlfriend and the boy's mother had called the ambulance. She told me how they were both known to use drugs, and that her son had spent some time in a rehab unit trying to kick his drug and alcohol addiction.

We called for another ambulance as they were so far into their drugged state they were in a real danger of blocking their own airways and choking to death. There was no way we could transport both patients.

So I stayed downstairs with the man. He was 6 feet 2 inches, built like a brick outhouse that has a hobby as a weightlifter. My crewmate looked after his girlfriend in the bedroom. Sometimes I draw the short straw ...

Eventually another ambulance turned up (we were having a very busy night), and we started to move the patients into the ambulances.

Unfortunately for me, the male patient became just a bit agitated and started waving his arms about. He managed to string together a couple of naughty swear words just for my ears. As we got him into the ambulance he managed to punch my crewmate and kick the FRU driver who had arrived to help us out.

As I was trying to strap him down onto the bed he swung an arm at me and caught me in the face.

My glasses went flying off my head, bounced around the back of the ambulance and landed in pieces at my feet.

I'd just like to state that without my glasses I score a 9/10 on the Mr Magoo Scale. This is about the level where you would pick up a skunk thinking that it was a pet cat while being just shy of walking into walls.

We took both patients into the local hospital, where the young man decided to kick off again. He tried biting a couple of us until the docs could dose him up with Haldol, which calmed him down.

I then called Control on our radio and let them know that I was no longer able to work – I don't have a spare pair of glasses, so there was no way I could continue.

Control sent one of our new duty station officers (DSOs) over for a chat – I've got to say I was pretty impressed with him, he seemed to have a good idea of what was going on and he talked a lot of sense. He told me that each night around ten ambulance crews are assaulted, which is a surprisingly large number given the shortage of ambulances on the road each night.

He also told me that when I got new glasses I should give the receipt to him so that he could do battle with the finances department and then I could claim the money back. Asking him if the patient would be made to pay by the LAS, I was told that this wouldn't be the case and that the money would come out of our normal funding.

I was told not to buy any solid gold glasses.

I find this a bit ridiculous. Here is a patient who has indulged in something illegal – he has assaulted a number of ambulance and hospital staff (thankfully no one was seriously injured) – he has wasted all our time and broken an essential bit of kit for the running of an ambulance. Because of him there was one less ambulance covering our area that night.

And he's going to get away without losing a penny.

I can see why we don't bother pressing criminal charges against him (I have read enough police and magistrate blogs to understand a little about the CPS), but you'd think that we could win some small civil action against him.

So, as it is, my new glasses are being provided by the taxpayer.

Thanks.

It took the LAS just over a year to refund me the money I spent on my glasses, no wonder outside contractors charge the NHS more for any work they do – it's to make up for lost interest while they wait for them to actually cough up the cash.

Helpful Demons

The government hates hoodies, the media lambast hoodies, people in the street are scared of hoodies. Hoodies are urban demons that do nasty things to people and then post them up on YouTube.

We were on a nice simple job – a woman had taken her child to the GP; the GP had called us because he thought that the child needed to go to hospital.

As we pulled up outside the surgery, a group of hoodies wandered up.

'What's happening?' they asked.

'Plane crash. Didn't you hear it?' My standard answer – anyone would think that children didn't learn about patient confidentiality in schools these days.

We entered the surgery and were directed to the patient. The GP was still with the two-year-old and the mother. It was nice to see a GP who continued to care for the patient while waiting for the ambulance.

The child had had some breathing difficulties during the day and the GP had already started treatment with some salbutamol nebulisers. The mother didn't speak any English so the GP (who was from the same ethnic group) explained what would be happening and we made a move to the ambulance.

Outside the surgery the hoodies were still hanging around. We opened the door to the ambulance to allow the mother and child to get onboard but she just stood there saying something to me in some Asian language.

We tried our usual attempts to communicate but the woman refused to get onto the ambulance.

'Here mate,' said one of the hoodies, 'she says she wants to phone her husband.'

'Could you tell her that she can phone him when she gets to the hospital? We haven't got phones on the ambulance.'

There was a bit of a dialogue between the two of them.

At the original hoodie's direction one of the others in the group pulled out a phone and handed it to the woman.

'She can use my mate's phone if you want then she'll be happier to get in the ambulance.'

There was some attempt to ring her husband, but unfortunately his phone was engaged. The hoodies then spoke to her and she agreed to get onto the ambulance.

We tried to assess the child but the mother wouldn't let us take his coat off.

Once again, our 'street thug' group translated for us.

'She says he'll cry if you touch him.'

The GP treatment had obviously worked well so we weren't about to argue the point. We would just take her and her child to hospital and one of the nurses there could translate for her.

I thanked the hoodies for their help before getting into the ambulance and driving off.

'No problem mate.'

So there you have it, these demonised members of society helped us and the woman by translating and offering the use of a phone. Of course, that won't make it to the front page of the newspapers. I'm old enough to have seen the reality of the cycles of media hatred and scapegoating. I remember skinheads being to blame for all society's wrongs, then the punks, then the ravers, now it's hoodies.

I'm sure that people older than me can go further back. I'm certain that some will remember everyone blaming the teddy boys in a similar way.

Silliness.

Absurd Council 'Thinking'

So picture the thought processes that went into these decisions:

You have a young woman who has already broken her ankle in a suicide attempt by jumping out a second-floor flat window.

So the council rehouse her ... in a fifth-floor flat.

When her husband attempts to protect her by installing metal grilling over the flat's balcony, the council threaten him with court action for 'defacing' the building.

We've just taken her to hospital because she was threatening suicide by jumping out a window.

Perhaps the council can rehouse her in an even taller building?

Twits.

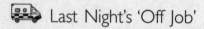 Last Night's 'Off Job'

Take off your shoe.

Now remove your sock/stocking.

Get a ballpoint pen (red for added authenticity).

Lightly touch the nib of the pen against the sole of your foot.

You are now looking at the same wound that I went to last night. As a Category A call.

The patient was a 25-year-old woman who had stood on a sliver of glass. The pain was apparently so bad that not only couldn't she walk, but the pain was travelling up her leg and into her chest.

Chest pain = Category A call = blue light response, get there in eight minutes or someone might die.

I had to wheel her out of her expensive riverside ~~flat~~ apartment.

Her husband told us that he would follow behind us in his car.

The only sound you could hear while she was being wheeled out was Reynolds grinding his teeth.

After she was safely dropped off at hospital I indulged in a little 'primal scream' therapy.

🚑 Wild Geese

This night shift was lovely and easy. One patient was a little old man who was 'not right' and had 'vague eyes'. His wife was terribly worried about him, but I suspect that there was little seriously wrong with him. We then got sent to a two-week-old baby with a flaky scalp. Once more, a nice easy job where we didn't even have to carry the patient.

Then we were sent to '54-year-old male with chest pain'. The call had come from a public telephone box so I wasn't too surprised when we received the update 'Patient has been drinking.' The area is a local haunt of our homeless alcoholics – there are public toilets, a nice churchyard nearby to hide and sleep in and a number of off-licences to buy their cheap tramp juice.

Both the FRU and us spent some time driving back and forth trying to find him, with no luck.

We got back on station before being sent on a similar call in the same area. I suddenly had a brainwave.

'I bet it's John Smith,' I said. 'He's an alcoholic homeless guy, normally as good as gold, but he calls us when his hostel kicks him out for drinking.'

We got an update: 'Patient's name is John Smith.'

Once more we chased around the area looking for him; at least this time I knew who we were looking for. Once more he had given us the slip. I'd never known him to act like this.

Still, next time I see him I'll have a little word in his shell-like ...

Three years later, I haven't seen him again. Perhaps we should check the churchyard for an extra set of remains?

Why You Should Pull Over and Let Us Pass (Or Hahahahahaha ...)

A quick thank you to one of the police cars of Newham.

There we were last night, driving on blue lights and sirens to a job that would ultimately prove to be as dull as ditchwater.

I was racing down Barking Road. I always race to high priority jobs, it's what I'm paid to do.

Ahead of us, at the junction with Ron Leighton Way, there was a police car. They saw and heard us coming so they pulled over to let us pass. Just then another car decided to overtake the police car in the middle of the junction, pulling out in front of us so that we had to slam on the brakes to avoid driving into them.

I may have honked our horn at them.

So it was with much merriment that I saw in our rear-view mirror the police car pulling the car over in preparation for a jolly good talking to.

We were laughing about it for the rest of our shift.

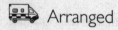 Arranged

I had two new experiences yesterday. I'll tell you about the job I had that left me unhappy that I couldn't help more.

We arrived at the same time as the police to find an Indian woman crying on her bed. We had been sent round to the house because she was supposedly threatening to jump from a window and there were signs of a disturbance all around the bedroom. The woman herself wasn't seriously physically harmed although she had a few scratches to one of her wrists, an obvious sign of attempted self-harm.

She was lying face down on the bed, sobbing uncontrollably. Her husband told us that he had 'done something wrong' and that she had got upset over it.

She was obviously in no fit state to remain at home but it took a long 20 minutes to persuade her to make a move down to the ambulance where we could have a private chat with her.

Her story was simple, yet one I hadn't come across before.

Her marriage had been 'arranged'; she had met the man who was to be her husband just four months before they married. The pair of them lived in a house with her husband's mother and sister. The husband was apparently seeing other women on the side and his mother had told our patient that this was normal in England. Our patient told me, between sobs, that her mother-in-law and sister-in-law both bullied her.

Her only family was out in India, and today when she had told her father about her troubles he had started crying. This is what had sent her into such a distraught state. She was distressed because she had made *her family* unhappy.

My only option was to offer her a trip to hospital so that they could clean and dress her minor wounds. The police officer, however, could offer more; she took my patient's mobile phone number and promised that she would pass that number onto the groups that deal with situations like this. All I could do was get her out of the house for a couple of hours so that she could collect herself and start thinking about what she could do next. As I often feel in such distressing cases I wished that there was more I could do for her.

I would imagine that due to the ethnic make-up of east London there are quite a few arranged marriages. I'm always suspicious about the marriages where a 40-year-old man is married to a 26-year-old female. While I'm not completely against the idea of arranged marriages, there does need to be specialist support for those people who are quite obviously powerless in the relationship.

Arranged marriages should not be about power over a woman being given to a man.

I hope that the woman whom we left in the A&E department will be able to get the support she needs and that the short period of time I knew her will be a turning point for her.

 ## Sugar

The Tate and Lyle sugar factory is pretty much smack bang in the middle of my 'patch'. When I was on the FRU and ordered to 'go and drive around – see if you can find someone injured', I would often travel past it. I'm a bit of a geek and factories full of pipes, chimneys belching strange smelling smoke and arcane bits of machinery interest me greatly. However, until today I'd never actually been inside this behemoth of a factory.

The call was pretty simple – the hydraulics of a forklift truck had burst, and the fluid had splashed into the driver's eyes. Luckily he had been wearing safety goggles, so had been spared the full brunt of the spray. The company's first aider/fireman had already washed his eyes out with plenty of saline so there was little for us to do except take him to hospital to make sure that nothing had scratched the front of them.

But that wasn't the fun bit ...

To show us where the patient was a security guard met us at the main gate then he jumped into a Vauxhall Astra and drove like a man possessed through the factory grounds towards the patient.

I was driving.

I got to chase him. I got to chase him the length of the factory.

More importantly I got to chase him through narrow turnings and under footbridges full of pipes. Smoke was billowing out from vents while I dodged between lorries and powered up ramps.

In my head the theme music to *The Sweeney* was playing.

I just *may* have giggled like a nine-year-old girl.

Yet another thing that I love about my work – I get to go into some strange places.

F-off

I have just felt a surge of rage.

Some bastard just told us to F-off simply because we dared approach *his* crossing point on blue lights and sirens and expected him to wait the second it would take us to pass.

Somehow (don't ask how) I managed to avoid jumping out and punching him in his gobby mouth.

... and breathe and relax ... breathe and relax ...

The Standard Weekend Night

I return to work for a Friday, Saturday, Sunday night shift.

Deep joy.

The standard breakdown for a weekend night shift is as follows:

19:00 – Clock on at the station.

19:01 – First call, normally to someone elderly, probably chest pain.

20:00 – Man with 'man-flu'.

21:00 – First assault of the night, outside a pub.

22:00 – 'Unconscious' male in street – normally a homeless guy.

23:00 – Another assault. Fuelled by alcohol.

00:00 – 'Unconscious' – drunk in street.

01:00 – Child with a high temperature – everyone in the house is awake.

02:00 – Young man with bellyache/young woman with dizziness. (*We are now the only ambulance running from West Ham.*)

03:00 – Nightclubs kick out. An assault who doesn't want to go to hospital.

03:30 – Drunk in the street or a drunk who has injured themselves.

04:30 – Get back to station.

04:31 – Matern-a-taxi.

06:00 – Another matern-a-taxi.

06:30 – Return to station – start watching the clock for sign off at 07:00.

06:57 – Get a job for a little old lady with cardiac chest pain, miles out of my area.

06:57:01 – Start swearing.

07:25 – After a 'scoop and run' return to station to sign off – all ready to repeat the night in just 11 hours and 35 minutes.

Moped Madness

So the first job of the night turned out not to be an elderly person with a common medical ailment, but instead a young man who had hit a car then while limping home had caused three people to call an ambulance.

Add in another call in the same general area and you had a potential for chaos. However, our Control staff are pretty good so everything was sorted out.

The patient had reached his home and then started hyperventilating, with all the symptoms that this brings. Luckily he wasn't seriously hurt and once he had calmed down it made for a fairly easy job and a pleasant trip to the hospital.

🚑 Sucking Lungs

The second job of the night is a two-day-old baby who has coughed up 'something white'. It's an easy job where the parent carries a healthy baby into the ambulance, I drive it 800 yards and the local hospital provides reassurance.

Forgiveness is also due because the birth was difficult and the baby was born two weeks early. Although there is some negative marking for thinking that the baby 'needed suctioning for amniotic fluid still in the lungs'.

I'd just like to say that my (female) crewmate finds babies cute.

I don't.

🚑 Persuasion

I used to swim. I used to swim a lot and so it was a nice surprise to be called back to one of the swimming pools that I used to spend so much time in. Unfortunately it was for a drowning.

Rather obviously we raced around to the pool. A member of staff kindly ran us to the first aid room where we would find our patient. During this run, carrying pretty much the entire contents of our ambulance with us, I was going through my mind about everything I knew about drowning – I was expecting a lot of work on this job.

We entered the first aid room, and the patient, a young lad, was wrapped in a space blanket, sitting up chatting with his friends. My crewmate and I both breathed a sigh of relief.

We spoke to the patient, his friends and the two lifeguards who'd pulled him out of the water. The patient had been unconscious on the bottom of the pool for around 30 seconds; after the lifeguards had pulled him out the patient had started breathing on his own. A short period of time after looking 'shocked' and 'shaking' the patient had made an apparent full recovery.

'I don't want to go to hospital,' he told me. 'I'm all right.'

My crewmate and I looked at each other.

I turned back to the patient. 'You haven't got a choice mate – you *are* going to hospital.'

As I looked at the patient the thing that was foremost in my mind (and the mind of my crewmate) was 'secondary drowning'. In secondary drowning there can be damage to the lungs caused by the inhalation of a fluid. The patient will then die a couple of hours after being pulled from the water.

He was going to hospital. I just had to persuade him. So I tried all the nice ways, the ways that won't worry the patient, the ways that maintain respect and autonomy and all those other hippy words that are apparently so important even if the patient is bleeding to death in front of you.

None of it worked.

Time for the big guns.

'OK mate,' I said, 'the reason why we are taking you to hospital is because of a thing called secondary drowning – you are all right now, but it can cause you to drop dead in a couple of hours, and there would be nothing we could do about it. So you *are* coming to the hospital with us – you have no choice in the matter.'

He agreed to come to hospital with us. He was a pleasant young man, and he was given the all clear a bit later that day.

My point is that despite the cries of the 'respect brigade', sometimes you have to become a patriarchal bully in the best interests of the patient. Sometimes it's the only way to get the patient the care that you know they need. I don't like bullying people, but sometimes it's the only way to protect both the patient – and my job.

So, sod it, sometimes I'm a bully.

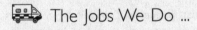 The Jobs We Do …

We arrived at the location at the same time as the FRU, one of those warrens of estate flats that cover our patch. It was gone nine in the evening and there were patches of rain. The job started well as I fell arse over tit up an unlit flight of stairs while carrying some of our kit.

Our patient was given as a 60-year-old having an asthma attack. After peering at door numbers in the dark and climbing three flights of stairs we finally managed to find the flat. Our FRU was peering at his watch, he was off work in ten minutes so was hoping that we wouldn't need his help.

A bedraggled woman opened the door; she was in her late fifties and was crying.

'She's dead,' she said to us, 'she's dead.'

I pushed past her, not knowing what to expect.

The body was lying on the floor, half in the living room, half in the hallway. Flies crawled over it, and there was the smell of death in the flat.

'I came home from shopping and she was just lying there,' the woman sobbed.

I wondered if I should check for a pulse on the corpse. But where is the pulse on a dead dog?

The deceased was a rather overweight collie dog. I walked over to it – while my expertise is in dead people, it was pretty obvious that the animal had been dead for some time. It looked like doggy CPR would not be needed. It would also take an hour to shave the dog enough to be able to stick our defibrillator pads to its chest. So we decided to step outside our guidelines and declare the patient dead without the customary heart-trace.

My crewmate looked after the human patient as I waved the relieved FRU goodnight. It looked like at least one of us would be getting off work on time for a change.

I looked around the flat; it was a bit cluttered and a little grimy but not too bad. Unfortunately there has been an explosion in the fly population in east London recently and I think that most of them came from this flat. One bit of flypaper had been hung and it was solid with the bodies of flies. The rest buzzed around us, landing where the dog had evacuated its bowels and then in our hair.

Lovely.

Our patient was incredibly upset that her dog had died and I have complete sympathy for this. It's awful to lose a loved pet and as this woman lived alone it was probably her only company. She'd become so upset she'd started to have trouble breathing. My crewmate had already done a good job of calming the woman down, but every time she saw the body she'd start crying again.

It also became obvious that the woman had some sort of mental illness; she had some strange beliefs that didn't affect her ability to look after herself and was a bit 'off' (which is obviously a highly professional medical term for 'somewhat eccentric').

The woman also refused to come to hospital.

But what could we do? All the council workers who would remove the dog would be home having their supper.

Once more it was down to the ambulance service to step outside our normal job of giving people a taxi ride to hospital.

Leaving my crewmate with the woman I made my way back down to the ambulance and radioed Control. After giving her the story there was silence on the other end of the radio followed by laughter. Once she had stopped laughing she asked if she could phone me privately. A few moments later my phone rang and I was greeted by Control giggling down the line at me.

Once the pair of us had calmed down a bit we decided to contact the RSPCA and see what they could advise. After a bit of toing and froing I ended up speaking to one of their inspectors. For some reason they are only really interested in animals that still have a pulse, but he did tell me that the Harmsworth animal hospital would take the dog in to be cremated if our patient agreed.

I checked with Control that it would be all right for us to do this; they agreed that it was in the patient's best interests and none of us wanted to leave her all night with an incontinent dead dog in her living room. We spoke to the patient and, after saying her final goodbyes, she agreed to let us take the dog.

I'd been in the job longer than my crewmate, so I made sure that I was at the head end, while she got the leaky end that was covered in maggots. She's worked with animals before so didn't mind.

Honest.

We wrapped the corpse in a sheet and started lugging the dead weight down the stairs.

Now, I know it's awful to lose a pet. I've known people devastated by the loss of a dog and can fully sympathise. But there was something inherently funny about two ambulance folks carrying a dead dog out to an ambulance at the dead of night. So I'll admit that there were a fair few giggles. All the time we were hoping that no one would look out of their window to wonder what we were doing.

Finally we made it to the ambulance and loaded up. Just then a police carrier crept up to us and asked if we needed any help with anything (for we were on *that* kind of estate). We told them the story. I think they enjoyed the entertainment.

We then found ourselves driving across London with a dead dog in the back of our ambulance. My crewmate spotted me checking the corpse in the rear-view mirror – there then may have been some suggestion that I thought it was a zombie dog and that it was waiting to attack ...

We reached the Harmsworth hospital and signed over the dog to the very helpful nurse. I'm not sure what the people in the waiting room made of two ambulance people carrying a dead dog past them in a sheet, all four legs stiffly pointed in the air.

Then it was a case of mopping out the back of the ambulance (where the dog had ... leaked) and getting on with finding some less hirsute patients.

Now, some people might think of this as a waste of an ambulance, but we did what we had to do in order to help the woman, to stop her having stress-related breathing difficulties. We also filled in one of our 'vulnerable adult' forms to refer her to the social services in order to help with her fly infestation and maybe have someone formally assess her mental health. Sorting out someone's health by removing a dead dog is a new treatment – perhaps I could get a grant to research it?

On Dealing with a Brain Surgeon

I was sent to a twelve-year-old whose hand had been burnt. The address that we were given was in the street so we could expect anything.

Outside the local newsagent was a group of 'feral' children, eight or nine of them aged 10–13 I'd say. I told my crewmate who was driving that we would 'scoop and run' as it was near the end of our shift and there was no way that I wanted to try to control a bunch of little thugs.

'Who's the patient?' I asked as I jumped out of the ambulance. I'd already spotted one lad holding his thumb; sure enough he identified himself as the patient.

'OK then, on the ambulance.' I opened the door and bundled him in.

About six of the other children all wanted to come with him. I wasn't going to hang about to argue so, after discovering that there was no relative or adult present, we made our way to the hospital leaving his friends by the side of the road.

The child had decided to spray some deodorant into a glass jar then drop a match in it. As the fumes caught light his hand had received a minor but painful searing. The skin wasn't even red.

Still, we have a nice burns dressing that smells lovely and can ease the pain so I wrapped his hand in one and asked him why he had done such a daft thing.

'Dunno,' was this particular brain surgeon's answer.

I told him, in no uncertain terms, that playing silly buggers with chemicals and fire would only lead to him getting even more hurt. Did it do any good? Well I doubt it, but surely it was worth a try.

Here comes the confession – I was a little short with him. Not only do I think that a 'there, there, everything will be all right' approach would have been wasted on him, but I also wanted to make sure that he knew exactly what an idiot he'd been. I wanted to embarrass him, I wanted him to pay attention and most of all I didn't want him doing similar things in the future. There may have been some sarcasm; hopefully he'll remember that more than if I'd been all motherly towards him.

My brother is a teacher – he uses sarcasm when needed to control his classes; he can be nice and he can be a right evil sod, it all depends on the child and on the situation. So on that day I took a leaf out of his book.

I just hope that I don't end up returning to that child after he's torched his parents' house.

Forgetting Your History

The first patient of our shift this morning was a classic example of how patients can often forget a potentially useful part of their medical history. The patient was an elderly man with a general sort of abdominal ache. We quizzed him about his history (nothing especially relevant apart from some possibly constipating drugs); our initial idea was that the patient had constipation.

It was only as we were wheeling him out of his front door that he mentioned that he had diverticulitis – a medical condition that can cause exactly the type of pain he was describing.

At least he mentioned it to us rather than waiting and telling the nurses, making us look like fools, something that happens with some regularity (they'll then go on to tell the doctors something additional, thereby making the nurses look bad).

🚑 A Warning

Dear Opiate Addict,

Just a quick letter to give you a warning – especially if you are in the east London area (although I do not know how far the distribution of drugs stretches).

It appears that there is a batch of illegal opiates on the streets of east London. What is unusual about this particular batch is that I believe it to be cut with a little less chalk/rat poison/talcum powder than usual. I can tell you this because my friends and I have come across a number of regular users of these substances who have overdosed.

Signs of an overdose include a reduced desire to breathe, purplish lips and ending up being buried in a cemetery in a wooden box called a coffin.

As a suggestion – if you desire to inject/smoke opiate-based drugs, try a little less than you normally use, and make sure that there is someone 'straight' to watch over you. If your rate of breathing drops below ten breaths a minute they should call for an ambulance. Tell the caller not to worry, the ambulance service and the hospitals don't involve the police. If they wish, just ask them to leave the door open before they run away. A note pinned to your chest may also be useful.

Try not to vomit. It just makes a mess.

I would also ask that when we revive you, try not to attack the ambulance crew for 'ruining the buzz' – trust me, we only do this if we think that you are about to die.

At least you know that the rest of the batch you have may last you a little longer than expected.

Keep safe out there!

Yours,

A friendly ambulance person

🚐 Bloody CPR

I'd give his friend 11 out of 10 for sheer guts – he did something I wouldn't have done in a million years.

They'd left him sitting on the garden seat enjoying the afternoon sun – last night had been a heavy drinking session and he was a bit sleepy. He was fine half an hour ago, but when they next saw him he was covered in bloody vomit and he wasn't breathing.

I was working solo on the FRU car when I got the call as 'bad hangover – sleepy – not breathing'. As I didn't know any better I was thinking about what I would say to them when I arrived to find the patient breathing, something about ambulances not being needed for hangovers … Still – no matter; as always I drove there as quickly and safely as possible.

His friends opened the front door for me and I walked into the house. One of them, in a thick Eastern European accent, asked me to follow him. He led me out to the garden; lying on the patio in front of me was the patient. He wasn't breathing, he was covered in bloody vomit and he was a nasty shade of mottled purple. One friend was doing good chest compressions while on the phone to our Control.

Another friend was giving him mouth-to-mouth … through the bloody vomit covering the patient's nose and mouth.

I've got to say that this impressed me a huge amount. It also made me feel a little ill.

To be honest, if his friends hadn't been doing CPR I probably would have recognised death right there at the scene. As it is, if someone starts CPR then we have to continue all the way to the hospital. I started doing my job – breathing for the patient using my ambu-bag and pounding on his chest to keep blood flowing to the essential organs.

Every time I pressed on his chest a little geyser of bloody vomit erupted from his mouth. With an airway in the patient's mouth, that gush of fluid can travel a long way. The ground around the patient was also covered in his vomit so I couldn't kneel down. I ended up doing the chest compressions standing with my feet five feet apart while bending over the patient.

My back started to twinge.

The ambulance took *ten* minutes to get there. To be fair, they did have a long way to travel, and there were some heavy roadworks between them and me. We scooped him up into the ambulance and drove quickly to the hospital while I continued to do chest compressions and the ambulance attendant kept breathing for him.

As suspected there was nothing that we or the hospital could do – another man in his mid-forties dead.

I had to go back to the house to pick up the FRU car. The patient's friends came out to meet me; only a few of them spoke English. I had to explain that the patient had died. The ambulance service doesn't like to use the word 'died'. Unfortunately it was the word I had to use. I let them know that they had done everything correctly but that the patient didn't have much chance of surviving despite his friends' best efforts.

I left them trying to phone the patient's mother so that they, in their native tongue, could explain what had happened.

 Stabbings and Sex Politics

I arrived on station this morning to hear the news on the television that there had been 50 stabbings over the bank holiday weekend.

'Hmm,' I thought, 'a few more than normal, but hardly news.'

Then I realised that they were talking about the whole country and not just London.

So now I was surprised at just how low the number of stabbings was.

I don't know if it's just east London having a higher number of stabbings than the rest of London, thereby causing me to overestimate how many we have, but I wouldn't be surprised if there were nearly 50 stabbings every weekend in London alone.

I went to a stabbing yesterday. We'd normally wait for the police to arrive to escort us into the house but the way that the job was sent down to us over the computer terminal let me think that we could approach safely.

The doorbell was answered by a young man with an obvious wound to the upper arm.

Getting him onto the ambulance I learnt that he had 'come clean' to his long-term girlfriend about cheating on her two years ago. During the course of the argument she had then stabbed him in the arm with a kitchen knife.

Thankfully the wound, while deep, wasn't especially serious – for the ambulance side of things it was a simple job to dress the wound and take the patient to hospital. The doctors at the hospital would have to be more cautious as the nature of the wound meant that the bone, or the layer of tissue covering the bone, might have been damaged, in which case infection was a bigger worry than normal.

The police arrived and got the whole story – the first words out of the patient's mouth were, 'I don't want her charged.' So the case will be referred to the domestic violence team but it probably won't go any further.

On the way to hospital I let the patient know how lucky he was. I've been involved in a couple of jobs where a domestic argument has turned into murder when the man has been stabbed by his girlfriend/wife. One was on Christmas Eve.

My advice to everyone is that you shouldn't have an argument in the kitchen ...

At the hospital the patient's girlfriend arrived with tears in her eyes. As soon as the nurse had finished assessing the wound the couple pulled the curtain across the trolley bay and hugged each other for a long time.

It's strange, but I know that I'd feel different about the situation if it had been the woman who had been stabbed. If he had stabbed her, then I would be thinking of how the woman was a victim. With a male being stabbed I'm thinking more about how daft he was in causing the argument in the first place.

With a male being stabbed by a woman, it is kind of expected that he will just 'get over it', while if a woman was stabbed by a man I would start imagining that this could be a possible start, or fatal ending, of a longer term abuse.

I'm vaguely comforted by the thought that if this was more a case of prolonged abuse I'd be just as sympathetic for the victim whatever their sex.

It's strange to examine your thoughts and see such a hidden prejudice. I guess that somehow, while being brought up to act as a gentleman, I was programmed to see women as needing protection.

And to think I always considered myself a feminist.

New Terms

I've just discovered a new phrase that the police use: 'TACAU', which means 'Treat All Calls As Urgent'. It's used to flag an address so that if there is a 999 call from it they run there as quickly as possible.

In this instance it was because a young man decided to beat his mother-in-law over the head with a broom before threatening to kill other members of the household.

Everyone was rightly concerned that he might return to the house to make good on his threats, which is why the policeman in attendance flagged the address.

The mother-in-law had such a swollen cheek her face was twice the normal size.

Back when I was an A&E nurse I would have put her somewhere quiet so that she could try to relax, especially because she couldn't speak English and her relatives were still at the house dealing with the police.

Unfortunately the nurse in charge was a little less sympathetic and put her out into the waiting room. So I ended up leaving her looking upset and confused, surrounded by people she couldn't understand. While it might have been the 'clinically correct' thing to do, I wouldn't have thought it was the *right* thing to do.

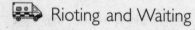 Rioting and Waiting

Apparently there are near riots in the Canary Wharf area.

Today I have been working alone on the FRU car.

I've just spent an hour and 20 minutes sitting on scene with an 86-year-old woman waiting for a 'real' ambulance to take her to hospital.

Why so long?

Because all the ambulances were dealing with (presumably) drunken rioting idiots.

It's also typical that the one time I work outside of my normal area we get the 'fun' of rioting.

☕ Not with Your Ten-Foot Barge Pole

You know you've been doing this job for a long time when someone mentions that your patient is a heroin-smoking, weed-puffing drug addict who funds her habit with prostitution – and you don't blink an eye.

Maybe it's because I'm used to working in Hackney.

Like all the prostitutes I've met, I wouldn't touch her with a ten-foot barge pole. Heaven knows the sort of people who are so starved of sex that they would consider paying good money to have it with them.

☕ Not All Bad

It's not all drug-addled prostitutes in this part of the world.

I've just been cheered up out of a funky mood by watching some youngsters practising Capoeira dancing in a bandstand. They have these little bongos to provide the music.

The sun is out and, yes, I still love London.

🚐 Minimalist Blogging #1

Second least fun thing yesterday – trying to hold still the leg of a five-year-old boy while he waved it around. I was feeling the broken ends of his leg grinding together.

Minimalist Blogging #2

Least fun thing yesterday – looking after a 72-year-old man. His wife of 50 plus years had died in his arms and there was nothing we could do for her.

 Minimalist Blogging #3

You've got to be careful in this job, because the thought that will keep you lying awake at night covered in a thin film of sweat is simply this:

Any action, inaction or wrong action tomorrow at work may well mean I kill someone.

I suspect doctors have this a lot worse than us ambulance people.

 Minimalist Blogging #4

I like east London; with the mix of cultures and languages it's like living in the 'cantina' scene out of *Star Wars*.

 Minimalist Blogging #5

Despite being an atheist, I still feel uncomfortable walking in my boots into a mosque, especially while the prayers are still going on. At least the people who ask me to remove my boots understand why I can't do as they ask.

🚑 Community Care

One of the things that the newspapers seem to like to do is to stir up trouble between different racial groups. One need look no further than the amount of press given to a demonstration against 'police brutality' held on my patch – less than 100 people turned up, and yet it was 'important' news.

Actually living and working in Newham gives you a much better picture of how people get along, and it has nothing to do with the mainstream media's attempts to split us apart on behalf of various vested interest groups.

I was sent to a little old lady who had fallen over earlier in the day; she had been found by her next-door neighbour who looked after her.

My little old lady was white British, while the family who looked after her were Bangladeshi Muslim.

For a number of years they had helped her and her husband, checking in with them to make sure that everything was all right. The son of the neighbours would help out around the house.

When my patient's husband had died, the family had stepped up the amount of help they gave her.

It was the neighbour's son who had found her and called us. It took us some time to deal with the patient – she had an obviously broken hip and we needed to give her a large amount of painkillers before we could move her. During this time the Bangladeshi mother and son stood watching, making sure that she was all right. The mother spoke no English, but even I could recognise her prayers.

As we loaded the patient into the ambulance both the mother and father were praying, and it brought a smile to my face when their son shouted at them, 'Will you both stop that, we aren't in the village any more.'

When the patient's real son turned up he appeared more concerned about the inconvenience that his mother's fall was causing him. The neighbour's son was more concerned with her health.

This is what I see: communities working together and looking after each other, not because of government-sponsored 'multiracial community days' but because, quite simply, we all live together. It is a shame that you don't hear about these small acts of humanity when so-called 'community leaders' are shouting about perceived unfairness.

Things that Make Me Want to Go Stabby

Sometimes we meet lovely people, who look after one another, who do their bit for the community and who are just *nice*. But in all things there is a balance, people who are not quite so nice. Such is karma ...

Some of my station workmates were parked at the hospital on Wednesday night booking a patient in. Someone broke into their ambulance and stole the satnav monitor (which won't work as all the actual electronics of it are buried deep in the motor itself).

They also stole a drugs pack with little else in it besides some Calpol and some vials of adrenaline. So keep your eyes open for someone with a fast heart rate running around Newham with sachets of Calpol in their pockets.

What this means is that we will have one less ambulance on the road while it is getting fixed (the whole dashboard was pulled out). Also that night there was a strange man walking around the station at 3 a.m. He stole some cigarettes and when challenged replied, 'You're open 24 hours ain't you.' He then acted threateningly towards one of our female crews before leaving. Shame I wasn't there ...

I wonder if the people that did this care that they are robbing the community of an ambulance.

I suspect that they don't.

Why I Keep Telling My Mother that I Would Rather Wear Glasses to Work than Contact Lenses – Namely Their Protective Quality

As the subject line says: it's so that when I get sprayed in the face with someone else's blood it goes onto the glasses rather than into my lovely, virus-absorbing eyes.

It was the last job of our shift, just down the road from the hospital – it was given to my crewmate and I as 'Throat cut. Serious bleeding.' Now, I've been at this game long enough to realise that a cut throat can be anything from a near beheading to a shaving cut.

As an aside, my mate got sent to a 'stabbing', it turned out that the landlord of our 'victim' had poked him in the chest with a finger ...

So we rushed down there, fully prepared to see a man with a slight scratch to his neck, probably from an irate girlfriend.

As we got there, the first few things that I saw made me think that this was a 'proper' job.

There was someone laying on the floor in the street with a dark puddle of liquid around him.

There were two policemen leaning over our patient.

The police were looking worried.

There was already police 'incident' tape strung around the area.

I leapt out the cab of the ambulance, grabbed my response bag and jogged over to the patient while my crewmate parked the ambulance and started getting the stretcher out of the back.

Our patient was an 18-year-old man; he was covered in blood although thankfully he was screaming. Screaming is good; it means that you are alive.

The police had saved his life – one of them had bunched up the patient's T-shirt and was pressing it against the wound. When I removed the T-shirt to look at the wound I found a small cut under the jaw, but one that had severed an artery. The wound was still spurting blood at high force which caught us all a little by surprise.

Through this cut of perhaps two centimetres, the patient had lost about a litre of blood. Without the quick thinking of the police, he would have bled to death on the scene. As it was the patient was entering the second stage of shock brought on by loss of blood. This was serious.

I jammed a couple of dressings on the wound, and knowing that just tying them wouldn't work I spent the rest of the job applying pressure with both hands while trying to reassure the patient. It was here that the patient gave a cough and I felt the familiar feeling of someone else's blood being splattered across my face. Given the proximity to the hospital we 'scooped and ran', putting the patient into the ambulance and blue-lighting it into Newham hospital.

One of the policemen travelled with us. The patient was, quite understandably, frightened by his predicament and asked for someone to hold his hand. As I was clutching the dressings to his neck I didn't have a spare one, yet the policeman, also covered with the patient's blood, didn't hesitate to hold the frightened patient's hand.

When we got to the hospital the patient asked if we were all white. I have no idea what was going through his head to ask that question, perhaps he had been brainwashed to believe that all white people in uniform don't give a damn about young black men. To be honest I hadn't given it a thought and I doubt that the policeman had either, all we saw was someone who needed our help.

It's what drives me nuts about the media, and to a certain extent members of the public and community leaders. Everyone is so quick to jump onto the bandwagon of criticising the police over, for example, a raid where they believed they had good information about a chemical bomb, yet you never seem to hear about the numerous small acts of kindness that they perform daily.

This is why I think that if you really want the truth of the situation you need to go to the people who are actually there – this is why blogs and websites have taken off in popularity and in authority.

We got the patient to the hospital where he was seen by the trauma team. The surgeons got a bit splattered by blood themselves; unlike me, however, they had plastic aprons on.

So then it was a simple case of washing my face and arms, mopping out the back of the ambulance and going home to sleep ...

... only to be kept awake by drunken football fans.

The Usual Suspects

I never knew it, but it seems that we local ambulance crews have been having a holiday!

Two of our regular attenders (both alcoholics) had disappeared, while another was in prison. Oh, the glory of never having to go to the familiar call of 'female fitting' on Green Street, or the 'man collapsed' at Woodgrange Road.

Unfortunately, it seems that with the nice weather the usual suspects have returned.

Three especially are particularly unwanted. One, who is possibly the most disgusting-smelling man alive, has reappeared from who knows where. He'll have an ambulance called for him because he (a) drinks too much and falls asleep in the street, and (b) looks half dead – well, he *smells* dead. He has been picked up *eight* times in one day. I watched him as he was dropped off at hospital by the ambulance, then five minutes later he was staggering off looking for the nearest off-licence.

We are a bit stuffed to be honest – people call us and we have to go to them, we have to take them to hospital because there is no other place we can take them. There is no chance of them being cured. We just have to wait until they drop dead. Then they are replaced by younger 'up and coming' alcoholics.

Our second caller is less smelly, although with the recent death of his landlord I don't think that'll last too long. He has possibly the world's most broken nose and often phones us up to let us know that a man has collapsed. If you aren't quick getting there then he'll sometimes wander off and you never find him – instead you ~~waste~~ spend 20 minutes trawling the streets. I was sent to him the other night. I saw him standing in the public phone box still talking to Control so we sidled up to him. He never noticed us.

'Control,' I called up on the radio, 'is our "collapsed" patient still on the phone?'

'Roger that.'

'Well, he's the most upright collapse I've been to in some time ...'

I don't mind this one too much as he walks onto the back of the ambulance, sits fairly quietly while we have a chat, and then walks off the back of the ambulance at the hospital.

The regular I'm going to write about here (for have no doubt, there are *many* more) vanished for nearly a year. She also is particularly smelly, occasionally abusive and will call us four or five times a day. She had been living with some nuns, but they got fed up with her and threw her back out on the streets.

So there you go – too annoying for nuns ...

It's sad to have people in this state, there is nothing anyone can do to help them and their lives are disappearing down the neck of a bottle of cheap cider. Sometimes I think that their whole social circle revolves around drinking, riding in ambulances and sitting in hospital waiting rooms. It also drives you crazy when you are just about to have your first cup of tea of the shift and you get sent out to them. Once or twice I've had to bite my tongue as I sit in the back with them while Control is desperately radioing for a free ambulance to go to a sick child.

But what can you do?

Since writing this all of the people mentioned in this entry are now dead, and as predicted they have been replaced by some new 'up and comers'.

 Maybe

There is a little old lady. She sits alone in her house. Mainly she stays in one room – there is no radio, there is no television.

She sits at her table and shuffles paper.

She has a mild form of dementia.

Her carers arrive, they give her some medication. They change her incontinence pad; they get her dressed and washed.

Meals on wheels arrives; she has something to eat.

In the evening there are more carers, they change her incontinence pad and give her some night medication. They put her to bed.

She lives, isolated in her house.

Her carers don't like her because she shouts and she repeats herself.

One day she falls over. She is found by her carers.

So the ambulance service is called. We pick her up, but she doesn't want to go to hospital.

We watch the carers bully her so that they can change her soiled incontinence pad. The carers are aggressive. Their tone of voice and the words that they use are harsh.

Our patient tells us that the carers that visit in the morning have hit her. Given the attitude and actions of the carers that I have seen this doesn't surprise me.

We contact her daughter – this isn't the first time that she has made this claim; her daughter has reported it to the social services.

We leave the patient as she doesn't want to go to hospital and we cannot kidnap her. We return to station where we fill out a 'vulnerable adult' form. This goes off to our Control where it is dealt with by a specialist team.

A week later I'm asked to phone the social services person dealing with the case.

They ask me what I've seen, what I've heard.

Explaining over the phone it feels that trying to express the atmosphere in the house is impossible.

But for once I have faith in the social worker; I don't know why but I do.

I don't know how this story ends.

The little old lady needs people to not hit her; she needs company and she needs *care*.

Maybe our attendance will be the tipping point that will start that care. Maybe the social services needed to hear from someone else the reports of abuse. Maybe the carers tiptoe around the daughter when she is there. Maybe something will get done.

I hope so.

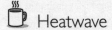 Heatwave

London (soon to be the rest of England) is under a bit of a heatwave at the moment; temperatures of 30°C have led to all sorts of announcements. The Met Office has raised the Heat-Health level to 3. The next level up is a National Emergency.

The advice given is as follows:

Stay out of the sun. Keep your home as cool as possible – shutting windows during the day may help. Open them when it is cooler at night. Keep drinking fluids. If there is anyone you know who might be at special risk, for example an older person living on their own, make sure they know what to do.

When they suggest drinking plenty of fluids I don't suppose that they mean beer. So please stop stripping your top off, drinking nothing but pints of Stella and then thinking it's amusing to run out laughing in front of ambulances travelling on blue lights. It's not big, it's not clever and one day my eyes will be elsewhere and it'll be all I can do to wave at you as you bounce off my windscreen.

I've also seen news that over the past few days the number of calls described as 'Collapse' is up 48 per cent, while calls to asthmatics are up by 13 per cent.

Calls are up all over London. While we've got used to dealing with 3800 calls a day, our rate is now around *4500*. With no extra ambulances you can imagine how busy we are. Remind me to tell you sometime how we are expected to work without a break.

🚑 Blue, Blue, Blue and Blue

I have a bit of luck; a brand-new shiny relief has drawn the short straw of working with me for four days. This means that I know who I'm working with for this period of time, which makes me a more relaxed ambulance person.

She asks that she be described here as 'sexy, smart, kind-hearted and with a nice bum', or something like that. I was too busy laughing at her after the first few words.

She is actually a very nice person and I think she'll fit in well with the rest of our complex. I'm enjoying working with her.

... except ...

Last night, with one exception, all our patients were so ill we had to 'blue' them into the resuscitation room at the hospital. 'Blueing' in a patient means that we find ourselves racing to hospital on blue lights and sirens because we are concerned about their well-being.

Our first call was a 'classic': a frail, demented 90-plus female in a nursing home who had become semi-conscious. We arrived at the home to find that the FRU had arrived before us. He shouted out of the window at us that the patient 'wasn't well'.

Breathing at 60 times a minute, she barely flinched as we lifted her across onto our trolley bed. She looked so unwell I connected her to our defibrillator machine just in case.

As is usual with these cases the nurses at the nursing home couldn't give us too many details on the patient; they had no idea how long she had been ill for and had to be persuaded to call for the next of kin.

Our next job was for a man who had collapsed and was having a seizure in the street. He had a cycle of coming out of a seizure then having another one. This continued in the ambulance so once more we found ourselves 'blueing' into the hospital. The patient continued to fit until some rather strong drugs were given.

Our next patient was another 'fitter'; this one, however, was a two-year-old girl. As we arrived she was still fitting. Prolonged fits can result in a lack of oxygen to the brain, so this justified another 'blue' into hospital. As we arrived at the hospital the child woke up and seemed fine.

I hate children – when they are ill they really put the wind up me.

Our last blue call of the shift was to another child; this one was five years old and had fallen four feet out of a bunk bed. He had a painful shoulder and neck, a huge bump on his head and was very drowsy.

I didn't like how drowsy he was. It's normal for a child to be sleepy after an accident, but this seemed a more profound drowsiness than is to be expected.

As the child was a funny shape I couldn't fit a hard collar to his neck (to protect against the possibility of injury). Trying to put a collar on a child normally has them squirming and crying, but this child just lay there wanting to go to sleep. I had to make do with wrapping his head in a blanket roll, an old-fashioned way of immobilising the head, but one that I think is often more effective than the specifically designed equipment that we have.

So once more we found ourselves heading into hospital under blue lights and sirens and I'd like to thank my shiny new relief for a nice smooth ride. It's easy to get fired up in the moment, to start driving hard, all the while forgetting that your crewmate is getting bounced around in the back of the truck. This didn't happen, which made me grateful, as I would have been the one bouncing around in the back.

Once we got to hospital the child seemed to make a full recovery. I suspected that the hospital would observe him overnight before sending him home.

I'm thankful that there was a nice doctor receiving the patient; she understood that I had my concerns even though the child now seemed fine. It's the curse of the ambulance service that in the nice controlled atmosphere of a resus room things rarely seem as bad as they are out on the road.

Still, no one ever lost their job by 'blueing' in a patient who didn't need it. I'd rather be a bit of a worrier than have someone drop dead as I calmly wheel them through the doors after convincing myself that 'they aren't *that* sick'.

So a busy night but one in which we both felt we'd done some good work above and beyond the normal 'pick up drunk, take to hospital, mop out vomit' that I often find myself doing.

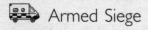 Armed Siege

Suddenly I find myself involved in an armed siege on my patch. It's never good when you have to make a rapid dash for cover ...

I've got to give the armed police their due – they turned up *very* quickly once the call went out.

It started out sounding like our usual sort of call, an assault in the street. A nice simple job for a pleasant afternoon in Newham.

We arrived and found six police officers around a Russian man and his girlfriend. There was a lot of shouting and screaming on the part of the man, mainly because he'd had his two front teeth knocked out.

Suddenly one of the police turned to me and said, 'Quick, we are moving to another area.'

'Why is that?' I asked.

He pointed to a house window across the road. 'Because there is a man there with a gun.'

Thirty seconds later my ambulance, my patient, my crewmate and most importantly me were 200 yards down the road behind some houses and a very solid brick wall.

Policemen with big guns appeared from nowhere and they laid plans about what to do about the situation.

To cut a long story short, the police negotiated the release of a child from the house and after around seven hours the siege was ended peacefully.

My patient managed to smoke all of one policeman's cigarettes.

Working for Your Pay

A friend of mine has just come back from a job as a solo responder.

A small child was choking on a bone. He managed to clear the child's airway so the child didn't choke to death.

I let him know that I was impressed with the way that he had saved the child's life; without him being there the child would have died.

'You've earned your pay packet for today,' I told him.

He didn't seem too impressed with me commenting on the incident, saying, 'It was nothing.'

So, consider this being 'Mentioned in Dispatches'.

Top bloke.

Boating

I'm sitting on standby next to the Thames, waiting for someone to fall ill (or fall over on a Sunday football field). As I sit here I've been watching canoeists paddling up and down, and I am terribly jealous.

One of the things I've always wanted to do is boat up Regent's Canal; I can only imagine the sights I would see.

Instead, I'm sitting, sweating and dreaming.

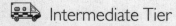 Intermediate Tier

I need to give you a bit of background before I talk about today.

There is a breed of ambulance called the 'Intermediate Tier'. Staffed by two crew who have had less training than for a regular ambulance, they attend to the lowest priority jobs, the so-called 'Green calls'. Green calls are the sort of calls that, while an ambulance may be required, it is not essential to have it speeding to you with two fully trained staff on blue lights and sirens. They also deal with 'GP Urgent' and 'Non-Urgent' calls, those patients whom a GP has seen who need treatment at a hospital but, again, don't require a full response.

So far it has worked well. Some emergency ambulance people loathe doing Green calls, as they are often not very exciting. (I like them because they are normally simple jobs.)

As I am a long-term single (without a regular crewmate since she broke her foot), I have been working with lots of different people. Today I was put onto an Intermediate Tier vehicle with a woman who normally works on it.

I'm always happy for a bit of a change of scenery. As I have no idea how the paperwork/assessment/handling of these patients differs from my normal emergency work it was suggested that I drove.

The first job was to someone with quite severe back pain. While not life threatening the patient needed to go to hospital for some really good painkillers and there was no way that they could get there on their own. Severe back pain is annoying as there is little that we can do to help; the patient often has to walk as the pain gets worse if they sit in our carry chair. However, after some pain relief with 'gas and air', the patient was able to make their way to the ambulance.

At the hospital I bought myself an overpriced hospital sandwich and settled down for breakfast.

Another snippet of background. In my mouth there is a broken tooth; I've had it for ages and it seldom bothers me. I have so far ignored it.

As I bit into the sandwich I felt an incredible shooting pain running from the tooth, under my tongue and jaw and into my feet. I started to sweat and feel sick. I couldn't talk because I had pins and needles in my tongue.

Finally the pain died down into a dull roar and I suggested that we had a drive over to a dentist so I could make an appointment.

I entered the dentist's surgery and found it empty. The staff were about to start their lunch break. The nurse behind the counter looked me up and down, asked me a few questions about the pain and disappeared. She came back moments later and told me that the dentist would fix my tooth for me now.

Fifteen minutes and £50 later I became the proud owner of a temporary filling. I was ecstatic with my treatment – they were very kind seeing me in their lunch break, and the dental treatment was first class. The nurse behind the counter said, 'We can't have you saving lives with bad toothache can we?' Sometimes the ambulance uniform is an excellent thing to be wearing. I blessed them all for working during their lunch break. I may have offered one of them a marriage proposal.

It has been more than 20 years since I last visited a dentist (and, yes, I know that this only confirms the American view of English dental care), not out of fear, but more that if it didn't hurt me then it wasn't worth the trouble.

I'm also grateful that there were no Green calls that needed our attention at that time.

There were two more calls for us this shift. Another woman with back pain and a man who was so heavy I worried that he was going to break our carry chair. Normally we need to tip the patient back on our carry chair. This is considerably tricky to do when he weighs more than you do and you find your feet lifting off the ground.

With the exception of my tooth it was a lovely shift, and a nice change of pace.

🚑 Double Fall

'Report on arrival'; it's something that Control asks us to do when a call seems serious. It's also a way of reminding us that there are extra ambulances or even the helicopter doctors available to help us with a difficult call.

This job was to a 'fall from height'. To be honest, I was a bit worried about what we would find.

The patient was a 95-year-old man; he had needed to change a lightbulb on his upstairs landing. He had got a stepladder, climbed up it and in the process of undoing the bulb had toppled backwards.

He'd fallen, cracking his head on the lintel of the bathroom door. He'd then rolled down his stairway before coming to rest halfway down the stairs.

When we arrived he had picked himself up and was sitting on the downstairs sofa. His concerned neighbours (who were the ones who had called us) had already changed the lightbulb for him.

A quick examination showed exactly two injuries. He had a small bleeding wound on his arm and he also had a bump on the back of his head.

He hadn't hurt his neck, he hadn't been knocked out, he hadn't broken any of his frail-looking bones.

He was also a very nice chap.

While I can often examine someone to decide if they have injured their neck, and indeed this patient apparently didn't have any neck injury, in this case I thought that it would be best to err on the side of caution. Ninety-five-year-olds tend to have crunchy bones.

Half of this job is how you relate to people, so I told the patient that I was going to strap him down to our spinal board so that when he got to hospital he wouldn't be sent out into the waiting room but would instead be seen immediately. It's sometimes better to say this than 'You may have broken your neck and I don't want you dying as we go over one of the many speed-bumps on the way to hospital.'

So we took the patient to hospital. They saw him straight away and it was determined that he had, indeed, only minor injuries.

He was a very lucky fellow. And we didn't need the Helicopter Emergency Medical Service (HEMS) team, which is good because when I *do* need it it means that someone has been seriously injured.

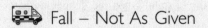 Fall – Not As Given

The call was to a 28-year-old female who had 'fallen down, unable to get up'. So far, so dull. We drove to the house on blue lights as, for some reason, it was rated as a high priority job. As an aside, one of my pet hates is that a little old lady who has fallen over and is stuck on the floor without any physical injury gets a very low priority, while a 20-year-old with a cough is often a high priority.

We arrived at the house, grabbed our bag full of equipment and made our way inside. A man was standing by the door hopping from foot to foot. He said something about 'she's had it' and 'funny breathing'. We fully expected to see a woman lying on the floor having a panic attack.

We climbed the stairs into a room full of mattresses and clothes lying around the floor. There were four females in the room. Our patient, her sister, a next-door neighbour ...

... and a newborn baby girl, still attached to the mother by a glistening umbilical cord.

Time to switch into action mode.

I jogged back to the ambulance to get our childbirth delivery packs while my crewmate started to assess the patients. He is only a couple of months out of training school but handled himself really well. He cut the cord and I looked after the baby while he took care of the woman. My immediate impression was that everything had gone smoothly. The mother had minimal bleeding and with a bit of rubbing on my part the baby soon 'pinked up' and didn't seem to be in any sort of distress.

I spoke to our Control on the phone and they promised us a midwife. In a case like this, what we normally do is get a midwife out to assess the mother and child and do the normal things that occur in the hospital. Then if they are happy with both patients we can leave them at home. Much nicer than taking them to the hospital when the dangerous part has already passed.

However, the midwife seemed to be taking a bit of a time to arrive.

Here is a rough time-line.

00:10 Baby born.

00:15 We arrive, experience mild panic.

00:16 Cord cut, everyone is happy.

00:20 Ask for midwife.

01:00 Ask where midwife is. Control tell us that there is difficulty in getting one.

01:30 Still waiting.

02:00 We are informed that there *is* a midwife who will come out. Midwife is waiting for taxi as there are no ambulances available to bring her to scene.

02:40 Midwife arrives, does various technical things.

03:00 We are clear from scene and are ready to do another job.

The mother was in occasional pain from needing to deliver the placenta and didn't want to hold the baby. The father was worried that he would drop it. So it was up to me to cuddle it and keep it warm while awaiting the midwife. So for three hours I was left holding the baby.

I have an idea of why the call didn't come down to us as a 'birth at home'. I imagine that the sister phoned for the ambulance, said something about the patient lying on the floor, which the call taker then typed into the computer. Then the sister told the call taker that the baby was coming out and so the call taker had to talk the sister through the fun and games of childbirth. They were then so busy that while the call taker bumped the priority of the call up for immediate dispatch, they forgot to type in that the woman was having her baby.

Perfectly understandable, and it's nice to be surprised every so often.

🚑 Faux Pas

It's 5 a.m. and we are attending to the now traditional early morning 'matern-a-taxi'.

Two women leave the house; one is obviously pregnant while the other is wheeling the pregnant woman's case.

'Hello,' says my crewmate, motioning to the pregnant woman, 'you must be our patient.'

The patient nods an affirmative.

'And you,' he continues to the woman following, 'you must be her mother.'

'Erm, no,' she replies, 'I'm her sister.'

I would like to apologise to all the people in that street for waking them up with my laughter.

My crewmate was a tad embarrassed and, of course, I didn't let him forget it for the rest of the shift.

🚑 'Cheating' to Get Care

I've mentioned before about how we in the ambulance service have procedures in place for the elderly whom we suspect of being at risk. If there is a risk of abuse or violence then we can fill in a form, fax it off to Control as soon as we reach a hospital and the team in Control will make sure that social services are made aware of our concerns.

It works pretty well to be honest. I've done a few of these 'vulnerable adult/vulnerable child' referrals and have got good feedback on most of them.

Unfortunately, there is no easy way to alert social services to a 'non-emergency' cause for referral.

We were called to an elderly lady who had got out of bed and had slipped. She had fallen on the floor and couldn't get up. Also in the house was the woman's sister, also in her eighties. Her sister had tried to help, but the patient was heavy and the sister was frail. Our patient was stuck.

I'm more than happy to go to these sorts of calls (a 'Nan down' call) mostly because if the cause of the fall is a simple trip or slip we can pick them up, check them for injuries and more often than not leave them at home. The patient is happy to be off the floor and not being dragged to hospital, and we are happy because we feel that we have done something useful for a change.

In this case it was a simple slip that had caused the patient to fall and she had not hurt herself. We picked her up off the floor and after an examination were more than happy to leave her at home.

I asked the patient and her sister if they had any carers, anyone who came in and helped them with the day-to-day stuff. She replied that there was a district nurse once, but that she had disappeared without doing anything.

With my inexpert eye I looked around the flat. I could see where some handrails could be useful, where some modifications to the bath could improve safety and where a better bed could prevent a recurrence of the fall. The patients could also do with a community alarm.

Community alarms are great, the person wears an alarm around their neck and if they fall over or get into trouble they can activate it and we turn up to help them.

So it appeared that someone had been there once, but since then the sisters had dropped off the radar.

There was no way that I could justify filling in a 'vulnerable adults' form for this, they weren't 'vulnerable', they just needed a proper assessment to provide some things that would make their life that little bit easier and safer. If I filled in one of those forms it would take time and resources away from those who really did need immediate action.

Unfortunately I'm stuck – we have no pathway in place to involve social services in any way other than in an emergency fashion. Our emergency care practitioners can refer patients to social services, but only if they live in certain postcodes (where Primary Care Trusts – PCTs – fund the ECPs; it all gets horribly complicated).

The LAS could do with improving this. We need a way to bring patients to the attention of the social services that doesn't require it being an 'emergency'. Let's face it, we see hundreds of people each day (around 4000 calls each day at the moment), who better to keep an eye out for people who might be at risk, yet who haven't yet had any social services input?

Maybe the social services don't trust us to do their job for them. Maybe they are so overstretched that they can't deal with a raft of new referrals that we would make.

Well, in this case I've 'cheated'. I gathered the patient's details, spoke to a friendly receptionist (actually all the receptionists at the hospitals are friendly) so I could get the GP information and I've now written a letter to the GP detailing my concerns. I've done all I can do about this situation, which means that I can sleep at night, but wouldn't it be better if we didn't have to 'cheat'?

I hope that the GP/social services don't get snotty. I hate having to shout at people.

🚑 Oh FFS!

Can you imagine the ambulance response ...

We are driving along on blue lights and sirens, traffic is heavy and we are on our way to a potentially life-threatening call.

From the side of the road we see a member of the public gesticulating angrily at us. He is shouting, swearing and indicating something to us.

He is angry because our sirens are so loud they are disrupting his mobile phone call.

Obviously it is a more important phone call than our emergency journey.

One member of this ambulance crew may well have made a rude hand signal at this pillock, I wouldn't like to say which one.

I happen to think it was justified.

🚑 Shattered

I am absolutely knackered – twelve-hour shifts followed by running around taping TV for my travelling family has had me sleeping around five hours a night in a strange bed, in warm weather that does not aid rest.

During today's shift I have had an ominous feeling that I am in some sort of trouble, just waiting for the call from management to come into the office for 'a chat'. I had no idea why I was feeling this way until I pondered the stimulant effect of the four cans of Red Bull that I have drunk in order to remain upright. I'm suffering from fatigue and drug-induced paranoia.

Not fun.

At least the work I've been doing has been pretty stress-free, nothing too much like hard work. Today's trickiest job was a demented 96-year-old with serious difficulty in breathing. Living in a nursing home we noticed that the staff were keeping well out of arm's reach. The FRU who was already there warned us that she was a bit 'punchy' and he was trying to sneak some medicine under her nose to open up her airways.

'Hello dear,' said my crewmate, 'we need to take you to hospital to sort out your breathing.'

'FUCK OFF!' came the rather loud reply.

We tried to persuade her to come with us but she was having none of it. A couple of times she tried to grab us but experience has taught us to keep all vital bits of our bodies away from these sorts of patients.

I often tell patients that I can't kidnap them, but when the patient is demented like this then they lack the capacity to refuse our treatment. Using our super-secret martial arts techniques (grab her arms and wrap her in a blanket), we managed to safely transfer her to the ambulance. She was cursing us all the time.

We 'blued' her into the hospital as, although we couldn't get any vital signs on her, we could see that she was seriously ill.

It's all a bit sad really; she lives in a typical nursing home, is demented and angry most of the time and ends up feeling very unwell and being kidnapped (using as soft a force as possible) by two men in green. No matter how bad my day was, hers was worse.

 Tilt

It's normally pretty easy to get a patient out of a house. They either walk, or we put them on our collapsible carrying chair and carry/wheel them out. Occasionally you come across a job where that simple approach isn't going to work. This is often a satisfying job as you have to solve a problem for a change.

We were sent to a teenager who had hurt her leg playing football in the garden. We arrived to find the girl lying on the living-room floor. Also present was her mother, older brother and baby sister. The girl had, indeed, been playing football and, due to circumstances that I shall obscure for reasons of privacy, had broken her leg right up where it joins with the hip.

This is often an injury related to age, old people fall over and break their hip, and this was the exact same injury. The problem with this is that we can't really carry them out on our chair because of the pain and further injury that can be caused by the two ends of the bone grinding together, chewing up muscle and nerves and potentially damaging the main artery that supplies blood to the leg. If you damage that it's very easy to bleed to death.

'No problem,' we thought. The girl herself was light and the mother and older brother were sensible people. So we warned everyone involved that it would take a bit of time to remove the patient from the house in as safe and pain-free a manner as possible.

Now, with a patient like this we would normally put our scoop underneath, strap them in a bit and then lift them onto our proper trolley bed. Unfortunately, in this case, the angle to the front door was such that we wouldn't be able to get our large trolley bed into the house, and giving the scoop a dry run, we wouldn't be able to fit that out the front door either.

Didn't those people who designed houses 80 years ago consider modern ambulance stretchers? Typical really.

So we sat and thought for a moment. The patient was calm (and by now the pain relief we had given her was working), the mother was calm, the older brother was calm, baby sister filled her nappy (that or my crewmate farted but managed to keep a straight face). Could we go out through the garden? Nope, there was no access to the street through that route. Could we open the living-room window and pass her out that way? Nope, the design of the window precluded us from doing that.

Brainwave!

If we strapped the patient to the scoop *really* well then we could tilt it up by 50 degrees and fit it (and the patient) through the door.

However, this involves a lot more strapping in a way in which we don't really get much practice. You have to follow it up by a bit of faith that when you lift the scoop up the patient isn't going to slip out the bottom of it and end up in a painful heap on the floor.

So we explained what we were going to do (Rule #1 in keeping patients calm: explain what you are going to do) and spent the next ten minutes tying her to the scoop, hoping that we were doing it right.

Then came the moment of truth: we lifted her up, carried her towards the door and tilting her up held our breath.

It worked perfectly, she didn't move an inch, she didn't cry out in pain and, most importantly, we didn't drop her.

From there it was a simple job to carry her to the ambulance where we travelled as carefully to hospital as possible in speed-bump-infested east London.

She was seen pretty much immediately by an A&E consultant.

Job was a good 'un.

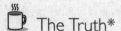 The Truth*

'It started off pretty easy, writing my book. I mean, there was always plenty of material, people would fall over and injure themselves and I'd

*By 'The Truth', I actually mean 'Completely Made Up'. This section was inspired by a joke from the very funny Scaryduck who, incidentally, has a book for sale.

write about it. I mean, for God's sake, I work in east London it's not as if we are short on stabbings and shootings.'

The author looked down at the half-drunk bottle of cheap cider.

'But, of course, as the editor read my progress he started demanding more from me. It wasn't good enough for him to read about some bloke falling off his bike and skinning his knee. He wanted blood and gore; failing that he wanted "heart-warming" or "shocking". I mean, I try to do as little work as possible, but now I found myself having to go *looking* for patients and interesting ones at that.'

Taking a swig from the bottle he looked around as though frightened that someone walking their dog across the deserted park would overhear him.

'Well, it started off pretty simply, but then most bad ideas do. We'd be driving down the street and I'd see some old woman looking a bit unsteady on her feet. I'd give her a blast on the sirens and see if I could make her fall over. Did I mention that the editor liked little old ladies being injured? I'd get some good comments for a nice "Nan down" story. But it still wasn't enough, he demanded more. So then I graduated to pushing small boys' heads through park railings. I'd go to a house and the first thing I'd do was to go into the kitchen and look for a nice large pot. My crewmate would look after the patient while I worked on jamming it onto a kid's head.

'It went well for a time, but that editor, that damn editor, demanded more. So we took to cruising the streets at night looking for drunks winding their way home from the pub. My crewmate would hide the ambulance around the corner and I'd jump out from behind some bushes and beat up the patient. Then we'd "discover" another case of "inner city violence".'

The author took another swig from the bottle and stared at his hands.

'I suppose publishing the evidence was a bad idea. The book had become a kind of confessional, detailing my crimes against humanity. Where once I would have dry spells without an interesting job, now I only had to stalk the night carrying a root vegetable, some stockings, a half-brick and a length of garden hose and I'd have a section worthy of the best tabloid papers.

'My stationmates started asking questions about why I kept getting such interesting jobs. I thought I'd thrown them off the scent with a few blatantly made-up stories, but who would believe that I'd go to a drug addict with a heart of gold, or would find myself trying to save a pigeon with a broken wing? So I got found out. The service couldn't stand the shame so they quietly "retired" me.

'Still it wasn't all bad – the BBC needed a replacement presenter for *Animal Hospital* for Rolf Harris. A TV programme where vets look after cute little creatures is pretty simple. I could get viewers crying over injured little animals; I mean, people cry over sick animals a lot more than sick people.

'Now if you'll excuse me, I have to prepare for tonight's programme. I have a baby deer to kneecap. These things don't run out in front of cars on their own you know.'

The author stood up and walked off into the sunset swinging his favourite claw hammer while whistling a happy tune.

Why Your Train Yesterday May Have Been Delayed

Sometimes, even when it's cold and dark and raining on your head, you have to go a bit slow.

I was working on the FRU last night. My crewmate is still off sick and will be for at least the next four weeks so finding myself without a partner and being asked to go 'on the car' is fairly common.

I'm sent to a job marked as 'Male fell onto train track, head injury, ***track current off***.'

It's that last bit that I like to see.

I get there and park up at the normal parking place for the police and the ambulance. Just as my handbrake goes on a British Transport Police (BTP) van screeches up behind me. A policeman jumps out, shouts, 'He's on platform three', and runs into the station. I gather my equipment bags and waddle after him. (All the equipment we carry tends to slow us down.)

I'm led to the patient by one of the staff. Even though we are both walking quickly and with purpose a passenger still tries to stop the station worker to ask if there is a replacement bus service. I'm guessing that obviously leading a heavily laden ambulance worker to a patient is less important than her trip home.

The patient is, indeed, lying on the tracks of the Docklands Light Railway. Around him are several BTP officers and station workers so I know that the area is safe. They have already covered him with two blankets and put a dressing on his head wound. Wisely they haven't moved him, so he remains pretty much facedown. They have been talking to him although they say that he isn't making much sense.

I jump down onto the tracks (it's about a five-foot drop) and start to get a feel for what has happened and how badly injured the patient is. He's not behaving normally; in fact, he's acting 'post-ictal', which is a side effect of having had a seizure. There is what I would call a reasonable amount of blood swilling around the puddles on the track. I know I'm going to get bloodied in this situation, so I dive on in.

I'm not happy with the distance that the patient fell. One of the station workers was talking to him as he fell onto the tracks and his head bounced off one of the rails, which explains the blood that is covering everything. The worker then tells me that, after falling and hitting his head, the patient had a fit for about a minute. It's all starting to come together.

'When you talked to him, before he fell, did he sort of go all stiff?' I ask the station worker.

'Yes, his eyes kinda went funny.'

413

So now it looks like the patient started to have his fit while standing on the platform, fell back onto the tracks and landed on his head. I'm not happy about moving him. His head has travelled about eleven feet, and I can't rule out a serious injury to his neck. So now there is little I can do besides give the patient oxygen, try to reassure him and get rained on.

Thankfully the ambulance crew are quick to arrive. I explain what has happened and they agree with me that the best course of action is to 'collar and board' the patient before moving him off the track. We do this to protect the patient's neck and back. If he has damaged his neck then the hard collar and head blocks that we fit around him will reduce the chance that moving him will damage his spinal cord. A damaged spinal cord can result in paralysis or death so we don't want to make any injury worse.

Unfortunately this takes time, especially when you are dealing with a wet, semi-conscious patient in the dark. As we are preparing to secure the patient he has another fit. Then he has another one as we are trying to strap him to the scoop so that we can lift him off the tracks. Thankfully he has a clear airway throughout and the fits don't last too long. It's one of those situations where you need to go slowly in order for the patient to receive the best treatment.

Throughout this we can hear the station tannoy announcing delays due to 'a person on the tracks'. So now, dear tube traveller, you have an idea what is going on when your train is similarly delayed.

The Transport police have been very helpful throughout and now they and the station staff help us lift the patient onto the platform and then onto the trolley. The police want to know how the patient is going to do; if the injuries are life threatening then a much more in-depth investigation needs to be carried out.

I tell the police that, to be honest, I don't know how seriously the patient is hurt. While the fall may have been caused by an epileptic fit, the head injury might be nothing too serious and the further fitting might be his normal pattern of epilepsy. Or it could be that the patient may not be epileptic at all and may have just fainted onto the tracks and that the fitting is being caused by fatal bleeding on the brain.

We load the patient onto the ambulance. Now he is in the warm, dry and well-lit ambulance we can cut off his clothes and make a proper inspection of him. Physically he seems unhurt apart from the seizures and the head injury. We need to decide which hospital to take the patient. We could take him to Newham hospital, which is about three minutes down the road. While this has a good A&E and is very close it doesn't have the resources of our second choice, the Royal London. We choose the Royal London mostly because if the patient does have bleeding on the brain, then that hospital has neurosurgeons that can operate on him. If we took the patient to Newham hospital and he needed neurosurgery then he'd have to be transferred, all of which takes time.

So we go (under blue lights and sirens) the further distance to the Royal London. I travel with the crew in case something nasty happens during the transport. The patient has a further two fits while on our way to the hospital.

However, we safely reach the hospital. Wheeling the patient into the resuscitation room he chooses that moment to start to lose control of his airway. It's annoying; we look after him all this time, then as soon as some doctors see us the patient gives them the impression that we have been letting him choke to death.

Nevertheless, he is safely in the hands of the doctors. We have done our job by not letting him get any worse. By bypassing the nearest hospital we have got him to a centre that specialises in his potentially serious injury. A job well done and the crew and I feel happy that we have helped someone who really needed it (unlike my mate who went to a young woman with period pains).

The only problem is that the back of the ambulance looks like a bomb has hit it. I'm covered in blood up my arms where my gloves stop and my hi-visibility jacket is likewise covered in blood and train oil and possibly other substances. I have only one such jacket and, as I'm working for the next six days, I wonder when I'll be able to give it a wash.

Oh well, a dirty jacket is the sign of a hard worker. Right?

And I appear to have lost my wristwatch. Bang goes £20.

Three Glass Stories

Some injuries are like buses, you don't see any for ages and then two come along at once.

We were called to a young man with a cut foot. The trail of blood led up the garden path to a small pool of the same blood underneath a rather annoyed young man. While walking in the street he had stepped on a broken bottle, the glass had sliced through the sole of his trainer and managed a fairly nasty cut to the sole of the foot. It was a simple job to wrap his foot in a bandage and then stare in awe at the lump of glass poking through the trainer. He was a nice enough lad who hopped to the ambulance, and whose friend's mum had already put on a pretty good dressing. He just needed an X-ray to exclude any glass being left in the wound and a couple of stitches.

Our last job that day was also a foot cut on some glass; this time it was a 15-year-old girl who lives in a pub. She'd been barefoot, and as is typical with the pubs around our way, there had been a nice sliver of glass on the floor. Cue much screaming and a rather huge amount of blood. Feet tend to bleed a lot, partly because there are plenty of blood vessels in them and partly because gravity tends to make the stuff leak out of you. I'd give the people in the pub a medal, though; not only had they tried using a towel to stop the bleeding but they'd also laid her on the floor and lifted her foot above her head. If only all our patients had such sense.

She still had the sliver of glass in her foot and while we aren't supposed to touch such 'foreign objects', I believe that we have enough minor injuries experience to pull it out and better control the bleeding with pressure. It's a bit nasty to put pressure on a wound when there is a two-inch lump of glass in it. Needless to say the patient managed to leak the red stuff all over the floor of the ambulance and my crewmate looked as if she had performed surgery on the patient. The bleeding was controlled, the patient was taken to hospital and everyone was happy.

My final glass story happened the night before last. We were called to a 'collapse behind locked doors'. The relatives of a woman in her sixties had called us because they could see her lying on the sofa in her ground-floor flat but she wasn't answering the door or telephone. We arrived and the door was well locked – there was a deadbolt as well as the normal Yale, so neither I nor my martial arts master/built like a brick outhouse of a crewmate could kick the door down. At the relatives' request I smashed the bedroom window and, after some backbreaking limbo work, climbed in.

Unfortunately, the patient was deceased. It's never a nice thing to tell relatives that their loved one is dead and that there is nothing we can do to help. I tried to explain that the patient looked very peaceful and that she had probably passed away in her sleep. We waited for the police and left them to look after the family. I had to have a quick run back to the hospital so I could wash the blood off the brand-new cut I'd given myself on my hand. A minor injury that needed no treatment, and if it meant that the relatives thought we did all we could then perhaps worth it.

Although I have spent the last two shifts picking glass dust out of my hair/clothes/boots.

 Hit

I was working on the Fast Response Unit so I was on my own and pretty much left to my own devices. I'd spent part of the night driving around looking for a job to do, but there wasn't much going on for us solo responders. I had a bit of a hunger on me that I thought a quick trip to Tesco would cure. The one advantage of working on the car is that you can sometimes get decent food.

So I drove down there, parked up and went shopping. Plenty of chocolate and other unhealthy foods (I said you 'can' sometimes get decent food, but there was little point in me breaking the habit of a lifetime). I had just managed to put my shopping bags of goodies in the car when the computer terminal rang.

'Seventeen-year-old male, assaulted outside Tesco.'

Brilliant. The call wasn't the high priority calls that FRUs are supposed to be saved for, but as I was already on the scene it would have been churlish to complain. All our vehicles are tracked by Control on a big map of London – they know where you are at any point in time. It turned out that Control had seen me sitting there, realised that they were out of ambulances and so decided to keep me 'on scene'.

The patient was sitting inside. He had a brand-new hole in his forehead made by some form of weaponry and the Tesco staff had been taking care of him. A motherly manager was fussing over him, which I thought was nice of her as he wasn't a happy bunny. He was otherwise unhurt and while the cut was pretty big it wasn't anything too serious and it had already stopped bleeding.

'So,' I asked him, 'who did this?'

'Don't want to talk about it,' he replied.

'OK then, did you see what weapon they had?'

'Said I don't want to talk about it.'

Great, here was another young man who wasn't interested in throwing out any information. My psychic powers were tingling. It was pretty obvious that he knew the people who had hit him, and he probably knew the reason why he had been attacked. One thing that I've learnt from the years on this job is that truly random attacks are pretty rare and while it is wrong, you can generally understand why most of the people we see get thumped. I looked at my watch; there was no way I'd be able to put up with this fool playing the 'silent gangster' role while waiting for an ambulance.

'OK, come on, I'm not supposed to but I'll take you to hospital in my car.'

'Thanks.' While he was untalkative he was at least polite.

I let Control know what I was doing and because of the lack of ambulances they were quite happy I was bending the rules. We aren't supposed to transport patients in the FRUs; if something were to go wrong with my patient I would be stuck on my own in a car with no trolley and no assistance.

He sat quietly in my car while I ran him down to the hospital; my attempts at conversation were met with silence. While on the one hand this was an easy patient to deal with, on the other it would have been nice to know what had happened so as to better assess the injuries he received. He wasn't impressed that I was trying to talk to him. He wanted to go to hospital and get fixed and he wasn't interested in making my life any easier.

I asked him if he wanted the police involved and he refused, which is fine by me as it reduces the amount of paperwork that the police have to do. Unfortunately for him the police were there to meet him at the hospital. The Tesco staff had called the police on his behalf and had directed them to the hospital. I don't think that they got any additional information out of him.

Before I left him sulking in the waiting room I asked him one last thing, 'When you find the people who hit you, don't go and beat them up. It only makes more work for me.'

His reply was a sullen grunt.

I love teenagers.

🚑 Allergic Reaction

There is a reason that I came off the FRU, I don't like sitting on scene with patients that (for whatever reason) I can't transport. Sick patients need to be in hospital, not in their houses being stared at by my ugly mug.

I was working on the FRU and was sent to a child who was suffering an allergic reaction. These are normally pretty minor things; mum has changed the washing powder and the little 'un has a bit of a reaction to it.

Not so in this case; the child looked like something from a horror movie. The two-year-old's skin was covered in itchy and painful-looking blisters, his lips were swollen and he was generally a funny shade of red.

The first thing that I checked was his mouth. Allergic reactions can cause the tongue to swell up and if this blocks the airway then a person can easily choke to death. Luckily this wasn't happening to this child; while his lips were swollen his tongue looked fine. The next thing that you do is to get the stethoscope out and listen to the child's chest; an allergic reaction can have the same sort of effect on the lungs as an asthma attack. Once more the child's lungs sounded fine, maybe a bit of an infection, though.

I asked the parents what had happened.

They had realised that the child had developed a runny nose so they took his temperature and discovered it to be a bit high. Then, unlike the vast majority of the parents in the area, they had given him Calpol and Nurofen in order to keep his temperature down. This is something to be applauded, as there are large numbers of families who would call out an ambulance for such a thing.

As soon as he swallowed them – pop, pop, pop, the child developed the blisters and his lips started swelling. So it looked like the child was allergic to one of the ingredients in the medicine.

Now it was time to wait for an ambulance. I knew we were short of trucks that night, I'd been bouncing from call to call including a couple that I shouldn't have been sent on but had been asked to go because there was nothing else to send. So we waited, and waited and waited.

Then we waited some more.

And a bit longer.

And even more.

By now the parents were, quite understandably, beginning to get upset. Their child was a bit distressed, although not as much as most kids would have been. There was little I could do but monitor him and see if the reaction got worse. While I can give an injection of adrenaline/epinephrine (or whatever it's called today) to reverse life-threatening reactions, it's not very nice to give it to a patient whose tongue isn't swelling up.

I phoned Control to see if there was any chance of an ambulance. They told me that they had already put a 'general broadcast' out for this call, but there was only one crew at the hospital and they were the ones I'd just done a job with, so they would still be unloading the last patient.

I even tried phoning my station to see if there was anyone there who was waiting for an ambulance to dry after mopping out after a mucky job. There was a crew there, but they were tied up talking to an officer because they had been assaulted and they were also filling in one of our emergency referrals for a child being at risk. I know the crew well and if they could have come to my rescue then they would have.

I can't take small children to hospital as the FRU doesn't have a child seat and it's unsafe to transport a small child in its mother's arms. I asked the father if he had a car/child seat – but they use public transport. If the child was in danger of not breathing then I might have taken the risk, but while the reaction looked severe the child was more uncomfortable rather than likely to stop breathing – actually the child was having a great time playing with my car keys.

So all I could do was to monitor the child and keep him and his parents calm. I like to think that I'm pretty good at this because, perhaps due to writing my blog, I can explain exactly what is happening in quite simple language. I'm also not quick to panic and my general attitude tends to lend itself to keeping people relaxed.

Listening to the child's lungs he had started to develop a little wheeze, exactly what happens to asthmatics, so I gave him a salbutamol nebuliser (our treatment for this) and it settled down almost as quickly as it had started. His tongue was still the normal size although his lips had become more swollen.

Then the ambulance crew who had been to my last job walked in through the door. They had turned around their last job in just over 40 minutes, which is very fast, and had then ridden to my rescue. I love the look on parents' faces when they realise that the ambulance has arrived and I love the relaxed feeling in my gut when I have a sick patient and the crew walk in through the door.

It all worked out fine in the end. The child didn't need the injection and perked right up after some oral medicine. He spent the night and next day in the hospital under observation and made a full recovery. While it might sound daft it probably worked in his favour – at least they'll have a good idea what started this reaction and can plan on avoiding it.

While we go to a lot of rubbish on the car, this was a genuine job. It was just a shame that the ambulances in the area were probably going to drunks who had fallen over in the street or other minor incidents. While the FRU is mainly used to get the government-mandated targets it can sometimes be clinically worthwhile. This was such an occasion. I'd also like to applaud the parents for keeping calm while their child looked so ill; they were worried but polite and understanding. A rare combination.

After the Epilepsy Comes the Work

There is a genuine job that I dislike above all others, and that is someone who has had a seizure in a public place and is now 'post-ictal'. The post-ictal stage of a seizure is the period after the fitting has stopped when the patient can become very drowsy or, and this is the bit I hate, can be extremely confused. These patients can also become violent and very distressed. It's normal and something that we learn to deal with, but I still don't enjoy it.

We were called to a collapse in a supermarket. It's fun to go to these as you try to guess if the collapse is real or if the person faked the fit because they were caught shoplifting. Yes, I have a nasty, cynical and suspicious mind.

Out patient was a young woman in her twenties; she was being restrained in the first aid room by the security/first aid officer. They could see that she was confused but probably didn't understand why the patient was fighting with them and wanting to walk off. The problem that we have is that we aren't really meant to restrain patients, but on the other hand if I let her waltz out into the traffic I think I'd be getting some rather negative newspaper headlines.

So we tried talking to her but she was still very confused. A quick check revealed nothing physically wrong; she was just in an agitated post-ictal state.

So we found ourselves essentially frogmarching the poor woman out the door to try to get her into our ambulance; she was fighting us the whole way. Again we aren't supposed to do this, but I believe that we are protected under common law to prevent someone from hurting themselves. She adamantly refused to enter the ambulance but she was in no fit state to be left alone.

Then our angel descended from the heavens.

A girl, about ten years old, appeared from nowhere. To take one look at her you would instantly mark her down as one of those wasted youth who hang around on street corners. She came over and started talking to the patient; it turned out that she was her next-door neighbour. After asking us if our patient had had a seizure she managed to persuade her to get on the ambulance where we could do further checks and provide a bit of treatment.

After some talking (and some persuasion from our angel) the patient agreed that we could take her home and as she was starting to recover we thought that this was a reasonable idea. It's something we sometimes do – provide a bit of treatment until the patient recovers and then the patient will ask to be either left where they are or to get a lift home. This is one 'taxi-ride' we don't mind.

All throughout our angel was superb. She went back into the shop and bought the item that our patient had originally come out for, then she kept talking to her in order to keep her calm. Finally when we reached her address she made sure that our patient was safely indoors and offered to stay with her until her family returned home.

So because of our angel a very tricky job became much easier and much more pleasant for the patient.

The reason why I don't like these jobs is that all the public sees is us 'fighting' with an aggressive and confused patient and no doubt forms the impression that the patient is either drunk, on drugs or insane. I hate it for the embarrassment that the patient must feel afterwards when they realise what has happened. I hate it because it's such a show we get the maximum number of rubberneckers and you can hear people tutting as they walk past.

...And yes I hate it because I don't like forcing people into my ambulance.

Snails

There is a reason that I dislike working nights at this time of year. I suspect that it has to do with the love I have of animals, even the slightly squicky ones. During the night, when it is damp, the snails come out. Perfectly camouflaged against garden paths, each one is like a little landmine of guilt. I have size twelve feet, my eyesight isn't the best and each snail that I crush makes me want to weep. I watch them during the day, their friendly little eyes looking up at me as they go on their merry way. Little do they know my unwitting genocide against their species.

I found myself the other night picking my way through an overgrown garden to attend to an elderly man with a bellyache – nothing particularly serious but his garden path, long and dark, was full of snails, soon to be deceased.

So out came my torch and I carefully picked my way between them, my crewmate (hoof-footed fool that he is) managed to splat one of them by accident. After discovering that our patient wasn't too ill my crewmate helped him get his coat and keys while I snuck out in the garden and started picking the snails out of the way of the partially sighted patient. I'm sorry to say that in my eagerness to save as many as possible one died in a 'friendly fire' incident.

The patient came shuffling out of the house and, despite my feeble torchlight and my evacuation of as many of our shelled friends as possible, he still managed to step on two of them. Each one was a chain of guilt around my heart.

I know it is strange to think about such things but these are the kind that go through your mind at 2 a.m.

And, yes, I know that snails are considered pests to gardeners but I'm not a gardener, I think I'm a frustrated Jainist – although perhaps not as I'd quite happily roll some of our regulars into the canal.

I also have a horrible fear that one night I'll run over a fox – I think that'd be the day I have my long-awaited nervous breakdown.

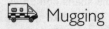 Mugging

I honestly can't believe it, a Friday night and I went to someone who had genuinely been mugged.

Please allow me to explain ...

Now, I may be accused of being overly cynical and those accusers may have a fair point, but given the amount of street violence that I see I have come to a few conclusions.

(1) Many people who get beaten up have done something to 'deserve' it, even if it is a stupid, childish or other pointless reason like 'respect'.

(2) As someone wiser than I said, 'For instant arsehole, just add alcohol' – a large amount of beatings are fuelled by it.

(3) Truly 'random' violence is very rare.

This is what gives me confidence when I'm walking down the otherwise frightening streets in the dangerous parts of town during the hours of darkness. I'm not involved in drugs or gangs. I have no bank of 'respect' that I have to protect and I'm not drunk and combative. This means that it is unlikely that I'm going to get myself attacked.

In the three and a half or so years I've been doing this job I can count the number of genuine muggings I've gone to on the fingers of one hand. This is obviously a good thing; I'd rather have frequent jobs to drug dealers who have beaten each other up than to an innocent who has just been robbed. With the former you can turn up and treat them while with the latter there is a distinct feeling that you will feel some sympathy for them – something that does your hard-bitten ambulance street-cred no good whatsoever.

426

The poor soul that I attended to had been punched in the face and the criminals had stolen his bag. The local kebab shop had taken the victim in, had called the police and ambulance and had sorted him out with a towel (for his bust lip) and a bottle of water. The unreported kindness of strangers often makes my job bearable.

We were first on scene and quickly determined that while shocked, he wasn't seriously hurt. He'd need hospital treatment for a cut lip and eye but wasn't in any danger to life or limb.

The 'street crime' squad arrived a minute or two after us. We let them use the back of our ambulance as an impromptu interview room so that they could get a description of the attackers. Two of the team questioned the patient and my crewmate attended to his injuries; meanwhile I stood outside (to give them room) and chatted with the final officer. As is often the case the police were sympathetic and professional.

With the details collected we took the patient and his friend to the local hospital. The problem patients like this have is that as the injury itself is fairly minor they are often a low priority and are sent out into the waiting room. But I think that the psychological trauma of being mugged should warrant a cup of tea and a bit of a sit-down somewhere quiet (not out in the waiting room with the noisy drunks). Unfortunately, this doesn't happen because there aren't the resources available and this is a damn shame.

This is why we try to make the transport to hospital as nice as possible as it's often the last time they'll get proper one-to-one care.

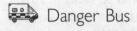 Danger Bus

The other night I was working with a friend of mine; he's built like the proverbial outhouse, is a martial arts master and looks scary. While I'm not an expert fighter I tend to have no fear.

That night we earned our name as the 'Danger Bus'.

It must have been that the police had fewer numbers than normal working as job after job was being sent to us as a 'Fight'. No injuries reported, just that there had been a fight (or that a fight was in progress). Sometimes we would get more details, sometimes it would just be that word.

There are two ways of dealing with a job like this. Officially we are supposed to hold back from the scene of violence until we are either sure that it is safe or we have a police escort. What often happens in real life is that we will take a look. We tend to know when a scene is dangerous and often don't want to bother the police who are as overworked as us. Sometimes something in the description of the call will give us cause to want the police there.

This job was one of them. It was given as 'Russians fighting in house'.

If you work with Russians in an emergency setting you will be nodding your head and agreeing with me that this situation was too dangerous for us to enter.

You see, I like Russians, they are fun, normally polite and tend not to make a fuss. However, when they have been drinking and fighting ... well, let's just say that when they fight they tend to play for keeps. I've seen 'friends' beating each other over the head with planks of wood then refusing to go to hospital as the inch-long gashes in their scalp were 'nothing to worry about'. Being between two fighting Russians is not a safe place to be.

So we waited for the police to arrive, which didn't take too long, then we advanced using them as a shield. It didn't look too good to need police to go into the job, especially when they were both female and were half the size of us. But you know that I'm no sexist so I knew that they were more than capable of handling pretty much anything. While it might not have looked good, I felt a lot safer.

The patient had a rather large split to the lip that would require an operation in a specialist unit, nothing life threatening but nasty nevertheless.

The next 'Fight' we went to was in a Docklands Light Railway station. The police had arrived before us and were told, to quote the officer we met, 'You can go lads, it was two teenagers and one of them gave the other a slap – I told them to stop being silly.' We could see the two teenagers slinking off into the night.

If people were nicer to each other I might be able to get a cup of tea once in a while.

Dog (Or, Why I Like Animals More than Most People)

I'm racing down the road on lights and sirens; there is a traffic-light-controlled pedestrian crossing so I have to slow down to avoid knocking over the people who think that it is a good idea to run across the road in front of me.

Sitting, quite calmly, on the side of the road is a guide dog for the blind. Amidst all these people running over the crossing, trusting that I'll try to miss them should they fall over in the middle of the road, the dog sits quietly and doesn't make a move.

The dog has more sense than the people of Newham.

Thursday Night

I've just been told to 'Fuck off' by one of our regular abusive alcoholics.

She then tried to push me over.

She's seventy-five.

I'm six foot one.

Funny, how we can laugh at these sorts of things. She's been left at home; no doubt someone will be called back to her before the night is over.

Thank You West Ham

A medal for my crewmate please ...

We picked up one of our ... erm ... 'less fragrant' frequent flyers. She stunk, as is usual with her, to high heaven.

I'm driving; my crewmate is in the back of the ambulance with the patient.

The people at the football at West Ham are just emptying out.

It takes us 43 minutes to travel the 500 yards to hospital while weaving through traffic that often leaves me a credit card's thickness of space on either side. It would normally take us a minute or two.

Every time I tap the brakes a wave of nauseating smell rolls from the rear of the ambulance into the driver's section.

My crewmate doesn't complain at all and just makes conversation with the patient – something that I wouldn't enjoy.

We arrive at the hospital to find another crew in the same situation more than 40 minutes in transit, only their patient has drunkenly urinated all over the floor of their ambulance.

This is exactly the sort of job that we don't get the recognition for.

🚐 My New Plan for Hoax Calls

Yesterday I had a call that I knew was going to be a hoax but would have to be investigated anyway.

The call came down to our computer terminal as 'Child on phone claiming to be 52-year-old male with difficulty in breathing, no answer on ringback, probably hoax, please investigate.'

While this seems pretty cut and dried it's probably for the best that we are sent to investigate; it only takes one misunderstanding and someone to die and the whole service would be dragged over the coals. I can just picture the headline 'Ambulance Thought My Dying Husband Was a Hoax Caller!'

So we went to the phone box and sure enough there was a gang of perhaps eight young teenagers standing opposite it. One of them did that annoying thing where they run into the middle of the road, stamp their feet then wave at you and shout that they have broken their leg.

We pulled up next to him. 'Call an ambulance did you?'

The teenager faked ignorance.

'It's against the law to dial 999 for no reason,' I continued.

He just laughed.

So in an uncharacteristic fit of quick-thinking I pulled out my mobile phone and took a picture of him.

He looked shocked and ran off to his friends and muttered something quickly to them.

My crewmate completed the illusion by pretending to talk to Control on our radio.

The gang of kids disappeared.

The good thing was that (a) it's not against the law to take a picture of someone in the street (he had no expectation of privacy), (b) if he'd done nothing wrong he'd got nothing to worry about and (c) if it was him hoaxing us, then it might give him a sleepless night worrying what we would do with the 'evidence'. Of course, there was nothing that we could do because we couldn't prove that he was the one to make the hoax call, so the prospect of a little guilt on his part was the best we could hope for.

I'm sure some social worker* would be upset at my actions, but when we are overloaded with calls such idiocy could cost someone their life.

On TV Dramas and Documentaries

I can't stand to watch TV medical dramas these days; they have all fallen into 'soapdom'. Where once upon a time they would have a storyline about an interesting disease, they seem a lot more likely now to have storylines about the staff having sex with each other.

Let me tell you something, working shifts for the NHS means that sex is the last thing on many of our minds. And no right-thinking ambulance worker would get naked on an ambulance trolley – we know exactly what sorts of patients we have on them – and it's just too yucky to even think about screwing on one.

It's not just the paucity of good stories, it's the errors made in the treatment of patients and in the characterisation of staff.

I could go on for hours about the apparent success rate of resuscitating dead people on TV and how it sets real relatives up with unreasonable expectations. I've lost count of the number of people who've asked me why I'm not 'shocking' their deceased relative, because they have seen it being done on the telly.

---

*Talking of social workers, a friend of mine went on a call last night where one got involved. Said social worker got out of his car, urinated in the gutter and then bullied an elderly but otherwise healthy patient into going to hospital. Words fail me.

The staff in these programmes are either angels (the medical staff) or devils (the management). The ambulance staff are assaulted and never fight back, the nurses are all incredibly caring all the time and the hospital management care for nothing but 'the bottom line' (whatever *that* is in a charity like the NHS).

But I don't worry about such things. I understand the pressures that TV works under, how something as simple as the sun starting to go down during filming means that the 'ambulance crew' have to get patients out of a crashed car in a way we never would. I understand that it's hard to show the myriad of emotions that runs through the average staff member every day.

I can understand the documentaries as well; they need to be interesting and the editing needs to be fast-paced. It's not the production company's fault if the editing makes the medical staff look criminally negligent in their treatment of a patient.

So I don't watch medical dramas if I can help it, and I don't watch documentaries either – after all it's a bit too much like a busman's holiday.

 Dotty

There is often something endearing about the pleasantly confused elderly, at least in the short term. For us it makes a difference from the confusion that has little old ladies grabbing your testicles because you are obviously 'a Nazi come to take me to the gas chambers'.

We were called to one of our less regular warden-controlled homes. I've been there a couple of times and have normally been impressed with the staff, not just because I had a cup of tea and a cake once when I helped them out a little outside of what is normally expected of us.

It was two o'clock in the morning as we pulled into the parking area of the home. We'd noticed a little old man in a heavy coat who was pulling a wheeled basket and being flummoxed by the automatic gate.

The warden, looking at the end of her tether, came out to meet us. She pointed at the man. 'There he is, he's confused and I can't do anything with him.'

The patient didn't really want to go to hospital; he wanted to go for a walk. Chatting to him I could tell that he wasn't in a right frame of mind. My crewmate expertly took the warden off to one side and got the information that we needed. I on the other hand worked on the patient.

Luckily he didn't need much persuading; after a bit of a chat I found out that he had a long-running problem with his elbow. I explained that 'as we are here', it would be our pleasure to pop him down the hospital so they could have a look at him. He was a really pleasant bloke, and I enjoyed having a (slightly muddled) chat.

So we had a nice little journey down to the hospital where we discovered the probable source of his confusion. Someone had cancelled his night-time sleeping pill. It's a well-known effect of stopping sleeping pills that (particularly in the elderly) it can cause night-time confusion, agitation and wandering. I believe that an early episode of *Scrubs* had a running joke to this effect. Still, at least the hospital could make sure that this was the cause for the confusion, not something more serious.

Unknown Aggro

Ah, the pure pleasure of being in the middle of a domestic dispute; oh how I love the shouting, the swearing and the pulling of hair.

We were called to a patient with a long-term illness; his daughter arrived at the same time as the ambulance and was crying before the front door was opened. Our FRU driver was already present talking to the patient and his partner (a surprisingly young-looking woman).

Barely had we set foot in the flat than the arguing started. It appeared that the daughter had some 'issues' with the patient's partner so they started shouting at each other over the (rather ill) patient.

They were shouting at each other so much that the patient's concern that he was about to be incontinent of faeces couldn't be addressed in time. Heaven knows we tried to get him to the toilet, but with both women screaming at each other it was perhaps inevitable that he would poo on the carpet.

Enough was enough, so I locked one of the women out of the house so we could actually find out what was wrong with the patient. The problem was pretty simple and not worth the aggravation that we were getting from these warring relatives.

Then the two women started to fight which resulted in some items of clothing getting torn. I managed to calm things down a little by threatening to call the police. We were all getting exasperated by now and just wanted the patient on the back of the ambulance and safely on the way to hospital.

Thankfully the son of the patient arrived and managed to calm his sister down; we were then able to 'load and go' to the nearest hospital.

I didn't know what the argument was about, and to be honest I didn't care. All I wanted was to look after the patient and go onto my next job. In the end neither of the women was any help to the patient (or to us). It's in situations like this that you have to bite your tongue and yet remain forceful enough to stop people beating each other up.

I don't know how the police do it day after day ...

I'd want to pepper spray everyone.

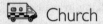 Church

Top call of the day ...

The call was given as 'Collapsed, not breathing', so we rushed around there to discover that the location was a cab office.

A woman had come into the office to try to persuade the cab dispatcher to go to church; he had buried his head in his hands and tried to ignore her.

She then thought he had died, panicked and called us.

The 'patient' was apologetic, he didn't know that we had been called, while the caller was convinced he had died and come back to life, despite being told otherwise by ourselves and the patient.

You have got to laugh.

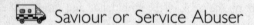 Saviour or Service Abuser

I had my first famous person in the back of my ambulance the other day.

Jesus Christ.

We were called to a 'Male, 51, schizophrenic, acting violently.'

So we waited for the police to turn up, for we are not stupid.

The door was opened by a woman; she said something to the police and they pulled out their ASP truncheons and loosened the straps on their CS sprays. They made their way upstairs and left the woman downstairs with us. I started to have a little chat with the woman and thought to myself, 'She's a bit strange ...'

The police came down the stairs, one of them took me aside and, indicating the woman, told me that *she* was the patient and was on leave from the local mental health unit. We took her outside where she explained that, yes, she was on leave from the unit but her father had suddenly developed schizophrenia.

I asked her if it might be her mania flaring up, and if she would like to return to the unit. She agreed that this would be a good idea, so the police asked her for her name.

'Jesus.' The policewoman and I looked at each other. 'Christ,' she continued.

'OK,' said the police officer, 'but do you have another name, perhaps one your parents gave you?'

The patient gave us her 'birth name' and, fetching her huge bag of anti-psychotic medication from under the sink, she hopped into the ambulance.

We drove her straight to the mental health unit that she was on leave from. We went into a side room to talk to the mental health nurse.

'What's the story now then?' she asked.

I told her.

The nurse tutted. 'She's not really mad, she's just playing up.'

I looked at the huge bag of medicines the patient took. 'But,' I said, 'why is she taking all these anti-psychotics?'

'Well,' the nurse replied, 'she is a bit mad, but she doesn't need to be in the unit.'

I wasn't in the mood to argue, after all it's not my place to question the long-term care of the mentally ill.

We started to leave the unit.

'Have fun with Jesus Christ,' I fired over my shoulder.

♨ Possession

Once upon a time, in the far depths of internet time, back when the Lynx browser was pretty much the standard, I signed up to be a 'Humanist Priest of the Universal Church' or some such. Don't ask me why, I think it was set up so that Americans could get tax-breaks. Not much use for myself who (a) wasn't American nor (b) as a student wasn't paying taxes at the time. I printed off the certificate, laughed and forgot about it.

If only I'd known that I'd end up working on an ambulance I might well have paid extra (that is paid anything) to get the advanced certificate. Let me tell you why ...

Every so often we get sent to 'person behaving strangely', sometimes this is an adult and sometimes it is a child. When we reach the patient we are told, with a straight face nonetheless, that the patient is possessed by ancestors/spirits/demons.*

Despite being an evangelical atheist, I have to take this sort of thing seriously. There is however a problem – our training guidelines pull us in two directions.

Direction one: we should respect the culture and traditions of our patients.

Direction two: we should never collude with, or reinforce the delusions of, someone who is psychotic.

(Psychosis is defined as 'irrational beliefs not shared by the patient's traditions or culture'.)

You can see the problem that we have.

I have been to a 13-year-old boy who has been possessed by spirits and, when the police arrived, ran off like Linford Christie. Of course, he reckoned without the police van coming around the far end of the street.

I've been to a teenage girl who was 'protected' from demons by some

*Delete as applicable.

wall hangings, but they might have found a way through and this was what was making her sick.

I've been to a mother who was channelling spirits in order to drive out the evil ancestors plaguing her daughter (who, unsurprisingly perhaps, had mental health issues).

I've been to members of an evangelical Christian cult who were trying to drive evil spirits out of their elderly relative by throwing salt at them.

I've been to countless people who have believed that they were possessed and have had near superhuman strength to prove it. I've seen them 'levitate' off beds despite their father sitting on top of them. I've seen them running down the street naked, covered in their own excrement, all in order to fulfil some direction from God.

So where do I stand? Do I respect the culture and agree that 'yes, it might be demons', or do I not reinforce their delusions by reminding them that a urine infection can cause similar symptoms? More importantly, where does madness end and religion begin?

The Humanity of the Officer of the Peace

We were sent to a 17-year-old boy who had been drinking too much of the nastily strong cider that our seasoned alcoholics seem to love; the sort of stuff that comes in blue plastic bottles and costs a pound for three litres. He had made his way to a friend's house and then collapsed on their kitchen floor. The family that he had 'gatecrashed' were concerned and had called us.

The people at the house were very nice, they realised that he was too drunk to be left alone but his family lived in Essex and had no way to collect him. It seemed pretty obvious that the young man needed to be in hospital; his was a case of alcohol poisoning and to leave him behind would have been dangerous.

We tried to rouse him from his slumber and were greeted with abuse and finally a thick stream of vomit, which he proceeded to lay his head in. The family told us that he was awaiting sentencing for breaking a man's jaw and that he was expecting two to ten years in prison. They mentioned this because they didn't want to see us punched by his, now puke-covered, fists.

We decided that it would be wise to call the police.

Two police officers arrived and, after apologising for calling them out, we explained the situation. We all agreed that the hospital would be the best place for him, but at a pinch the police could arrest him for 'breach of the peace' and then take him to the station where the police doctor would send him to hospital. A roundabout route, but in either event he would eventually be cared for in hospital.

One of the policemen spoke to the boy firmly but with compassion. He noted the signs of self-harm on the boy's wrists and took a fatherly tone. It was great to see the police officer persuade the boy to attend hospital when previously the patient had refused all offers of help.

Because of the chance of violence the police officer travelled in the back of the ambulance with my crewmate in order to maintain our safety. Thankfully, we reached the hospital with no further incident.

While waiting for the nurses at the hospital to accept the patient I started chatting to the police officer and he agreed that it was incredibly sad to see the patient in such a state, that he was starting down a life of alcohol abuse and crime. We could both easily see where this teenager would end up and we thought that it was both sad and frustrating that this descent would probably be inevitable.

It was the common humanity of this seasoned police officer that is so unrecognised by the media and the public that makes me privileged to work so closely with these professionals.

While cleaning the ambulance outside the department I saw a drunken patient ejected by security. Complaining loudly, the patient headed over to the same police officers and demanded that they 'do something'. The police officers calmed the drunk down and advised him to head home.

He climbed into his car and started to drive off.

The last I saw of this man was him, stopped by the police ten yards down the road, being breathalysed.

 Abandonment

I don't like it when we get 'dropped calls', where someone has called for an ambulance, yet put the phone down (or been cut off) before all the details have been given. I don't like it because without all the information in place it is hard to get a 'feel' for how dangerous the job might be.

I don't like the idea of being stabbed because I don't know what I'm walking into.

The call as we got it was 'child reporting mother cutting wrists', then the child hung up. This could run the whole spectrum of calls from a hoax to a psychotic woman running around with a kitchen knife. I've been to both types of call, and it's why I don't get too wound up by hoaxes.

We arrived to find the police already there. Control had called them in advance as they had realised that the scene might well be dangerous. The two police officers were standing outside the address; they had been unable to gain access and were contemplating kicking the door down.

'Is everything all right?' a woman shouted down from the flat above our position.

We explained that we were looking for the woman of the house and asked if the neighbour had seen her.

'She left about ten minutes ago; her and her husband got into a car and drove off.'

I used my finely tuned experience of watching *CSI* to note that there was no sign of blood in the area and drew my conclusion that the call had been a hoax.

'Hey! ambulance man with his nose to the floor looking for pools of blood,' the neighbour shouted again, 'her son is over there by your ambulance, maybe you can ask him.'

The police and I walked over to where we had parked; the child was talking to my crewmate, who rolled his eyes as we approached.

'I'm sorry I called you,' the ten-year-old said. 'My mum was angry at me so she locked herself in the bathroom and told me that she was cutting her wrists. So I called for an ambulance, but she was only pretending. Then Mum and Dad threw me out of the house and they drove off in the car. I don't know where they went.'

One of the police officers asked the child if he had any relatives he could stay with. The child knew of no adults to look after him.

'Sounds like a social problem,' I said to one of the police officers.

'Yep.'

'Not a job for an ambulance,' I continued.

'Nope.' The police officer looked crestfallen with the amount of paperwork that he was going to have to do. I've read enough police blogs to realise that any job involving children is a huge pain, more so I would think if the child has been through the experience this one had.

'We'll be off then,' I said with only a little *Schadenfreude*. I could trust the police to look after this situation.

Little was I to know that our next encounter would be with a stereotypical 'world's worst mother'.

🚑 Both Boxes Ticked

We were sent to 'Female, head injury, police on scene.'

The patient ticked both the 'crack user' and 'prostitute' boxes on the 'Is your patient a crack whore?' form.

She was in the garden of the house shouting and swearing at the lone police officer and the ambulance duty station officer who had been sent out as a first responder. Between near incoherent offensive language we discovered that the woman had a bit of a bruise to her head.

The mother had got into an argument with her 14-year-old daughter. After years of this sort of behaviour the daughter had finally snapped and hit her mother around the head.

I spoke with the police officer; he told me that the child had only recently been returned to the mother's custody. The social workers involved in the case had said, 'The mother needs to take some responsibility for caring for her daughter.' The police officer was the same one who had driven the daughter home from foster care.

The mother was well known to the police for the reasons given above.

The police officer was feeling guilty as apparently the child was a 'good kid'.

Our patient was complaining of all over body pain; my crewmate took her into the back of the ambulance and did a sterling job of calming her down. The drive to hospital was uneventful.

The daughter had to be arrested. We are all crossing our fingers that the mother won't press charges.

We meet such *lovely* people in our line of work.

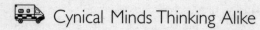 Cynical Minds Thinking Alike

We healthcare people can be nasty cynical-minded swines sometimes.

Sent to an eleven-year-old child suffering from an asthma attack, I arrive to find the child breathing normally. His oxygen levels are better than mine, his breathing is nice and relaxed, and on listening to his chest I can detect no wheeze or chest infection.

The child tells me that his chest is still feeling 'tight' even though he has no other symptoms of any difficulty in his breathing.

Why is it that I, my crewmate and the nurses at the hospital all have the thought that today is Monday and therefore a school day uppermost in our minds? Could the child be faking his illness just to get out of school?

As I say, we have nasty cynical minds.

Still, it meant a nice early trip to the hospital where I could score something to eat.

 Veil

I hate mornings; there is something deeply depressing about crawling into work while it is still dark knowing that for the next twelve hours you'll be run ragged.

The current topic of conversation in the messroom at the moment is the suggestion that Muslim women wearing full-face veils only divide communities as well as being harder to understand.

My patch has a large number of Muslims; some days I'll only attend to them. This isn't a problem for me as most of them are polite and don't get horribly drunk and try to hit me.

On more than one occasion I've turned around to discover that the patient I've been talking to has 'robed up', the woman has turned from a person into a black 'blob'. It's always surprising to see such a total change.

I'm a big believer in freedom of expression, and I have no problem with people wearing whatever they want, but the burka and its relatives can make my life difficult.

You see, I'm a bit hard of hearing, and if the person I'm talking to has a strong accent I tend to get more meaning from lip-reading rather than just listening to them. If the person has a full-face covering then it's often tricky for me to hear what they are saying. Add in the fact that the back of an ambulance isn't the quietest place on earth and the problem becomes a lot worse.

I don't want to offend people but it does annoy me to keep saying 'Pardon?' because I can't understand what the person is saying. I'm trying to be as nice as possible here but what is more important, the wearing of a veil or the ability for the ambulance man to understand you and your illness?

It's Ramadan at the moment so loads of people are fasting and again this can lead to offence.

I went to a gentleman who had fainted. As he was South-East Asian I asked him if he had been fasting (as this is a common cause of collapsing at this time of year). He told me that he was a Hindu rather than a Muslim, and that he hated all Muslims because of the fighting that had occurred between the two faiths in the past.

I apologised, and the patient wasn't bothered by my assumption, but another person might have taken offence and complained. It can be a minefield out there, especially given some religious adherents' near constant level of being offended.

Still it could be worse, we could be killing each other over which sect of a religion we belong to ...

... again.

🚑 A New Kind of Stupid

Every day I meet a new kind of stupid.

A woman, 35 years old, mother of two children, went to her GP. She had a swollen belly and pain that came and went in waves. She also hadn't had a menstrual period in over nine months. That morning, just after the pain had started, she had lost some fluid from her vagina. The pain was getting worse and the waves were getting closer together.

The GP did a pregnancy test that – surprise, surprise – came back positive.

The GP was incredibly relieved when we arrived.

We had just managed to wheel her into the maternity department when the baby made an appearance. My crewmate helped the midwife deliver the baby while I was hiding in the ambulance. I'm quite happy for any babies to be born without me being involved. I suspect the woman was quite happy I wasn't there as well.

Here was a woman who was fully aware of what pregnancy is like, but still the whole thing came as a complete shock. Her husband looked completely shell-shocked as well.

The whole thing really beggars comment.

🚑 Forked

I am currently so tired I'm not actually human at the moment – after a few litres of Coke I approach sub-human. This is not a huge disadvantage in this job.

Thankfully it was a pretty easy day today.

One call was to a teenage girl with abdominal pain, diarrhoea and vomiting. She described herself as an alcoholic. I let the nurses at the hospital know. Perhaps she'll get referred to the social services, maybe she is already known to them.

Then there was a homeless guy who was suicidal. The community mental health team wasn't interested in seeing him so he went to A&E where the nurse in charge took good care of him.

Another call was to one of our regulars, a child who keeps collapsing. He's a nice enough lad but so far investigations have shown nothing. It's believed that he collapses because of stress over bullying and various people are involved in his problem.

The final call of the day was to an ill person whom we never reached. On the way to the call we came across a four-year-old child who had been sitting on the crossbar of her father's bike. Somehow she'd got her foot caught between the spokes of the front wheel causing a crash. There was some serious swelling and bruising to her foot and ankle but thankfully she wasn't otherwise hurt. It's possible, but unlikely, that she could have broken a bone in her foot.

The child was really grown-up, hardly crying at all. She did keep giving me a sullen stare though ...

Darn kids can see right through me.

 Hypo

I think that there is something in the air. Yesterday we went to two diabetics with critically low blood sugars. It's a job that we sometimes do but isn't actually that common. The day before there were at least two others in our area, one of whom was quite ill.

The first was rather simple. A woman found her husband collapsed in the living room, she called us and we quickly diagnosed and treated the low blood sugar. When we found him he was unconscious, sweating profusely and he was rather ill looking. One injection and some glucose gel and an hour later the patient was playing with his very cute Doberman. We may have also been enjoying playing with the friendly dog as well.

The second person was a young woman in the workplace. I felt sorry for her as her work colleagues surrounded her and it was impossible for us to move her to a more private area. She wasn't as low as our first patient although she was very sweaty and was acting as if she were drunk. Once more we managed to 'cure' her with some sugary drinks sipped a little at a time. She was mortified that she was ill in front of her colleagues.

Both patients did not want to go to hospital and once their blood sugar was back to normal there wasn't much that the hospital would do. Traditionally, these are the sort of patients who refuse to attend hospital and are left behind by us ambulance crews.

Still, it is nice to be able to help people in such a profound manner; it makes a pleasant change from people who aren't actually ill.

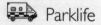 Parklife

'Male, 40 years old – fitting.'

The call was to a park, it was midday, so I didn't really need to see the update that said, 'Patient with two males, both appear drunk.'

I think that it is a law of the universe that your middle-aged, middle of the day, middle of the park fitter will be an alcoholic. That or they are an alcoholic who also happens to be epileptic.

As we approached the scene my crewmate asked where I thought it would be.

'Well, the drunks tend to hide down by that end, it's close to the off-licence.'

I was right. Our patient looked familiar but after a while all alcoholics start to look familiar. I did recognise his two friends, one had been picked up two days ago, and the other was another of our regular callers.

'He's had another fit,' said the slightly more sober one. 'He's had three today.'

'Yeah,' said the other taking a swig from a big bottle of cheap cider, 'he's epileptic but he doesn't take his tablets.'

Our patient had the same ground-in grime that you get from sitting on a park bench drinking all day, then falling over and going to sleep in the bushes before heading home at some point in the early hours of the morning. It was a simple job to load him up onto the stretcher, check him out, give him some oxygen and pop him into hospital.

My crewmate and I were inspecting him in the ambulance when I felt an urge to pass wind.

It was perfect timing, I could blame it on the semi-conscious patient.

My crewmate groaned, 'I think he's pooed himself.'

I told her the truth.

Honest.

By the time we reached the hospital the patient was a lot more awake, so we spoke to the handover nurse, put him on a trolley and went outside to clean up, finish off the paperwork and 'ahem' air out the back of the ambulance.

I think it was 30 seconds before we saw him walking out of the department.

Probably towards the nearest off-licence.

9010

Our code 9010 is for 'Assist only, not transported.'

It was a grey, horrible day. There was a constant drizzle of rain and when I got in my car to come to work it was so humid everything I touched was sticky.

Our first call of the day was to an elderly female who was believed to have had a CVA (cardiovascular accident), another word for a stroke. It's never a nice job so my heart sank.

We arrived to find the patient sitting in her living-room chair; also present were her friends (who have a front door key) and a carer who was preparing breakfast. The patient was lovely, she was sorry to have called us out and was, as is common with our older patients, worried that she was wasting our time.

She hadn't had a stroke; instead, she had been unable to get out of bed and so had crawled onto her landing on hands and knees in order to get some help. Her bed had recently been changed after she had been discharged from hospital a week ago and the rails that she should have used to get out of bed had been left leaning against the wall.

So my crewmate and I fitted her bedrails. Then we made sure that she could get into and out of bed. I then checked her physically to make sure that she wasn't hurt in any way. We then had a nice little chat, flirted with each other a bit and then, because the patient didn't want to go back to hospital, left her with her carer.

Throughout this call the patient was really worried that she was wasting our time. Personally, I think she had the chance of being our most worthwhile call all day – we turned up and fixed her bed (even though that wasn't our job), thereby providing her with some more independence. We left her at home feeling happy and more confident about moving around the house. This wasn't a job where we save someone's life but it was still hugely satisfying to help her out, even if it meant using common sense rather than following any protocol.

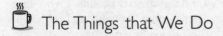

The Things that We Do

I'm an ambulance man. I'm supposed to pick up ill or injured people, right?

I'm not supposed to fix beds.

Or stairlifts.

I'm not here to fluff your pillows.

I'm not supposed to rescue you when your car breaks down, or get your car running again.

I'm not here to kick down your door because you have forgotten your key.

I'm not trained to fix your washing machine.

I'm not here to hand you a hanky when you break up with your boyfriend.

Nor am I here to help you shift a boiler.

At some point I should mention that I'm not here to settle an argument over a TV programme.

And I'm definitely not here to supply you with condoms because you've run out and need one now because 'my bitch wants screwing'.

But still I find people thinking that these are my jobs so they pick up the phone and dial 999.

☕ Helpful Passers-By

There is a secret(ish) forum for ambulance staff; one of the contributors there posted the following entry. While slightly tongue in cheek I thought that it would be shamefully wasted if it stayed on the forum. I reproduce it here for your reading pleasure. Send happy thoughts and wishes of quiet night shifts to 'The Saint' who originally wrote this.

Would all helpful passers-by please note:

If you really must ring for an ambulance for someone you see collapsed/dead/fitting/sat in a shop doorway, please ring then, and not three hours later, by which time – not surprisingly – the deceased has got up and left.

Two adult males sitting outside South Kensington tube station, sharing a bottle of Diamond White cider are NOT collapsed – they are having breakfast/dinner/lunch/a party. Singing, talking, vomiting and belching are all indications that the said males are alive.

Someone who is sitting in a shop doorway when it's pissing with rain is SHELTERING, not collapsed.

Just because someone with crutches is sitting down, they are not necessarily in need of medical intervention. Having hospital crutches is a clue. They have already been to hospital, and have been discharged.

If you really feel you just have to interfere in the life of a person happily sitting there drinking himself into alcoholic oblivion, when you ask him if he needs an ambulance, please take it as a massive clue when he says 'Faaaaaaaaaarrrrrrkkkkkk Ovvvvvvvvvvv!!!!!' This is his little way of saying 'Thank you for your concern, but I'm fine.'

When someone tells you they are fine, and they do not want an ambulance, please, please, please believe them. They are NOT lying – they know what they are doing.

Someone who is staggering between point A and point B CAN walk. The helpful clue is the movement of the legs and feet. If someone tells you that they cannot walk, but their legs are moving, THEY ARE LYING. Don't believe them.

Green stuff coming from a drunk's nose is NOT a reason for an emergency ambulance – it is actually a reason for an emergency hankie. Green stuff emanating from the patient's nose is very rarely Cerebro-Spinal Fluid, despite what you might have learnt from Casualty, ER *and* Holby City. *It is SNOT.*

If you see a pair of legs under a car, and the legs are surrounded by mechanic's tools, the person under the car has NOT been run over – he is more than likely to be FIXING it. Other clues are the radio playing nearby, and the deceased singing along to the music.

Talking of cars, if you happen to see several cars colliding with each other, and you can't get through to the ambulance service, have a look around you. Yes, the other twenty people with phones stuck to their ears are ALL calling the ambulance service. That's why you can't get through. And please tell us the right location – saying you are on Greenford Broadway when you are on Southall Broadway is less than helpful. And please don't insist you are right and the other twenty callers are wrong – it is highly unlikely.

Oh – and – please do not call the ambulance service if you see 200 people fighting on Fulham Broadway on Friday night. We are not remotely interested, and will not become interested until the police arrive. The police have guns, batons and CS gas, and can deal with a large fight a lot better than two female LAS personnel who are five feet nothing and jointly weigh 12 stone, and are only armed with rubber gloves and a frothy cappuccino from the Wild Bean Café. Please ring the police first – we'll pop along a bit later. Honestly. We will.

☕ Government Targets

The Healthcare Commission assesses and rates all NHS trusts.

The LAS got a 'Quality of Service' of 'weak'.

The reason?

We failed 'All ambulance trusts to respond to 95% of category B calls within 14 minutes (urban).' Possibly because we are chasing after Category A calls with not enough ambulances.

We also 'underachieved' at 'Deliver a ten percentage point increase per year in the proportion of people suffering from a heart attack who receive thrombolysis within 60 minutes of calling for professional help.' Is this because we don't do thrombolysis (giving a clot buster) in London? Instead, we take the patient to an angioplasty centre, which is much better for the patient.

So, once more we are punished for not having adequate resources and punished again for providing a service superior to that normally expected.

We are getting used to being underrated by the government.

Once again this is another example of how the government completely misses the point of what an ambulance service is for and what it does. We are underfunded and are forced to chase clinically irrelevant targets – it's no wonder we road staff feel rather annoyed.

Hectic

It all appears to have gone crazy in Newham. The hospital is full, they have no beds for admission and the A&E department is nearly overflowing. It's getting close to standing room only in the waiting room.

The ambulances here are pretty much fully staffed, yet the police are bringing in 'blue call' motorbike crashes because there are no ambulances to send to them.

West Ham football club is playing at home later this afternoon so that will mean more work.

Apparently the other hospitals in the area are in a similar position.

Whatever happened to Sundays being quiet?

 Beaten

I'm sitting in the back of the ambulance watching as a 16-year-old girl cries while explaining to the policeman why her father beat her.

Her tears are falling onto her clothes, leaving small salty circles.

While she is in pain, this isn't the reason why she is crying.

She uses up the last of our tissues.

Her jaw and chest are hurt where he used his fists and feet to beat her. I'd say that she has at least one broken rib.

I sit there listening to a long list of abuses her father has visited upon the whole family, from the seven-year-old up to his wife.

She didn't deserve this.

Her tears only stop once we reach the hospital.

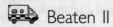 Beaten II

It would seem that when it comes to domestic violence cases, they sometimes come in groups. Just after dealing with one victim of violence we were called to a woman who had been assaulted. We arrived to find her talking to two police officers in her house. She had been punched in the face and would have a black eye coming up soon. They were getting details on the male who had assaulted her.

The story was fairly simple. The male was her ex-boyfriend but she had stopped seeing him some weeks ago. However, he kept coming to her place to persuade her that he still wanted to date her. This time, though, he had seen fit to break into the house and then to punch her in the face.

The police knew of the male and were trying to get the woman to press charges.

For some reason she didn't want to.

Was it because she knew him and worried that he would come back and kill her if the police were involved? Was it because she didn't want to go through the trouble of the courts? Or was it some other reason? I couldn't understand it myself, but then, having never been beaten, I don't expect I would.

So the police could only refer her to the domestic violence team and leave the patient in our care.

Sometimes I'd like more 'closure' in my work.

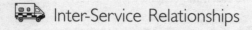 Inter-Service Relationships

Four jobs into the shift and none had wanted to go to hospital. It was a mix of the uninjured and the 'can't be bothered'.

The next call came.

'Two people stuck in a lift for two hours, one has collapsed. Fire service on scene.'

Great ... this could take hours.

This is not normally a problem, but in this case my crewmate really wanted to use the toilet.

We dutifully made our way to the train station where the lift was stuck and, after traipsing around a bit carrying our kit, managed to find the affected lift. There were a couple of firefighters, some station staff and three lift engineers. It turned out that two teenage boys had been jumping around in the lift causing the emergency locks to jam. They had been stuck for two hours and were making a lot of noise. From the shouts of both of them it was obvious that neither of them had collapsed.

There was little for us to do while waiting for the engineers to free the lift apart from chat to the firefighters and watch a fireworks display going on across the river.

Twenty minutes later and the lift was freed and the two little hooligans rolled out.

'Who's gonna take us to get a McDonald's?' were the first words out of one of the boys' mouth.

No 'Thank you', no 'Cheers for getting us out', and definitely no 'Sorry to waste all your time.'

We told the boys to 'ahem' 'Go home' and set about packing away our gear.

One of the firefighters turned to us. 'Fancy a cup of tea back at our station?'

My crewmate still needed to use the toilet so we agreed. It was a quick drive to their station to 'use their facilities' and have a nice cup of warm tea. Excellent company as we put the world to rights and five minutes later we were back on the road ready to continue. It was handy of them to offer us the use of their station as it was a lot closer than our ambulance station, so we were back on the road quicker than we could have been otherwise.

I'm occasionally dismissive of the fire service (mainly because they don't wave when we drive past each other), so it was really nice to be human to each other. And while I do take people as I find them, a simple cup of tea has meant that I can look at some of them in a much different light.

We should do it more often.

Actually I think that we should have ride-outs between us, the fire service and the police – it'd only help to improve our working relationships (although we ambulance people and the police tend to get on well anyway because we often attend the same sorts of jobs).

Ghosts of the Past

A tricky job to write up as it touches on a 'thing' that has squatted in the back of my head for a long time. Something I thought I had dealt with years ago but obviously haven't. My mum will read this and I don't think it's something I've ever really talked to her about, but I asked her if I could write this and she agreed.

We were stuck in traffic on our way to someone with a headache. It was a Green call so we didn't need lights and sirens, we just had to trundle there, pick up the 20-year-old and trundle into hospital. It was a nice easy job and got us a bit closer to the end of the shift.

Then we heard Control asking if there were any free ambulances to attend to a female who was giving birth; the nasty bit was that the woman was only 26 weeks pregnant. Control told everyone that the baby's head was visible. We called up and mentioned that we were on a low priority job and if they wanted to send us we would quite happily go.

A crew was already on their way and as the information came in that the woman had just given birth we were dispatched as a second crew to help out. If she had given birth to such a premature baby then every hand could help.

We were on the other end of our patch and the daytime traffic was hectic, but I drove like a demon and we were soon there. The job was at the top of a block of flats so we grabbed our kit, jumped in the lift and made our way to the right floor.

The doors of the lift opened and standing there was one of my mates with a tiny baby in his hands. It wasn't breathing.

'Do you want the baby or the mother?' he asked.

'Give us the baby, we'll run with it,' I answered. With that he handed us the baby and the lift doors closed.

We were met downstairs by the father, who had run down, so we rushed out to the ambulance to 'scoop and run', to get this baby to the hospital as quickly as possible. All I could look at was how tiny the baby was, it looked like the baby birds that you sometimes find fallen from the nest. Its arms were like matchsticks, it was covered with blood and there were no signs of life. My mate was in the back trying to resuscitate the baby while I drove us the, thankfully, short distance to the hospital.

We got to the hospital and the doctors there tried their best, but inevitably the baby was declared dead soon after we arrived.

It turned out that the woman, while believing that she was 26 weeks pregnant, was only 20 weeks so the baby didn't stand any chance at all.

This job shook me up because I believed that the baby had a chance.

I was less than a year old when my mother gave birth to my brother Mark; he was premature at 23 weeks' gestation. Today, survival rates for a baby at that age are around 17 per cent; back then in the 1970s they were much lower. After a few days of life my brother died.

I thought that it was something that I had put behind me many years ago, that I had a brother I'd never met, whose grave I've never seen. It's not something that we talk about much as it still pains my mum to think about it. Some years ago, for no reason, I started wondering what he would have been like if he had survived. I long felt I'd put those thoughts behind me, but looking at a child that I thought was 26 weeks' gestation brought those memories flooding back. I wondered if that had been what Mark had looked like.

At the hospital there was an officer. He told us to return to station to have a cup of tea and a 'de-stress' and to return to work when we felt able. Also, if we wanted to talk, he'd be around to listen.

A cup of tea helped, and I felt able to keep working after a little sit-down. But now, as I write this, I can feel the sadness in my chest – not for the child who never had a chance at life, but for the brother whom I never met.

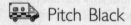 Pitch Black

It was supposed to be a simple job, pick the little old lady up off the floor and either take her to hospital or leave her at home. Unfortunately, there were a number of complications.

The first complication was that there was a power cut in the area. As it was the middle of the night the whole place was pitch black. We have lovely torches in our ambulances. Well, it turned out that we had 'a' torch.

It wasn't working.

Brilliant, all our actions would be under the light of our pen-torches.

We managed to find the house quite easily; there were two candles in the window. The patient herself didn't open the door, she was too scared. Instead, one of her neighbours had a key to let people in. He wasn't much younger than the patient herself and had been drinking a little.

We went in and, under feeble torchlight, managed to determine that she had a black eye, a cut on her shin and a small cut on her face. She refused to go to hospital. All she wanted to happen was to be put back to bed.

I looked around, I couldn't see a bed.

The patient sleeps on the sofa because she is too frail to climb the stairs to her bedroom. So she puts lots of pillows on the sofa and throws a blanket over herself. Because of the power cut she didn't have any heating.

Like Miss Nightingale before me, this (ex-)nurse was forced to clean and dress the patient's wounds under candlelight. My crewmate did a good job of holding the candle, only dropping it the once.

Still the patient refused to go to hospital.

I asked her if she had any carers. She told me that her son came every couple of weeks to stock her cupboard with food, but other than that she had no social services/care input at all. This is partly why she was sleeping downstairs on the sofa; she hadn't been offered stairlift installation.

I wasn't very happy to leave the patient at home, but she had the capacity to refuse treatment so I had no choice. In a case like this I like to have a GP come to visit to make sure that I haven't missed anything important (I know my limits). Unfortunately the emergency GP couldn't give us a time when he would be able to visit. The keyholder would be going to bed (it was edging on to 11 p.m.) so there would be no one to open the door for him.

So with some regret I arranged to have the patient's own GP come out to visit her in the morning. It was basically the best I could do for the immediate future.

Then the patient needed to use the toilet, my (female) crewmate took care of this (for which I'm very thankful). It was about now, about half an hour too late, that I realised that the light on my pocket PC made a really good torch.

For a longer term look at her care I filled in a 'vulnerable adult' form. This got faxed off to our Control which then deals with any concerns that we raise. In this case they will speak directly to the local social services and hopefully they will provide some help to enable this patient to live safely in her own home.

I have to do all this; it's how I get to sleep at night. If I'd just left her and crossed my fingers then I'd be worrying for days about her. By doing all the above I've done all that I can, and it is now up to the GP and social services to do their job.

A conscience is a terrible burden sometimes.

Of course, it would have all been a lot easier if there hadn't been a power cut, if it wasn't during the hours of darkness (when the regular services all vanish) and if she opened her own door.

Actually, it would have been much easier if I'd been able to persuade her to go to hospital.

For once I had some feedback from the 'vulnerable adult' form that I put in: the patient had agreed to go to one of the nicer warden-controlled flats just a few streets away. It's good to know that some people get a happy ending.

Google Health

I love Google, I really do. It does a wonderful job and helps me out in nearly endless ways.

But ...

It seems that more and more calls that I go to have a computer running in the background. These computers are often displaying a 'health information' webpage. While I think that having readily available information is a good thing, it is important to be able to interpret that information. It is not enough to read and understand the words that are shown on screen, they need to be filtered through some form of expert knowledge, even if it is just the skill to use a bit of common sense.

Take, for instance, a job I went to recently. The patient was a fit and healthy 25-year-old. He works on a building site and this involves plenty of heavy lifting. For the last two weeks he has had pain in his left arm. He'd already been to A&E because he was afraid that it was something serious. The hospital did plenty of medical tests, all of which came back normal.

So, why was he calling for an ambulance when the illness was so old? He'd looked on a website and it had mentioned that left-arm pain can be caused by having a heart attack. He'd read this then started to have a minor panic attack. As he continued reading it also told him that difficulty in breathing is another symptom of a heart attack.

Now, most people would realise that, given his history, it would be very unlikely that he would be having a heart attack lasting two weeks. But this patient read the webpage uncritically and so convinced himself that the cause of his pain was cardiac in nature.

Obviously this was one of our high priority calls so the FRU car was already there although we weren't too far behind. All I could really do for the patient was to reassure him, check his vital signs and symptoms, and then drive him to hospital so that he could be checked out. He was a nice enough bloke and he accepted that some of his symptoms were caused by his fear so for me it was an easy job and one that got me off shift on time.

I think that you need to develop an easy-going attitude to these sorts of calls; you can get very annoyed by those that seem like a waste of time. I just put it down to fear and lack of knowledge, not something a lot of people can do much about.

However, with that lack of knowledge, rather unfortunately, often comes a lack of critical thinking about what turns up on an internet search. While Google can be helpful, it isn't the be all and end all and you still need people who can interpret it.

🚑 Another Monday Night

Lots of anger tonight.

The local A&E departments are full, the nurses in charge are doing juggling acts in order to try to get patients in a position to be examined by the doctors. Waiting rooms are full and in at least one case there are no beds left in the hospital while plenty of patients need admitting.

I explained to one patient we brought in that this is why she had to go to the waiting room – there just wasn't room for her and her two-day-old headache to lie on a trolley.

'Fucking hospital, always some excuse!'

It took some restraint on my part to not shout at her to open her eyes and take a look at the crowded department she was standing in, to look at the staff charging around doing a dozen things at once, and to consider that this headache perhaps wasn't the highest priority illness that night.

The expectation of patients is much higher than the care which can reasonably be provided. Even when it is obvious that the department is being overloaded, the desire to get their 'serious' problem cured immediately leads to anger.

Patient tempers were flaring; the doctors and nurses were run ragged. Multitasking is an important nursing skill, especially when not only do you have to do all your normal nursing duties but you have to run crowd control on angry relatives and the normal cast of drunks.

So please explain to me why those complete 'expletive deleted' morons in the Department of Health are planning to close two of our local A&E departments? When the current A&E capacity isn't enough, and there is a year-on-year increase in attendance, shouldn't these people be supporting the A&E departments rather than cutting capacity even more?

Sorry, I forgot – we are supposed to be more 'efficient', people are going to be treated in the community (by ambulance staff at some point in the indeterminate future) and they won't need to go to hospital. Eighty per cent of our calls don't need an ambulance. But, and it's a big but, they might need an ambulance, X-rays, blood tests and the like to come to the conclusion that they didn't actually need that ambulance.

Of course, people will still want to go to hospital, and we are unable to refuse. Then when they get there and see queues running out of the door they'll complain and make life awful for the folks who work there.

This overloading of A&E departments is one of the things that led me to leave nursing – and I haven't missed the hassle nor the inability to properly care for terminally ill patients because there were no pillows or blankets in the hospital.

It's sad, but one of my favourite nurses is in the process of moving career because she's getting fed up with trying to bail out a sinking ship. I suppose that this is a governmental success; fewer departments and fewer nurses mean less wages, which saves money.

I don't know what they plan to do with the patients, though.

In the end the government decided not to close the departments, partly, I suspect, because of the Olympics coming to the area. It didn't stop them severely cutting the services available at one of them, though.

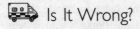 Is It Wrong?

Is it wrong to want to punch a patient after he tells you to fuck off and he's going kill you? After you have been extremely nice to them.

This is our first job.

It's going to be a long night ...

🚑 The Right Choice

There is a road on our patch that I'd never been to before; there are only 30 or so houses in it. However, in the past two weeks I've been there on four occasions.

Last night I was there because someone had slipped and fallen on the floor. Last week I was there for an ill child but it was the first two times I went there that will stick in my mind. They were both on the same day.

It was the first call of the evening, a 'difficulty in breathing' for an elderly woman. We entered the house to be surrounded by a large number of relatives. This wasn't unusual as it was an Indian family and they tend to be large. The patient herself was a very frail and bedbound elderly woman who had had many strokes in the past and was dependent on her family for her care. It didn't need the FRU paramedic to tell us that she was extremely unwell. The patient was unresponsive and had laboured breathing. She had a sheen of sweat on her, a sign that her body was struggling, and she was completely unresponsive.

It soon became obvious that the patient had pneumonia and wasn't shifting enough air to keep alive. We loaded her and one of her relatives onto our ambulance and 'blued' her into hospital. The relative seemed resigned to our patient dying; we couldn't disagree with them.

By the time we took our next patient into the same hospital, all the relatives had arrived. They had spoken with the doctors and it was decided that it was in the best interests of the patient to not pursue any active treatment, and instead to let her die. The relatives had asked if they could take her home, and the hospital was in the process of arranging transport for her.

It must have been a hard decision to make – having seen many, many futile attempts to save someone's life, it always seems to involve pain and suffering as needles are pushed through skin, drugs with nasty side effects are given and breathing tubes are inserted. It was brave of the patient's relatives to make that choice that this moment was the end of their loved one's life and that it should be as peaceful for the patient as possible.

It was less than an hour later that we were called back to the same address; the job was given as 'patient deceased'.

What had happened was that the hospital transport had taken the patient home and, before they left, the patient died. They then advised the relatives to call for an ambulance.

So we arrived and everyone decided that it was for the best not to resuscitate her. We offered our sympathies and arranged for a GP to come out to certify the death.

The family were lovely; they offered us tea and thanked both us and the hospital for what we had done. We hadn't saved her life but we had allowed her to die with some dignity at home, rather than being treated futilely on a hospital trolley.

When I went back to the same address a couple of days later (for the sick child), I saw the funeral notice on their front door. Last night when I went back to the same street for the woman who'd fallen over, one of the family came out and thanked us again.

Four times to one small street and for a family and a job that I'll remember for a very long time.

 ## The Slow Attrition of the Soul

It is 3 a.m., it is cold and dark and damp. I am tired and fed up and sad.

My heart is being broken by a deeply demented 65-year-old woman who can only whimper and cry for no obvious reason. She can hardly talk because of the dementia, crying quietly to herself is now the only thing she does.

She is clean and well looked after by her daughter who, a couple of months ago, suddenly had her mother-as-a-child, in addition to her own children, to look after.

It's jobs like that which slowly destroy your soul.

Knee

I have a problem with knees, partly it's because I'm slightly squeamish about them, partly because when they break or dislocate it is incredibly painful for the patient.

Our woman had slipped on a wet floor, she had landed on her knees and, after we drove across most of our patch to get to her, we found her lying on the floor.

Upstairs.

In a narrow corridor.

She wasn't a 'small' person either.

My physical examination led me to believe that she had broken or dislocated her knee – it was a bit tricky to examine her in the enclosed space she found herself, her weight didn't help either.

The patient was lovely; she understood why she had waited so long for an ambulance. She'd also taken some painkillers before we arrived, something that is an absolute rarity. She was nice to talk to and when I explained that we would take things slowly for her benefit she understood.

First thing that I did was to give her some of our painkiller gas Entonox. Then I slipped a splint around her injured knee. This combination seemed to help the pain a lot. She further proved to be a good patient by immediately understanding my instructions on how to take the Entonox – another rarity in our area.

The staircase that we needed to get her down was steep and narrow; there was no way we could use our carry chair. She would have to be strapped to our scoop and carried down the stairs that way. But we would need help.

I'm six foot one, my crewmate is five foot eleven and a half, not the best combination of sizes for getting a large woman downstairs on a scoop – although my crewmate would like you to all note that she (believes she) is the strongest one out of the two of us. So we called Control for assistance, namely another crew or an FRU person. We were assured that one would be on their way.

While we were waiting we placed the patient on the scoop and started the long process of strapping her to it so that, when we tilted it by 80 degrees to get her out of the house, she wouldn't slide out of the scoop like someone being buried at sea.

After some time one of our emergency care practitioners arrived and he gave us some much-needed help in manhandling the patient down the stairs and into the ambulance. We took the patient to hospital where X-rays showed a dislocated knee.

This is what I like about my job. This job wasn't about saving someone's life, it was about causing the patient as little pain as possible while solving the puzzle of how to get her out of the house all while keeping her as calm and happy as feasible. It's not a buzz, but it is the satisfaction of a tricky job well done.

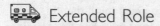 ## Extended Role

I had a job that required me to undertake an extended role.

The call came down as 'Patient's own hospital bed broken, patient stuck', rather predictably I had visions of some little old lady folded in half by a malfunctioning electric bed.

The 'patient' was sitting in her chair, her husband was running around flapping and the domestic carer was looking confused.

The bed was a type that I had never seen before. It had a hydraulic ram underneath it which tipped the mattress on end by 90 degrees, I suppose so the patient sort of slid into an upright position.

The bed was stuck in this upright position – if the sheets had been black it would have looked like the Monolith from *2001*.

After some fiddling around (a technical term) I managed to get it into the horizontal position and checked that it would raise and lower as designed. I'm grateful for my various experiences fixing broken things.

So ten minutes later, after pointing out the rather large print on the bed's instruction folder (which said 'Emergency out of hours technician ring 0800 xxxx'), we left another satisfied customer.

I decided to have a joke with Control.

'Control, the patient's bed is fixed. I'll do my paperwork for this job then I'll be ready for any blocked gutters or windows that need fixing.'

Funny how people panic and call us.

 ## The Stanford Experiment

I've written before about how I am a different person when I'm wearing a uniform, how I am more confident, more proactive and sometimes louder. The reverse is also true and I think that this is, in some way, because of the way that people treat me when I'm wearing the uniform.

People see me in uniform and permit me to direct them, advise them and do things physically to them. Without the uniform I can't do this.

It all became obvious on the way home from the centre of London one night. I was using the tube and, on travelling up an escalator while changing between lines, came across a man who had collapsed.

There were two members of the public with him, a station officer and a station cleaner. As I approached I saw that he was pale and sweaty; he triggered that bit of my brain that says 'this person is properly ill'.

I tried to walk past, I really did. I think I got two steps beyond him before turning around and returning.

'Hi there, I work for London Ambulance, can I help?'

He'd apparently become dizzy and then had collapsed. A little chat with him revealed a significant history of internal bleeding in the past. Feeling for his pulse I couldn't find one in his wrist, which meant that he had a very low blood pressure. This would explain his pallor and sweatiness.

I asked the station officer if he'd called an ambulance and he mumbled something in the affirmative. I tried to take control of the situation, but it all came out a bit vague and quiet. I put the cleaning bucket under his feet to try and raise his blood pressure a little and awaited the ambulance.

All the time this was going on I was feeling rather vulnerable, unlike when I am 'on the job'. I could also tell that the people I was with weren't taking me as seriously as they would had I been wearing a uniform.

The ambulance crew arrived and I handed the patient over to them. They didn't seem impressed, again probably because I wasn't wearing my uniform.

As I walked away I felt rather bad. If I had turned up in an FRU car then the job would have felt very different, but without my uniform I wasn't as confident.

It's funny what a green shirt can do for your confidence.

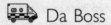 Da Boss

'Our eyes met across a crowded room.'

One of the things that Peter Bradley, the boss of the London Ambulance Service, does is to occasionally come out on the road and do a shift working on an ambulance. Last night he was in our area teamed up with a team leader, running an extra FRU car. Whenever he has been around I've not been working; however, last night I was working at the same time.

We were called to a 37-year-old man who was 'suspended', not breathing and with no pulse. Control told us that there was a hysterical woman on scene and that it was a child who had called us. We rushed around there and saw that a passing teenager had asked for us. Hopping out of the ambulance I saw an FRU pull up behind us. In it was a team leader ... and *Da Boss*.

My crewmate and I ran into the house and found the man dead. Sticking out of one leg was a needle and on a nearby workbench there was some citric acid, a spoon, a lighter and other drug paraphernalia. It looked like he had overdosed.

There was nothing that we could do except for wait for the police. The team leader and da Boss looked after the distraught wife and the man's young daughter, while my crewmate and I made sure that no one altered what could be a crime scene. It's very sad to see someone so young dead, and to leave behind such a young child is terrible. We try to rationalise this by saying to each other that perhaps she is better off without a drug user in the house, but ... I just don't know.

Da Boss and the team leader came back in with the police to show them the body and I bid farewell to Da Boss with a cheerful, 'Welcome to Newham, sir.'

The team leader seemed very eager to get him away from me, I have no idea why. This was a shame as I would have liked to have asked him how crap it felt to be screwed over by the government so much.

Actually, I think that may have been why the team leader was so eager to get him away.

I can still picture the house as I stood in it hearing the crying mother and child as the team leader told them that their husband and father had died.

🚑 Standing Back

There are times when it is simpler, and better for the patient, to stand back and let the relatives decide the best course of action.

I went to an older woman who had suffered from a stroke some time earlier. She had made as good a recovery as was expected and was being looked after in her home by her family and some paid carers. There was a lot of equipment in the house. Lifts and hoists had been installed; the patient had a modified wheelchair and a specialist bed. The reason why we had been called was because she had developed a chest infection – this can be very serious in someone who is essentially bedbound – and so she needed to go to hospital.

As I walked into the house I sensed a vague negative attitude towards us. It may have been that they were waiting some time for the ambulance (as it was one of our low priority calls), it may have just been that they were rightfully unhappy that their mother needed to go to hospital again. So the atmosphere in the house meant that I would have to handle the family carefully. They had a lot of experience with their mother so, where we would normally barge in and take control of the situation, I decided that I would discuss the best way to move the patient with them.

At every one of my suggestions I explained the reasoning behind my thinking, and I let the family use their equipment to carefully, and in their own time, move the patient to the hospital.

At the end of the journey the relatives were a lot happier, all because I let them do most of the work.

🚑 Two in Two Nights

It was a bit of a 'stabby' weekend. I don't normally do 'sexy' calls but for some reason I had two stabbings on two consecutive nights.

The first was a young man who had been attacked in the street. His main injury was a stab wound through his thigh. He'd leaked a fair bit of the red stuff but not enough to particularly worry us. He also had a slash wound across his chest but this was fairly minor. What made the job tricky was that there were around 40 youths milling around, all wanting to talk to their 'bruv'.

Our patient was more concerned with getting his mobile phone back from one of his friends. I'm guessing, given his demeanour, that he wanted to arrange some retaliation. Meanwhile, more and more of his friends were arriving and causing trouble for the police. For some reason the people of Newham seem to enjoy ignoring 'Police: Do Not Cross' tape.

We 'blued' him into the local A&E where he was treated (and probably discharged later that day).

The next day had another stabbing, this one somewhat different.

The patient didn't want his girlfriend to leave him so he stabbed himself in the stomach.

(No, I have no idea either, especially as this was the third time he'd done this to himself.)

What made it annoying was that the patient was pretending to be unconscious. As it was difficult to see how deep the wound went, and we had been told that it might be three inches deep, we 'blued' him into the local A&E. After the doctors there poked a metal probe into the wound they discovered that it was a minor injury. I left him in the A&E still pretending to be unconscious.

The police officer who came with us just wanted him to admit that it was self-inflicted then he could leave. He was only there to check that it wasn't the patient's girlfriend who had stabbed him.

As one wit mentioned to me, the reason that people ignore the police tape is because they think it only applies to the police – the tape should read 'PUBLIC: Do Not Cross'.

🚑 MHU Transfers

One of our more regular jobs is to the Newham Mental Health Unit (MHU). It is one of the more bizarre side effects of the way that the NHS is structured in that while the MHU shares a physical site with Newham hospital, they are completely different trusts.

As each trust has its own portering staff, if a patient needs to be moved from the MHU to A&E ... they call an ambulance.

So we get calls to patients who need to be moved a grand total of 400 yards down the road. I've worked in hospitals where you would need to wheel patients on trolleys for longer distances just to get them to the wards. Unfortunately neither trust will take responsibility for wheeling patients between the two buildings.

It doesn't help that I'm not enamoured of the medical care for people in the MHU.

Sometimes we will be called for something as simple as a chest infection, or that the patient needs blood tests or an X-ray. Sometimes you will go to something that sounds difficult but which ends up being something simple.

Take, for example, the last time I went there. The patient was a young girl and her diagnosis was 'pulmonary embolism'. This is a serious and life-threatening illness; it is a clot on the lungs which causes severe difficulty in breathing, shock and death.

This patient, however, had none of the risk factors or symptoms for this. She was shaking like a person with Parkinson's disease but her vital signs were all normal. She had also been in this state for a couple of days.

It looked to me like a toxic amount of one of her anti-psychotics.

Oh well, 400 yards later and she was safely in A&E where they quickly ruled out an embolism and sent her back to the MHU in one of the private contract ambulances. I'd be interested to see how much that trip cost the hospital.

The cause of her illness?

A higher than normal level of anti-psychotic in her blood.

No Boom Today, Maybe Boom Tomorrow

I was working a late shift when I got sent to an RVP (rendezvous point). These are normally used when there is a suspicion that there is some violence in the offing – the last ones I have been to were for the arrest of someone over firearms offences and for the possible stabbing of somebody in a domestic violence case. Both of which were uneventful; the arrest went calmly and the 'stabbing' was actually a 'stabbing pain' with a thick accent.

This one was different; someone had smelt gas and had called the authorities. The fire service had arrived and cordoned off the road, the police were there to manage the scene and we were called in case something went 'boom'.

We were left alone with these other services for quite some time. Normally there would be a DSO (duty station officer) at an event like this, but I think he was halfway across town. So I promoted myself to 'Ambulance (Non-)Officer In Charge of Scene'. It's what we are supposed to do with major incidents; the first person on scene takes charge until someone with some pips on their epaulettes turns up.

I promise that I didn't stroll around trying to look important.

I found the fireman with the white helmet (the white helmet means they are an officer) and had a chat with him; then I found the police officer in charge and chatted with him. I updated Control, then chatted some more with the police about the weather, our stab vests and why they make such good body warmers, and finally about the people who didn't want to be evacuated from their homes.

The man from the gas board came and went with various technical bits of equipment, then told the fire officer that he needed someone above him to declare it safe. The woman from the council's emergency planning group turned up and I had a chat with her, and managed to wangle an offer for a cup of tea.

So we waited some more, until our officer finally turned up and tutted that it was me there. In his words, 'Why is it always you at the centre of the chaos?'

I informed him that as I was in charge, there was no chaos.

A bit more of a wait around before the scene could be declared safe and we could all head off. I left just as they were about to dig a hole to see if the leak was worth repairing.

A nice easy job, no one was hurt, which is always nice, and it managed to last me until the end of my shift so I even got off home on time.

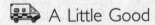 ## A Little Good

We were met at the door by a man whose face was covered in blood. The blood wasn't his.

There were two ambulances parked outside, one of which was mine. There was also an FRU. We had been given the job as 'Male, suspended' and if the manpower is there then Control will send two ambulances.

As we were both running from our station we had followed each other down the road.

We had arrived on scene to find the man, in his fifties, the only living person in the house. His mouth was covered in the blood of his childhood friend. Standing outside were a lot of crying women. Lying on the kitchen floor was our patient and he was surrounded by blood. There was blood on the cupboards and the walls; there was blood on the floor. In the sink there was blood and lumps of lung tissue.

It was obvious that we were not going to be able to do anything for him.

His friend had been doing mouth-to-mouth but the blood that filled his lungs had rendered this best of intentions useless.

The patient had been suffering from lung cancer. While watching the telly he had developed a coughing fit and, coughing over the sink, had showered everything with blood and then died.

So we did what we thought was best. After talking to the relatives, we cleaned the kitchen and our patient; we took away the blood-soaked clothes. Putting a dressing in his mouth to prevent leakage we placed our patient in a carry chair and took him upstairs and laid him in his bed. Once there we arranged him so that he looked like he was sleeping.

By the time we were finished the kitchen was spotless and the patient was clean and looked restful.

We then helped the family get in contact with the undertaker and with the GP. We offered them the only help that we could – they had lost their husband, their father and their friend. We couldn't save his life, but we could try to reduce the hurt in those whom he left.

And you go away from a job like that thinking that you did some good, even though you didn't save a life.

Anger

I'm writing this when I should be in bed, but I can't sleep. I can't sleep because you made me angry.

You could have been anything; you could have been a doctor, a teacher, a father. Your family didn't seem poor, you lived with them and now you are dead.

Twenty-three years old, a heroin addict.

We tried everything we could, two ambulances were sent. You had the best treatment you can get outside of a hospital, but I guessed that you would stay dead when I saw you lying on your bedroom floor. I was pounding on your chest and all I could hear was your mother crying. I tuned out that crying because we were so busy. There was a little girl, perhaps four years old, she was crying as well. Was it your little sister? I could only ignore her as well, for we were carrying you out of the house.

I didn't have time to register the crying, we were too busy trying to start your heart.

But what did register with me? Sitting outside the hospital while my crewmate was doing his paperwork I saw your grandparents being led away in tears. They were broken. Twenty-three years ago they probably thanked their God that you were born safely. Their dreams probably had you as a doctor, a teacher, a father.

Now you are dead, and why? Because you sought heroin; because you wanted that pleasure above everything else.

I don't care about you.

I care about your grandparents, your parents, your brothers and sisters. I want to go back in time and, like the ghost of Christmas present, show you where your path will lead. I want to slap you awake and show you what you have done to your family.

Was it worth that pleasure?

Yes. This job did piss me off. Sorry. And it did cause a sleepless night. I was told by someone much smarter than me that I wasn't a cynic, but that I was often disappointed by the failure of others to live up to their potential. I guess that this job hit all those buttons.

A Night on the FRU

Grief – a Saturday night alone on the FRU makes for a not very happy ambulance man.

I was just snuggling down for a little kip on station. It was about three in the morning and all seemed quiet, the temperature outside was somewhere around freezing, so lying on the sofa wrapped in my fleece was looking like a really good idea.

Obviously, the activation phone decided to ring and I soon found myself speeding far out of my area to a 'life status questionable'.

His life status wasn't questionable, his sobriety was. One of our friends from Europe, he had been drinking and decided to have a sleep in the doorway of a shop. Granted if I hadn't gone and woken him up he may have frozen to death. As he was a nice enough bloke I couldn't be too angry. It also put me very close to the Log Cabin, which meant I could go and have a hot, filling 'gob job' before trying to catch forty winks.

Of course, halfway through the cooking of this gastronomic delight I get another job. I could tell what sort of job it was going to be – someone had dialled 999, said 'Hello' then hung up. For some reason (maybe one to ask our Control), this was coded as another 'life status questionable'.

'I'll be back in a minute,' I said to the domestic goddess cooking my burger.

I dutifully screamed through the streets of Whipps Cross to find, to my utter surprise, an empty phone box.

'Hello Control,' I called up on my radio, 'I have a lack of any dead or dying people here, please cancel the ambulance, I'm calling it as a hoax.'

It was then a quick drive back to collect and eat my burger.

The drive would have been quicker had some drunk not tried to jump into the car so I could 'just take me up the road'. When I refused I was sworn at, but that didn't bother me much as I had a nice hot burger waiting for me.

The jobs I did that night were:

2 hoaxes

1 painful knee

1 hot child

1 drunk ...

and an alcoholic with liver failure.

This is not good when you need inspiration for writing.

 Attention

Everyone was ignoring the patient.

We'd picked her up after an episode of a recurrent illness. She was going to be fine but I felt sorry for her. Hardly anyone was talking to her; they were all distracted by her partner. I worried about how safe her partner would be in the back of our ambulance. It turned out that it wasn't a problem.

When we got to the hospital the staff there were more concerned with the patient's partner and she did cause a few organisational problems although she was a big hit with the department. A few other patients looked a little worried by her presence.

It made me feel bad. I felt that the patient was being ignored with everyone paying full attention to her partner. So I made sure that I talked to the patient. I'm guessing that although she was used to such reactions she would still feel upstaged.

'I bet you get ignored a lot when you are with her,' I said to our patient.

'Yes, but you have to get used to it,' she replied.

But why was all this attention being lavished on our patient's partner?

Because our patient was blind and her partner was a guide dog.

Sure, it's an unusual thing to have to deal with a guide dog in an A&E department (although when I worked in A&E we had a regular), but it still surprised me that playing with the dog or talking about it seemed to be more important than putting the patient's mind at ease. Maybe it's because I've got a mate who is registered blind, but it just seems *rude* to put all your attention on their dog, no matter how cute they are.

Meal-Breaks

For the first time ever, ambulance crews are going to have rest-breaks.

For too long we have been working twelve hours a day without a break. Sure, we may be able to sneak a cup of tea at hospital, but if we take longer than half an hour to unload the patient, hand over to the nurse, clean and restock the ambulance and finish our paperwork so that the patient can't sue us, then we often get asked if we could 'green up' for another call. Trust me when I say that it can easily take longer than half an hour to do all the above.

We rarely get to see our station; too many people call us and we simply don't have enough ambulances to deal with all the drunks, cut fingers and coughs and colds that we get sent to.

European legislation means that we should all get a short rest-break. If you work for twelve hours, is it really too much to ask for a half-hour break at some point?

Apparently it is too much to ask for the *Sun*.

Some journalist, who can no doubt have plenty of cups of tea during her day, decides to attack our service for (a) following the law, and (b) treating its staff like human beings who need feeding and watering.

You can see the headline now, 'My Mum Died While Medics Drank Tea'.

It can be hard work on an ambulance. While a lot of our work is fairly simple, there are days when, not only are you run ragged, but you also have a string of tricky jobs. Why shouldn't we be like everyone else and get a break? The police have meal-breaks, nurses have meal-breaks, doctors have meal-breaks and the fire service has meal-breaks (if I were being uncharitable I would say that the fire service has occasional breaks in their meals for work).

So why should we be any different?

We make enough sacrifices for this job – shift work knocks years off your life, wrecks your health and social life. We go into dangerous situations on a daily basis, get beaten up and sit in enclosed spaces with infectious patients. We also don't get paid enough considering how the government keeps expecting us to hold together the tatters of the NHS. Until we got breaks we would also be eating unhealthily, wolfing down fast food between jobs. Physical fitness is a concern for us – gym memberships are a waste of money when we work half the time they are open.

So the *Sun*, rag that it is, wants us to work like robots. Instead, they should ask why, despite meeting targets, regardless of an annual increase in calls, and despite being told we should cover the shortfall in GPs and

A&Es while the government takes money away from us, we can't have more ambulances. Ask why we have to go to people who have stubbed their toe, got a wart on their foot or have 'man-flu'. Ask why, after dark, it's us and the A&E departments against the world as all the psychiatric teams, social workers and care home staff vanish along with the sun.

Maybe that would be proper journalism.

I'm already hearing about crews getting abused because of the newspapers writing articles speculating about patients dying while we sit down and eat some grub. One person has already reported being shouted at while having a sandwich, while another received abuse from a patient with a cut finger (needing only a plaster) – all because they think we should be running around saving lives. It only needs someone to abuse me on this subject and they would get a lecture on how you shouldn't believe everything that you read in your newspaper.

In reality meal-breaks won't make much difference in responding to emergency calls. It just means that the 'stubbed-toe brigade' will have to wait half an hour for their free taxi to hospital, while true emergency calls will be covered as well as they are at present. Being able to have a protected break may also mean crews will be refreshed so that they will 'green up' that bit faster, improving our response to those genuine calls.

🚑 Battered

The radio squawked into life. 'Can anyone assist with an emergency call in Alice Street?'

We were around five miles away and there were three ambulance stations between us and the call. Obviously, everyone else was further west than us or already busy on their own calls.

'Sod it,' I said to my crewmate. 'It'll be fun for you to have a decent run on blue lights.'

So we made our way there as quickly as we could in the traffic that seems to come from nowhere at 11 p.m. in east London.

As we approached the scene we saw our FRU already on scene along with a van full of police. My heart sank, I knew that this wasn't going to be a simple job as I could see the police stringing the 'Do Not Cross' tape around where our patient was lying. The locals, as usual, were ignoring the tape; the police were getting exasperated.

Jumping from the ambulance I headed over to the patient. Our FRU paramedic was leaning over the patient's head and as he straightened to greet me I saw that the patient's head was ... well ... mushed.

He had huge swellings around his eyes and head; he was semi-conscious and covered with blood and vomit.

'Apparently,' our FRU told me, 'he's been hit once with a lump of wood.'

Looking at his head I wondered why, if he'd only been hit once, it was such a strange shape.

'OK,' I said, 'we aren't going to hang about, let's run him to hospital.'

There was some commotion as his drunken friend gave his story in fractured English to a police officer, while more locals ignored the police tape which was cordoning off the crime scene. I needed to know how many times the patient had been hit, as it would change my treatment of him. His friend was adamant, he was only hit the once and his face normally looked misshapen. It wasn't outside the realms of possibility that our patient was just ... ugly.

As we lifted the patient onto the trolley he let forth a long stream of vomit which managed to lightly splash my boots.

In the light of the rear of the ambulance I could take a closer look at our patient – he did have a very lumpy head along with plenty of soft tissue injuries to the face. One eye was swelling up and he was still leaking blood from a large cut on his scalp. He was still semi-conscious and I made the decision to 'blue' him into hospital.

But which hospital? If I was sure he had a brain injury then I could take him a couple of extra miles to a hospital with a neurology unit, but if his drowsiness was as a result of alcohol (and we had been told that he had been drinking a lot) then the much closer local A&E was a better bet. In the end I decided on the closer A&E, they would be better able to assess him and if needed could easily transfer him to the hospital with the neurology unit.

So, after making sure that he hadn't been stabbed or shot (not unheard of in east London), we started towards the local hospital.

The police officer who travelled with us asked if our patient's injuries were life threatening. I could only reply that it was a possibility but he'd have to wait until the hospital ran some more tests.

It was only as we were pulling into the hospital that I noticed one of his pupils was getting larger where previously they had been equal. This is not a good sign as it is an indicator of a serious head injury; it's normally quite a late sign, though, and he didn't look that neurologically impaired. Still it was too late to change our destination. During the transport he had turned his head to vomit on the floor, and on arriving at the hospital did the same on the lift of the ambulance.

Straight into resus and I gave my handover to the doctor in charge. The team descended on him and, after booking the patient in, we left to begin the long, smelly and mucky task of cleaning out the back of the ambulance (and changing my now spattered uniform).

We went back to the hospital later to find out what had happened to our patient. After exhaustive tests it was found that his facial bones had been broken in several places and he had a fractured skull. His friend had obviously been lying when he told us that he had been hit only the once. The reason why the patient's pupil had started to change was because the optic nerve had been damaged. There was a strong chance that he would lose the sight in the affected eye.

Thankfully, I'd made the right decision. After CT scans it was determined that there had been no brain injury and that the reason he was so out of it was because of the alcohol he had drunk over the night.

It later transpired that the beating was in part due to the 'inter-tribal' warfare that often takes to the streets of London. Country 'A' hates Country 'B', and so they decide to beat each other up. The ambulance service and A&E departments along with the police are the lucky souls who get to pick up those pieces.

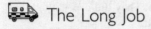 The Long Job

'Patient is suspended.'

We rushed to the scene. The FRU had arrived seconds before us. The patient, an elderly man, was lying on the floor. He wasn't breathing, he didn't have a pulse and he looked dead.

'He's dead, isn't he?' asked his wife. I could tell by the look on her face that she knew he was dead.

I could only tell her the truth. 'He isn't breathing at the moment and his heart isn't beating. We are doing everything that we can for him, but you should expect the worst.'

She nodded; she'd seen the colour of him and seemed resigned to his death.

My crewmate put the defibrillator pads to his chest – he was in 'VF' (ventricular fibrillation), a rhythm that we shock. So we shocked him and did some CPR, all according to our training. Then we shocked him again, gave him some drugs, breathed for him, shocked him again and eventually (and surprisingly) got a pulse back.

We all looked at each other – this sort of thing doesn't happen to us. Normally our dead patients stay dead.

We packaged him up for hospital, three times his pulse stopped but after a couple of minutes of chest compressions he'd get it back. Surely this wouldn't last, eventually he would die.

His wife seemed confused but happy. Perhaps he wouldn't die after all.

We rushed him to the hospital. I think he lost his pulse twice more, each time we got it back. By the time we reached the hospital he was chewing on the breathing tube.

The hospital worked on him for a long time – still he didn't die. They tried everything, they even gave him a drug that costs more than £600 in the hopes that it would help stabilise him. They did everything; they thought that he might have a chance as well.

His wife had hope. The last we heard was that he was transferred to another hospital where there was an intensive care bed. I'm guessing that I'll never learn what happened to him in the end.

I wonder if it was for the best that we saved him. My guess would be that, even if he does make a recovery, he will have some form of brain damage – he went without CPR for too long. The alternative is that he never leaves hospital. I wonder if his wife will continue to hope until he fades away in ITU.

From her acceptance that he was dead, to a probably vain hope that she would get him back, I wonder if it was cruel that our resuscitation was 'successful'. At the time we have no chance to make such decisions, we do what we do and get on with it. It's later, as you see the family around the patient, the monitoring machinery showing life but the patient making no movement, only then do you wonder if it is right.

I can't remember many of the people who die despite my best efforts (the cynical would suggest it's the sheer numbers I see that make it hard to remember). But this one will stay with me for some time.

I found out that the patient died two weeks later – it seems cruel now that we dragged his death out like that, but that is a thought that only comes with hindsight.

🚐 Christmas

Half past five and I'm getting up for work. How is that right or fair? It's not all bad, though, I'm working with one of my favourite people and she is bringing food.

The shift runs from seven until four. With any luck it'll be a nice easy one.

6:52

Preparing the ambulance for the shift, making sure it is fully kitted. All the while drinking a big mug of tea.

8:25

Got called an 'angel' by our first job at five past seven, a very nice 63-year-old chest pain. Patient called the emergency GP first which, considering his cardiac history, was probably the wrong thing to do. Cardiac chest pain = 999 in my book.

9:26

A little old lady who tripped and cracked her head open. She broke my heart and I found myself emotionally bullying the nurses with the phrase 'we need to show some Christmas spirit'.

9:46

Bless them all – loads of businesses got together and sent us food for Christmas. I'm devouring the chocolate now.

11:34

Another little old lady who fell over last night but 'I didn't want to bother you' so waited until this morning to call us. A lovely woman who may have cracked a rib. She has lots of friends who were all concerned for her and were very helpful for us (again, a rarity).

12:43

A run out of our area for a 50-year-old with a cough that he has had for three weeks. Quite a thin chap, which always makes such things look worse.

13:37

Matern-a-taxi.

15:38

Another little old lady; this one fainted. Both her and her family were lovely.

Half an hour until the end of shift. Will I get another job?

16:11 – Hometime

No late job (thanks to the kindness of Control) so now I'm heading home for the family dinner and the exchange of swag.

Back tomorrow for more of the same ...

16:38 – Or maybe not ...

... And of course as I go to drive to my mum's for dinner, the battery on my car decides to stop working. So I'm sitting in the car, in the dark, awaiting a pickup.

Merry Christmas all.

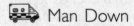 Man Down

You are going to love this ...

I'm at work, it's 7 a.m. and I'm checking the ambulance to make sure that all the kit is there and that it is placed where I can find it. As it is 7 a.m. and I'm not a morning person I drop the electronic thermometer, part of which falls under the trolley bed. I get down on hands and knees to retrieve it ...

... and hear a pop in my right knee.

Lots and lots of excruciating pain follows.

So I collapse onto the floor and scream a bit.

One of my stationmates hears me and comes to investigate. 'What the bloody hell* are you doing down there?'

*He may have used words stronger than 'bloody hell'.

He goes and gets some help. Help to stand there, point and laugh at me. He includes some trainees in the mockery. I think he is getting his revenge because I keep calling him tubby.

I get given some Entonox, a painkilling mixture of nitrous oxide and oxygen. Nitrous oxide is better known as laughing gas. For some people this gas does nothing, for me, three puffs in and I'm giggling like a schoolgirl and can feel hardly anything. That which I do feel doesn't seem that important. I laugh a lot, use my good leg to get onto the ambulance trolley, and have some more Entonox.

Mobile phone photographs are taken.

The trainees take my blood pressure, pulse and the like. I refuse to take my clothes off as I am a *bad* patient. I am also, as the young people say, 'off my head' on the Entonox. It's good stuff, and to think they give us huge bottles of it to play with.

At the hospital, in between giggles, I am assessed by my favourite nurse (who, sadly, is escaping that A&E department soon) and I get seen by an emergency nurse practitioner. I get a full exam, a justification for an X-ray and good clinical skills.

The X-ray shows an effusion and maybe some ligament damage. I may get an MRI scan in the near future.

My duty station officer arrives. His first words? 'If I'd known it was you I wouldn't have bothered coming. I thought it was one of the trainees.'

He is, of course, joking.

So I'm hobbling around on crutches, with painkillers should I need them and an appointment to see the knee surgeon in a little while.

A big thanks to everyone involved, from my stationmates to the folks at the hospital, the care was excellent.

🚐 Pre-Christmas Crisis

Our patient was in his mid-forties. He had called us from his mobile phone to tell us that he had suffered a fit. While I'm used to people calling us if someone has a fit in front of them, the patient themselves phoning us is unusual (and normally means that they haven't had a fit at all).

We found him sitting on the ground, beside a bus stop. It was one of the really cold days and so it came as no surprise to me that he felt like a block of ice. Our ambulance is warmer than an A&E department so I decided to sit and chat with him a bit so that he could warm up.

He told me that he was an alcoholic and that he hadn't eaten or slept for the past three days. A look into his eyes and I could see that it wasn't just alcohol that was his problem. I questioned him further and he admitted to taking 'speed'. If he was taking speed then I wasn't surprised that he hadn't slept for the past three days.

I checked him over to see if the cause of his seizure was anything we could treat. All his vital signs were normal although we couldn't check his temperature as our electronic thermometers stop working if it gets too cold.

His home address was on the other side of London, so I asked him why he was on 'my patch'.

'It's my daughter, you see,' he told me. 'She's in foster care around here, but I want to see her for Christmas. I even bought her a present.'

I looked around in vain for something that might be a Christmas present for a little girl.

'I sold it so I could get some cider.'

He'd been sleeping rough and in hostels after losing his daughter to social services. He'd been drinking so much that he had started to have alcoholic seizures. Instead of eating properly he had been drinking cheap strong cider and taking amphetamines. Then he had bought his daughter a Christmas present and sold it for a few cans of cider. If I left him where he was there was a good chance that, without a decent meal inside him, he'd freeze to death.

So I did the only thing that I could do – I took him to hospital.

Then I had to put it out of my mind and do my next job.

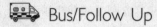 ## Bus/Follow Up

We were at the Royal London hospital; I was working with someone who is fairly new to the job. I like working with new people, they tend to not have any bad habits and I can sound like the voice of experience. My crewmate was one of those steady guys, he'd been out of training school for some time and I could rely on him not to do anything daft on scene or on the back of the ambulance.

As I mentioned, we were at the Royal London hospital having taken in the latest 'difficulty in breathing' that was, in reality, a runny nose. The whole shift had been like this, 'nothing' jobs that were simple walk-on, walk-off affairs.

'Attention all cars, attention all cars – ambulance required for a Bus vs Lorry RTA in Barking.'

I was driving, my crewmate was the one looking after patients; he looked a bit excited.

'Might be a good job,' he said.

'No mate,' I replied. 'We'll turn up and it'll be a fender bender.'

But we offered up for the job, although it was miles away, and sped off.

During the drive there I could hear another crew getting sent to the same location, then the location of the accident changed – luckily I had planned this into my route to the scene so we came across the accident first.

The bus had driven, at slow speed, into a JCB digger. The bus window was broken but there wasn't any other damage and as my crewmate jumped out he was just as quickly waved off – there were no injuries. We called Control and told them to cancel the other ambulance.

'Told you it would be nothing,' I said to my crewmate. 'It's against the laws of the universe for me to get an interesting job.'

Curse of the Observer

I had a writer from *Casualty* out with me a couple of weeks ago. He lives locally to the area and the BBC likes the writers to do at least one ride-out so that they can get the gist of what the ambulance service is like. I know, I know, it doesn't show up on the screen, but the thought is in the right place and as the BBC have been really nice to me in the past I'm more than happy to help them out.

He was a nice chap and before the shift started we had a little chat. He was shown around the back of the ambulance and I told him that I don't do 'heartbreak and trauma', more 'drunks and drunkards'. I explained all about the 'Curse of the Observer' – whenever there is an observer with a crew, they get nothing but 'crap' jobs all shift. We then settled down for our first call of the day.

So it was only a few minutes into the shift when we found ourselves rushing out to the ambulance for a 'Two-month-old child, not breathing.'

I turned around to the writer and explained that it was probably a child with a runny nose, it normally was. Then I realised what time of the day it was – 7 a.m. It wasn't outside the realms of possibility that this could be a genuine job. Maybe the parents had slept through the night and woken happy that their child hadn't disturbed them, only to find them dead in their cot.

I told the writer that as soon as we arrived at the house he should jump into the passenger seat and try to keep a low profile.

We arrived at the house at the same time as the FRU. I jumped out of the ambulance and struggled getting the equipment out the side storage; my crewmate ran into the house.

I heard the mother from the ambulance – she was making a noise, the mixture of crying and screaming that will turn anyone's blood cold. I didn't need to go into the house to know that the baby was truly dead.

Entering the house I passed the mother to get to the rear bedroom. The father was pacing up and down, nonsense words were spilling from his lips. My crewmate and the FRU were kneeling around a tiny baby. She was lying flat on the floor, motionless. A drop of blood had formed under her nose.

It was a 'scoop and run' job. There is plenty that we can do for people whose heart has stopped, even for children and babies. We are trained in the resuscitation techniques that the hospitals use. In these cases, though, we'd rather let the paediatric consultants deal with them; they are much better trained than us and, with lots of staff in a well-equipped resus room, young patients stand a better chance.

So we did some interventions on the scene while the mother got some shoes on then we rushed out to the ambulance. I drove us to the hospital, the writer next to me. Each time a car did something stupid the writer muttered that they should 'get out the fucking way'. We made it to hospital in a few minutes and left the child with the resus team.

Unfortunately, there was nothing that the hospital could do.

Once more, sitting outside the A&E department doing my paperwork, I heard the mother's scream from the relatives' room as the doctors broke the news to her that her baby was dead.

The writer was surprised at the speed and co-ordination that we showed in dealing with this job – even though I wasn't working with my regular crewmate, we worked as if we were one person. He was also surprised at the idiot drivers who refused to get out of our way. In my eyes the drive to the hospital wasn't a bad one, but then I have developed a high tolerance for driver incompetence.

We spoke to the police. There was nothing unusual about the circumstances of the death, the drop of blood on the child's face could have been caused by the parents attempting to breathe for the child and the police seemed satisfied that everything was above board.

Our Control asked if we were all right; they do try to look after us. We were all fine, but a team leader appeared to check up on us anyway.

Thankfully the rest of the day was fairly peaceful.

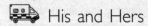 His and Hers

I'd never been to the patient before although the person I was working with told me that the household was a regular place to visit. Two people lived there, an elderly man and his wife. He has diabetes and leg ulcers and finds it hard to get around the house because of Parkinson's disease. His wife has quite far reaching dementia although she is physically fitter than her husband.

Social carers come round a couple of times a day.

Apparently the normal calls to this house are for him feeling unwell with his diabetes or for her hurting herself moving around the home.

We arrived on blue lights as the morning carer had called us and told us that the husband had collapsed.

He was beyond 'collapsed', he was lying on his back in the living room, his trousers around his ankles and his entire body shaking. When I tried talking to him all I could get out of him was incomprehensible grunts and groans. When I tried to touch him he would become combative and try to push me away.

I looked around, the carer had vanished. Unfortunately, this isn't unusual and to be honest often they aren't missed.

My first thought was that he had a low blood sugar – a nice easy job, give him some sugar and wait for his gratitude as we 'cure' him.

His blood sugar was within normal limits. This wasn't going to be as simple a job as I'd hoped for.

I did a full examination and there was nothing that would suggest the reason for his collapse or for his confusion. Every time I tried to do something to him, whether trying to examine or dress him, he would try to strike me so my examination wasn't perhaps the best.

His wife was alternating between pacing and sitting talking about shoes – thankfully she wasn't distressed. Actually she was quite cheery. I guess that she is used to us folk, dressed all in green, coming into her house and making things better. There was no way that we could leave her at home while we took her husband to hospital, she would have to come as well.

We made the decision that we wouldn't be able to look after both of them. I would have my hands full with my patient and there was no way that I could also keep her out of trouble. My crewmate called up Control and asked for another ambulance to take our patient's wife into hospital.

The second crew soon arrived and took control of the wife while I and my crewmate got our patient onto the trolley. Once we got him onto the back of the ambulance he immediately settled down, it was as if someone had flipped a switch in his brain. We went from wanting to 'blue light' him into hospital with me holding him down to being able to drive normally there while I had a friendly chat with him.

So once more we left the patient at the hospital – the nurses there would also have to look after his wife while they investigated why he had become confused and collapsed. At the end of my shift the hospital's theory was that he had suffered a transient ischaemic attack, or 'mini-stroke', which had resolved on its own.

And they did take good care of his wife.

On the Possible Causes for a Collapse

It is funny how you find yourself going to the same people. I'm sure that some form of 'Power Law' applies to patients as much as everything else. While sometimes you can get seeming 'clumps', other times the reasons for the repeat calls are easy to understand.

Take, for instance, a twelve-year-old boy. He had a history of collapsing at home and at school and previous medical tests had been performed to see if there was some cause for this. When I first met him he was waiting for an MRI scan.

He had collapsed at home. My immediate feeling was that this was a family that cared for him very much, nothing tripped my 'spider sense' that there was anything wrong. My own examination of him didn't show anything unusual; his behaviour didn't lead me to think that he had had a seizure. His blood sugar was normal, which ruled out him being an undiagnosed diabetic, and everything else I did drew a blank.

He'd been to hospital a day earlier and, after a battery of tests, they had discharged him. The tests had shown nothing. I was more than happy to take the boy to hospital, his family was nice and I've developed a 'risk averse' attitude to leaving children at home.

I later talked to the unit and they told me that, although they could find nothing wrong, the paediatric team was going to admit him overnight for observation.

It was only a day or two later when I got called to him again; he had collapsed on a public green on his way to school. One of his teachers was next to him. This time he wasn't moving or talking but a quick assessment told me that he wasn't really unconscious. So I got him up and took him to the ambulance. One teacher went to phone his parents, the other stayed to talk to my crewmate.

Once more all his vital signs were normal and once his father turned up we took him to hospital.

It was only after we put him into the paediatric waiting room that my crewmate turned to me and told me what one of the teachers had mentioned to him. The teachers suspected that he was being bullied although the child would not say anything to them about it. We passed this information on to the hospital and, after checking with the notes of his last visit, the hospital let us know that the paediatric consultant was thinking along the same lines. Various meetings were going to be planned with the school and the social services to fix this problem.

I'm glad that the hospital was taking things seriously. We've all heard of schoolchildren who commit suicide over bullying so it is important to have support services like this. This isn't the first time that I've seen a child become physically ill because of bullying; I suspect that, unfortunately, it also won't be the last.

For my part I'm glad that I could provide a safe and reassuring environment for the time he was with us. He might not have been physically hurt but that didn't mean that we would ignore his mental health. It's not all about bandages in this work, and sometimes it's the stuff like this that makes you feel that you are doing the right job.

Non-Carers Who Care

It had been a busy day running from A to B and back again dealing with some rather unwell patients, so a call to an elderly lady with a cut leg was going to be a nice change of pace.

We'd been told that she had fallen on the bus but was now at her home. As we pulled up we could see one of the council's buses parked outside; they are used to take the vulnerable elderly to day centres and the like. The pavement was soaked in soapy water.

The driver of the bus met me and he looked a little worried as he showed me to our patient. She was sitting in a chair, her leg was raised and although the bus driver and his mate had used a towel to try to stop the bleeding her leg was still leaking a fair amount. Still it was a fairly simple job – bandage up her leg and drive her into hospital where they could properly clean and close the wound.

All throughout my treatment of her, the patient was more concerned with making sure that the bus workers didn't get into any trouble. She was a little bit ... 'dotty', which her neighbour assured us was normal for her. She wasn't worried about her leg, nor really about the amount of blood that she had lost (not a huge amount, but it looked like a lot), all she was worried about was the bus crew.

For their part the bus crew had done a lot of good, especially given the fear that a lot of council workers have of being sued when acting outside their 'protocols'. They had made her comfortable, had given her some effective first aid and had cleaned up the pavement and her garden path. They had even brought her shopping in and put the frozen things in the freezer. Given what a lot of others would have done, they had acted above and beyond their duties.

And all *they* were concerned about was that the patient got better.

It's so refreshing to come across some council workers who actually care; unfortunately, it is rarer than I would like.

🚐 Canvas, with Handles

We have a huge amount of equipment on the back of our ambulances, from the complicated hydraulic trolley through various splints, oxygen delivery systems, a defibrillator and ventilator to the machine that can measure the carbon dioxide that a patient breathes out.

But it's often the simple bits of kit that are most useful.

We were called as a second crew in order to help with a 'difficult removal'. It wasn't a good sign when we arrived on scene and had to make our way up four flights of narrow communal stairs to get to the front door of the flat. Then we had to negotiate another narrow stairwell to get to the bedroom where the patient and the other ambulance crew were.

The patient was one of those generally unwell people – nothing specific and he would need further tests in hospital. The problem was that he was too weak to move – that and his blood pressure was incredibly low, dangerously so.

The original crew had given him a load of fluid into a vein in an attempt to raise his blood pressure enough to get him out of the house – for some reason this wasn't happening. The crew were concerned that if they sat him up to put him into the usual carry chair the blood would drain out of his brain. This would be a *bad* thing.

So we put our minds together and decided to use one of the simplest bits of kit on our ambulance: a carry sheet.

A carry sheet is, at its simplest, a canvas sheet with handles attached. You put the patient on the sheet, all grab a handle and use it like a very soft stretcher. I believe that it is going out of favour because health and safety gurus think that it is bad for our backs. The thing is, out in the real world, you sometimes need to use equipment in an 'unapproved' way in order to get the job done. The need to improvise is just one of the reasons why I love my job.

We dutifully explained to the patient and his wife what we were going to do then rolled him onto the carry sheet and prepared to carry him out of the bedroom, down the stairs, across the walkway, down four flights of stairs and out to the waiting ambulance.

Head first.

I would imagine that it didn't feel very safe, four sweating, puffing and groaning ambulance workers carrying you down all those stairs. Narrow stairwells are a complete nightmare when you are moving at three abreast. Then you have to *bend* the patient around corners. All head first in order to allow the blood to flow to his brain by keeping his head lower than his body.

By the time we huffed and puffed him into the ambulance his blood pressure had raised a little.

Fear of being dropped will do that to you.

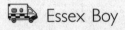 Essex Boy

It was one of those days when the sun was shining, everything seemed right with the world and both my crewmate and I were happy to be working. Normally these feelings don't last long as you find yourself wrestling with an aggressive drunk or something – but we were enjoying it while it lasted.

Our call came in as 'pregnant female, fell over', not a huge problem – people fall over all the time and babies tend to be pretty well protected while still in the womb. Reaching the scene we found a woman who was doing a good show of not being distressed. She had tripped over and now couldn't feel the baby moving. There was no pain or bleeding, and everything else checked out fine.

The LAS policy is that we should take the patient to their 'booked department'. This patient's department was a fair way out of London, it was actually in Essex. As it was so far away (it would take us 40 minutes to get there), I called up Control to ask permission to go there; they agreed that it was in the patient's best interests and so we started the drive.

I'm glad we have satellite navigation, that's all I'll say ...

As we pulled up to the hospital the patient's mother arrived and was very grateful that we had brought her to 'her' maternity unit. We then handed over to perhaps the nicest midwives *ever* and went to do our paperwork. While there we waved a 'hello' to a confused-looking Essex ambulance crew. We don't often get out that far from London.

'Greening up' we returned to our patch and continued working.

It was only a few jobs later that we found ourselves going into the Royal London hospital. This was a good thing as we were getting hungry and the Royal London has a McDonald's opposite – great for the healthy ambulance diet that I, and my belt, have become accustomed to. I wandered in there to get my cheeseburger, fish burger and Big Mac when who should I bump into other than the ambulance crew we waved at back in Essex.

They had done a transfer from their hospital into London and had decided to grab a similar meal for the long drive back to their area.

It can be a small world.

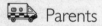 Parents

When dealing with children in a basic ambulance job there are two types of parents: the calm sensible ones and the flappers. Calm sensible parents are preferred; they keep the child calm, can give you a full and complete history and are a pleasure to have in the back of the ambulance. Flappers are another matter.

Our call was to a nine-year-old girl with a nosebleed. The family lived less than two minutes from their local hospital and the presence of a car in their driveway had me rolling my eyes. The patient's mother opened the front door, she was literally running backwards and forwards with tears streaming from her eyes. She could hardly talk because she was so upset and her breathing was just a shade short of becoming full-blown hyperventilation.

Obviously, I had a moment where I thought that the child was more seriously ill than a simple nosebleed.

Then our patient walked around the corner; she had a bit of kitchen towel held up to her nose but there wasn't any active bleeding. There were one or two drops of blood on her blouse and otherwise she looked fine.

I finally got the mother to calm down enough to explain what had happened. Well, I say calmed down, what she actually did was thrust a piece of paper into my hands. The child had ITP, an often mild clotting disorder. Examining the child it seemed that the nosebleed had already stopped and there was a large jelly-like clot in her nose. The best thing to do is to leave well enough alone and give the wound plenty of time to clot – if you start fiddling around with it then the chances are good that the bleeding will start again.

There wasn't enough blood loss to fill an eggcup.

But still the mother cried, ran up and down and generally did her best to inadvertently scare the child. While the child seemed quite sensible (she'd done the right thing in clamping the kitchen towel to her nose) she was obviously frightened by the mother.

So I turned on my 'everyone keep calm' demeanour. I tried to calm the mother down; I told her how it wasn't serious, how the bleeding had stopped and how the blood loss was tiny. I showed both of them the vital signs that I took and explained how they were all fine and if it were anything serious then the pulse would be higher, the blood pressure would be lower and the breathing more rapid. But the mother didn't listen.

Instead of going to the local hospital (with a perfectly fine paediatric department) the mother demanded that they go to the Royal London where the child was under the haematologists. I explained that the Royal London didn't have any paediatric beds (because we'd just come from a transfer from there to another hospital) and that the local hospital would be able to cope just fine. But the mother flapped and fretted and so I agreed that we would drive past the local hospital and down the road a few miles so she could go to the Royal London.

So we set off for the hospital, the bleeding remained stopped and the mother seemed to calm down a bit. But then every few minutes she would dart forward and scream 'It's red!' and pluck the kitchen towel from the child's nose causing the patient to cry.

Later in the day I could contrast it with a ten-month-old baby who had had two febrile fits in the space of two days. The parents were sensible, calm and a pleasure to deal with. The parents were more than happy to go to the local hospital for a check-up and the baby was fine by the time we got there. The calmness of parents tends to keep the child calm – and a calm child makes for a happy ambulance person.

A Query on a Phone Call

The first job of our night shift was to an overdose. Sometimes these jobs are nasty, sometimes they are easy. Sometimes you know what the job is going to be like from the information sent down to our ambulance.

'Fifty-five-year-old man, overdose on diazepam and alcohol. How long? Amount?'

My psychic powers kicked in and I predicted an alcoholic who had taken many tablets of a low dose of diazepam (a muscle relaxant and sedative) with rather a lot of alcohol. Probably nothing too serious in a physical sense, but it never hurts to get there as quickly as is safely possible.

The FRU was already there, along with the patient's sister. Our patient had drunk a huge bottle of whisky along with around eight tablets of very low dose diazepam. He'd taken about double the daily dose, which meant that he was going to be sleepy but it wasn't likely to be life threatening. He'd still need to go to hospital to be sure and so he could have a psychiatric referral.

I asked the sister about the patient, was he a heavy drinker? She replied that he wasn't just a heavy drinker but that he was an alcoholic, not that I really needed to ask – one look at the state of the patient's house told me that.

The patient had taken the overdose in the morning then rung his girlfriend to tell her what he had done. She was out at work and so the message was left on the answerphone. In the evening his girlfriend had returned home from work, heard the message and phoned his sister, who lived closer. The sister had called us and went round to open the door.

What I wanted to know was, did the patient really want to kill himself and left phoning his girlfriend until he knew she would be out in order to make sure he was dead before she got the message? Or, more likely, was he so drunk while taking the tablets that he didn't know what the time was when he made the phone call?

It never ceases to surprise me how people who take an overdose act. They take a handful of tablets then phone a friend. They then act surprised when the ambulance arrives.

Thankfully this patient was drowsy and compliant (he was a big man and I didn't fancy wrestling him into the ambulance). He'd slept the day away, spent some time sleeping in the A&E department and the last I saw of him was him walking into the patient toilet.

So an easy job, a sensible sister and a puzzle on the nature of a phone call.

Wheelchair

I heard a great story from a relative of our patient last night; it had my crewmate, our patient and me in fits of laughter.

We were called to a patient I've been to previously. They are a nice family and the patient is lovely. Unfortunately, the patient has a long list of medical problems and needs an electric wheelchair to get around. He had been taken ill and, after a four-hour wait, had finally got an ambulance to take him to hospital.

He was in his bed and we would use our carry chair to get him out of the house. First, though, we needed to move the patient's own electric wheelchair. Now I'm experienced enough to know that I really shouldn't touch these things because I'll only end up breaking them, so we called for the patient's son to come and move it.

He tried moving it by standing next to it, but the patient said something to him in his own language and the son climbed into the wheelchair and steered it away.

As he did this he told us the story of having to take the wheelchair to the hospital on his father's previous visit.

You see it's hard to stand next to a wheelchair to steer it via the joystick so he climbed in it and rode it to the bus stop.

The problem was that there was a load of people standing waiting for the bus watching him.

He felt too embarrassed to climb out – it would look a bit ... well ... 'funny'.

So the bus came and the bystanders helped him get on it then they helped him get off at the other end of his journey. He even gave them a wave of thanks as the bus pulled away.

The son told this story so well we were nearly wetting ourselves with laughter; his animated demonstration of the wave at the end was a sheer brilliant flourish.

Even the father had a (slightly gap-toothed) smile.

The thing that was so funny was that we could all put ourselves in his place and we couldn't really say that we wouldn't do exactly the same thing. It was like a Basil Fawlty sketch, a weird mixture of not wanting to offend people and so getting yourself into a silly situation.

As I say, the patient and his family are really nice and he was one of the very few people during the shift who said thank you at the end of the job.

 ## More of the (Shameful) Usual

As is normal these days the nursing home that we went to was 'well known' to us. The patient had the normal 'difficulty in breathing' which I have learnt means anything from a cold to the patient not breathing at all.

As we arrived I spotted two healthcare assistants standing outside smoking. 'Another ambulance,' one of them commented. 'This place is a right dump.'

I couldn't really disagree with them.

So we made our way up to the patient. No one was there to show us where to go; again not an unusual situation. Our FRU was already there. He's a good bloke and I trust his clinical skills completely. He'd already done a full assessment and was talking to the nurse in charge. From the sound of the patient's breathing and his high temperature it was obvious that he had pneumonia.

So I asked the nurse how long he had been coughing and having trouble with his breathing.

'Ten minutes,' she replied.

Now, you don't need to be a medical genius to realise that his breathing must have been horrible for quite some time. But given the amount of times I've heard that 'the patient was fine until five minutes ago' from a nursing-home nurse – if that is true then I suspect that there are a whole load of medical books that need rewriting.

The patient was seriously ill, and you don't get like that in ten minutes. My guess would have been that he was unwell for at least a day, yet no one had thought to call a doctor or us until it looked like the patient might die.

Yet again the nurse in charge of his care didn't seem to know anything about the patient. When I asked about him the nurse seemed to think that giving me a list of his medicines counted for this. Sadly, this is also not unusual. I did my usual trick of pretending not to know what a certain drug does then asking the nurse to see if they know. It is essential that a nurse knows about the medication that they are giving someone so that they understand how they work and the side effects that can occur. Unfortunately in many of the nursing homes we go to this is a rarity.

In this case she was unsure as to why he had been recently prescribed some antibiotics.

I used my 'ex-nurse' knowledge to write a quick entry in the patient's nursing notes – that way nothing can be added after we have left. It's a little trick of mine that satisfies my bloody-mindedness.

So we moved the rather ill patient to the ambulance and while treating him waited for the accompanying member of staff. We waited and we waited. I was considering just driving off. Eventually one of the usual foot-shuffler 'nurses' made an appearance and we left for the hospital.

It's depressing, and I've written about this before, but it's all too common to find this sort of neglect going on in nursing homes. The companies who run these places make huge amounts of profits, yet the care is what I, in fact what most people, would call substandard. If the number of people with dementia continues to increase then more people will need nursing care, and if the care isn't there at the moment I dread to think what it will be like in the future.

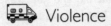 Violence

We ambulance crews are verbally and physically abused on an almost daily basis – it has become so common that we tend to ignore the verbal abuse that we get. It's only with the increasingly common physical assaults that we fill in the required forms.

Let me give you an example from my last night shift, a not unusual job.

We were called to 'woman collapsed in the street' at gone midnight. We arrived to discover our patient lying under a bus stop with what appeared to be her worldly possessions in a plastic bag. There was no one else around except for the minicab driver who had called us from his office in front of which she had 'collapsed'. While my nose can no longer detect alcohol my crewmate for the shift was able to tell me that the patient smelt as if she had been dunked in a brewery sewer.

A quick check in her bag revealed nothing obviously medically wrong with her (no medic alert bracelet or 'I am an epileptic' card). It did, however, reveal that the woman had been released from custody earlier in the day.

I tried to wake her, but she screwed her eyes tight and refused to talk to us. The problem was that we couldn't leave her on the street; someone else would call us and we would be back and forth all night. Likewise if she froze to death we would be to blame and if she were stabbed later in the night we'd also probably be to blame. The police wouldn't be interested. They have stopped taking people who are drunk; one too many deaths in custody is to blame for this. So, as she refused to go home or to her hostel, the only place that we could take her was to hospital.

I was in a good mood so I explained all this to her, that we couldn't leave her here, and that if she didn't come with us the police would probably be called and that they might take a dim view of her drunkenness (a bit of a bluff, but it sometimes works).

So she started to swear at us, she threatened to hit me and she was generally rather rude ...

Again, this is all water off a duck's back to me. At one point she tried to kick me, but I'm an old hand at drunks in the street and by the cunning tactic of stepping out of the way managed to avoid a scuffed shin.

Eventually we managed to hoik her up and into the back of the ambulance where, after a bit more swearing, she settled down.

She did give me a dirty look at the end of the journey though.

I would say that I get a patient who is verbally abusive at least once or twice during a night shift. I don't mind violence from people who are medically unwell (e.g. diabetics with low blood sugars, post-seizure epileptics). But can I really count 'drunk' as a medical problem?

I also count myself lucky that I work where I do – unlike the hospitals where people become frustrated by long waiting times and perceived injustice I'm often seen as a friendly stranger who makes everything better.

Increasing Calls

It is a regular story in the media that the ambulance service is getting an ever increasing number of 999 calls.

One of the reasons that some people have suggested for the increase in calls is the recent British Heart Foundation advert urging people to call for ambulances if they get chest pain. In my own experience there hasn't been a huge increase in calls because of this; in my area people don't need any encouragement to call us out.

When I started working for the ambulance service we got around 2500 calls across London each day – now it isn't unusual to get 4000 plus. While a government spokesperson says that there are more ambulance staff than in the past (which is true), it doesn't follow that there are more ambulances. Ambulances which used to be covered by staff on overtime are now manned by relief crews – so while there is more manpower the actual number of ambulances on the road is pretty constant.

I don't think that there has been an increase in the actual number of ambulances in the last 15 years; yet we have increasing call numbers and an ever expanding role.

I would say that there is a number of reasons why there is an increase in calls:

The lack of GP services 'out of hours': since GPs were allowed to stop covering out-of-hours services the quality of primary care during the hours of darkness has plummeted. Because of decreased GP cover we are going to more and more primary care situations, jobs that would normally be under a GP remit.

The increasing 'I have the right' brigade: people who know that they have a 'right' to an ambulance as a free taxi to hospital. All thanks to the 'Patient's Charter'.

People want healthcare when they want it, rather than when it is available: waiting for an appointment to have your foot wart removed is such a chore. You want it off now? Call an ambulance to take you to hospital.

A general lack of education: a simple chest infection in an otherwise healthy person isn't going to kill you; however, some people do believe that a cough is something life threatening.

A lack of magic cures: I've lost count of the number of people I've been to recently who have seen their GP for a chest infection, have taken two of the prescribed antibiotics and yet they aren't feeling better. Then they call an ambulance. Here is a hint: there is a reason why there are 28 tablets in the pack ...

Increased population: more and more people are living in smaller homes; buildings are being thrown up all over London, yet there isn't a corresponding increase in healthcare provision. There is also a big move in converting houses into five or six bedsits, each bedsit housing a family.

Twenty-four-hour licensing: I know it's an unpopular view in some circles, but we are going to more drunks and alcohol-related calls than ever before. As I write this the latest figures are that in London the number of calls we go to that are related to alcohol has increased by 12 per cent.

One of the problems is that we are trying to solve all these issues by throwing ambulances at them, ambulances and staff that we just don't have. We are covering for reduced GP hours by implementing ECPs (emergency care practitioners, GPs on the cheap). What patient is going to want to get an appointment for a GP when you can dial 999 and have someone turn up at your door when you want?

As a whole, health education in this country is dreadful – barely going beyond 'safe sex' and 'stop smoking' messages. Drunks in the street are going to a nice friendly A&E department rather than a less comfortable police cell where they are charged with an offence.

We aren't refusing ambulances to people who don't need them. Partly it is because we are mollycoddling people for fear of being sued and having a bad press or making a mistake. If the ambulance service continues this way then I can't see things getting any better.

We are also having to change the way we work in order to meet the government's useless targets. This will lead to problems with patients and crews.

Without a sea change in society as a whole and in the funding and measurement of targets in the ambulance service, despite the LAS's best intentions, things aren't going to get any better.

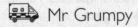 Mr Grumpy

I suspect that I'm going to have two complaints put in against me this week. Not from patients, nor from relatives, but from random members of the public.

You see, I've been 'rude' to two of them.

Take the first one. We were called to a teenager who'd been run over by a car. He had quite a nasty injury that threatened the health of one of his limbs. So I parked in the road as there was nowhere else to park that wasn't on top of his head. We did a few bits at the side of the road then scooped him up into the ambulance. We then had to do a lot more clever medical stuff to him before heading off to hospital, partly to stabilise his injury and partly to make sure that his big obvious injury was, indeed, the only thing wrong with him.

I then heard a knock at the back door of the ambulance and, thinking it was the police, went to have a look.

It was the driver of one of those big stretch limos – the kind that are hired out by hen parties. He wanted me to move the ambulance so he could drive down the street.

I tried to explain that I'd got a seriously ill patient in the back of the ambulance, and that it needed both of us crew to look after him. I say I 'tried' to explain but the man wouldn't let me get a word in edgeways – he just wanted me to move because he had 'kids and their parents' in the back of his limo. I was conscious that my crewmate might need me in the back of the ambulance. Trust me, I was not being purposely obstructive.

Well, the red mist started to rise at the corner of my vision, so I told him to (and my exact words were), 'Shut up!'

'That's a bit rude,' he said, and then drew breath to moan some more, but I interrupted him. 'Yes! I know!' I then stormed back into the ambulance to deal with my patient. (I may have flounced back into it; my arms do get a bit flappy when I'm angry.)

The limo driver then miraculously managed to squeeze his huge vehicle past the ambulance despite me not moving it.

The second one was last night. The ambulance bays at the Royal London were packed with ambulances. There was also a bloke in a private car parking in one of the bays. I was trying to park so that the 18-month-old who had just had a fit could get into the hospital to see a doctor. This car was blocking my way, and blocking the ambulances who might want to get out for another job.

'Excuse me sir,' I called after the driver, 'you can't park there, it's for ambulances only.'

'Where am I supposed to park?' he shouted back at me.

'Well, sir, if you go around the back of the hospital you can park there.'

'But then I'll have to walk,' he shouted back.

I noted the 200 yards he'd have had to walk.

'So,' I shouted back at him, 'you ignore the big "No entry" sign, the big writing on the floor that says "Ambulances Only" and stop me from being able to park my ambulance THAT ALSO HAS A SICK PERSON IN IT!' My arms might have been a bit flappy as well.

He turned around and headed into the hospital. I'm not sure that he heard the shouted 'Pillock!' after him. I thought long and hard about putting a brick through his car window.

I decided not to.

Needless to say this was highly amusing to the other ambulance crews in the area.

I wouldn't mind but I'm normally very placid. And again this person could put in a complaint against me and I'd have to defend myself to people much higher than me in the ambulance management food chain. Remember, my only complaint against me so far has been from someone who assaulted me and was horrified when I told him that he 'slapped like a bitch'.

But I'm only human.

 Yellow Card

I picked up a patient who appeared to be having a nasty reaction to 'Picolax', which is a laxative used to prepare the bowel before a colonoscopy.

I've given a fair amount of this stuff in my previous life as a nurse and can't ever remember anyone having this particular reaction.

As we took the patient into the hospital we were met with disbelief – the patient in the next bed had exactly the same symptoms from the same use of the drug.

Weird.

It's currently being reported to the people who look after this sort of thing under the 'yellow card' reporting procedure. Perhaps it was a bad batch, both patients were given the drug by the same hospital: maybe it was just a coincidence.

I wonder if there will be any more this shift ...

🚐 Fat Bastard

I'm not as thin as I used to be. Come the end of April and I shall be engaging in that thing called 'exercise'. My belly is resembling a pot and I get out of puff walking up two flights of stairs. This is not good for a youngish man such as me.

It's good to see that my own mental image of my body is current though, otherwise I may well have got myself in some serious trouble.

We were called to a 'trapped behind locked doors'. We arrived and the police were waiting for the 'enforcer', a ram that they use to knock down doors. Given that she was a little old lady lying on the floor, whom they could see through a window, they didn't fancy smashing her door to pieces.

Then I noticed an open window ...

I looked at it, it was a very narrow opening but I thought that I would be able to make it.

The thing is, I'm a big kid at heart – give me a door to break down or a window to climb through and I'm a happy soul. It's not so much for the patient's benefit (although obviously I am thinking about them), it's more for the fun of the experience.

One of the police found a garden chair that I could stand on and they eyed me suspiciously as I tried to slide through the window.

The fleece that I was wearing was padding me out too much so I took it off.

I tried again, this time it was my pen, pen-torch and scissors in my shirt pocket that got in the way. I moved them into my trouser pocket.

One of the police asked if it would help if I were buttered up.

I pretended not to listen to him.

Or to the giggles of my crewmate.

I managed to get my head and chest through the window then my gut got in the way and there was a momentary fear that I would get stuck in this position, half in, half out of the window. I sucked in my stomach and thought 'thin thoughts'. I managed to slip through the window, nearly killing myself in the sink.

I had a little ego boost as, panting heavily, I opened the door so that my crewmate could get in and we could look after the patient who was actually rather ill.

So yes ... I need to lose some weight and get fitter than I am at the moment, especially if I want to keep being able to climb through windows.

On the Failings of My Stab Vest

It's coming up to 1 a.m. and there have been another stabbing, a 'glassing', and two head injuries caused by blunt weaponry.

For the first time in ages I've put my stab vest on. It's not a nice way to realise that I've put on a bit of weight since the last time I wore it.

We were sent to the 'glassing', but were informed that the assailants were still on the scene so we decided to wait for the police to turn up and make sure that we wouldn't get to be another stabbing.

Unfortunately, it was all for naught as a passing ambulance got flagged down by the victim's friends. So there we were, hiding down the end of the road listening to the crew giving details of their 'running call'.

Luckily the assailants had disappeared.

Meanwhile, we were sent to a man who was so drunk he couldn't stand up. He didn't want to come with us, but it was too cold to leave the drunk and incapable 'patient' in the street where he might freeze to death. So we dragged him up and went to go to hospital.

The problem I had was that this incredibly drunk man kept pawing at me then tried grabbing my arse while leering at me.

My crewmate found it all incredibly amusing.

It was at the hospital I discovered one of the weaknesses of the stab vests we are given as part of our uniform. In his drunken flailing around he managed to strike me in the testicles – needless to say I dropped to the ground like a sack of potatoes, gasping like a fish.

Thankfully it was 'just' a glancing blow; so it only took half an hour for the pain to go. The patient was thrown out of the hospital by the security staff.

Another normal night in Newham.

Unfortunately.

🚑 Broken Finger

We found ourselves going to a woman who had a 'broken finger, bone sticking out'. This looked like it was going to be a pretty simple job; finger injuries are normally.

Not this one.

As we entered the room we could tell that it wasn't a 'standard' broken finger. The workmen in the room had wrapped her hand as best they could and then held it above her head.

The patient had completely degloved the finger – her ring had got caught on a fence and had torn the skin off the finger. The skin was bunched up around the top joint of the finger and held in place by her ring. There was no way that we were going to be able to remove the ring and the skin was white and chalky. What this needed was immediate medical treatment before the tissue completely died.

So we 'blued' her into the local hospital where they cut her ring off and started to arrange transfer to a plastic surgery centre. Unfortunately, the first choice was unavailable as they had no beds. The next nearest facility was actually outside London; my crewmate and I volunteered to take the patient there and Control agreed. It's nice if you can keep up this continuity of care and I soon found myself driving 28 miles on blue lights to the hospital.

Of course, when I got there I didn't have any idea where the ward we were transferring the patient was so I asked one of the local paramedics directions and he jumped into the ambulance to direct us. The patient was soon safely on the ward, slightly dazed on morphine, and with the best chance that she had (however slim) to save her finger.

The paramedic who helped me emailed me the day after to apologise for not taking us straight up to the ward, but his Control were already on his back. I still find it a bit weird to be 'recognised' if only because people talk to me after I've left them ...

🚑 Returnee

We have a number of policies concerning the care for patients, what we should do to them and what should happen if we don't take them to hospital. Sometimes we come across situations that fall outside our policies – it's for those that we have to rely on our experience and our common sense.

We were called to a 16-year-old with 'learning difficulties' who was refusing to eat. The address seemed familiar and, sure enough, as we pulled up outside the door I recognised that I had been here a few days ago.

On that first visit the girl was complaining of leg pain, she was lying on the floor and very upset. I'm no expert but it seemed that the mental age of this girl was somewhere around that of a four-year-old. She was looked after by her mother; the father hadn't been seen since the birth of the child. She was screaming in pain and seemed, at first, to be inconsolable.

That all changed as we looked after her; she brightened up and was laughing and joking with us by the time we reached the hospital. The pains in her legs seemed to have vanished. She doesn't have good mobility at the best of times so it's always hard to assess any change.

So we were returning to the same girl. This time her mother was telling us that she wasn't eating. The girl was lying on the same spot on the floor, covered with a blanket and crying. As soon as we walked into the room a large grin broke out across her face and she started laughing. It seemed pretty obvious that the girl wasn't sick.

Her mother told me how the girl had cried when she had to leave the hospital. She had returned to hospital twice more in the last two days so it appeared that this was a repeating pattern.

It seemed pretty obvious to me that the girl was manipulating her mother so that she could go to hospital where she was the centre of attention. Of course, this was all assumption and I wondered if there was any way I could get proof of this.

I get on really well with the receptionists at our local hospital; they are all extremely lovely people. So I phoned them up and asked what the girl's previous medical notes said. This was probably going against a whole load of guidelines and protocols, but I needed to know if, by taking the patient in, we would be reinforcing her behaviour.

The medical notes basically agreed with my assessment of the situation – she had told the doctors that she liked being in hospital because 'home is boring'.

The hospital was arranging for a follow-up appointment with the paediatricians and it was also liaising with the social services to get the mother and her daughter the help that they needed.

So after some discussion with the mother, we came to an agreement that we would leave her daughter at home, her mother would keep watching her and we would see if it could break the pattern. We agreed to help the mother wash her daughter for bed, even though her daughter was now throwing a 'bit of a strop' as she knew that she wouldn't be going to hospital.

So she was left at home; a risk for us because if she were to drop dead it'd be us to blame – even if it were for a completely unrelated cause. But I'm of the mind that sometimes you have to be cruel to be kind.

And kudos to my crewmate – as the female in our party she got the job of helping the mother clean her daughter while all I had to do was talk on the phone.

We had another 'returnee' that same night: a 20-year-old man who called us with abdominal pain. He didn't tell me that he had been to the hospital earlier that day but had left after ten minutes. I think he'd have a bit more waiting to do after that particular abuse of the service ...

 Another Good Job

For the second time in two weeks I did a job where we did some actual good. To be completely honest it put my crewmate and I on a bit of a buzz for the rest of the day.

The job started out as a bog-standard chest pain: 41-year-old male, pain in the chest radiating down his left arm. He was originally from the Indian subcontinent and people from this part of the world tend to have a lot of heart problems.

It didn't seem like a big job to be honest. He didn't look like he was having a heart attack – he wasn't sweaty, the pain got worse when he breathed in (often a sign of non-cardiac chest pain), he didn't have the 'feeling of impending doom' that is described daily in ambulance training schools across the world.

But he just didn't look right. I have no idea what it was about him but there was something that set alarm bells ringing.

So we popped him onto our carry chair and wheeled him out to the ambulance in order to do a few checks before taking him to hospital.

His blood pressure was high, but everything else seemed fine. As we were preparing to do an ECG (electrocardiograph, a tracing of what is going on in the heart) my crewmate and I agreed that no matter what it showed we would be 'blueing' him into the local hospital, just based on the feeling we had about the patient.

His ECG printed out and we realised that we wouldn't be going to the nearest hospital around 400 yards away ...

There is something that the LAS do exceptionally well, and that is to diagnose heart attacks (properly called myocardial infarctions, or MIs). We have good experience of spotting ST segment elevation MIs and dealing with them accordingly. Not so long ago the treatment for an MI was to have a 'clot-busting' drug, which worked most of the time but had the possibility of some serious side effects (like bleeding onto the brain and death). Recently, in London at least, some specialist hospitals have been offering 'primary angioplasty', which is a surgical procedure where a wire is threaded from your groin into your heart and the blockage is cleared manually. It's done under a local anaesthetic and is the gold standard treatment.

So now the LAS will diagnose a heart attack and instead of taking you to the nearest hospital for substandard treatment, will take you to the specialist unit for the best treatment possible.

This patient was having a massive MI. Absolutely life threatening.

He had been waiting for a same-day appointment to see his GP about the pain, but as it got worse he'd wisely called for an ambulance.

We gave him aspirin, morphine and GTN (glyceryl trinitrate) – good, immediate treatment for his MI – and 'blued' him to the specialist unit.

As we arrived we showed the receiving doctor the ECG heart trace. He told us, 'That's all I need to see, bring him straight through.' We moved him onto the hospital's trolley and left him in the care of the doctors while they assessed him for surgery.

Then his heart stopped pumping blood.

He was dead.

Rapid, effective treatment by the doctors restarted his heart within a minute and he was soon asking them if he had just fainted. During this I was explaining to his wife what was happening. English wasn't her first language so she was confused by what was going on.

He was rushed into the surgery room and the doctors asked if we would like to see the procedure. As we were doing our paperwork we agreed.

An X-ray image of his heart came on the screen as they pumped a contrast agent into his blood to show where the blockage was.

There are two main arteries feeding blood to the heart; one of these was completely blocked. The doctor described it as 'the widowmaker': a severe blockage in exactly the wrong place. This was almost certainly why his heart had stopped beating while they were preparing him for surgery.

We watched as they did a bit of delicate plumbing work to remove the blockage and restored the flow of blood to his heart.

While he will almost certainly survive this episode, I wonder what damage has been done to his heart; the MI causes part of the heart to become starved of oxygen and this can reduce its function.

If he'd waited the hour to go and see the GP, he would be dead.

If he hadn't called for an ambulance, he'd be dead.

If we weren't routinely trained to recognise MIs and take them to the right place, he'd be dead.

If the primary angioplasty wasn't available, he'd probably be dead.

Everything went right on this call, we felt that we had saved his life (a rarity in this job), and it let us feel that we had earned our pay today.

Another 'good' job done.

For the medically minded, he had a VF/VT arrest, corrected after two shocks, and a complete blockage of the LAD (left anterior descending artery) about three millimetres from the base. He walked out of the hospital a few days later.

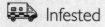 Infested

I called up Control on the radio after dropping our patient off at the hospital.

'Control, I need to return to station to clean out the back of our motor – we've just transported one of our "local legends". Is there any infection control policy for patients who are infested with insects?'

'Erm ...' came the reply, 'just scrub everything really well.'

So we returned, used every cleaning product that we had and then used the ambulance jetwash to hose out the interior.

I woke up the next morning and found myself covered in insect bites. So the itchiness I had while cleaning the vehicle wasn't imagined ...

🚑 Small Annoyances

I took in a woman whose one-year-old child had vomited. Once.

The woman rolled her eyes and pulled a face when I told her that we would be taking her to the nearest hospital (about half a mile away) rather than her local hospital at Basildon, which, you know, isn't even in London.

Then both she and her husband both pulled a face and rolled their eyes when they realised that they wouldn't see a doctor immediately.

Apparently it was all my fault.

Most of the time this sort of thing rolls off me like water off a duck's back.

But then there are some days when it drives me potty.

🚑 Friday

Another teenage boy has been stabbed to death on my patch. I had reason to go to the receiving hospital just after it happened; already the friends and relatives were gathering. I saw the now familiar emotions of grief and anger. During the night more people came and the emotions seemed to settle into a stunned silence. Questions were asked but it seemed that there were no answers.

The hospital staff looked after them in a professional manner. It's unfortunate but seems that we are getting more practised with such things.

A crew wheeled a drunk teenager, clothes torn and barely able to raise her head, past the grieving relatives. It's a strange feeling to take in such a patient; you almost feel embarrassed to bring such an idiot in while parents and brothers and sisters are weeping.

Not a good night in east London.

But, sadly, not unusual.

The Same Old Story

I was being sent to one of our regular nursing homes. I'd been to Rose Cottage a few days earlier for a patient who 'wasn't eating' and had a low blood sugar. This time it was for a patient with chest pain.

It's not the worst nursing home that I go to. The place is clean and tidy, some of the nurses speak good English and the patients aren't beaten. But it's still not as good as it should be; the normal problems of the staff not knowing about their patients and the usual cold cups of tea sitting just outside of the patient's grasp render it an impersonal and borderline-neglectful place.

We arrived to find that our patient was a 93-year-old female, bedbound and only recently discharged from hospital. She also had dementia, although more of the 'pleasantly confused' type. I have found that there are two main ways that dementia manifests itself in nursing homes: the 'constant screaming, scratching and crying' type, and the 'pleasantly stoned' type where the patient is dotty but fairly happy.

This tiny little bird was of the second type. She looked at me as I walked in the room and gave a big toothless smile.

Our patient had been discharged from a good hospital less than 24 hours ago. She had been in hospital because, even though she is bedbound, she managed to break her hip. While she was in there she caught a chest infection but had since recovered enough to go home where she would continue to be nursed.

Fat chance of that.

The nursing-home staff had called the GP, who had decided that the patient should go to the hospital. Like most out-of-hours GPs he saw us arrive, threw a letter at me and ran off.

For some reason they don't like talking to other medical people they can't bamboozle in person.

The doctor had decided that the patient needed to return to hospital – fair enough, at the end of the day it's what I'm here for.

'She has chest pain,' the nurse told me.

I asked the patient if this was true.

'Only when I cough.' She was just finishing her course of antibiotics and this was to be expected.

It was obvious that the patient was dehydrated; the heating in the room was high and a full cup of water sat out of reach.

'She hasn't been eating or drinking,' the nurse told me.

'Would you like a drink?' I asked the patient.

'Yes please,' she replied.

So I did what nurses are supposed to do with patients like this – I helped her have a drink of water. At this point the nurse scuttled out of the room to 'photocopy the notes'.

I noticed that she had a recent cut that was undressed and some bruises to her arm – probably nothing as she does have frail skin, but I made note of them anyway. I lifted her onto the trolley and, wrapping her up, took her back to the hospital.

'It's a Rose Cottage special,' I said to one of the doctors. She replied that she could tell that from a distance without needing to speak to me. The charge nurse whom I handed over to spotted the cut to her arm before I had a chance to mention it, which put me in a good mind about the sort of care she'd get at the hospital.

So she returned to hospital where she would probably get another chest infection, and this one might kill her.

Even while the patient was in hospital the care home would be charging in the region of £500 a week for the empty bed. Is it any wonder they call for an ambulance at the drop of a hat? I would imagine that a care home with all its patients in hospital would be very good for the shareholders.

 Yellow

I came out of the house and started coughing. I'd needed to leave so I could get some fresh air.

Picture the house, an elderly married couple, both chain-smokers, both requiring home oxygen for emphysema, both suffering from recurrent chest infections. As our patient put it, 'I think they are fed up with me down at the hospital, I was only there a few days ago.'

The walls were yellow-brown. Actually *everything* was yellow-brown. An old Labrador had wheezed its way up the hallway to greet me, its tail wagging furiously. My crewmate was attending so I was free to play with the dog.

Thankfully it was nothing serious; a chest infection that hadn't gone with the first round of antibiotics, our patient would need something stronger.

I could feel the tar seeping into my skin, there was a horrible taste in my mouth and I started wondering what the lethal dose of nicotine was. Would it be a good idea to get our hazardous rescue team out in their noddy suits?

They were a lovely couple, rattling and wheezing away, rows of cigarettes lined up like soldiers. Cigarettes already placed into cigarette holders, something that I haven't seen except in movies set in the 1950s.

Hundreds of souvenirs, all covered with a patina of tar, nicotine and heaven knows what else, told me of their life before they became housebound. They were quite happy in their life, they had each other, they had their 'little sin' and they weren't hurting anyone.

They were lovely, we had a little laugh and a joke with them, I stroked the dog a bit more and we took our patient off to hospital.

But I could taste that house for the rest of the day.

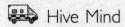 Hive Mind

There I was, sitting outside the newsagent's shop at the end of the hospital road. The newsagent whom I'm sure I keep financially stable with my purchases of large amounts of caffeinated beverages. As I finished off the paperwork from my previous job one of our ambulances raced past me on the way to a job. A woman chose that moment to cross the road without looking first for big lumps of yellow metal and blue flashing lights moving at speed.

The ambulance missed her, but she stood in the middle of the road and swore at it. She then continued to walk across the road and I noted that she had spotted my ambulance ...

She stalked over to me and banged on my window. I wound it down a notch.

She was angry.

'Do you know that ambulance?' she shouted at me.

I told her the truth, I had no idea who it was.

'Yes you do!' Small flecks of spit hit the window of the ambulance. 'You ambulance drivers think you own the fucking road!'

She continued in a similar vein with much more swearing. Most of it directed at me. She wouldn't let me get a word in edgeways.

I considered stepping out of the ambulance and punching her on the nose. I reconsidered as it was not a good career choice.

I told her to go away. Maybe a little less politely than policy would suggest.

Apparently, because we all share a uniform we all share a hive mind. Also I suspect that she wouldn't shout at me if she were to come across me in the street wearing my jeans and hoodie.

From Sun to Scum

It was a beautiful day, early afternoon and the sun was making everything in Newham look lovely. A stationmate had been showing his young children around the back of our ambulance when we got the call.

'Male, overdose, not breathing.'

So we whizzed around to find two FRUs already there. We climbed three flights of stairs and entered the flat.

Disused needles everywhere, unwrapped foil, empty drink cans, and the odd lighter fuel can on the floor. Two men were agitatedly pointing at our patient on the floor. The patient wasn't breathing, so one of the FRU pilots was breathing for him with a bag and mask. The other FRU was getting venous access.

The patient had injected some heroin and then stopped breathing. It's one of the things that sometimes happens when you inject a potent dose of heroin.

I busied myself with drawing up the antidote.

'He'll be all right,' I could hear one of his friends say. 'They'll give him an injection and it'll reverse it – I've seen it before.'

The other man agreed. 'I've had it happen to me six times.' It was almost a badge of pride.

The antidote duly given, our patient soon woke up. He was a bit agitated and wouldn't stop talking about getting work building things for the Olympics. We led him down to the ambulance and worked hard to persuade him to attend the hospital. One of his friends was trying to dissuade him. He wouldn't believe that the antidote often wears off before the heroin and it's very common for the patient to have to have a second dose.

Finally the patient agreed to attend the hospital and talked to me throughout the trip. Well, I say talked *to*, actually I mean he talked *at* me. I suspect that there may have been some amphetamines involved; he had that highly annoying behaviour.

So from a beautiful spring day to a drug den in the space of a few minutes.

He walked out of the hospital less than half an hour later. I'm glad that they didn't have to spend too much time with him.

What a waste.

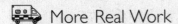 More Real Work

I have my new permanent crewmate. This makes me happy and I think that we will work well together. She says that she never gets a serious job; something that I think applies to me as well.

So, of course, on our first two days together we ended up with some really rather seriously ill patients.

It's been unseasonably hot and we had already been called to an elderly man who had collapsed. We ran our full barrage of tests and it looked like it was because of a few too many layers of clothing. We'd also been to a woman walking around in the middle of the day wearing a Puffa jacket, who was feeling dizzy. Probably something to do with the high temperature.

We were called to another collapse. We arrived and thought at first that he was dead. His whole body was either white or purple and it was only because our first responder was talking to him that we knew he was alive. Gradually a bit of colour came back to him and he told us about the abdominal pain that he had been suffering with from earlier in the day.

As he was lying flat out in the kitchen and we needed to get him to the ambulance we gently sat him up in order to get him into our wheelchair. His eyes rolled back into his head and we quickly lowered him back down to the floor. Again he lost all his colour and I quickly checked that his heart was still beating.

This needed a rethink. A quick examination showed a pulsating lump in his abdomen. This is typically a sign of an abdominal aortic aneurysm (a 'triple-A'), which, should it start leaking or burst, will kill you. The only treatment is surgery. This meant getting him to hospital *very* quickly. So we grabbed our scoop stretcher and carried him out flat. It's a lot more awkward and took more time, but if he was going to collapse every time that we sat him up it was the only way to get him out of the house.

A few quick checks on the ambulance to make sure that he wasn't having a heart attack (and would, therefore, have gone to the angioplasty unit) and we 'blued' him into hospital.

As I hopped out of the driver's seat and opened the door I noticed that his colour had improved greatly and he was a lot more talkative. As we wheeled him into the resuscitation bay I said to the doctor, 'Well, on scene he looked like a triple-A.'

We left the hospital to it and did a few more jobs.

It was only later that we saw him being wheeled out for a transfer to another hospital – it seems that our initial suspicions were correct and he was, indeed, having a slow bleed from his triple-A. While he was currently stable (stable enough, apparently, to transfer him without a nurse or doctor escort), I guessed that he would still be needing surgery.

Once more, a 'good' job; one where we made a difference. I don't know what is going on – all these genuine jobs ... Whatever happened to nice simple broken fingernails and watery eyes that walk on and off my ambulance and mean little work on my part?

 More Strokes

We had been on a rest-break, but Control had interrupted it in the last 15 minutes (which was fine by me as we get financial compensation, and I'd rather not be named as 'Medic on Tea-Break While My Child Died' in the *Sun*).

The call was given as 'elderly woman collapsed behind locked doors, possibly deceased'.

We got round there as quickly as possible (after taking a detour because of a council rubbish truck sitting in the middle of the road; obviously picking up some cardboard boxes was much more important than whatever we were going to). Our FRU was already there, as was the patient's nephew.

The front door was shut and our FRU pilot was nowhere to be seen. We knocked on the door and it opened a crack. The familiar face of our FRU appeared in the gap.

'She's lying in front of the door – I climbed in from the neighbour's back garden.'

We made our way through the neighbour's house and stepped over the two-foot fence that separated their gardens.

The first thing that I noticed was that the house was spotless; it was obvious that our patient was originally in good health.

Then I saw her lying in the corridor.

She had been there for probably 24 hours; there was no carpet so she had been lying on the tiles overnight. The entire right side of her body was a huge bruise.

As you get older your skin becomes less resistant to damage, so you bruise easily, tear the skin easily and can get pressure wounds. The weight of a body can cause the flow of blood to become interrupted and unless you move (which is what people normally do) then the skin and underlying tissue can die.

You end up with terrible wounds that never seem to heal.

The entire right side of her body was likely going to become one huge wound.

It became obvious that she had suffered a stroke – she wasn't moving the right side of her body. Her left hand kept snaking out and grabbing at us and you could see the fear in her eyes.

She was also as cold as a block of ice. Being unable to eat or move, stuck in the draught from her front door in an unheated house meant that she was suffering from one of the worst cases of hypothermia I'd ever seen.

Her core body temperature was 28°C (82.4°F).

We carefully removed her to hospital – any sort of physical shock at this temperature can cause the heart to stop. All we could do was to make her as comfortable as possible, wrap her in blankets, hold her hand and talk to her.

With a hypothermia this severe the hospital can rinse warm fluid around a patient's internal organs after making a surgical hole in the abdomen. In this case though the risks to a patient this frail meant that they stuck to the safer warming blankets and warmed fluid into the veins.

It was unlikely that she would survive this episode. I hope that the stroke affected her mind and that she wasn't aware of what was happening to her. I can't imagine what it must have been like, to lie there for so long, unable to move, gradually getting colder, not knowing if help was ever going to come.

I hope that it affected her mind, but with the look in her eyes I think that she knew exactly what was happening.

It's not a good way to end 80 plus years on this planet.

Not unsurprisingly she died a day later. When I think about this job I can still feel how cold her hand was as I held it to try to comfort her. Yet another job that always springs to mind when I drive past the address.

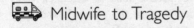 ## Midwife to Tragedy

'Midwives to tragedy.'

It's an awful phrase that came to me as we were returning to station after our latest job. We often are there at a transition between a normal happy life and one that has taken a sudden, permanent and terrible turn for the worse.

When the job came down the computer terminal we thought it would be one of our regular types of calls – a 35-year-old man was complaining of numb hands and legs. This sort of thing often turns out to be someone having a panic attack, a frightening but fairly harmless condition.

We arrived on scene and were met by the patient's wife, a number of small children milling around her feet. She led us upstairs to her husband and I could see straight away that it wasn't a panic attack.

He was unable to talk to me or to use the right side of his body. Surely he couldn't be having a stroke?

But further investigation ruled out anything else. He was having a stroke and there was little that we could do about it. So we carried him downstairs and rushed him to hospital.

Half an hour before he had been fit and well then, moments later, he was struck down with a debilitating illness. His wife had gone from looking after her children, with a husband who provided for her, to someone who would end up nursing him, possibly for the rest of his life, and would need to rely on disability benefit.

He wouldn't be able to dress himself, or clean himself after going to the toilet – he would rely on his wife to do these basic things for him.

As it gradually dawned on his wife that their life together was changed for ever she looked at me in the hope that it was not true.

And me? It was another job, another life-destroying event that I was a witness to. There to watch as the realisation sunk in that their lives would never be the same as we tried to ease the patient's and their relatives' transition into a different, more tragic life.

Another patient to go on the list whom I can no longer remember.

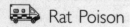 Rat Poison

There comes a time as you approach the end of your shift when you start looking for an 'off job'. This is a job that will put you at your local hospital as the clock ticks over the shift end. It's nice to get away from work only half an hour after you officially end. So you try to arrange things so that you are free 45 minutes from the end of your shift so that you can do that final job.

Then you can go home, sleep and do it all again in eleven hours.

We'd just dropped our patient off at the hospital and had 50 minutes until the end of our shift when we heard a call go out for a 33-year-old man who had eaten some rat poison. It was just around the corner so we called up for it and were there in a few minutes.

The man was visiting his sister's house. He'd forgotten that there was rat poison behind the sofa and had pulled the sofa out a bit to sit on the floor against it and eat some rice. His son and his nephew had crawled behind the sofa and reached the rat poison which looked like crumbled biscuits. One of the children was at that age where everything goes into its mouth.

The children had played next to our rice-eating patient and when he had looked down and seen what had happened he'd thought that maybe the children had put some of the poison into his rice. When we arrived he was really rather nervous.

He asked us to take him to hospital.

I suggested that we took the two children as well. He didn't understand why until I suggested that the children may have eaten some of the poison as well.

So we found ourselves driving to hospital with three adults, three children and myself in the back of the ambulance.

It took an extended time to book the patients into hospital because this family was of a culture that had half a dozen names for each of them, which meant repeated running backwards and forwards asking if they were ever known as one of a handful of names.

Then it was time to fill in three sets of paperwork.

You wouldn't think that you'd ever get writer's cramp in this job.

Still, it did see us off in time.

All the patients were fine – apparently you have to eat huge chunks of rat poison for it to have any effect on you.

Filth

Picture the scene.

You are in a house that hasn't been cleaned in years – the walls are filthy, there are carpets rolled and stacked in the stairways. The occupant, our patient, lives alone in a tiny room at the top of this house. His heating is a paraffin burner and there are half-full cans of fuel dotted around the room. Actually, I nearly hang myself on a bit of string stretching from one corner of the room to the other. I can't see the carpet because of all the rubbish on the floor.

Our elderly patient has obviously been wearing the same clothes for weeks on end.

The patient's ex-wife is the one who called us; she is pawing at me, telling me not to let him die. He isn't going to die today; his blood sugar is low and he has had a diabetic collapse. We give him some sugar and he comes around.

But there is something 'not right' about him. I don't think that it will be safe to leave him here; besides his diabetes there is a good chance that he'll burn the place to the ground one day. He seems somewhat confused; he won't talk to me although his ex-wife is clear that he can speak English. We'll need to take him to hospital.

So it boils down to 'capacity to refuse': does he have enough presence of mind to refuse treatment and be left at home. I tell him this but he doesn't answer me. I explain that if he wants to stay at home he has to talk to me – he just says 'No.' We recheck his blood sugar level and it is back to normal; there is no obvious medical reason for him to be ignoring us. I consider that he may have something neurological going on inside his head, for example a stroke.

Without him answering me, I can't tell whether he has capacity to refuse. This means that in the patient's best interests I can forcibly take him to hospital.

I don't like doing this.

Actually I REALLY don't like doing this.

So after half an hour of trying to persuade him, during which he blatantly ignores me, we realise that we will have to get him out via other means.

If his house wasn't such a tip we could maybe wrap him in a blanket and strap him to our chair and carry him out. But the amount of rubbish in the stairwells means that we'd probably break our necks.

So we have to try to drag him out. This is also something that I don't like doing. It's night-time, there is no one else around besides the police at this time of night. I really hate calling them out in order to help us get a 65-year-old, five-foot-nothing-tall man out of a house.

That and they'd probably send two five-foot-nothing female police officers to assist us – which would damage my ego even if I did know that either of them could kick my arse without breaking a sweat.

So we drag, pull and try to get him to let go of the door handle – he finds that just by sitting down we are unable to move him. We get to the point where I'm considering doing painful things to him out of spite. Then the FRU (who was first on scene and had left to do his paperwork) returns. I explain what we are trying to do.

'Mr Smith,' the FRU says, 'come downstairs into the ambulance.'

And, of course, he does.

So then he sits happily in the back of the ambulance, still ignoring us, and we take him to hospital.

We tell the nurse we hand over to about the situation at home, and we tell the nurse in charge of the department – I advise them that he'll need some sort of input from the social services before he gets discharged.

So when we see him being wheeled out to the private ambulance to go home without any apparent social service input we fill in the LAS 'vulnerable adult' form detailing the self-neglect and the fire hazard. We'll make sure that he gets help even if it seems no one else cares.

🚑 Why I Like Old Folk

We'd just dropped our last patient off at the hospital, twenty seconds later we were sent another job – business as usual then.

The job was given as 'fall, cut leg'; an 'Amber' call, and the FRU was already outside.

Our patient was an 80-year-old woman who'd fallen over in her very small toilet. A large lady, she was stuck there. She also had a 30-centimetre-long cut to her leg that had leaked a fair amount of blood – probably more than half a litre.

Her family was there, and they were lovely – they didn't moan that they had been waiting 18 minutes for an ambulance, they didn't moan that they had been sent a solo responder in a car, and they didn't moan that we were going to have to take the removal of the patient a bit slowly.

In fact, the family and the patient were all lovely people. The family was happy to help us by carrying some of our kit and by moving furniture. Our patient was in good spirits despite a nasty cut to the leg and the FRU was happy just to see us.

Three bandages later and we'd managed to control the bleeding from the leg and we moved her out to the ambulance.

The patient told me that her blood pressure was high, and after I measured it I let her know that it was a pretty good blood pressure. As quick as you like she replied, 'I suppose all that bleeding has lowered it a bit, perhaps I should cut myself more often.'

We got her to the hospital, and I explained, 'In a minute I'll get you to cuddle me so we can slide you across onto the hospital bed.'

She nearly leapt across the bed to give me a hug.

The family collapsed with laughter. 'He said in a *minute*!'

A really nice job – unfortunately, the hospital were unable to deal with the wound so she had to be transferred to a plastic surgery department at another hospital. It's always a shame when bad things happen to nice people.

As an aside, it used to be that the FRU only ran on 'Red' calls. Now, after being told off for concentrating too much on Red calls and not enough on Ambers, the FRUs are sent off to these lower priority calls in order to 'stop the clock' so that we meet our ORCON time target to please our governmental overlords. When an FRU reaches the scene the clock is stopped and the job is deemed a success. It wouldn't do for us to have more ambulances would it?

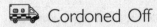 Cordoned Off

It is coming up to half past six in the morning.

I've just come into work and I'm brewing two cups of tea while my crewmate is making sure that the ambulance is fully stocked.

The clock clicks over to six-thirty and the activation phone rings.

There is a major incident at the local hospital and some of our workmates are involved. We are being sent to relieve another crew who are on standby to make sure that none of the firemen hurt themselves.

We drive there to discover a dozen fire vehicles (including command and control base vehicles) and the whole access road to the hospital blocked off.

We liaise with the officer in charge of the situation. He tells us that some men came into the hospital via ambulance and it was discovered that there might be a chemical contaminant involved.

There is a double cordon in place, our HART team are there. (The HART team are paramedics who are trained to use breathing apparatus and can go into the 'hot zone' of a situation. I think that they also run into burning buildings.)

It's all quite calm. The policeman standing in front of the 'Police: Do Not Cross' tape has only had to have one argument with a woman who wanted to walk through the centre of the incident.

We sit in our ambulance watching the sun come up while drinking tea – it's a hard life sometimes. We are listening to the chatter on the posh new radio that we were given as we arrived.

Then it's all over – the patients have been treated, the hazardous materials people have given the hospital the all clear, and I hear over the radio, 'Incident over, everyone stand down. You in the ambulance, don't forget to bring our nice radio back.'

We have a little chat with the HART team as they pack up to leave and get the full story and that everyone is fine. Then we make ourselves ready and head off for another ordinary day.

Invisible Dogs

I've mentioned it before that if I have the chance to climb something or to clamber through a window then I will – so when we got a job described as 'Child fallen off seven-foot-tall fence', I was hoping that he was on the other side.

It was a good job he had fallen on the other side – he had a softer landing. I say softer, instead of landing on concrete he'd landed in a bed of nettles.

Climbing over the fence was no problem; landing on the other side was a little trickier as my knees are getting old.

The story that we had from the large number of friends that were present was that our patient had been chased by a 'big dog', and in order to get out of the way the boy had scaled the fence and fallen over the other side.

We didn't believe him for a second. He'd been with friends (who smirked somewhat as they told his story) and the garden that he landed in belonged to a derelict house, the windows and door sealed with metal plates. I'm sure that I'm not the only person reading this who used to play on disused land.

The dog, obviously, was nowhere to be found.

I suggested that I could call the police to let them know that an aggressive dog was on the loose – the friends let me know that it wouldn't be necessary.

The trouble, of course, was that our patient was on the other side of a seven-foot-tall fence. He'd also injured his ankle and I suspected a fracture.

Did I mention that as well as the rather tall fence we would have to lift the patient over it was dark and we were surrounded by a dozen teenagers?

Actually, his friends were as good as gold. They helped me out by holding torches and mobile phone lights on the patient and by keeping him occupied while I got his leg into a splint.

After I'd assessed him I noticed that he was wearing female socks (pink and sparkly). I find that sometimes the best form of distraction therapy is to mildly mock the patient. I asked him if he usually wore women's socks. Bless his friends as they tried to cover for him by telling me that they were the latest fashion.

His mother arrived on the other side of the fence and let us all know that he was wearing her socks because he didn't have a clean pair of his own. She then shouted over to (jokingly) ask if he was wearing a pair of her knickers as well.

We explained to the mother what had happened and she was really sensible and not a worrier. She reminded me a bit of my mum actually – if you hurt yourself and you obviously weren't dead or missing any important bits of your anatomy you became fair game for those magic words, 'I told you so.'

To get our patient out we called out ~~Trumpton~~ the London Fire Service and they lashed some ladders together each side of the fence and one fireman came over to help me. I'd strapped our patient into our scoop and we would use that to get him out. Let's just say that lifting him to waist height was no problem. The 'jerk and lift' above our heads was a different matter (for me at least).

But after a bit of lifting and grunting (again, mainly on my part) we soon had our patient and his mother in the ambulance. Some further assessment and we were off to hospital where it turned out that the patient had only sprained his ankle rather than broken it.

A 'fun' job, no one seriously injured but a bit of thinking needed on our part, an amusing patient and a sensible mother. I could hardly have asked for anything more.

Why the Government Hates Us

I have a theory as to why the government refuses to properly fund ambulance, A&E and social care services.

Most of the people who use these services are old.

The above services prolong the lives of old people.

Despite the fact that old people pay all taxes except national insurance, the government, along with a lot of the population, seems to believe that they contribute nothing.

Therefore, if the services aren't properly funded then more old people will die and save the government money.

Simple really.

Thanks to a Bystander

'Funny place to be drunk,' I said.

We were being sent to a 'not breathing' at one of the bridges around my patch. Most 'not breathing' calls to public places are drunks, but this one didn't smell right. Sure, there is a pub underneath the bridge, but there was something about it that made me think that it might be genuine.

It doesn't make a difference to my driving what I'm thinking – I'll get there as quickly and safely as I can, even if I know it's one of our local drunks.

The bridge is a dual carriageway with a divider down the middle and as we approached we could see them on the other side of the road – there were two cars parked and a person standing there waved at us as we drove past. He didn't look too bothered.

We spun around the roundabout at the end (narrowly missing some idiot who not only doesn't know how to give way at a roundabout, but jumps out on ambulances that are all lit up) and approached the two parked cars.

It immediately struck me that there was a man lying his back, with another man doing very effective CPR on him. Looked like the call was a genuine one!

I stopped the ambulance and told my mate to grab the 'shock box' and look after the patient; I would get the trolley off the back of the ambulance and we would 'scoop and run'.

The patient had been a passenger in his son's car when he had suddenly collapsed. The son had pulled over to find that his father didn't have a pulse. A man driving behind them had stopped to offer some assistance. He'd recognised what was wrong and had started the heart massage.

By the time I'd managed to get the trolley and manoeuvre it through the traffic (which was whizzing dangerously close to us) my crewmate, who has been out of training school for less than a year, had diagnosed the patient's heart rhythm and had given him a 'shock' from our defibrillator.

It was about then that another ambulance and an emergency care practitioner (ECP) arrived. We loaded the patient onto the ambulance and started some advanced techniques. I kept bouncing up and down on the patient's chest.

Then the patient got their pulse back!

And he started breathing!

Time to drive to hospital.

When we got to the hospital the patient was given a good chance of surviving his 'death'. He had the best chance an outdoor cardiac arrest ever has. While what we did was important it was what the man who was driving behind the patient, stopping his car, pulling the patient out and performing very effective heart massage for the eight minutes it took us to get there.

And, while I may often gently mock the St John Ambulance Service, the man who was doing all this was one of their members.

So if the patient survives, and he has a pretty good chance, it'll all be because of the help that bystander gave. Unfortunately, I was too busy to tell our Good Samaritan this, so with a bit of luck someone who reads this might know him and pass on my thanks. He deserves to know what an effect he had on this patient.

The patient survived and walked out of hospital after a few weeks. Sadly, I never managed to thank the St John Ambulance person.

Smoky

The universe has a strange sense of humour. I can say this because no sooner than I ask for something a little different from the tales of doom and gloom I have been 'entertaining' my family with than one drops in my lap. This one made my mum really happy and proud of me.

The call was given as 'House fire – persons reported inside', an interesting job. So at 1 a.m. we flew through the streets to find firefighters having just doused the fire that had wrecked a house. I spoke to their officer in charge and he told me that they had checked the entire house and that there weren't any people inside.

It was then that I looked down to see a firefighter on his knees giving oxygen to what I thought was a baby.

With a longer look I was extremely happy to see that it wasn't one.

It was a cat.

The poor little soul was covered in soot and was having real trouble breathing – it was panting like a dog and the rate of its breathing was incredibly fast. The firefighters were giving it oxygen and trying to keep it warm (as it'd been soaked by the firefighters' hoses).

One of the firefighters seemed a bit upset. 'Don't lose it; we had a cat die on us last week.'

I let them know that we would take the cat.

So we picked it up and took it into the back of the ambulance; the neighbours who'd all gathered to watch the show seemed bemused. Unfortunately, the owners of the house couldn't be found, so the cat had suddenly become my responsibility. We dried it off and gave it oxygen using the McIlroy funnel that is used to give oxygen to neonates.

This was the first (and hopefully only) time I'd ever needed to use it.

The cat really didn't look well. I'm no vet and I've never kept a cat, but I could see that this was serious.

I listened to its chest and it sounded ... well ... kind of normal. But I had no real idea what it should sound like.

I radioed our Control.

'Hello Control, erm ... This is going to sound weird.' How best to phrase this?

'We have no human casualties at this call, but I do have a very sick cat with smoke inhalation. I'd like to take it to the 24-hour veterinary hospital at Wanstead. Mainly so that I can sleep tonight. Can you ring them and let them know that we are on our way, please?'

There was a long pause; the controller was probably talking to her senior.

'Roger that ambulance – we'll show you headed to the hospital. Do you know their phone number?'

I let them know that I didn't.

Then another crew who had been listening in on the conversation broke in and gave Control the number for the hospital.

We whizzed down there and were met by a vet and veterinary nurse who did lots of clever things to the cat, including giving aminophylline and doing the world's smallest venous cut-down. Its breathing became a lot better and the staff seemed hopeful for its chances. We gave them the address of the house so that they could reunite the animal with its owners.

Now some folk will moan that we used an ambulance to look after an animal but this 'patient' was the only one who actually *needed* an ambulance that night, we'd been dealing with drunks for much of the shift. So if you want to moan, then moan away, but it was good for the mental health of my crewmate and me.

I'd like to just say a big thank you to the Control staff who let us run to the veterinary hospital and also to the staff there who helped us out.

Also thanks to the crew who gave Control the phone number to the hospital. Because of them I can write about this and can sleep soundly knowing that we did the best we could.

Even if it did make the ambulance smell of wet smoky cat poo for the next hour.

I was contacted by the neighbour of the house that caught fire. I had asked them to make sure that the owners knew where their cat was. I'd left a note but I know how such things can go missing when your house has been wrecked.

They let me know that not only had the owners been reunited with their pet, but that he was apparently doing very well. I like happy endings.

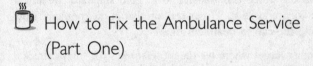

How to Fix the Ambulance Service (Part One)

To recap: the main target that the government has set ambulance services around the country is that of ORCON. This, at its simplest, states that we should reach our high priority calls in under eight minutes and our medium priority calls in under 14 minutes.

The problem that I have with this is twofold. First, in a supposed 'evidence-based' NHS there is little clinical reason for the eight minutes as opposed to four minutes. Second, and much more importantly in my opinion, it directly impacts on patient care.

In order to meet the eight-minute target ambulance services are removing double-crewed ambulances from the road in order to increase the number of fast response units (FRUs). The reasoning is that if an FRU is on scene then the 'clock stops' and the job is a success. It's not a success for the FRU if they are stuck on scene with a stabbing, an unresponsive asthmatic or with a child with meningitis.

People who are seriously sick need to be in hospital, not having a solo responder holding their hand while praying in desperation for an ambulance.

Ambulance folk can do a lot to stabilise a patient, but as a trainer I know wisely says, 'The place for a sick patient isn't the back of an ambulance.' Nor is it in their own home waiting for an ambulance to turn up.

So, what are we to do? We need to check on the performance of NHS trusts, that much is certain.

My solution is to have more targets.

But targets which will have an impact on patient care.

Let's have a target where we improve the number of heart attacks that we diagnose in the home and transfer to a 'gold standard' treatment centre. I think we are at 95 to 97 per cent on that at the moment. How about improving the call to treatment time?

Let's have another target where we diagnose strokes (or 'brain attacks' in the jargon of today) and transport them to a specialist centre. Of course, we might need a few more places to become specialist centres first, but isn't the NHS a 'joined up' organisation?

Let's have a target where we try to reduce the number of patients with asthma who need admitting to hospital. Better, let's reduce the number of people who need to stay in ITUs because of asthma. Of course, it isn't the sole job of the ambulance service to do this, but our targets should inform other aspects of the NHS, just as theirs affect ours.

How about improving the measurement and treatment of pain? It's something that we aren't too good at, given that in most cases our choice of pain relief is restricted to Entonox or morphine. We carry aspirin, but that is for heart attack treatment, not the treatment of minor pain. We also have paracetamol for children. How about nasal diamorphine? Improving the measurement and treatment of pain will directly better patients' experiences.

How about improving cardiac arrest survival rates? We've managed to improve these greatly over the past few years. Unfortunately, the government doesn't 'reward' us because of our improvements in this area, perhaps they should.

Time until a patient is reached is important in some cases, so we'll keep a target for reaching patients, but let's change it to only having the clock stop when a proper double-crewed ambulance arrives on scene. The other targets (like cardiac arrest survival) will be met by FRUs getting there quickly, but this will mean that there is less chance of FRUs being manned at the expense of proper ambulances.

How about a target of increasing the amount of paramedic cover in an area? Or how about a target for improving the training of people on the road? Better trained staff means better care for patients.

Maybe there should be a target to increase the number of ambulances on the road. Even better would be a target to have a certain amount of spare ambulances. We should have a slight excess capacity of ambulances at all times, not have people waiting for ambulances to finish with one patient before they can be attended to.

We should definitely have a target to have our ambulances fully stocked with blankets and drugs and oxygen and other essential bits of kit that make our turning up to patients actually worthwhile because we can treat them.

Finally, how about a 'staff satisfaction' target? A happy workforce is a more effective one.

Some of these targets are more important than others and by giving individual targets a separate weighting we could come up with a total 'score' that would show improvement, but could also be broken down to show where further improvement could be made. For example, the number of people who get diagnosed and treated at a specialist centre for a stroke could be worth ten times as much as the number of people who get painkillers for their broken arm.

We could even keep the ORCON target, but give it a more reasonable weighting of importance.

This system would have the advantage of being better based on current evidence and would highlight areas where changes can have an immediate effect on patient care and outcome.

There is a reason why I get a warm and fuzzy feeling when I diagnose and take to a specialist centre someone having a heart attack. It's because I've done something that will have an effect on patient well-being. It's a feeling that I don't get when I reach somewhere in under eight minutes or meet an FRU who has been on scene for 40 minutes.

Right, how do I get to be Minister in Charge of Sensible Ideas for Ambulances?

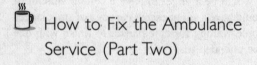

How to Fix the Ambulance Service (Part Two)

More ambulances, more ambulance staff and to stop trying to run the service like a business and run it more like a charity.

The government to decide if they want to fund the service properly in order to give the public what they expect of an ambulance service, or to work on lowering the public's expectations to something more fitting the current budget sheet.

More money in general, really.

🚑 Hidden Abuse?

We were looking for the last job of the day, something simple that would leave us close to our home base. The job which came down our vehicle's terminal wasn't ideal, but it wasn't awful either.

'Thirty-six-year-old female, assaulted. Currently in the police station.'

It wasn't ideal because she would be going to a non-local hospital, but it wasn't too far from our station. We'd be getting paid overtime to drive back.

Our patient was sitting in the front of the police station talking to one of their civilian support workers. With her were two of her neighbours. All three came from the Indian subcontinent. Our patient didn't speak any English at all and the neighbours were translating as was the police's civilian support worker.

Out patient had physically a small injury – nothing too awful, it would be sorted out by a quick visit to hospital.

We set about getting a history of what had happened to her via the different translators.

Our patient was married to a 60-year-old man. She had been assaulted by him and by her daughter.

Except the neighbours told us that the daughter wasn't her daughter – she was the 60-year-old man's other wife.

She was aged 13.

The neighbours had basically rescued our patient and brought her to the police station in order to get this state of affairs out in the open – the assault had been the final straw for them.

Our patient kept crying, partly because of what had happened, but also because she thought that the police, and us, would beat her up.

There are some weird (compared to how I was brought up) power dynamics in some of the communities around our area – young girls marrying men very much older than themselves is just one of them. This is the first marriage I have come across where the other wife has been under the legal age.

But then I wonder – in this community families live in large groups, perhaps I've taken more than one underage wife to hospital. If they are described to me as a 'daughter' or 'sister', how am I to know? I've got so used to seeing lots of people packed into one bedroom that I don't think about it any more. Is there a huge amount of child abuse going on that I have no way of knowing about?

I used to think that these large families were a good thing – the community would look after their own elderly population. I've often been very impressed with the round-the-clock care that large families can give. But perhaps there is a dark side to this.

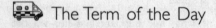 The Term of the Day

'Fitting female.'

The address was one of those tricky ones. Places in that area tend not to have door numbers on them and in the rough area of this address there is a homeless hostel (which has a lot of people fitting because they are alcoholic) next door to a disabled person day centre (where a fair number of their clients have epilepsy).

We had to take a guess as to which of the two places the call came from – we guessed wrong because as soon as we walked into the hostel the man behind the desk looked very confused and in broken English asked us why we were there. To give them their due they do normally know when one of their lodgers has taken a bit sick, as they are normally the ones who phone us.

So we walked to the large house next door where some of the local disabled people have a day centre. We were met by a member of staff who led us to a young woman lying on the floor. In the corner of the room was a woman dancing to some music with a wheelchair-bound patient.

One of the day centre staff told us what had happened – the patient had suffered a short fit, and as part of their care protocol they had to call an ambulance.

I tried talking to our patient but she wasn't saying much. I asked if she understood English and they told me that she spoke it perfectly. They also told me that she wasn't deaf and that she was normally quite chatty. I tried talking to her again and there was still no answer.

I sent my crewmate to fetch the trolley bed. It was tricky to get it in but it would serve us better than the carry chair. Meanwhile, I checked the patient out a little further to make sure that she wasn't hurt and got a bit more of a background from the staff.

In a strange coincidence the member of staff who was talking to me was an ex-patient of mine, I'd taken him to hospital when he had had a heart attack at work. Nice to see that some of my patients do get better ...

As soon as the trolley was brought up to her my patient sat upright and told me that she 'wasn't going to go on one of them' and that she would much prefer to walk onto the ambulance. So after struggling with the trolley to get it into the centre we had to struggle to put it back on the ambulance.

Our patient and a carer walked onto the ambulance and, after a few more checks, were soon on the way to hospital.

I'm a friendly chap and will quite happily talk to my patients so I started getting her medical history. Epilepsy was pretty easy to get out of her, but how do you ask someone what their particular mental 'disability' is? I always feel that it's like calling someone stupid or insane. I'm also never quite sure which politically correct term is flavour of the month.

In the end we settled on 'learning disabilities' and then settled back to chat about all sorts of things, including her telling me that doctors keep asking her if she has a boyfriend, something that she finds rather rude. We chatted about other things, of course, like her going to college and the other people in her family.

Eventually we reached hospital and left her and her carer there so that she could wait for her mother to come and pick her up and take her home.

At the end of the day I don't think that she really had a seizure – her recovery was too quick and she was too eager to go to hospital. I'm guessing that she really just fancied a day at home rather than at the centre. But who am I to judge? Unless I see the fit myself I don't know if it has been faked or not. No ambulance person ever lost their job taking a willing person to hospital.

And I had a nice chat as well.

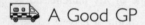 ## A Good GP

I often moan about GPs. Mostly it's when I go to a really sick patient who is sitting out in the waiting room. On more occasions than I can count I've been called to someone who looks like they are having a heart attack and the GP is nowhere to be seen – instead they are dealing with a nasty case of nappy rash.

I understand that GPs are under time pressures, but sometimes the care that people who are actually sick receive makes me spit feathers.

So when I meet a GP who knows what they are doing I feel like shouting it from the rooftops.

I was sent (miles out of my area, but that is nothing unusual) to a person having an allergic reaction in a GP surgery. I've got to admit that I fully expected to walk in and see the patient sitting in the waiting room clutching a letter from the GP while the GP was hiding in a back room.

But no.

Instead, the GP had recognised a fairly severe systemic allergic reaction. He'd laid the patient down, was giving oxygen and, by the time we arrived, had given two drugs via injection and put in an intravenous line. Because of the GP's actions the patient's allergy was resolving nicely.

And the GP was incredibly polite to my crewmate, the first responder and me. I've got to say that I was mightily impressed with the actions and attitude of this GP. The GP had also made some suggestions as to what had caused this new allergic reaction and had all the patient's notes printed out for us.

The only thing about this that is a shame is that I find it so surprising and unusual to come across such a good GP. I'm always aware that I only tend to go to the bad GPs and that the area in which I work probably isn't high on the wish-list of jobs for GPs who can interview well elsewhere.

Still, it is nice to see someone else out there doing a decent job in a crappy system.

A Tale of Two Cardiacs

Patient number one

He's 34 years old and lives (like an increasing number of my 'client group') in a hostel. We have been called because he has 'chest pain'. Chest pain calls are pretty much all 'Cat A' calls and therefore we whizz round there on blue lights to jump through the government-mandated eight-minute hoop.

He has chest pain and is feeling a bit dizzy. The most likely reason behind this is the four lines of cocaine and five ecstasy tablets that he took a few hours ago. His hugely dilated pupils stare up at me as he tells me how worried he is about the pain. To try to stop the pain he has also self-medicated with some illegally gained sleeping tablets.

This isn't the first time this month he has been in the back of the ambulance for chest pains – last time the pain came on after smoking some cannabis. He asks me not to tell the hostel owners about his drug use as if they find out they will throw him out on the street. It's a Christian faith-based hostel and it strikes me as a particularly unchristian thing to do. But what do I know? I'm just the Hell-bound atheist that looks after him and takes him to hospital. I agree that I won't tell the hostel staff about it; it's never been my job to be an informant if no one else is getting hurt.

In the back of the ambulance I do an ECG – cocaine is well known for causing heart attacks. Thankfully it's all normal. We then talk as we travel into hospital. He tells me of all the things that he has lost because of his drug use – his girlfriend, his family, his friends. He tells me about losing the middle part of his nose due to all the drugs he'd been stuffing up there. He starts crying.

A month ago he had been 'clean' for six months then for reasons he can't, or won't, tell me he started using again.

What can I do? I tell him that he is foolish to start using again, and that drugs, while nice in the short term, never solve any problems – they only create them. I tell him that he should talk to the nurses so that they can refer him on to someone who can hopefully stop him backsliding.

What else can I do?

Patient number two

He's in his late seventies and as fit as a butcher's dog. He'd been to the GP for the first time in years and had been diagnosed with a simple heart arrhythmia (atrial fibrillation for the medically minded). He'd been referred to the hospital for further assessment and treatment. This would be in a few weeks.

Then he got some chest pain and, like many men, ignored it for a while. Then it got a bit worse so he called for a cab and made his own way up to the hospital. I saw him when he walked in and told the receptionists that he had chest pain.

Twenty minutes later I was transporting him to another hospital for a primary angioplasty in order to treat the heart attack he was having.

If he'd called an ambulance we would have diagnosed the heart attack and transported him straight to the specialist centre, cutting out the middleman of the local hospital. It hadn't crossed his mind to dial 999 and ask for an ambulance.

I gently told him off. I also told him that, seeing as he'd spent his whole life working to pay his national insurance contributions, it would be a good idea to call an ambulance if he had chest pain again and that it would be our pleasure to pick him up.

He'll make a good recovery but I wish he'd called us first rather than getting a cab. We spend so much time going to people who don't need an ambulance it drives us mad to see genuine patients muddling through without our help.

Two jobs in the same night. Both with the same job description. Both very different.

Twit One and Twit Two

I've just finished the fifth twelve-hour shift of seven and I am both tired and angry. It's been a slow build with very few 'worthy' jobs, the normal roster of drunks and people who can't be bothered to see a GP.

But I have a story of pure stupidity to entertain you.

A man brings his little child into A&E because she has suffered a very minor injury, no treatment required to be honest. While in the department he starts to feel unwell.

So he goes home.

And dials 999 and calls for an ambulance.

Which he obviously gets, and is returned to the exact same department that he recently left.

I wonder how he can breathe and walk at the same time.

We do sometimes get people who turn up at the A&E department, decide that they don't want to wait, so go home and call an ambulance thinking that it will get them seen quicker. This is the first time that I've heard this particular variation on a theme.

My last job of the shift is for a drunken 16-year-old girl who has called an ambulance because 'She has drunk too much.'

So we whizz round to the hostel and find her just having vomited on her carpet. We start off being nice but she is obviously playing us around so I decide to be honest with her.

'Why did you call an ambulance?' I ask.

'Because I don't feel well,' she replies.

'Why do you think that is?'

'Why do you think!' she pretty much shouts at me.

'Is it because you drank too much alcohol?' I remain polite throughout this questioning.

'Yes.'

'Don't you think that ambulances have better things to do than pick up drunks?' I venture.

'No.'

'I mean, I should be going to dying babies and people having heart attacks shouldn't I?'

'No.'

'No? Is that because you consider yourself the centre of the universe and therefore much more important than other people?'

'Yes.'

'More important than babies choking to death?'

'Yes – stop being rude!'

'I'm not being rude. I'm just asking some questions.'

'Be quiet.'

'OK. Please be comfortable on our trolley bed, but do try to stop spitting on the floor of the ambulance, I find it most disgusting.'

And then we take her to hospital where she will no doubt sleep it off on a comfortable hospital trolley before returning home and getting someone else to clean up the vomit burns to the carpet. But, of course, I am the one who has to mop out the ambulance where she has been spitting.

I do wonder why I do this job sometimes.

Two Amusing Things

We had a lot of simple and ultimately uninteresting jobs last night, but two slightly funny things.

The first was our initial call of the day – a man who had fainted in a betting shop. When we arrived we were told by the other patrons of the shop that the patient had already left. They shoved us to the door and pointed in the general direction of the busy street.

'There he is!' they shouted at us, waggling their hands in a general direction of 'outside of the shop'.

'Who?' I asked. 'There are loads of people out there.'

'Him – the one with the head.'

I was a bit surprised by this description.

'They all have heads you silly sods!'

We didn't find him in the end, he can't have been that ill to outrun an ambulance.

The second started off as one of our usual types of calls, a four-year-old boy who had been vomiting. His mother was concerned and so we agreed to take him to hospital. As there was no other adult in the house the mother had to take the boy's sister with her.

Our patient was fine, fairly happy and there were no further signs of vomiting.

The sister, however, waited until we were within sight of the hospital before puking all over the floor of our ambulance. It seems that we are making people sick (literally) in the back of our ambulance.

I correctly identified the child's dinner as chicken and sweetcorn. Then I had to mop it up.

It's a glamorous job I have.

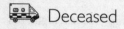 Deceased

We were met downstairs by a young man. He was leaving the block of flats but stopped long enough to tell us, 'I think she's passed away but I couldn't bring myself to tell her mother. She's old. I thought I better call an ambulance.'

We had been called to a 40-year-old woman – 'Drunk? Passed away?'

I was met at the flat door by a woman in her seventies. She didn't seem distressed as she led us into the living room. Everywhere I looked there was evidence of her daughter's alcoholism. The flat was cramped and squalid. Her mother had been visiting her.

Her daughter was obviously dead, her skin was yellow and waxy, and she was in full rigor mortis. It was obvious that she had been dead for some time.

I had to tell the seemingly oblivious mother that her daughter had died.

I sat her down and explained that her daughter had passed away some hours ago and that there was nothing that we could do to help her.

I braced for tears, or a scream, or an 'I thought so'.

The mother didn't cry, she didn't scream, she just sat there and whispered a quiet 'oh'.

The daughter had come out of her bedroom the night before and told her mother that she didn't feel too well and had lain on the sofa. Her mother had fallen asleep in the armchair. When the mother woke up she couldn't wake her daughter.

She'd then sat with her for at least six hours before knocking on the neighbour's door to see if he could wake her up.

Talking to the mother it was obvious that she was suffering from early dementia. I'm not sure if she secretly knew that her daughter was dead, but wasn't letting herself accept it.

It was strange – no tears were shed, but several times we were treated to the mother's life story.

We had to stay around for a few hours with the police because there was a chance that the death may have been suspicious, although it was more likely to be natural causes.

It was saddening to see the mother wandering around, her dead daughter lying on the sofa covered only with a sheet just a few feet away. Sad talking to her about the changes that the area has gone through, about her dead twin and about her other daughter.

Had she sat alone with the body for so long because she couldn't face up to the truth, or did she really not realise what had happened? Either was possible, and I'm not sure which one gives most comfort.

It's the sort of job that will stick with you for some time.

 Fuming

I'm going to try to write this without swearing – honest.

Our first job was the now traditional 'drunken Eastern European'; this time he was on a bus. He had a cut to the bridge of his nose and no ability to speak English. He had that immensely annoying way of pawing at us with his big blood-soaked hands. I think that he was trying to argue with us; it certainly sounded like it but you can never be sure with Russian (or Lithuanian, or whatever he was speaking). On more than one occasion we thought that we would have to get the police.

It's actually incorrect to say that he didn't speak any English; he could say 'Eeeennglisssshhh' and stick his middle finger up at us.

It would have been nice to leave him where we found him, but we'd only keep getting called back to him.

So far, so good – a slight annoyance but nothing out of the usual.

Our next job, however, was a young man who was really rather close to dying. It took us a while on scene to basically save his life during which I was running back and forth to the ambulance.

When we loaded him in to go to the hospital I realised that in my rush I must have left the ambulance unlocked.

Some filthy thieving scumbag had stolen the satnav screen and my crewmate's bag.

I informed Control and spent the next five minutes fuming as I drove the ambulance to the hospital. We were met by one of our managers who made sure that we were all right and sent us off for a replacement vehicle and a much-needed cup of tea.

Dear thief,

We ambulance folk work long twelve-hour shifts in all weathers, at all times of the day. Because of working shifts our health and relationships suffer, our social life is a nightmare. I take home £10 (about $14) for every hour that I work, whether that is two in the afternoon or three in the morning. We do a job that has us verbally abused, assaulted and spat at. We go into the worst parts of town and treat the lowest scum of humanity with dignity and respect. We put ourselves at risk of catching serious diseases like HIV, hepatitis and TB from rich and poor alike. We get used by the police to go to domestic assaults when there are no police units to send. We serve the community; we are always there when we are called, even if it is for the most minor of things. This is what we do – when you hurt we help, when you are dying we provide comfort. We do all this and, like oxygen, we are always there.

And this is how you repay us.

By stealing something that is of no use to you, by stealing the medical books that we use to treat you. By seeing that we are in a house treating someone and thinking not 'I hope the person they are seeing to is all right', but rather, 'They won't be back for a while I wonder what I can nick from that ambulance.'

Because of shift work I'm cutting my lifespan. I already have illnesses that are work related. When you get stabbed, I'll be the person to come and make sure that you don't die.

And this is what that sacrifice of every ambulance person is for? For worthless scummy bastards like you?

Your actions have taken an ambulance off the road; in the morning there will be one less to go to people – maybe it will be your mother who is ill and will have to wait longer for the ambulance, maybe it will be someone who you don't know. Either way you have made our job that much more difficult and put people's lives at risk.

I wish I knew who you were – I'd fight you to get our kit back.

And then, without doubt, another ambulance would treat you.

Tom Reynolds.

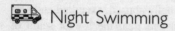 Night Swimming

It was a beautiful clear night and the full moon shone down on her, colouring her dark hair a shade of silver. She would often walk alone at night, the dark and the quiet calmed her, kept her mind from becoming too busy, too full of the things that worried her.

She slipped through the park, it was nearly midnight and the drunks had gone home. She had the park to herself.

Sure, people would be worried when they discovered her gone; her mother would panic and call the police.

But it didn't matter – this night was for her.

She slipped into the cold waters of the lake, the moonlight had turned it into a mirror and her entry cast ripples from shore to shore. She wasn't bothered by the stones on the bottom of the lake as she continued to wade out. She had kept her shoes on.

Finding the depth she started to swim – strong powerful strokes. Her muscles, initially frozen by the waters of the lake, began to warm. She was alone in the dark, water below her, the moon above.

... OR ...

She had escaped from the house. Her mother had locked the door but she had watched her as she hid the key. Tonight her search for death would be fulfilled.

She ran to the lake, it was peaceful here – no one would interrupt her, no one could stop her as she ended her pain.

She ran into the water – if she swam out to the middle she could simply let go and drift down to the bottom where she could let her lifeless body lie.

... OR ...

She was a princess. All princesses need a challenge; they need a knight in shining armour to save them. If she swam out to the island in the middle of the lake someone would come and save her.

She needed saving.

... OR ...

She didn't know why – she just wanted a swim.

It was after midnight and we'd been called to a woman who had been swimming in the lake. The parks police in one of their final rounds of the night had spotted her. They'd pulled her out and wrapped her in a blanket. She wasn't saying much but they managed to find her mother who let them know that she had 'mental health problems'.

I asked the mother about her daughter's mental health problems; she couldn't tell me what the doctors had diagnosed. The patient just sat there, dripping wet. I asked her why she had been swimming in the lake at night.

She never answered me.

I'll never know.

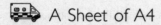 A Sheet of A4

I came across a patient yesterday who had a really good idea; it was an idea that helped us, helped her and helped the hospital.

We had been looking for a job to last us until the end of our shift and had thought we had got it with a drunk in the street. It would have been fine if he'd let us take him to hospital, but unfortunately he woke up and wandered off home. So we were stuck with 40 minutes until the end of the shift. We would have to hope for a nice quick and easy job – something like a two-year-old with a head injury.

Two-year-olds with head injuries are easy jobs because the injury isn't severe, it's normally stopped bleeding, we don't have to do any serious observation taking and the mum or dad looks after the child while we essentially act like a taxi.

Of course, what we wish for is often very different to reality.

From our 'patch' we were sent to a train station miles away in the middle of London.

At least it was Sunday, so the traffic wouldn't be so bad.

Our patient was having an asthma attack. The first responder on the scene was asking for an ambulance as quickly as possible so it was obviously something a bit serious.

I don't like people having asthma attacks – they can tend to go wrong very quickly. Also the patient was having a very hard time of it and it's never nice to see that. I heard a description of an asthma attack once as 'trying to run a marathon while breathing through a drinking straw' and that description has stuck with me for years.

So we got there as quickly as we could through unfamiliar streets to find *two* motorcycle responders there. They had been waiting a long 29 minutes for us.

Our patient was still receiving the nebuliser treatment that the two motorcycle responders had started. They told me that the patient's chest had nearly been silent when they had arrived. This is a sign of a very serious attack.

Our patient had obviously been in this situation before as she produced a neatly typed sheet of paper with all her details, her allergies, her previous medical history and the type of treatment options that worked best for her. It told me that she was a 'brittle asthmatic', which always makes me 'blue light' these patients to hospital when they are having an asthma attack. If you are having an asthma attack it can be difficult to talk so all our patient had to do was hand over the sheet of paper to whoever was looking after her.

It was a good thing that she had that bit of paper because every time she removed the nebuliser mask from her face to talk her oxygen saturations (a measure of how well she was breathing) dropped rather quickly.

So we loaded her up and sped to the nearest hospital.

I wish that all our patients had such a bit of paper. Where I work there is often a language barrier, even heavy accents can make my life difficult, so a little sheet like that would make my life so much easier. Also I find myself going to patients who *don't know* what is wrong with them.

All they know is that they take a 'little white pill in the morning and two brown pills in the evening'. Of course, this is more a failing of the primary healthcare provider in not making sure the patient is kept informed about their health.

More importantly imagine going to a 'collapse in the street' only to see a bit of paper stuck to their jacket saying, 'I'm OK – I'm just drunk.'

Tough as Old Boots

Let's call her Gladys. I meet a lot of people called Gladys in my work. Gladys is in her eighties.

Gladys had taken a tumble but not your average tumble; she had fallen down an escalator at one of our tube stations.

Not just a few steps. She'd fallen down at least *30* of the hard metal stairs.

Two members of staff met us at the now familiar 'rendezvous point'. You can spot them outside the stations; they are the little plaques with 'RVP' written on them.

I arrived to see Gladys sitting on the now stationary escalator surrounded by Underground staff. I'd come fully expecting to see someone covered in blood who would need to be 'collared and boarded' out.

Instead, she was sitting up, apparently not in pain and in good spirits.

Now, I'm a bit of a 'nervous Nelly' when it comes to people injuring themselves in such a manner – I have a strong desire to take them to hospital to be looked over by a doctor.

Unfortunately, Gladys was refusing.

I checked her out. She had a lovely lump on the back of her head and that was about it. I checked her neck and she told me that there was no pain. I wanted to make sure that she hadn't collapsed or fainted. She told me that it was her luggage that made her fall backwards. I let her know that I wanted to take her to hospital; she refused.

I did manage to persuade her to come to the ambulance for a blood pressure check, and there I was able to confirm that, apart from the bump on her head, she seemed unhurt.

A little trick for my fellow ambulance personnel: after an accident people will often feel fine and this is the effect of adrenaline pumping around the body. Then, as the adrenaline leaves the bloodstream, the person becomes a lot more 'shaky' and may feel sick. It's best to wait until this 'shaky' time is over before you leave them. Sometimes the effects of this will let you persuade the patient to come to hospital.

Gladys didn't get shaky.

I sat chatting to her for 20 minutes, and she was fine throughout. She was adamant that she be allowed to continue on her train journey home. If she'd lived in London I would have taken her home myself. Unfortunately I think that Control would have had a dim view of me wandering across into Kent.

And this is where I was impressed by the staff at the Underground station – not only had they looked after her really well while they called for the ambulance, but they then arranged to have her met by staff at the other end of her tube journey. The staff would also talk to the tube driver so that he could keep an eye on her. Then one of the Underground staff stayed with her on the platform until she got on the train.

Top service.

I wasn't hugely happy about her heading off on her own, but she seemed a sensible soul and she wouldn't be on her own sitting in a busy tube train. She also promised to call an ambulance if she felt unwell at any point, and as she lived in a warden-controlled flat she wouldn't be alone there either.

All that was left to do was the paperwork (meticulously written to cover my back should anything happen to Gladys), then get ready for the next job.

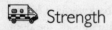 Strength

The wife looks at me and my crewmate as we lift the chair with her husband in it onto the back of the ambulance.

'You both must be very strong,' she says.

I reply with a joke, normally about how my crewmate, half the size of me, is actually the stronger of the two of us.

However, what I want to say is that the lifting is the easy part; the real strength is needed with the things we see and the patients that we deal with.

It's the strength that you need when you have to pick up the fourth severely demented patient in a row. They curl up on our trolley having been unable to move for many years, their arms and legs contracted into the foetal position. Their bodies are skin and bone, as we pick them up their joints creak and crack and they shriek in our ears, long nails dig into our arms.

It's the strength that you need when driving the ambulance and you hear them start to cry in the back. Your crewmate holds their hand and tries to reassure them but they can't get through. Instead, all you can hear is the sobbing and the noises that are all that are left to them now that language has gone. They can't tell you if they are in pain or are scared – instead all they can do is moan, and cry and scream.

It's the strength you need when you walk into a nursing home full of the demented elderly. Stuck on the walls outside the doors to their rooms are photographs from their prime. Happy mothers holding their children; proud men standing to attention in military uniform. Sepia memories from the past; what they were, not what they are. You open the door and the person in the photograph is lying on urine-sodden sheets, legs heavily bandaged from ulcers that will never heal, with hands constantly grasping for something imaginary that floats just out of reach. The person that they were is gone; all that is left is the shell, no expression behind the face that smiled all those years ago for the photo outside the door.

Then one takes hold of your hand and looks up at you with bright blue eyes and asks if you are their dad, long since dust.

And your heart breaks.

I don't know how much longer I can do this.

END CREDITS

END CREDITS

Unlikely Plotpoint

The job I'm writing about today would, if shown as a *Casualty* episode, have me groaning at the screen at how unlikely the events were.

We were sent to a 'male, collapsed', on the screen was the patient's name – it was a name I was somewhat familiar with.

It was a name I used to go by (sometimes I feel like Old Ben Kenobi remembering his time as Obi wan Kenobi with the amount of names I had ...).

I've mentioned my father once on my website – in 2005 I wrote this:

The short version of my history with my father is that he left home when I was around fourteen (my brother was around twelve), and married another woman (without divorcing my mother first – an oversight on his part, he is after all barely literate). Since then I haven't seen or heard from him, which was a bit strange as the split between Mum and him wasn't acrimonious.

So my attitude towards him has basically been 'Fuck him'. It appears that he wanted us out of his life as quickly as possible, and he has succeeded admirably on that point.

So ... why was I thinking about how I'd love to meet with him, tell him how excellent my life is? I'd love to let him know that my brother is an excellent teacher and is getting well paid for his work. I'd love him to see how his walking out on us only freed both my brother and I to go on to do things that we love doing. I'd love to show him how relaxed and chilled out my mother is now. I'd love someone to read this blog out to him, so that he could know that I'm doing better without him in my life.

Actually ... I wonder if he is still alive?

So – for one moment after not thinking about him for years, I'd love to rub his nose in how good my family and I have it now he isn't on the scene.

And now I find myself going to someone who could well be him ...

We arrived on scene, I was driving and I'd been telling my crewmate about my history with my father. It looked like the place where I'd last seen him more than 20 years ago, but I wasn't sure.

Then we entered the flats and from the tickle in my memory it was obvious that this was where he lived.

He was laying on the floor with one of our FRU people already looking after him. The FRU looked at us and started to give us a handover.

'This is *Firstname* *Secondname*,' he said.

'I know,' I replied, 'it's my dad.'

'Hey, your son is here,' the FRU said.

'He probably wouldn't recognise me,' I said back as my father turned to look at me.

The job itself was fairly simple, carry him downstairs, into the lift – then, after running some tests, off to hospital.

I wheeled him into the lift, it was small so his 'wife' had to walk down the stairs – leaving just me, my crewmate and my dad alone in the lift.

He looked up at me and said the only two words he would say to me during the time we spent together that night.

'Say nothing.'

Now, if I had even the slightest care about him, those two words would rip out my soul and stamp on it. It would break my heart. That his son, whom he hasn't seen for 20 or more years, is here, saving his life and all he wants is for me to say nothing to him.

He has his new life, and he wants nothing to do with me, or my brother.

'Fuck him' would indeed seem to be the right attitude to have had over him, and I'm very glad that I've not worried, fretted or even given a moment's consideration to the man that walked out on me and my brother. Now I knew why we'd never had even a birthday card from him.

He had obviously wanted to wash his hands of us.

So I switched to 'full on professional' mode. I spoke to his 'wife' (who seemed quite a nice person actually) to get his history and I drove him to hospital.

After dropping him off I asked my crewmate if she thought it would be a good idea if I walked in to him, told him how well our family is doing without him and then walked out.

She rightly pointed out that despite her wanting to give him a slap when he'd said 'Say nothing' to me, it would do no good.

So we left him at hospital – I don't know if he lived or died. To be honest I don't care – I care less than I would were he one of the strangers I pick up normally.

I told my mum about it, and she was furious – I think she would have quite liked to have turned up at the hospital herself to give him a piece of her mind, but I assured her that once my shift was over I'd stopped thinking about him.

So yes, stranger than *Casualty* – although I'm sure that *Casualty* would have had us reconciling ...

(I include this story in this book because I know that *Sirens* has a plot-line about a father, and it's not as unbelievable as what happened in real life.)

🚑 Lexicon of the Ambulance Service (or What 'Punter' Means)

999 – The number you dial to get the ambulance. Equivalent to the American 911 or European 112.

A&E – 'Accident and Emergency', also known as 'Casualty' or 'ER – Emergency Room'. The place where we take our patients in an effort to make them feel better. In reality, quite unlike how they are portrayed in TV programmes.

Alkie – An alcoholic.

Amber call – In contrast with 'Cat A' calls these are the calls that are deemed less serious. Stuff like simple accidents, broken legs, epileptic fits where the patient has stopped fitting.

'Ambo', 'big white taxi', 'motor', 'truck', 'drunkmobile', 'barely working shitheap' – Ambulance.

AOM – Area operations manager. The boss of a number of stations that are grouped into a 'complex'. Often the highest-ranking officer most staff see. They concern themselves with the strategic and logistical management of the ambulances working under a complex.

ASP truncheon – Straight, expandable Armament Systems and Procedures truncheon used by the police.

BASICS – British Association for Immediate Care. A charity of mostly doctors who attend accidents in public places. They can be extremely handy when the brown stuff hits the fan. We have an excellent one on my patch at the moment.

Bent – Wrong, illegal, corrupt, or a derogatory term for a homosexual. Used as 'That car radio is bent', 'That bloke is bent' or 'All the police are bent.' Also used as 'running back bent', meaning going for food/back to station without letting Control know about it; sadly running out of usage as all vehicles now have satellite tracking installed.

Bloke, fella – Male person.

BP – Blood pressure. Everyone has blood pressure but some have high blood pressure. Without blood pressure all your blood would pool at your feet, which would be bad for the brain.

C/EC/NE/NW/SE/SW – The sectors of the London Ambulance Service: Central, East Central, North East, etc.

CAC – Central Ambulance Control, full of people who actually take the 999 calls, and others who dispatch us to the jobs. They have air conditioning and don't actually smell the patients that they send us to. They also work under pressures that you would not believe. See http://www.neenaw.co.uk/ for further details.

CAD number – Computer aided dispatch. Each job has its own number. These are refreshed each day. Because of this I can tell you that the LAS goes to more than 3800 calls every day, more than 4500 on a bad day.

Cannulation – Placing a needle into a patient's vein for the purpose of delivering drugs. Also a **cannula**, the needle itself.

Cat A – A high-priority emergency call. This is the priority that cardiac arrests get, along with chest pains, difficulty in breathings and the like. These are timed with ORCON, which I often rant about ...

Chav – Like a scrote, only with more money.

CO – Carbon monoxide, an odourless gas that causes illness and death. Has been discovered poisoning ambulance crews in the older vehicles of the fleet. These vehicles are still in service. This is one of the reasons why we drive with the ambulance windows open.

CPN – Community Psychiatric Nurse, an often useless person who visits people with mental health problems in the community.

CPR – Cardiopulmonary resuscitation. The process of pounding on the chest to move blood around the body while forcing air into the lungs either by mouth to mouth (urgh!) or by using an ambu-bag. Often seen on telly being faked unconvincingly because to do this on someone whose heart is still beating is incredibly dangerous.

DSO – Duty station officer. Two rungs up the management ladder from road staff. They carry out administration duties, check on staff welfare, handle disciplinary procedures and sometimes cover for absences.

ECG (EKG) – Electrocardiograph. An examination of the heart using electrical impulses generated by the heart. If you are in an ambulance and the crew start to look worried at the printout you may be in trouble. Used to diagnose heart attacks, angina and other cardiac problems.

EMT – Emergency medical technician. Like a paramedic but we don't have to pay dues to an organisation that exists solely to discipline them and get them sacked. We often work with a paramedic and we do our best to keep them out of trouble.

EOC – Emergency operations centre. Our 'Control', which answers the 999 calls, uses a computer system to prioritise the calls and then dispatches us to the address. A real pressure-cooker environment I couldn't work in as you are constantlly being watched by managers. See http://www.neenaw.co.uk for the view from there.

ETA – Estimated time of arrival. How long we or the police have to wait for the other to turn up. Sometimes people dial 999 again to see how long the ambulance will be.

FRU/RRU – Fast/rapid response vehicle manned by a solo member of staff. These cars are used to reach patients quicker than an ambulance. In reality they are used to stop the ORCON 'clock'. Because of the design of the vehicles and the logistics of working on them they cannot be used to transport patients. This results in the solo responder trying to make conversation with the patient while they wait for the 'proper' ambulance.

GBH – Grievous bodily harm. An assault that breaks a bone or other serious injury. Someone who is likely to bleed over the back of your ambulance.

GP – Family health provider. Sadly we only get to see the crap ones who sit patients having heart attacks out in their waiting room and don't even give them an aspirin. Occasionally we meet a good one – this gives *us* heart palpitations of shock.

Green call – Lowest priority: cut fingers, coughs and runny noses. Often mistaken with Cat As because people who call ambulances for a cough often complain of chest pain and difficulty in breathing. Having said that some incredibly ill patients still come up as 'Green calls'.

GTN – Glyceryl trinitrate. A treatment for angina and some other heart complaints. Also used to make explosives.

HEMS/Paraffin parrot – Helicopter Emergency Medical Service. In London the medical helicopter that flies out of the Royal London hospital. Staffed with a doctor and a paramedic, they fly out to serious cases. Funded by charity and corporate sponsorship. Sometimes very helpful; sometimes a pain in the rear. Although when you need them they are worth their weight in gold.

Intubation – The passing of a plastic tube into an unconscious patient's airway to enable us to assist their breathing, or take over their breathing completely.

ISIS-2 – The study group that discovered taking an aspirin when you have a heart attack is a good idea.

IV access – Securing a cannula enabling staff to give drugs directly into the bloodstream.

IVDU – Intravenous drug user. Someone who injects illegal drugs intravenously, mainly a heroin addict. Often 'unkempt'.

LAS - London Ambulance Service, the organisation I work for. Also called 'Da Firm' by those of us on the ground floor. Run by 'Da Boss' Peter Bradley, who is generally tolerated by us grunts for the sole reason that he is considered a hell of a lot better than his predecessors.

LOL – Not, as internet people will tell you, 'laugh out loud', but 'little old lady'; a group of patients who spend half their time throwing themselves on the floor, breaking their bones and having urine infections. Normally, a pleasure to deal with.

Matern-a-taxi – What an ambulance turns into when transporting a near-term pregnancy who is having contractions every 'two minutes' yet you don't see anything approaching a contraction during the 30-minute journey. While an 'easy' job it is traditionally hated by ambulance crews, especially at five in the morning.

MDT – Mobile display terminal. The computer screen installed in the ambulance that, in between crashing, gives us the details of jobs. Also enables EOC to send messages to us, normally telling us to hurry up and make ready for the next patient.

Mmol/l – Millimoles per litre. Something to do with chemicals. In our job the unit we use to measure the amount of sugar in the bloodstream. Important for diabetics to keep an eye on.

Native – In east London a person from an ethnic minority, mainly because there are more ethnic minorities than 'White British'. This isn't actually an insult, more a running joke.

NHS – The National Health Service. The 'free at point of access' healthcare system of the United Kingdom. Paid for by taxes, it is slowly being privatised. Split into a number of 'trusts' which include hospitals, GPs and ambulance services.

NHS Direct – Another telephone advice service, staffed by nurses who will tell you to call an ambulance for having a cold. Ring 0845 46 47 for 24-hour advice. Often disparagingly called 'NHS Redirect'. We don't mind going to patients who have minor injuries who have tried NHS Direct first only to be redirected to us.

NICE – National Institute for Clinical Excellence. An organisation that provides advice on the best (and most cost-effective) treatment for patients. It is believed, though never confirmed, that one year of life is worth £20 000.

ORCON – Operational Research Consultancy. Report produced in 1974 that stated if a patient had a cardiac arrest an ambulance should be there within eight minutes. The government only read a bit of the report and decided that the eight minutes should be the measuring stick by which all ambulance services are assessed. The eight minutes applies to all Cat A calls, not just cardiac arrests. Get there in eight minutes and it's a hit; get there in eight minutes and one second and it's a miss, even if you save somebody's life. The chasing of this target directly reduces resources for better patient care. This target (which, after further research, was found to be no longer clinically significant) is the cause of a lot of problems for the ambulance service in its shortsighted desire to please the government.

Paramedic – An ambulance worker who is allowed to perform some advanced skills like intubation and cannulation on patients. They also have a few more drugs to play with. Many of them started out as EMTs. They have plenty more opportunity to get themselves into all sorts of trouble.

Plod, boys in blue, Old Bill, fuzz, coppers – The police; a bunch of folks we tend to get on well with, especially if they let us off speeding when they find out who we work for. Very handy for breaking down doors and sitting on patients who are throwing a wobbly. I have a lot of respect for them.

Popper – Someone who injects drugs subcutaneously; a handful died in Glasgow a while ago from an infected source, leading to much merriment from the local ambo crews.

Punter – A patient (or 'client', 'service user' or 'stakeholder' if you want to sound like a management twit); from a slang term, often used by second-hand car salesmen, meaning a gambler, or one who is about to make a gamble (so, therefore, a stunningly accurate description of our patients).

Purple, purple plus – A dead body; the 'plus' indicates a body that has been dead for some time; often recognisable when you walk in the front door and are hit by the smell.

RTA – Road traffic accident. The British version of the American MVA (motor vehicle accident). Now called a 'road traffic collision' in an attempt to stop lawyers getting their clients off the hook by telling the court that the police have already called it an 'accident'.

Scrote – An often alcoholic person who has more tattoos than teeth, bad hygiene and a poor attitude towards employment. Scrote is also short for scrotum.

TAS/CTA – Telephone Advice Service/Clinical Telephone Advice. When someone calls for an ambulance for some minor crap they may sometimes be diverted to the TAS desk at CAC for advice. They save us, service wide, from going to about 200 calls a day across London.

Tramp juice – Super-strength lager or cider, sold cheaply. Examples include White Lightning and Tennent's Super. Empty cans of which, when found in the street, signify the less salubrious parts of town.

VF/VT/asystole/PEA – The beating of the heart is normally 'sinus rhythm'. VF/VT/asystole/PEA are the names of heart rhythms that are ultimately fatal. VF (ventricular fibrillation) and VT (ventricular tachycardia) can be shocked with a defibrillator to try to restore a normal heartbeat; asystole and PEA (pulseless electrical activity) can't be shocked. Don't watch TV programmes expecting to be educated in this as they are always doing the wrong thing ...

Wanker – Technically someone who masturbates. In reality, a fairly mild insult.

Watersquirters, LFB, mobile drip stands, Trumpton – The London Fire Brigade; a bunch of part-timers who get to sleep all night as there are very few fires in London and no one cares if cats get stuck in trees during the night. Unlike the USA, we are two very separate services. We show our solidarity by sounding our sirens outside their sleeping quarters at five in the morning.

Acknowledgements

This book wouldn't have been possible without the input of many other people and it is only right and fair that I draw your attention to some of them.

First a book needs a publisher, and I'd like to thank Scott Pack and Heather Smith of The Friday Project for working with me to bring this book to print; they are both superbly professional and extremely nice people. They have been incredibly supportive when dealing with my mild neuroses. I'd also like to thank Carol Anderson, the copy editor whose job it was to batter my words into some form of grammatical sense; it can't have been the easiest text to work with. I'd also like to thank all of Press Books from layout to marketing and all other arcane sciences in between for making this book possible.

My mum who, in addition to giving birth to me, has taught me all the skills needed to survive in a post-apocalyptic wasteland and, by extension, to be a decent ambulance worker, and my brother, who constantly reminds me that I'm not the smartest person in the room, have also been amazingly supportive of me.

I mustn't forget my workmates at the London Ambulance Service. Cynics to a man (or woman), they have also been very kind to me. I know that I'm writing the truth because they would loudly let me know if I started bullshitting.

Respec' is also due to the BWTS mob. They keep me honest.

Also, big thanks for the Communications department of the LAS for not shutting me down when I started blogging. David Jervis, Alex Bass and the others have been complete stars.

I thank the police, who are often incredibly helpful and will gladly get 'stuck in', and the London Fire Brigade, who give me hours of joy by being asleep as I whizz past their station on sirens at three in the morning.

The comments and support from the readers of my blog, from which this book is drawn, are also vitally important. Without their feedback I almost certainly would have grown tired of writing many years ago. I can't name them all, but do feel free to go to my website and join in; 'batsgirl', 'dungbeetle', 'vic', 'EmT Vessel', 'vivdora' and all the other commentators are very welcoming.

Finally, and most importantly, I thank my patients. They have run me through every emotion, they have made me examine my own life and the life of others, they have made me grateful for what I have and have shown me what is really important in life. While they can infuriate me they can also inspire me; they are a mirror in which the world is reflected.

Tom Reynolds/Brian Kellett/Just another ambulance person.

Blogging regularly at http://randomreality.blogware.com